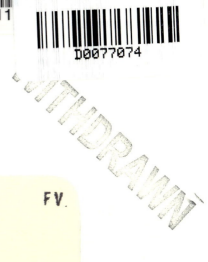
FV.

STEPPARENTING

Recent Titles in
Contributions in Sociology

Changing Jewish Life: Service Delivery and Planning in the 1990s
Lawrence I. Sternberg, Gary A. Tobin, and Sylvia Barack Fishman, editors

Alienation, Community, and Work
Andrew Oldenquist and Menachem Rosner, editors

High Risk and High Stakes: Health Professionals, Politics, and Policy
Earl Wysong

Immigration and Ethnicity: American Society—"Melting Pot" or "Salad Bowl"?
Michael D'Innocenzo and Josef P. Sirefman, editors

The Poverty Debate: Politics and the Poor in America
C. Emory Burton

Diffusion Research in Rural Sociology: The Record and Prospects for
the Future
Frederick C. Fliegel

Consciousness and Culture: An Introduction to the Thought of Jean Gebser
Eric Mark Kramer, editor

Community in Transition: Mobility, Integration, and Conflict
Hanna Ayalon, Eliezer Ben-Rafael, and Abraham Yogev

Cultural Conflict and the Swedish Sexual Myth: The Male Immigrant's Encounter
with Swedish Sexual and Cohabitation Culture
Sven-Axel Månsson

For Democracy: The Noble Character and Tragic Flaws of the Middle Class
Ronald M. Glassman, William H. Swatos, Jr., and Peter Kivisto

Social Oppression
Adam Podgórecki

Eastern Europe in Transition: The Impact on Sociology
Mike Forrest Keen and Janusz Mucha, editors

STEPPARENTING

Issues in Theory, Research, and Practice

Edited by
Kay Pasley
and
Marilyn Ihinger-Tallman

Contributions in Sociology, Number 108

Greenwood Press
Westport, Connecticut • London

Library of Congress Cataloging-in-Publication Data

Stepparenting : issues in theory, research, and practice / edited by
 Kay Pasley and Marilyn Ihinger-Tallman.
     p.   cm. — (Contributions in sociology, ISSN 0084-9278 ; no.
 108)
     Includes bibliographical references and index.
     ISBN 0-313-28502-0 (alk. paper)
     1. Stepparents—Family relationships.   2. Remarried people—Family
 relationships.   3. Stepchildren—Family relationships.   I. Pasley,
 Kay.   II. Ihinger-Tallman, Marilyn.   III. Series.
 HQ759.92.574   1994   93-25073

British Library Cataloguing in Publication Data is available.

A paperback edition of *Stepparenting* is available from Praeger Publishers,
an imprint of Greenwood Publishing Group, Inc. (ISBN 0-275-95381-5).

Library of Congress Catalog Card Number: 93-25073
ISBN: 0-313-28502-0
ISSN: 0084-9278

First published in 1994

Greenwood Press, 88 Post Road West, Westport, CT 06881
An imprint of Greenwood Publishing Group, Inc.

Printed in the United States of America

The paper used in this book complies with the
Permanent Paper Standard issued by the National
Information Standards Organization (Z39.48-1984).

10 9 8 7 6 5 4 3 2

Dedication

To Carolyn and Ernie Pasley, who have been my own personal cheering section for as long as I can remember.

K. P.

To James and Megan, Kelsey and Jacqueline, and Teddy and Fiona, whose expectations, choices, decisions, and problem-solving skills will help shape the future family.

M. I-T.

CONTENTS

ILLUSTRATIONS

PREFACE

The chapters in this volume focus on a family type that is rapidly becoming the norm. Remarriage (and the stepfamily that it typically establishes) was once called an incomplete institution (Cherlin, 1978), in part because people who remarried were not sure of what rules or standards to establish, how to enact their roles, and so forth. However, high rates of divorce and remarriage during the past 25 years have ensured that a large proportion of American adults and children either have experienced or will experience stepfamily living at some time during their lives. From their cumulative experience, researchers are beginning to discern some common patterns of behavior.

The increase in numbers of people who live in stepfamilies results in a need for those in the helping professions (e.g., clinical psychologists, marriage and family therapists, and social workers) to learn more about stepfamily living in order to assist their clients who are members of stepfamilies. One purpose in putting together this collection is to present some of the most recent findings from current research on stepfamilies to those who work with them. Additionally, we hope that this collection will be useful to those who address the needs of stepfamilies in educational systems and in the legal profession, as well as other professionals whose daily work connects them with adults and children living in stepfamilies. Moreover, we hope that students and researchers who study stepfamilies also will find this material useful.

The four section of this volume are divided according to these purposes. Chapters 1, 2, and 3 provide an overview of the current state of the research and discuss two new theoretical conceptualizations. Chapter 4 through 9 report research findings from several studies. These researchers attended to and have overcome the methodological weaknesses of earlier research by designing longitudinal studies, collection information from multiple sources, and using data from large, random samples. In some cases, multiple methods were used. Chapters 10, 11, and 12 focus on three social institutions: the clinical, educational, and legal. The authors review the issues facing those who work within these institutions and offer suggestions on how to effectively serve their clientele who live with stepfamilies. The final chapter examines the other chapters and delineates the common and unique contributions made to advancing our understanding of stepfamilies and of ways to better meet their needs.

We hope that this collection is useful to readers looking for the most up-to-date research and thinking on the subject. We selected research topics that were heretofore neglected in the literature, such as stepmother-adolescent stepchild relations, former spouse relations, and loyalty conflicts of fathers. Finally, we hope we have offered information that is useful to practitioners who work with stepfamilies. Whether we achieve these goals is yet to be determined. However, we already have achieved a feeling of success when we recount the pleasure and gratitude of working with the cooperative colleagues whose work is represented here. Like our first edited volume on the topic, this book was a joint effort on behalf of a group of scholars. We are extremely appreciative of their commitment to excellence and their unending good will in working with us in the editorial process.

We have come to believe that edited volumes are a labor of love. When deadlines come and go and the prospects of ever completing the work seem more fantasy than reality, or when the text needs more attention and revisions appear endless, the process definitely feels like labor. It is the finished product that results in the glow of a task well done. In addition to the product, were it not for the opportunity to work with some of the finest scholars writing on remarriage and stepfamilies, the labor would have felt more overwhelming and much less rewarding.

Valued assistance came from other people as well. Without the excellent secretarial support of Kelly Murrell and Terry Rakestraw and the attention to detail provided by two graduate students, Carmelle Minton and Amy Lofquist, at the University of North Carolina at Greensboro, the project would have been cumbersome to complete. George F. Butler, Acquisitions Editor of Social and Behavioral Sciences for Greenwood Press, and his editorial staff were encouraging, helpful and most understanding as our deadlines were inevitably postponed.

This book represents yet another collaboration for the coeditors: one of many in a long and valued shared history together. While the other commitments in our separate professional lives made this project more complicated and challenging than any of our past efforts, we continued to be enriched by our ongoing professional and personal relationships. It is our friendship that is most highly valued and that prompts us to find new ways in which to work together.

Chapter 1

REMARRIAGE AND STEPFAMILIES: MAKING PROGRESS IN UNDERSTANDING

Kay Pasley, Marilyn Ihinger-Tallman, and Amy Lofquist

Since the publication of our first edited volume on this topic (Pasley & Ihinger-Tallman, 1987b), scholarly interest in remarriage and stepfamily living has exploded. This is evident when we compare the numbers of empirical studies published before and after 1987. In the earlier volume, we reported that as of 1987, the bibliography of the Focus Group on Remarriage and Stepfamilies of the National Council on Family Relations included some 550 citations from the professional literature (empirical studies, clinical discussions, books, book chapters, and reviews of the literature) and 150 citations from the popular literature (Pasley & Ihinger-Tallman, 1987a). Since then, the professional literature has grown by some 350 citations, of which 60% represent findings from empirical studies. What this suggests is that families that are formed through remarriage are of increasing interest to family scholars. Given this interest, we need to ask, what has been learned from these studies? Have all aspects of the remarried family now been investigated, or are there research areas that require additional attention? Where have our scholarly efforts fallen short? In this chapter we (a) critique the extant literature, (b) delineate the progress that other scholars have made in providing knowledge about remarriage and stepfamilies, and (c) investigate whether the particular methodological problems identified in earlier publications have been addressed.

In order to accomplish these goals, we discuss the early critiques of the literature and then examine the empirical literature since 1987 in light of the critical comments offered. Our primary purpose was to determine whether scholars writing since 1987 have addressed the theoretical and methodological concerns noted in the earlier critiques. In addition, we were interested in identifying areas of neglect and topics that have received adequate attention.

This review is not intended to be inclusive. Instead, we discuss individual studies only as examples of the kind of studies available in the literature. Finally, this review is limited to empirical studies published in professional journals and books.

CRITIQUES OF THE LITERATURE

The first critique of the literature on remarriage was published in 1979. In that piece, Furstenberg (1979) identified problems facing remarrieds that were "theoretically compelling and amenable to empirical investigation" (p. 12). His intent was to identify issues deserving the attention of researchers in order to gain a clearer understanding of the interaction processes in what he called the "reconstituted family." As such, he identified seven areas needing attention: the consequences of marital experience on the transition to remarriage, the effects of divorce adjustment on remarriage, the effects of remarriage on other events in the life course, the effects of remarriage on the individual, the changes in conjugal roles from the first marriage to the second, the nature of the former-spouse relationship, and the maintenance and changes of child rearing functions and extended kin relationships after remarriage.

Unlike Furstenberg, Price-Bonham and Balswick (1980) focused their critical comments on the methodological and theoretical limitations of the empirical literature. While they concluded that there had been advances in terms of gaining breadth of understanding, they suggested that there was limited depth of understanding (p. 967). Methodologically, they saw several weakness in the empirical efforts: (a) inconsistently defined concepts and the use of nonstandardized instruments, (b) failure to assess multiple factors which resulted in oversimplified generalizations, (c) lack of longitudinal designs, and (d) use of nonrandom samples. They also noted the lack of a theoretical underpinning in many of the studies and recommended the use of existing theoretical orientations in future research, including general systems theory, social exchange theory, family development theory, and stress theory.

More recently, Esses and Campbell (1984) argued that the study of remarriage continued to be limited by a scarcity of rigorous studies. However, they believed that this lack of rigor was endemic because of the complex methodological issues facing family researchers in general. They suggested that, whereas family research in general was difficult to conduct, research with remarried families was challenged by even more difficult problems. They identified several issues faced by scholars studying remarriage that had not been addressed in earlier critiques. For example, they argued that there was a lack of an adequate model of stepfamily functioning to direct the formulation of research questions and a general insensitivity to structural variation in stepfamilies. Moreover, adequate sociodemographic information that assists the identification of representative samples was ignored by those who study remarried families. Like Price-Bonham and Balswick (1980), Esses and Campbell also noted the failure of scholars to use sufficiently large samples so that more complex questions might be addressed, and they bemoaned the continued use of nonstandardized measures.

Similar limitations were discussed in a review of the literature on the effects of remarriage on children (Ganong & Coleman, 1984). These authors called for empirical studies that offer "well-designed sampling and measurement techniques" rather than "a report of clinical impressions based on data gleaned via clinical observations from a unique sample of unknown size and characteristics" (p. 315). Using different terms, they advocated more within-group comparisons, the use of multiple sources of data, multiple methods of data collection (which should not be limited to self-report), and larger, random samples. Furthermore, they identified several content areas that were in need of additional attention: stepmother families, the effects of remarriage on stepchildren of different ages, and children who lived in well-functioning stepfamilies.

The concerns addressed by these writers were echoed recently by Coleman and Ganong (1990) in a critical analysis of the literature published in the 1980s. The recency of their critique calls into question whether scholars have addressed the limitations noted in earlier reviews.

ADVANCES IN SUBSTANTIVE TOPICS

Since 1987 we identified 133 publications that were empirically based. From these publications, we noted that several topics received more attention, while others remained virtually unexamined. The areas receiving more attention included studies that (a) provide descriptive information about the population of remarrieds and stepfamilies and aid in building a demographic profile, (b) determine the effects of remarriage on children, (c) examine the effects of remarriage and stepfamily life on the marital dyad, (d) address the overall adjustment issues of the family, (e) focus on child rearing by stepparents, and (f) examine various kin relationships (e.g., former spouses, grandparents). A commentary on these six areas follows.

Descriptive Studies

Of the 133 studies, 23 (17%) were descriptive in nature. These studies commonly reported the findings from large, representative samples, such as the National Survey of Families and Households (NSFH) or Current Population Surveys (CPS). As a result, demographers are able to provide a more detailed profile of this population (as examples see, Glick, 1989b; Glick & Lin, 1987; Thornton, 1991; Wilson & Clarke, 1992). Other descriptive information is provided in specific areas: probability of childbearing following remarriage (Lin, 1990; Wineberg, 1990); probability of marital dissolution (Bumpass, Martin, & Sweet, 1991; Wineberg, 1991); changes in the payment of child support following remarriage (Teachman, 1990, 1991); mobility and marriage order (Speare & Goldsheider, 1987); timing of remarriage (Smith, Zick, & Duncan, 1991); courtship patterns (O'Flahtery & Odells, 1988); probability of remarriage among professional women (Cooney & Uhlenberg, 1989); and characteristics of specialized populations, such as those individuals convicted of sex offenses (Erickson, Luxenberg, Walbek, & Seely, 1987; Gordon, 1989).

Interestingly, descriptive studies on remarriage have continued to be characterized by breadth rather than depth of treatment of the topic. Recently, the special issue of the *Journal of Family Issues* edited by L. K. White offered several good examples of empirical work that begins to build on the information now available from descriptive studies and, thus, to provide more in-depth understanding of the phenomena. As an example, Booth and Edwards (1992) tested five models linking "remarriage-induced attributes to an increased probability of a decline in marital quality and divorce" (p. 179). These five models, which they felt had potential for explaining the higher probability of dissolution of remarriages, were "(a) incomplete institution, (b) willingness to leave marriage, (c) selection, (d) socioeconomic status, and (e) remarriage market" (p. 180). They found that individuals in remarriages were more likely to be poorly integrated with parents and in-laws, more willing to leave the marriage, and more likely to be poor marriage material, have low socioeconomic status, and age-heterogeneous marriages. All factors but socioeconomic status are found to explain declines in marital quality and rises in level of marital instability (p. 179).

Effects of Remarriage on Children

Much of the empirical work on remarriage and stepparenting has children as the focus, addressing the question of how they are affected by the marital transitions of their parents. (Much of the earlier literature is summarized in comprehensive reviews by Ganong & Coleman, 1984, 1987a). Thirty-three percent of the citations since 1987 dealt directly with child outcomes, although the nature of the outcome varied. Several outcomes were addressed more frequently, including self-concept and self-esteem (as examples see, Parish, 1987; Pasley & Healow, 1988), academic achievement or success (as examples see, Marsh, 1990; Zimiles & Lee, 1991), behavior problems (as examples see, Bray, 1988; Tygart, 1990), child well-being defined broadly (as examples see, Dawson, 1991; Zill, 1988), and child abuse (Giordano, 1988; Gordon & Creighton, 1988).

The most popular child outcome in the research literature was self-concept or self-esteem (almost one-fourth of the 44 studies). Typically, these studies reported no significant differences in level of self-esteem between children raised in various family structures (intact, first-marriage families, single-parent families, and stepfamilies). As Coleman and Ganong (1992) concluded, there is little need for additional studies of child self-esteem in which family structure is the primary independent variable. It has been argued that between-group comparisons provide less helpful information than studies that make within-group comparisons (Clingempeel, Flesher, & Brand, 1987).

Similarly, no differences were found on measures of academic achievement between children from stepfamilies and those in first-marriage families (as examples see, Dornbusch, Ritter, Leiderman, Roberts, & Fraleigh, 1987; Marsh, 1990). However, the results of these studies do suggest that children of divorced, single-parent households may be at greater risk for academic difficulties than children from either of the other two types of families.

The study that focused on child abuse was descriptive and examined the incidence of abuse. In attempting to identify children at risk for abuse findings researchers suggested that adolescent, first-born children were at greater risk for being sexually abused than were younger children or children in other types of families (Gordon & Creighton, 1988).

Regarding behavioral problems in children, most studies attempted to determine the effects of stepfamily living on the frequency and nature of behavior problems. The findings varied somewhat. For example, studies of antisocial behavior found that children of divorced, nonremarried mothers and girls in stepfamilies had a higher use of controlled substances than children in either intact, first-married families or boys in stepfamilies (Needle, Su, & Doherty, 1990). Research also indicated that children of divorced, nonremarried mothers were diagnosed with more conduct disorder problems, while children in residential stepmother families whose mother had died had more neuroses (Steinhausen, VonAster, & Gobel, 1987). Bray (1988a) found that children in stepfamilies were reported to have more overall behavioral problems than children in other types of families.

Studies that examined the general well-being of children assessed well-being in a variety of ways. Some studies used measures of ego development, while others assessed impulsivity. Typically, these studies used family structure as the primary independent variable and attempted to determine whether children in step-families had poorer "adjustment" than children in either intact, first-marriage families or those residing in single-parent households. The findings were mixed. Some studies reported that children in stepfamilies had poorer adjustment (Amato & Ochiltree, 1987; Baydar, 1988; Zill, 1988), while other studies found no differences in children's adjustment or well-being (Kurdek & Sinclair, 1988; Marsh, 1990).

Another child outcome that has received recent attention is the "nest-leaving" behavior of young adult children. Specifically, two studies on nest leaving found that children in stepfamilies left home earlier than did children in other family structures (Goldscheider & Goldscheider, 1989; Wiser & Burch, 1989).

Factors Affecting Child Outcomes

A number of other studies examined a variety of factors affecting child outcomes. Using data from a large study of school children in California, Dornbusch, Ritter, and Leiderman, et al. (1987) found that while family structure per se had little effect on the academic outcome of children, parenting style was predictive of school performance. Using NSFH data, Fine, Donnelly, and Voydanoff (1991) reported similar findings. They found that positive child adjustment was associated with lower use of parental punishment, higher use of parental rewards and consistency, more parental consensus regarding children, and less anger toward the mother's remarriage. Two studies found that parental conflict had a greater impact on children than did family structure (Kurdek & Sinclair, 1988; Coleman & Ganong, 1987b).

One of the most consistent findings regarding factors affecting child outcome was the sex of the child. Vuchinich, Hetherington, Vuchinich, and Clingempeel (1991) found that stepfamilies with stepdaughters had more adjustment problems than stepfamilies with stepsons. Earlier studies also reported this finding (as examples see, Santrock & Sitterle, 1987; Zill, 1988). Other research suggested that contact with nonresidential fathers and paternal grandparents differentially affected boys and girls in stepfamilies under the condition of different lengths of stepfamily duration. Bray and Berger (1990) found that frequent contact and a good relationships with a nonresidential father was related to better behavioral adjustment in boys in families remarried 6 months and girls in families remarried 2.5 years. What these studies suggest is that family structure alone may be less helpful in understanding child outcomes than other aspects of family interaction, such as conflict and parenting behaviors.

Effects of Remariage on the Marital Dyad

Much of the literature on the marital dyad examined differences in marital quality, happiness, or satisfaction between first-married and remarried couples. Recently, Vemer, Coleman, Ganong, and Cooper (1989) reported the results of a meta-analysis of 34 studies of marital satisfaction in remarriage. They found few differences between individuals in first marriages and those in remarriages. In addition, no differences in marital satisfaction were found between stepfather and stepmother families, those with residential and nonresidential children, nor those in simple and complex remarried family structures.

Several studies examined the factors influencing marital quality. These studies moved a step closer to answering more complex research questions and going beyond simple description. The factors influencing marital quality include quality of the stepparent-stepchild relationship (as examples see, Brand & Clingempeel, 1987; Hobart, 1988), presence of a "common" child (Ganong & Coleman, 1988), age of the child (Kurdek, 1990), role clarity and satisfaction (Roberts & Price, 1989), and agreement over decisions (Keshet, 1990; Orleans, Palisi, & Caddell, 1989). Only one systematic finding was evident: the quality of the stepparent-step-child relationship is the strongest predictor of marital quality as the outcome, an idea first introduced by Crosbie-Burnett (1984).

Marital conflict was the focus of a few studies. Hobart (1990, 1991) compared first-married and remarried couples and found no difference in the frequency of marital conflict. However, he did find that the issues that generated conflict differed between groups. First-married couples had more conflict over household tasks, while remarrieds had more conflict over children. A study comparing intimacy among first-married and remarried couples (Larson & Allgood, 1987) suggested no differences between groups in intimacy. Important to marital conflict was Larson and Allgood's finding that the level of conflict resolution (one type of intimacy) was significantly lower among the remarried couples.

Several new areas of investigation related to the marital dyad have appeared in the literature since 1987. Two studies examined the decision to remarry from the perspective of ethics of care (Byrd & Smith, 1988; Smith, Goslen, Byrd, & Reece, 1991). Their findings suggest greater emphasis on self-other orientation in the decision to remarry. Two studies examined boundary ambiguity to determine the frequency of such ambiguity in different types of remarried families and its association with marital adjustment (Pasley, 1987; Pasley & Ihinger-Tallman, 1989). The findings from these studies suggest greater boundary ambiguity in stepmother families; however, boundary ambiguity was not associated with measures of marital adjustment. Kurdek (1989b) examined the association between social support and psychological distress in first-married and remarried couples. He found that the family of origin provided less social support to remarried persons and that satisfaction and frequency of contact with social supporters was negatively associated with psychological distress. Kurdek (1990) and Kurdek and Fine (1991) also pursued research that addressed the cognitive aspects of remarriage. Kurdek examined the cognitive correlates (e.g., ambiguity of the stepfather role, optimistic perspectives on stepfamilies, and myths about stepfamilies) of marital and parental satisfaction. Kurdek and Fine investigated the association between intrinsic/extrinsic motivations for remarriage and marital quality. Two studies addressed financial issues in remarriage (Coleman & Ganong, 1989; Zick & Smith, 1988). Their findings suggest that remarriage positively affected the economic well-being of widows and that pooling resources was associated with closer adult-child relationships but had little effect on the marital relationship. Last, Furstenberg (1987) focused on conjugal roles and role expectations following remarriage and found more similarity than dissimilarity in beliefs about the spousal relationship and marriage and household expectations in first-married compared to remarried individuals.

Stepparenting

About 5% of the studies focused on the stepparent role and/or stepparenting behaviors. Findings on the role of the stepparent that used data from the larger population suggest that people perceive greater variability in the role of the stepparent than in that of the biological parent (Schwebel, Fine, & Renner, 1991). Also, the stepparent role is perceived as pejorative (as examples see, Fluitt & Paradise, 1991; Ganong, Coleman, & Jones, 1990; Sauer & Fine, 1988).

Some research examined the factors affecting stepparenting. Of all the step-relationships, the stepmother-stepchild relationship is more problematic. One study (Guisinger, Cowan, & Schuldberg, 1989) identified two conditions under which adjustment in stepmother families can be improved: enhancing the stepmother-stepchild relationship and having a biological father who helps with household and child care tasks. Several studies focused on the sex of the stepparent as an influential factor (as an example see, Santrock & Sitterle, 1987). These studies suggest that children in stepmother families are at the greatest risk for poor adjustment, a finding that is supportive of the work prior to 1987.

In one of the few longitudinal studies of stepfamilies, Bray, Berger, Silverblatt, and Hollier (1987) examined the parenting behaviors in stepfamilies and first-marriage families. They found that stepfamilies demonstrated more coercive behaviors toward children and had poorer problem-solving skills than did first-marriage families. Also, stepfathers were either more authoritarian or more permissive and less consistent in their limit-setting behaviors than were biological fathers. These parenting styles have been associated with poor outcomes for children, such as poor school grades (Dornbusch, Ritter, Leiderman, et al., 1987). Other studies found stepparents to be less involved with their stepchildren than biological parents (Santrock & Sitterle, 1987). However, over time, involvement with stepparents increased (Amato, 1987).

Stepfamily Adjustment

No study since 1987 has addressed the overall adjustment of the stepfamily. Palisi, Orleans, Caddell, and Korn (1991) came close to this goal. In their study they found that prior parenting experience positively affected the adjustment of stepfathers.

Some attention was directed toward understanding the factors affecting stepfamily adjustment, specifically, the effects of the age of the child on stepfamily adjustment. Coleman and Ganong (1987b) found greater boundary clarity and more positive stepsibling relationships among older children.

Kin Relationships following Remarriage

Few scholars examined the nature of kin relationships following remarriage, although there is a growing interest in this area. Since 1987, only 7% of the studies addressed this topic. Several studies focused on the ex-spouse relationship following remarriage; however, few common themes or findings have emerged. The evidence suggests that former spouses have limited contact following remarriage. Contact is more likely to be maintained when proximity is not an issue (Ambert, 1988; Furstenberg, 1988). James and Johnson (1988) attempted to identify how different types of former-spouse relationships affected martial satisfaction and psychological adjustment in remarriage. They found that a cooperative relationship fostered satisfaction and adjustment in remarriage, while competition negatively influenced satisfaction and adjustment. Masheter (1991) found that quarreling between former spouses was associated with preoccupation with each other, that such preoccupation diminished following remarriage, and that quarreling also diminished following remarriage.

Studies dealing with kin relationships have typically focused on the grandparent role following divorce and remarriage. One study of college students suggested more desire to be involved with, and feelings of closeness to, biological grandparents than with stepgrandparents (Sanders & Trygstad, 1989). Two studies found the relationship between stepchildren and stepgrandparents to be more remote than the relationship between biological grandchildren and grandparents (Doka & Mertz, 1988; Henry & Ceglian, 1989). Johnson (1989) found that grandparents redefined their relationship to stepgrandchildren because they wanted to maintain access to their own adult children.

Other Substantive Topics

The influence of remarriage on outcomes for older adults was addressed by several recent studies. Findings suggest that remarriage is associated with better health and well-being (as examples see, Bulcroft, Bulcroft, Hatch & Borgatta, 1989; Burks, Lund, Gregg, & Bluhm, 1988). Another study examined the correlates of family satisfaction for remarried individuals who were 50 years of age and older (Pasley & Ihinger-Tallman, 1990). Only frequency of disagreement and use of both neutral and negative forms of conflict resolution was associated with lower marital satisfaction in men. For women, frequency of sharing problems with spouse, low frequency of disagreements, and infrequent use of negative strategies for conflict resolution were associated with, and were strong predictors of, perceived emotional closeness, greater commitment, and higher satisfaction with one's family.

Miscellaneous Studies

A number of topics appeared in the literature that could not be readily categorized into substantive topics, such as studies of negative stereotyping. Several studies found stepfamilies to be stereotyped more negatively than other family types (as examples see, Bryant, Coleman, & Ganong, 1988; Coleman & Ganong, 1987a). Another set of studies assessed intervention strategies (almost 4% of the total number of studies examined). The typical finding among these studies showed some form of positive outcome as a result of participation in specially designed programs (as examples see, Currie, 1989; Webber, Sharpley, & Rowley, 1988).

A final group of studies examined the incidence of remarriage and characteristics of remarried individuals in other countries (as examples see, Flinn, 1988; Holman & Woodroffe-Patrick, 1988). Thirteen percent of the studies fell into this category. These studies suggested that, for the most part, the incidence of remarriage has increased, but the characteristics of the remarried population are unique to the country under investigation. In addtion, these studies reveal a declining preference for remarriage in other societies. For example, Blanc (1987) found that nonmarital cohabitation rather than legal marriage was overwhelmingly the preferred type of second union in both Sweden and Norway. Cohabitation contributed significantly to a decline or delay in remarriage.

METHODOLOGICAL ADVANCEMENTS FOUND IN THE LITERATURE

Suggestions from scholars to improve the quality of research on remarriage and stepparenting have identified the need to use larger, random samples; explicitly stated theory; standardized measures; within-group comparisons; multiple methods, measures, and sources; a consistent definition of constructs across studies; multiple rather than single factors; and longitudinal designs. With these recommendations in mind, we again examined the 133 studies conducted since 1987 to determine whether researchers had addressed these concerns.

Many recent studies included analyses of data from large, random samples. Almost 34% used data from large datasets such as national surveys and census data (as examples see, Bumpass et al., 1991; Dawson, 1991; Glick, 1989b). Another 9% reported findings from moderately large (over 300 subjects), randomly selected samples (as an example see, Needle et al., 1990), and almost 13% used nonrandom samples with a sample size of more than 300 subjects (as an example see, Hobart, 1991). The remaining studies used either small, nonrandom samples (49.6%) or small, randomly selected samples (2.3%).

Few of the citations (12%) made explicit reference to theory. Of the theories that were explicitly drawn from, systems theory was the most frequently mentioned (as examples see, Bray & Berger, 1990; Cissna, Cox, & Bochner, 1990).

While scant attention was given to the explicit incorporation of theory, greater attention was paid to the use of standardized measures; almost 37% of the studies used at least one standardized instrument as part of the data collection procedure (as examples see, Hutchinson, Valutis, Brown, & White, 1989; Pill, 1990). Moreover, when comparisons were made, 41.4% of the studies reported findings that offered between-group comparisons; typically, the comparison was between first-married and remarried persons. A few studies made strictly within-group comparisons (2.3%), comparing stepfather families with stepmother families (as examples see, Marsh, 1990; Pasley & Ihinger-Tallman, 1989). Several studies (10.5%) offered findings from both between-group and within-group comparisons (as examples see, Coleman & Ganong, 1987a; Pasley & Healow, 1988).

The majority of studies remained inattentive to the recommendations for stronger efforts to include data from multiple sources with multiple methods and measures. However, a few studies since 1987 have done so. Of the studies examined, 14.3% reported results from multiple sources using responses from both the husband and wife or from the adults and a target child (as an example see, Kurdek & Fine, 1991). Nine percent of the studies used multiple methods and multiple measures (as an example see, Bray & Berger, 1990). Last, with the use of larger sample sizes, researchers were able to perform analyses that examined multiple versus single factors. Thus, the research questions that they addressed and the models they tested were more complex than was evident in earlier studies (as examples see, Bryant et al., 1988; Giles-Sims & Crosbie-Burnett, 1989).

While some studies incorporated standard nominal definitions of constructs, a similarity in operational definitions was less common. The greatest consistency in operational definitions occurred in three areas: marital satisfaction and quality, family adjustment, and child outcome. Spanier's Dyadic Adjustment Scale and the Locke-Wallace Marital Satisfaction Scale were common measures of marital satisfaction and quality (see Bray et al., 1987; Kurdek, 1989a). FACES (II or III) and the Family Environment Scale were common measures of family adjustment (see, as an example, Roberts & Price, 1989). Child outcome was commonly measured with Achenbach's Child Behavior Checklist and a measure of self-esteem, such as the Rosenberg Self-Esteem Scale (as examples see, Bray, 1988; Pasley & Healow, 1988).

Only about 7% of the studies used longitudinal designs (as examples see, Bray & Berger, 1990; Vuchinich et al., 1991). While the results of longitudinal studies are limited, this percentage represents an increase in the number of publications providing results from longitudinal designs compared to studies conducted before 1987.

CONCLUSIONS AND RECOMMENDATIONS

There continues to be a need for additional research on most topics associated with remarriage and stepfamilies. Of the seven topics that Furstenberg (1979) first identified, most topics remain unexamined. For example, we still know little about the consequences of the experiences that precede the remarriage and their effect on later adjustment to stepfamily life, especially for adults. Little is known about the effects of remarriage on other events in the life course, and little is know about changes in cojugal roles from first to second marriages. The nature of the former-spouse relationship and the maintenance and changes of extended kin relationships after remarriage remain relatively unexamined. Further, little is known about (a) stepmother families, especially those that deal with nonresidential, visiting children, (b) the effects of remarriage on young children, especially those under 9 years of age and over age 15, and (c) children who live in well-functioning stepfamilies.

In 1984, Esses and Campbell argued that there was not an adequate model of stepfamily functioning. To date, little progress has been made in delinating the characteristics of good stepfamily functioning. In other words, we do not know what works in stepfamilies. We know far too little about how successful stepfamilies develop and progress over time, the conditions under which successful functioning is fostered, and the variety of interaction patterns that are likely to assure positive functioning. If such knowledge were available, it would not only reveal the secrets of successful family dynamics, it also would provide sound empirical evidence on which to base the development of intervention programs.

At the same time, progress has been made in our understanding of some topics, such as the maintenance and changes in child rearing functions after remarriage. Researchers have begun to examine the nature of family interaction that affects children. Scholars have moved beyond simple comparisons of children by family structure to assess the conditions under which male and female children adapt to stepfamily life and the factors that mediate certain outcomes. Some recent studies have focused on issues of family process. These efforts have helped address concerns expressed by earlier critics.

As with the research on certain child outcomes (such as self-esteem), more research that examines the similarities and differences in the marital quality of first-married and remarried couples would be redundant. We know that the step-parent-stepchild relationship is a key predictor of marital quality; findings from studies of the factors affecting the marital dyad beyond marriage order are less clear. However, more studies that examine the frequency of conflict and the topics that generate it will be less useful to understanding stepfamily dynamics. Instead, attention should be directed to the problem-solving behaviors of spouses and family members that facilitate positive family or marriage outcomes. Knowledge of the factors that inhibit or enhance the ability of remarried couples and families to resolve conflict would provide a greater understanding of family communication. Also warranted are studies that attempt to replicate existing findings in order to validate them. Because of the limitations of past use of small or restricted (e.g., all white) samples and of certain methodologies (e.g., social surveys), we reiterate that future studies need to incorporate large, representative samples and multiple methods. Attention to these methodological issues will result in studies that provide information about complex family dynamics and patterns across groups which is currently not available.

While attention has been directed to understanding stepparenting behaviors, the role of the stepparent requires additional attention. Research that continues to address stepparenting behaviors that facilitate positive child outcomes and enhance member adjustment in stepfamilies warrants additional effort. More specifically, studies have yet to delineate how various members of the stepfamily perceive what is appropriate behavior for a stepparent. The conditions under which such behavior varies (e.g., by sex of the stepparent) need to be specified. In addition, we have little knowledge about the effectiveness of certain stepparenting behaviors over time or which ones remain effective over the family life course. These would be worthy topics to pursue.

Some research focused on kin relationships. However, we continue to know little about the ways in which the interaction between former spouses changes following remarriage and how such interaction affects stepfamily members. Also important may be studies that advance our knowlege of the nature of the relationship that is developed between the same-sex, nonresidential parent and stepparent, how that relationship affects child well-being, and how the nature of the relationship changes over the duration of the remarriage. Further research on the ways in which other kin relationships (siblings, uncles, aunts, grandparents) affect the development of a mutually satisfying relationship between stepparents and stepchildren and the ongoing relationship between the biological parent and child is needed.

We believe that a valuable contribution could be made from additional studies that address the effectiveness of various intervention strategies, including clinical interventions. There is a good deal of clinical literature that recommends some strategies over others; however, there is little empirical evidence to demonstrate their effectiveness. Well-designed evaluation studies are rare. Those cited here used small samples and poor assessment techniques.

Demographic studies of remarriage in various countries are encouraged, as this is a good first step to understanding cultural variations of the remarriage phenomena. Such studies will assist with an understanding of the factors and processes that are unique to a society or cultural group, as well as show the similarities between societies and cultures. To understand patterns of change over time, longitudinal studies are needed using sufficiently large samples so that complex issues can be addressed. We argue that future research must continue to move beyond simple comparisons between different types of families, as family structure per se seems to be less salient to understanding child and adult outcomes. Increasingly, research must further our understanding of why some outcomes are so consistent. For example, why does the stepmother role and the relationship between stepmothers and stepchildren place children in stepmother families at the greater risk for poor adjustment than children in stepfather families? Why does a stepdaughter have more difficulty than a stepson after a parent's remarriage? What factors facilitate effective parent and stepparent communication about children, and how does this affect marital adjustment? Concerning heretofore neglected issues, we ask, how does problem solving differ in well-functioning compared to dysfunctional stepfamilies? What roles do kin, especially those of former spouses, play in enhancing the marital quality and the quality of family life for stepparents, parents, and children?

Finally, our understanding of stepfamily life would be fostered by an increased use of standardized measures, multiple informants, and multiple methods. Studies with these qualities would allow researchers to learn how family communication, interaction, and affection patterns change over time. The use of multiple measures of a single construct is encouraged. The the data from many of the existing national surveys (e.g., NSFH or the National Survey of Children) come from representative samples, some of which are longitudinal in design. However, these studies are limited by the size of their surveys, and they typically include only a single item to measure constructs; psychometric properties of the measures are suspect.

In conclusion, it is our assessment that the quality of research has dramatically improved since 1987. Researchers have attempted to fill the substantive void as well as improve the quality of research design. However, much is left undone, and we challenge current and future scholars to continue to attend to the concerns expressed here as well as those offered over a decade ago; they continue to be relevant today.

KEY CHAPTER POINTS

1. Some progress has been made in examining certain substantive topics, such as child rearing following remarriage and the effects of remarriage and stepparenting on child outcomes.

2. Studies continue to focus on marital quality and child outcomes; a few studies that examined these topics moved beyond simple comparisons by family structure.

3. Greater success was evident in addressing the methodological weakness noted in earlier reviews, such as through the use of larger samples, mutliple informations, and longitudinal designs.

4. Studies continue to be needed that use large, diverse samples and mutliple methods to (a) track changes over time, (b) delineate the conditions under which change occurs, and (c) determine the effects of change (and accompanying conditions) that result in positive outcomes for members of stepfamilies.

NOTE

1. The *Theory, Research & Clinical Literature on Remarriage and Stepparenting* is updated annually by the members of the Focus Group on Remarriage and Stepfamilies of the National Council on Family Relations. Copies are available for $30 (hard copy) from Margaret Crosbie-Burnett, Department of Educational and Psychological Studies, University of Miami, 313 Merrick Building, Coral Gables, FL 33124.

Chapter 2

A MULTIDIMENSIONAL COGNITIVE-DEVELOPMENTAL MODEL OF STEPFAMILY ADJUSTMENT

Mark A. Fine and Lawrence A. Kurdek

Several recent reviews of research on stepfamilies have noted the lack of well-articulated theories in this area (Clingempeel, Brand, & Segal, 1987; Ihinger-Tallman, 1988). The absence of such theories makes it difficult to understand the complex processes by which members of stepfamilies adapt to the unique stresses and challenges of this type of family (Coleman & Ganong, 1990).

This chapter presents a multidimensional cognitive-developmental model of stepfamily adjustment that: (a) conceptualizes the stepfamily as a four-tiered system, (b) describes each member of the system as an information-processing organism attempting to make sense out of experiences related to the life course of the stepfamily, (c) depicts adjustment along a continuum from maladaptation to adaptation, and (d) provides a framework for deriving testable hypotheses to guide future research with stepfamilies.

To simplify the model, the stepfamily system considered in this chapter consists of a biological mother who is divorced from the child's biological father, a residential stepfather in his first marriage, one child, and a nonresidential father. Certainly, we realize that these restrictions limit the generalizability of the model. The experiences of other types of stepfamilies, those with stepmothers, those formed following the death of a spouse, those that have more than one child, and those that have spouses who both have children from previous marriages, may be quite different than those of stepfather families (Clingempeel et al., 1987).

The chapter begins with an overview of the multidimensional model and then considers each dimension in detail. This overview is followed by a discussion of the relation between cognitions and adjustment. Empirical support for the model is noted whenever possible. Finally, the implications of the model for future research on stepfamilies are reviewed.

THE MODEL

General Overview

The core elements of the multidimensional cognitive-developmental model of stepfamily adjustment are presented in Table 2.1. As shown in the table, the model is comprised of four dimensions. The first dimension describes *units in the step-father family system*. These include one-person units, two-person units, three-person units, and the entire four-person system. In two-person units, only direct relations between members of the unit occur. In three-person units as well as the four-person unit, direct and indirect relations between and among members of the units are possible.

Table 2.1

Dimensions of the Cognitive-Developmental Model of Stepfamily Adjustment

Dimension 1: Units in the Stepfather Family System
  One-person units (mother, stepfather, child, and nonresidential father)
  Two-person units (e.g., the mother-stepfather marital subsystem)
  Three-person units (e.g., the mother-stepfather-child residential subsystem)
  Four-person unit (the mother-stepfather-child-nonresidential father system)

Dimension 2: Types of Cognitions
  Perceptions
  Attributions
  Expectancies
  Assumptions
  Standards

Dimension 3: Continuua of Adjustment
  One-person units: individual psychological adjustment
  Two- and three-person units: adjustment of subsystems
  Four-person unit: adjustment of entire system

Table 2.1 (continued)

Dimension 4: Developmental Stages of the Stepfather Family System
    Dating and courtship with eventual stepfather
    Cohabitation (if it occurs)
    Early remarriage (0-2 years)
    Middle remarriage (2-5 years)
    Late remarriage (more than 5 years)

The second dimension describes five general *types of cognitions* (perceptions, attributions, expectancies, assumptions, and standards) relative to stepfamily life which each member of the four-person stepfather family system is posited to construct. In the multiperson units, the key issue is the extent to which the cognitions held by members of the unit are consistent (i.e., the extent to which members have cognitions that are similar and compatible with those of others in the unit).

The third dimension describes the *adjustment* of each unit along a continuum from maladaptation to adaptation. Further, cognitions and adjustment are thought to be reciprocally related, as is the adjustment of each unit member to other members of the unit.

The final dimension of the model is the *developmental stage* of the stepfamily. It is argued that cognitions, and the link between cognitions and adjustment, change over the life span of the stepfamily through such stages as dating and courtship with the eventual stepparent, cohabitation, early remarriage (0-2 years after remarriage), middle remarriage (2-5 years), and late remarriage (more than 5 years).

Dimension 1: Members of the Stepfather Family System

One-person units. Because the mother, stepfather, and child live together, they are one-person units in the stepfamily system. In addition, the nonresidential father is included as a one-person unit of the stepfamily system because data from national surveys indicate that a sizable minority of divorced fathers remain active figures in their children's lives in such areas as paying child support and providing input into child-rearing decisions (Furstenberg, Morgan, & Allison, 1987; Seltzer, 1991).

Multiperson units. The systems perspective adopted here necessitates that relationships within the stepfamily system be examined in terms of subsystems. Subsystems are viewed as structural units consisting of stepfamily members (including the nonresidential father) who have a shared background and a stable pattern of relating to each other. Consider, for example, the two-person mother-child unit. Within a stepfamily, the mother and child form a parent subsystem that has a history and pattern of interaction distinct from the history and pattern of relating that are characteristic of interactions between the stepfather and the child (the stepparent subsystem), the mother and the stepfather (the marital subsystem), the child and the nonresidential father (the nonresidential parent subsystem), and the mother and the nonresidential father (the coparental susbsystem). Because the relationship between the stepfather and the nonresidential father is typically formal and distant (Ahrons & Wallisch, 1987), the stepfather-nonresidential father subsystem will not be considered in depth here.

Direct and indirect relations. In each unit, direct relations occur when members of the unit are involved in the same interaction. For example, both mother and child are directly involved in an interaction in which the mother insists that the child stay home until his or her homework is finished. Only direct relations can occur in two-person units because there are only two individuals involved. Indirect relations occur in three- and four-person units when one person in the unit is simultaneously involved in multiple direct interactions involving different subsystems. For example, in the mother-stepfather-child subsystem, the mother described earlier may angrily issue a homework mandate to her child while she is arguing with her husband over the phone bill. In this example, interaction in the marital subsystem indirectly affects what occurs in the mother-child parent subsystem, and interaction within the mother-child parent subsystem indirectly affects what occurs in the marital subsystem.

Another three-person unit is the mother-nonresidential father-child subsystem. In this unit, the quality of the nonresidential father's relationship with his child is likely to depend on the extent of cooperation he experiences in the coparental subsystem. For example, the father may be able to maintain a positive relationship with his child if he and his former wife have resolved any remaining feelings of attachment and anger toward each other (Berman, 1988; Emery & Wyer, 1987; Masheter, 1991; Visher & Visher, 1988a).

The full four-person mother-stepfather-child-nonresidential father unit involves more complex patterns of direct and indirect relations. Two examples illustrate this complexity. First, interactions within the mother-stepfather marital subsystem may be affected by the nature of the nonresidential father's involvement in the child's life (the nonresidential parent subsystem). If the nonresidential father and the child are able to maintain a consistent and mutually satisfying relationship, this may have a positive impact on the mother-stepfather marital subsystem. On the other hand, if the nonresidential father is erratic in his contact with the child and the child is frequently disappointed by the father's inconsistency, this is likely to tax the mother and stepfather's relationship.

Second, interactions between the mother and nonresidential father (the coparental subsystem) may affect the extent to which the stepfather is directly involved in child care and discipline (the stepparent subsystem). If the biological parents are able to cooperatively and consistently discipline their child (i.e., develop a "parenting coalition," as described in Visher & Visher, 1988), the stepfather is unlikely to be actively involved in child rearing.

Dimension 2: Cognitive Elements of the Model

Baucom and Epstein (1990) described cognitive phenomena as "natural aspects of the information processing that are necessary in order for individuals to understand their environments and make decisions about how they will interact with other people" (p. 47). Cognitions provide meaning, order, and a sense of control. Because the model described in this chapter is designed to explain functioning in stepfather families, cognitions relevant to stepfamily life will be emphasized.

Baucom and Epstein (1990) described five types of interrelated cognitions that affect interpersonal relationships. We will use their taxonomy to organize this discussion of salient cognitions in the stepfather family context. These cognitions are *perceptions* about *what* events occur, *attributions* about *why* events occur, *expectancies* regarding what will occur, *assumptions* about the roles people play and the way in which relationships work, and *standards* regarding how individuals *should* perform their roles and the way in which relationships *should* work.

We conceptualize cognitions as being relevant to both the one-person and the multiperson units in the stepfather family system. For the one-person units, these cognitions are individual psychological phenomenon, whereas for the multiperson units, the consistency of the cognitions held by each member of the unit is of primary importance. The five types of cognitions held by individuals are discussed below. To illustrate each type of cognition and to indicate that family members may have different cognitions of the same event, all examples will refer to an event that affects all four members of the stepfather family system. In this scenario, the stepfather attends the child's Parent Teacher Association (PTA) meeting with the mother, and the nonresidential father is informed of this when he calls the mother to arrange a visit with the child.

Perceptions. Perceptions are those aspects of a situation that an individual notices and fits into meaningful categories. Here is included any aspect of stepfamily living that a member of the stepfamily system notices, gives meaning to, and regards as important. Because perceptions determine what will be attended to, they occur prior to the other types of cognitions. However, one's expectations, standards, assumptions, and attributions also influence what aspects of an event will be noticed (Baucom & Epstein, 1990).

In the PTA scenario, although members of the stepfather family system all noticed the same basic event, they may differ in the aspects of the situation to which they give meaning. The mother's perception might be that the stepfather is showing an active interest in the child. The stepfather's perception might be that he is cooperating with his wife in child rearing. However, the child's perception might be that the stepfather is "butting into" his or her life by inappropriately attending a meeting intended for "real" parents. Finally, the nonresidential father's perception might be that the stepfather is "crowding him out" of the child's life. As this example demonstrates, other cognitions, such as the various attributions for why the stepfather is attending the PTA meeting, influence perceptions.

Attributions. Attributions regarding outcomes in the stepfamily refer to beliefs about the causes of positive and negative events in the family. Attributions serve several purposes, including to help one understand family members, give one a sense of control over his or her life, protect and enhance self-esteem, predict events in one's relationships, and enhance one's image of one's partner or others in the family (Baucom, 1987; Baucom & Epstein, 1990).

Family members' attributions, particularly to the extent that they are stable over time, help them maintain a sense of order and consistency in their family relationships. One's attributions of another's behavior are dependent on earlier information processing (Bradbury & Fincham, 1990; Weiner, 1985). For example, family members have general impressions of, and desires for, themselves, others, and their relationships; these, in turn, often form the basis for the attributions that they generate to explain specific behaviors.

Returning to the PTA scenario, because the mother wants her husband and child to have a good relationship and believes that her husband shares this desire, she attributes her husband's willingness to attend the meeting to his wanting to be directly involved in the child's life. Because the stepfather seeks to strengthen his marriage, he attributes his own behavior to an attempt to please his wife by showing her that he cares for his stepchild. Because the child does not believe that the stepfather is genuinely interested in him or her, the child attributes the stepfather's behavior to pressure from the mother. Finally, because the nonresidential father believes that the mother is encouraging the stepfather to replace him as the child's "father," he attributes the stepfather's attendance to the mother's "pushing" the stepfather to attend the meeting.

As with the other types of cognitions, attributions should not be regarded as "accurate" or "objective" appraisals of the causes of behavior; rather, they are often biased so as to maintain one's general impressions of oneself and others (Bradbury & Fincham, 1990). Thus, even though individuals behave in diverse ways, attributions of their behaviors tend to be quite similar in order to maintain a sense of continuity in impressions of others.

In order to provide a comprehensive assessment of the attributions constructed in family relationships, Bradbury and Fincham (1990) argued that four dimensions must be considered: locus, stability, control, and globality. The ends of these continua include whether the cause of the event (the stepfather attending the PTA meeting) is internal ("I'm interested in my stepchild's welfare") or external ("My wife made me go"); whether it is unstable ("I felt like seeing what it was like at least once") or stable ("I always want to show an interest in my stepchild"); whether it was under the person's control ("I chose to attend the PTA meeting") or is uncontrollable ("I had to go or my wife would have been upset"); and whether it was specific ("I have nothing better to do tonight") or global ("All my evenings are free"). Describing attributions along these continua will be helpful in determining the extent to which they are adaptive for members of the stepfather family, particularly with information related to whether the event is positive or negative (Bradbury & Fincham, 1990) and whether the attribution is "relationship-enhancing" or "distress-maintaining" (Camper, Jacobson, Holtzworth-Munroe,

& Schmaling, 1988).

Expectancies. Expectancies represent beliefs about the likelihood that certain events will occur in the future under certain circumstances (Epstein, Schlesinger, & Dryden, 1988) or, more specifically, what consequences will follow a particular action (Baucom & Epstein, 1990). These expectancies may be based on a history of interactions with actual members of the stepfamily unit or on generalizations made from previous interactions that are carried over to the stepfamily unit.

Using the PTA scenario, the child's stepfather may initially have been reluctant to become involved in child-rearing activities. Now that he has become involved, his wife might expect that he will participate more actively in future activities related to the child. Further, she might expect that her child will be appreciative and will feel closer to her husband. The stepfather might expect that his wife will express her appreciation to him for his decision and might expect that his stepchild will treat him with more respect and kindness. Because the stepfather does not attend actively to the nonresidential father's reaction, he may not have an expectation about how the child's father will respond.

The child might expect that this initial step by the stepfather means that he will continue to "intrude" into the child's life. Further, the child might expect that in future disagreements, the mother will agree more often with the stepfather and less often with the child. The nonresidential father, because his relationship with his child is the most salient aspect of the stepfather family system to him, might expect that the child will want to visit him less and that his ex-wife will make it more difficult for him to continue to see him or her.

Assumptions. Assumptions refer to cognitions regarding how certain types of people typically behave, how relationships usually work, and the way in which one sees oneself in certain roles. These kinds of cognitions may represent stereotypes or prototypes that are derived from lifelong experiences with other people (e.g., children in remarried families have more problems than do children in intact families; see Ganong, Coleman, & Mapes, 1990). Assumptions may also be internalizations of cultural prescriptions regarding role behavior (e.g., the belief that mothers are typically nurturing and self-sacrificing; see Thompson & Walker, 1989).

The mother's primary assumption in the PTA scenario might be that the child needs as many supportive parental figures as possible. As a result, she assumes that stepfathers typically behave as additional parents. The stepfather, on the other hand, might assume that most stepfathers do not actively participate in child rearing because children are better off when their two biological parents make most of the decisions. However, he might also assume that husbands in successful marriages support their wives and often sacrifice to make them happy.

The child might assume that most stepparents are not actively involved with their stepchildren, particularly in school-related activities. The child also might assume that stepfathers will, at times, do what their wives tell them to do. Based on information derived from observations of friends who also are divorced, the nonresidential father might assume that fathers who do not live with their children usually have considerable contact with them. He also might assume that stepfathers typically treat their stepchildren as their own.

Standards. Standards differ from assumptions in that they refer to how things *should* be rather than how they are. Standards represent an ideal comparison level against which actual experiences are compared. Whether the resulting comparison meets or exceeds the standard will affect levels of perceived satisfaction (Rusbult, 1983).

In the PTA scenario, the mother might hold the standard that stepfathers, like biological parents, should be actively involved in their stepchildren's lives. The stepfather might believe that he should support his wife in an area that is important to her, but he himself may not hold the standard that stepfathers should be actively involved in child rearing. The child and nonresidential father might believe quite strongly, at least at this time, that stepfathers should not participate in child rearing activities.

Consistency of Cognitions in Multiperson Units

In multiperson units, the key issue is the extent to which the cognitions held by each member of the subsystem are consistent and in balance with those held by other members of the subsystem. A balanced subsystem is one in which the cognitions of the relevant members are consistent with each other, while an unbalanced subsystem is one in which members' cognitions are dissimilar and incompatible with each other.

The people in the PTA scenario can be used to exemplify both balanced and unbalanced subsystems. If both the mother and stepfather believe that men are primarily responsible for the outdoor maintenance of the home and that women are responsible for the indoor maintenance, they have compatible beliefs. Thus, the marital subsystem is balanced, at least in this aspect of spousal roles. However, suppose the stepfather and child differ in their assumptions regarding the stepfather role. If the stepfather believes that stepfathers are actively involved in discipline and the child assumes that stepfathers have no "right" to discipline them, the stepfather-child subsystem will be unbalanced. Further, conflicting cognitions in the two-person units may indirectly affect the three-person units and the entire four-person stepfather family system. For example, should conflicting cognitions arise between the mother and the nonresidential father regarding assumptions relevant to the stepfather's role, this will likely affect the functioning of both the residential stepfamily subsystem (mother-stepfather-child) and the nonresidential parenting subsystem (mother-nonresidential father-child).

Dimension 3: Continuum of Adjustment

Outcomes are proposed to occur for each unit in the model. Each outcome is depicted as a continuum of adjustment ranging from maladaptation to adaptation.

For each one-person unit, individual psychological adjustment is the relevant dimension. For the two-person units, adjustment is seen as a global evaluation of the functioning of the parent subsystem, the stepparent subsystem, the marital subsystem, and the coparental subsystem. It is important to separate these stepfamily subsystems, as some function well while others may function poorly. For the three-person units, adjustment is conceptualized as a global evaluation of the functioning of the residential stepfamily subsystem as well as the nonresidential parenting subsystem. Finally, the adjustment of the full four-person stepfather family unit is viewed as a global evaluation of how well the entire stepfamily system functions.

Dimension 4: Developmental Stage of the Stepfamily

The developmental component of the model proposes that cognitions and adjustment change over the course of a stepfamily's life span. While life-cycle perspectives have been common in the family literature (Suitor, 1991), they have only recently been applied to the stepfamily literature. For example, Hetherington (1989) distinguished between early stages of remarriage (the first 2 years) and later stages. She argued that the early stages of remarriage are devoted to adapting to the stress of a new life situation, while the later stages are spent negotiating family roles and relationships.

We extend the life cycle of the stepfamily to include time before the actual remarriage. Because remarried persons are likely to cohabit before marriage (Bumpass & Sweet, 1989), premarital interactions between the mother and the stepfather-to-be may set the stage for the way in which family roles and responsibilities are negotiated after the stepfamily's formation. Thus, the life cycle of the stepfamily is viewed as consisting of the following stages: dating and courtship with the eventual stepparent, cohabitation (if it occurs), early remarriage (the first 2 years which are likely to include the child as a residential member of the stepfamily), middle remarriage (2-5 years, a period still likely to include the child as a residential member of the stepfamily), and late remarriage (more than 5 years, a span that is likely to include the child's leaving the mother-stepfather home).

THE RELATION BETWEEN COGNITIONS AND ADJUSTMENT: A SELECTIVE REVIEW OF THE LITERATURE

The relation between cognition and adjustment has been more extensively examined in individuals and in dyads than in families. This literature is selectively reviewed below for each of the five cognitions of interest, with an emphasis on how this relation manifests in stepfamilies.

Whereas the focus of this chapter is on the stepfather family system, we expect that the relation between cognitions and adjustment is similar in more complex stepfamilies. Further, we predict that changes over time in cognitions are similar across stepfamilies differing in complexity. However, complexity increases the number of subsystems and makes it more difficult to establish a well-functioning family. For example, in stepfamilies in which both spouses have children from previous marriages, there are more adults and children, increasing the number of multiperson units in the family system. With this increase comes a larger number of subsystems that need to be balanced so that the entire family system can function well.

Perceptions and Adjustment

Because perception is an active psychological process (Baucom & Epstein, 1990), what is perceived is affected by transitory emotional states as well as by stable personality characteristics (Bradbury & Fincham, 1990). Cognitive therapists working with individuals (Beck, Rush, Shaw, & Emery, 1979), couples (Baucom & Epstein, 1990), and families (Epstein et al., 1988) have emphasized that individuals differ considerably in their perceptions of events in their lives. One important consideration is the degree to which individuals view their experiences realistically. For example, depressed and anxious individuals tend to view themselves, their environments, and their futures in consistently negative ways (Beck et al., 1979).

Extrapolating these findings, stepfamily members who tend to have negative cognitions about themselves and are distressed may be expected to consistently attend to the negative aspects of stepfamily situations and may interpret these experiences as undesirable. By contrast, on the positive end of this continuum, individuals who have realistic cognitions about themselves may view their stepfamily experiences in a balanced and adaptive manner, attending to both the positive and negative aspects and explanations of family events.

Because remarried individuals typically have experienced a distressful prior marital relationship and divorce, it has been suggested that they may perceive marriage more pragmatically and less romantically than persons in first marriages (Brody, Neubaum, & Forehand, 1988; Furstenberg & Spanier, 1984/1987). Although the relatively high divorce rate for remarriages may be consistent with this view (Martin & Bumpass, 1989), the motivations to be married of first-married and remarried persons do not differ greatly (Kurdek, 1989a).

Attributions and Adjustment

Studies of marital relationships have indicated that attributions may bias family members' perceptions and influence subsequent interactions. For example, in comparison to nondistressed couples, distressed couples are more likely to attribute negative partner behaviors to global and stable characteristics of the other person (Bradbury & Fincham, 1990). Such attributions may lead to escalating cycles of anger and conflict.

Leslie and Epstein (1988) have suggested that the structure of stepfamilies increases the number and combinations of factors to which problematic family behaviors can be attributed. On the maladaptive pole of the adjustment continuum, stepfamily members may believe that anything unpleasant that occurs in a stepfamily is the result of being in that family (Visher & Visher, 1988a). Such beliefs reflect stable and global characteristics, as living in a stepfamily is perceived as causing unpleasant outcomes over an extended period of time and across many different situations. Attributing negative outcomes to living in a stepfamily creates potential problems. For example, such attributions may lead to dichotomous thinking (i.e., the tendency to perceive a stepfamily as either all good or all bad) or to a sense of hopelessness by portraying the causes of problems as unchangeable and pervasive (Epstein et al., 1988).

On the adaptive end of the adjustment continuum, pleasant and unpleasant family outcomes may be attributed to a number of factors, including those associated with living in the stepfamily. Here, stepfamily members have realistic assessments of the factors that lead to desirable and undesirable outcomes. Living in a stepfamily can, and often does, contribute to stress and family conflict; however, it is unlikely that the stepfamily itself is solely responsible for family problems. Rather, living in a stepfamily is one among many factors that contribute to both pleasant and unpleasant family experiences (Leslie & Epstein, 1988).

Expectancies and Adjustment

On the maladaptive end of the adjustment continuum are expectations that are inconsistent with the realities of daily living in stepfather families (Leslie & Epstein, 1988). Visher and Visher (1988a) reported that stepparents often have unrealistic expectations ("stepfamily myths") of themselves and their new families, including the beliefs that stepfamilies are functionally equivalent to first-marriage families, that stepfamily adjustment will be attained quickly, and that loving and caring feelings will develop instantly between stepfamily members. These are considered unrealistic because stepfamilies are not functionally equivalent to first-marriage families, stepfamily adjustment does not occur quickly for most stepfamily members (Papernow, 1984), and feelings of love and care between stepparents and stepchildren typically do not develop immediately.

Such beliefs may lead stepparents to hold the expectations and behaviors characteristic of first-marriage families. This, in turn, may lead to frustration when the expectations are not met (Leslie & Epstein, 1988). In support of this notion, Kurdek and Fine (1991), in a study of stepfather families, found that unrealistic expectations were related to lower satisfaction with family, marital, and personal life for mothers and to lower satisfaction with parenting for stepfathers.

On the positive side of the adjustment continuum are expectations of stepfamilies that are consistent with the realities of daily living for most stepfather families.

Such expectations include the following: adjustment in stepfamilies is a gradual and slow process, caring and warm feelings toward stepkin take time to develop, stepfamilies are qualitatively different (although neither better nor worse) than first-marriage families, and hard work on developing relationships with stepkin does not necessarily lead to immediate improvements in intimacy (Visher & Visher, 1988a).

Members of stepfamilies also may have the expectancy that stepfamily living has the potential to be satisfying and that stresses are challenges to be met rather than oppressive burdens. Such beliefs may act as a buffer against some of the stresses experienced in stepfamilies (McCubbin & McCubbin, 1987). Stepfamily adjustment is believed to be facilitated when family members are able to consider their experience as an opportunity to grow and develop (Crosbie-Burnett, 1989a). It should be noted that such expectancies are likely to be adaptive when family members consider stepfamily living to have the potential to be satisfying, but not when individuals believe that stepfamily living *must* be satisfying.

Assumptions and Adjustment

Assumptions about the social roles that people play and the way in which relationships work also may affect the level of adjustment. Cherlin (1978) proposed that the stressful experience of stepparents is partly caused by the absence of clear and societally institutionalized norms regarding what is proper behavior in step-families. Without clear role prescriptions, members of stepfamilies may develop dysfunctional ones.

Role clarity is a central concept in the stepfamily literature. It is defined as the extent to which individuals have a clear idea about how to fulfill a particular role. The negative extreme of role clarity, role ambiguity, has been described as the core difficulty encountered in many stepfamilies (Crosbie-Burnett, 1989; Giles-Sims, 1987a). Role ambiguity includes uncertainty about (a) the scope of one's responsibilities, (b) the specific behaviors needed to fulfill one's responsibilities, (c) whose prescriptions for role behavior should be met, and (d) the effects of one's actions on the well-being of oneself and others (King & King, 1990). Many stepparents, their spouses, and stepchildren lack clarity about appropriate and desired behavior in their home lives, potentially leading to adjustment difficulties (Kurdek & Fine, 1991).

The adaptive end of the adjustment continuum is represented by stepfamily members who have a clear idea about how to function in each of their roles. It should be noted that role clarity is conceptually independent from the adaptability of a particular role, as one may have a clear perception about one's role and yet the content of the role may be maladaptive.

Maladaptive outcomes may be related to dysfunctional assumptions based on the generally negative stereotypes of stepparents or from a desire to overcome them. Several studies (see Ganong, Coleman, & Mapes, 1990) have concluded that people perceive "stepfamily" positions, particularly stepparents, more negatively than similar positions in intact families. The stereotypes of the "wicked" stepmother, "abusive" stepfather, and "neglected" stepchild may negatively affect family interactions by influencing family members' cognitions about stepfamily life, possibly leading to unreasonably high or low expectations.

Other assumptions regarding how families typically function may be transmitted from an individual's family of origin (Epstein et al., 1988). For example, if one's parents maintained traditional beliefs about appropriate family functioning, an individual may consider divorce a "failure" and believe that remarriage and step-family life are undesirable. On the other hand, if a variety of family arrangements were considered viable by one's parents, the individual may hold more optimistic cognitions regarding remarriage and stepfamilies.

Finally, marital satisfaction for both first-married and remarried couples has been related to the kinds of assumptions that spouses make about how relationships function (Eidelson & Epstein, 1982; Kurdek, 1991). Persons reporting high marital satisfaction tend to believe that disagreements can be helpful to a relationship, communication is important in making one's thoughts and feelings known, partners can change their behaviors, and all sexual interactions need not be perfect.

Standards and Adjustment

Marital satisfaction for both first-married and remarried couples has been related to the kinds of standards that spouses have about how relationships should function (Kurdek, 1991). The general pattern is consistent with that described above for dysfunctional assumptions. That is, marital satisfaction is negatively related to endorsements that disagreements should be destructive to a relationship, mind reading should be expected in relationships, partners should not be expected to change their behaviors, and all sexual interactions should be perfect (Kurdek, 1991).

There also is consistent evidence that marital satisfaction is related to an individual's appraisal of the extent to which the current relationship meets or exceeds some internal standard of what a relationship should be like (Rusbult, 1983). This standard may not necessarily be realistic. In stepfamilies, this internal standard of how relationships should be derived in part from family members' beliefs of how relationships typically function in intact families. As noted earlier, Visher and Visher (1988a) reported that parents and stepparents often have the unrealistic standard that stepfamilies should be functionally equivalent to intact families. Particularly in the areas of intimacy and cohesion in relationships, this standard is likely not to be met, and frustration may result (Leslie & Epstein, 1988).

Consistency of Cognitions and Adjustment in Multiperson Units

The consistency of cognitions held by members of a subsystem is of particular importance in multiperson units. We hypothesize that adjustment will be positively related to the degree of consistency in the perceptions, attributions, expectancies, assumptions, and standards held by the members of the subsystem.

Consistency of perceptions. Variability in adjustment may be related to the degree of similarity of unit members' perceptions of the social interaction. Difficulties in resolving marital conflict may be related to attention by the spouses to different aspects of the problem behaviors (Gottman & Krokoff, 1989). For example, wives are likely to attend to the emotional aspects of marital interactions, while husbands are likely to attend to the rational aspects of these interchanges (Thompson & Walker, 1989).

In the PTA scenario, the mother and stepfather attended to the positive aspects of the stepfather attending the meeting, while the child and the nonresidential father attended to the negative aspects of the stepfather's behavior. Such differences in perceptions, and in their emotional valences, may lead to later conflict. Conversely, similarity in perceptions should be related to more harmonious relationships.

Consistency of attributions. Although Bradbury and Fincham's (1990) review of the role that attributions play in marital satisfaction is mostly limited to studies investigating the link between an individual's attributions for events and his or her level of marital satisfaction, it is easy to see how contrasting attributional styles can lead to marital or family problems and how consistent attributional styles can lead to constructive problem solving. For example, a mother who explains her daughter's hostile behavior toward the stepfather as due to temporary adjustment problems which will pass is likely to disagree with a stepfather who interprets this same behavior as willful sabotage. On the positive side, mothers and stepfathers who enter remarriage with the perspective that marital and family events are under their own control will likely approach the inevitable difficulties with positive problem-solving strategies. Differing attributions in the PTA scenario may result in later conflict, as the mother and stepfather have positive (i.e., relationship-enhancing), although differing, explanations for why the stepfather attended the meeting, while the child and nonresidential father have negative interpretations (i.e., distress-maintaining).

Consistency of expectations. Leslie and Epstein (1988) indicated that conflict may occur in stepfamilies when there are inconsistencies in family members' expectations of what will occur. For example, Crosbie-Burnett (1989) indicated that at the time of remarriage, some stepfathers have little intention of contributing to child rearing. If the wife expects that her husband will share parenting responsibilities, marital conflict may ensue. On the positive side, if a stepfather expects to be a disciplinarian of his stepchild and the stepchild shares this expectation, the stepchild is likely, however grudgingly, to accept the stepfather as a legitimate authority figure.

Consistency of assumptions. Problems also can arise when different members of the stepfamily system have differing assumptions of how roles in the stepfamily, particularly the stepfather role, are to be filled. For example, the stepfather may see his role in regard to child care as active. However, his attempts to set and enforce rules may surprise and displease both the mother and the nonresidential father, who may see the stepfather role as merely supporting the decisions made by the parents.

Hetherington (1989) and Bray (1988a) found that stepfamilies functioned most effectively when the stepfather at least initially refrained from becoming actively become involved in parenting and instead performed a "monitoring" function that supported the biological parent. We speculate that part of the reason may be that mothers, stepfathers, and children in these families had clear perceptions of, and agreed about, the nature of the stepfather role.

Consistency of standards. Baucom and Epstein (1990) suggested that marital problems will arise if two spouses have differing standards for their marriage, even though both may have reasonable expectations. When both spouses have incompatible and unreasonable standards, their problems are likely to be compounded.

Such inconsistencies in cognitions may be more likely to occur in stepfamilies than first-marriage families, because stepfamily members' beliefs about family life have been formed while in other family units (Leslie & Epstein, 1988). Positive outcomes in stepfamilies are likely to occur if members of these families integrate or modify their beliefs until some degree of consistency is attained.

Developmental Changes in Cognitions and in the Relation between Cognition and Adjustment

The major stresses associated with divorce are thought to dissipate by about 2 years after the event (Hetherington, 1989). By this time, the single-parent family unit typically has achieved some degree of stability and equilibrium. The transition from the single-parent system to the stepfather family system is a major one, because the balance of the single-parent system may be upset by reallocating the mother's time and attention, changing roles and responsibilities, and introducing into the family system a stepfather who knows little about the specific dynamics of the single-parent unit, and its family life in general.

Because the transition from single-parent family to stepfamily may be stressful, particularly for children (Hetherington, 1989), we propose that cognitions related to stepfamily life will show reliable developmental changes. During courtship between the mother and stepfather-to-be, cognitions, particularly expectations, assumptions, and standards, are likely to be highly unstable within individuals and inconsistent across family members because there are no well-defined ways for the mother's boyfriend to enter into the single-parent system (Cherlin, 1978).

When the stepfather becomes a member of the residential family unit, whether during cohabitation or in the early phases of remarriage, cognitions are expected to begin to stabilize and become more consistent as new patterns of relating are developed and new traditions and routines are established. Further, cognitions are thought to be influenced, not only by the developmental stage of the stepfamily, but also by the age of the child in that family. For example, a stepfather may perceive that he should actively discipline a young child but not an adolescent.

It also is proposed that cognitions will show reliable changes over the life span of the stepfamily. Particularly in well-functioning stepfamilies, family members will (a) develop increasingly clear role perceptions, (b) adopt more realistic expectations of stepfamily life, (c) acquire more balanced attributions regarding the role of living in a stepfamily as a cause of pleasant and unpleasant family events, and (d) be less likely to hold the assumption or standard that stepfamilies are functionally equivalent to first-marriage families. Dysfunctional stepfamilies would be expected either not to show these developmental changes or to have changes in the opposite direction.

It also is hypothesized that the degree of consistency in cognitions in the stepfather family system will increase over time. In well-functioning stepfamilies, differences in perceptions, expectations, assumptions, attributions, and standards will be explicitly acknowledged and discussed. Such differences may be reduced through constructive problem solving and negotiation. For example, in the PTA scenario, the mother and stepfather may realize that they have different standards for how stepfathers should behave. After acknowledging this difference, they may be able to arrive at a consensus on how the stepfather will behave with respect to child rearing. In dysfunctional stepfamilies, cognitive inconsistencies may not be acknowledged or, if they are, not constructively resolved.

Whereas cognitions relevant to stepfamily living are expected to show developmental changes, the basic nature of the relation between cognition and adjustment for each stepfamily unit is expected to stay the same. In general, adaptive cognitions will be positively related to adjustment in individual members, and consistencies in the cognitions of family members will be positively related to adjustment in multiperson subsystems.

IMPLICATIONS OF THE MODEL FOR FUTURE RESEARCH

The model presented in this chapter leads to a number of testable hypotheses, examples of which have been presented throughout this chapter. The two major hypotheses are that (a) family members' cognitions (particularly role clarity, realistic assumptions and expectations, and reasonable attributions for the causes of family events) and the consistency of cognitions in multiperson units will be related to adjustment; and (b) cognitions will change over the life span of the stepfamily, with increasingly clear perceptions of roles, more realistic assumptions and expectations, and more reasonable attributions of the causes of family events developing over time. Further, the magnitude of these cognitive changes is expected to be positively related to the extent to which the stepfamily subsystems are functioning adaptively.

To test these hypotheses, considerable work needs to be done before the constructs in the model, particularly cognitions, can be reliably and validly assessed. Whereas there are numerous measures of individual, dyadic, and family adjustment (see Corcoran & Fischer, 1987; Touliatos, Perlmutter, & Straus, 1990), there are relatively few measures that assess *cognitions*. The Relationship Beliefs Inventory (Eidelson & Epstein, 1982) and its modifications (Kurdek, 1991) tap potentially unrealistic assumptions and standards that spouses hold about their marriages. There also are some measures that assess biased attributions (Epstein et al., 1988) and assumptions of dysfunctional families (Roehling & Robin, 1986).

However, few instruments have been specifically designed for use with families or stepfamilies. Measures of the clarity of the stepfather's role and expectations of stepfamily life have been developed that can be administered to stepparents and biological parents (Kurdek & Fine, 1991) as well as adolescents (Fine, Kurdek, & Hennigen, 1992). However, the psychometric properties of these instruments need to be established, particularly given concerns about the construct validity of already existing measures of role ambiguity (King & King, 1990). Because cognitions are often tied to specific family events, a promising assessment methodology is to ask individuals to report their perceptions, assumptions, attributions, standards, and expectancies in response to standardized family situations described in brief vignettes (see Schwebel et al., 1991) or to family events that are of relevance to the respondents.

Once adequate assessment instruments have been developed, the designs of studies that test the model ideally should include the entire stepfamily system, including nonresidential parents, because the degree of cognitive consistency in various family subsystems is expected to be related to adjustment. In addition, to monitor changes in cognitions and the adjustment correlates of these changes, family members should be studied longitudinally. As the model has posited four stages (five if cohabitation occurs) in the life span of the stepfamily, family members could be assessed in each of these time periods. Finally, although this chapter focused on simple stepfather families, stepfamilies varying on a number of variables (e.g., quality of overall adjustment, simple versus complex family structure, race, socioeconomic status, or whether divorce or death of a spouse preceded remarriage) could be investigated to determine the model's generalizability.

KEY CHAPTER POINTS

1. The stepfamily must be viewed as a multiperson system with several inter-related subsystems. An examination of the subsystems (e.g., mother-child, stepfather-stepchild) is essential to understanding stepfamily adjustment. Interactions and communications in one subsystem have both direct and indirect consequences for other subsystems in the stepfamily.

2. Stepfamily members actively process information related to their experiences. The nature of the cognitions involved in this processing (as well as their consistency and compatability across family members) affects adjustment. Positive adjustment is related to clear role expectations, realistic expectations, balanced attributions about the causes of family events, and a recognition that stepfamilies are not functionally equivalent to first-marriage families.

3. Adjustment is conceptualized as a continuum extending from maladaptation to adaptation. Outcomes are proposed to occur for each subsystem in the model, and some outcomes are more salient for one subsystem than for another. For example, for the individual subsystems, the psychological adjustment of each family member is the most salient outcome, whereas for the marital subsystem, adjustment within the marital relationship of the couple is the primary outcome.

4. Cognitions and adjustment change over the course of the life span of a stepfamily. To the extent that the subsystems in the stepfamily are functioning adaptively, stepfamily members develop increasingly clear role perceptions, realistic expectations, balanced attributions regarding the causes of family events, and reasonable beliefs about the uniqueness of stepfamilies. Furthermore, the cognitions of stepfamily members are expected to become more consistent and compatible over time.

Chapter 3

COMPARISON OF IMPLICATIONS OF THE JUSTICE AND CARE PERSPECTIVES FOR THEORIES OF REMARRIAGE AND STEPPARENTING

Jean Giles-Sims

Scholars of remarriage and stepfamilies have emphasized equity and power relations in the family. In their effort to do so, scholars have relied primarily on theories that assume the presence of rational self-interest, traditional norms and values, and structural influences such as the distribution of resources. These theories do not recognize that individual family members have subjective definitions of justice that evolve from individual motivations, including care for others' needs and couple or family interactions in specific situations. Use of normative resource theories of power and social exchange theory have led to important developments in research on remarriage and stepfamilies. However, research from this perspective does not answer important questions about fairness or mutual needs in families. Specifically, existing power and exchange theories do not adequately account for care of others that is not motivated by self-interest, nor do they account for the importance of the subjective definitions of fairness and feelings of being well cared for. A new perspective is needed that includes subjective assessments and distinctive patterns of care and responsibility to explain remarriage and stepfamily phenomena.

Empirical evidence indicates that subjective definitions of fairness and objective standards of equality do not always match. Thompson (1991) has encouraged family scholars to redefine distributive justice. This redefinition includes a greater focus on a sense of fairness that acknowledges how well cared for people feel and how responsive they perceive their partners and family members to be rather than only on a perceived standard of equality.

This chapter compares the assumptions and usefulness of a redefinition of justice based on responsiveness and care with those of established theories of power and equity, as these apply to remarriage and stepfamilies. It begins with a description of a relatively new and potentially useful conceptualization of justice and fairness: the theory of marital responsibility. It is based on two assumptions. One is that family members either do or do not meet each others' needs in their interactions. A second assumption is that fairness in the relationship involves relational morality, a subjective definition of fairness that is unique to the specific situation rather than defined on the basis of an objective criterion. Both the immediate and the broader social contexts influence family interaction and will be conceptually explained. In addition, this theory of marital responsibility uses four interactional concepts that are important to relational morality: attributions, disclosure, empathy, and cooperativeness. Discussion of this theory and its concepts will focus on its value and contribution to researchers and practitioners concerned with remarriage and stepfamilies. The methodological feasibility of research and theory development using concepts associated with the theory of marital responsibility also will be addressed. A final section evaluates the benefits and continued relevance of social exchange and normative-resource theories and compares them to those of the theory of marital responsibility.

A BRIEF OVERVIEW OF THE CARE AND JUSTICE PERSPECTIVES

The theory of marital responsibility based on relational morality draws on the *Care Perspective* described by Gilligan (1982), Noddings (1984), and Thompson (1989, 1991). It emphasizes that definitions of justice are derived from the meaning of interactional attempts to meet one's own needs and those of other family members in a specific, immediate, and sociohistorical context rather than from universal principles. It further emphasizes that the definition of justice in a particular relationship evolves through interactional processes of attribution, disclosure, empathy, and cooperation. In contrast, power and equity theories rely on an abstract assumption that justice is measured by an equitable split in contributions or value of contributions. These assumptions of power and equity theories are abstract ideas about what should be considered fair based on principles. Gilligan, Noddings, Thompson, and others have labeled this type of thinking the *Justice Perspective.*

Briefly, the Justice Perspective emphasizes the attributes traditionally associated with men (e.g., autonomy and independence) and assessments based on self-interest, rational causal thought processes, and accepted principles of rights and justice (Gilligan, 1982; Thompson, 1989, 1991). Social science traditionally valued these attributes and rational processes, and family theorists have extensively relied on assumptions consistent with the Justice Perspective. Family researchers using the Justice Perspective emphasize fairness and equity as the indicators of morality in marriage, particularly in the distribution of resources, division of labor, and decision making. This has been the dominant paradigm for examining fairness in marriage. In contrast, the Care Perspective emphasizes nurturance, understanding, interdependence, and contextual analysis.

The Care Perspective was identified and popularized by women theorists. The Justice Perspective, and particularly power and social exchange theories, were primarily developed by men. Thompson's (1989, 1991) arguments implicitly claimed that most women emphasize care, disclosure, empathy, and cooperation more than do most men. Traditional gender roles in the dominant social groups produce those differences between men and women in society. Historical gender differences, however, are not biologically inherent. If patterns of socialization and male dominance change, and if both parents share child care, those differences will largely disappear. Thus, as social norms change gender roles, theoretical models need to be adapted to include more emphasis on the variety of motivations and behaviors that people bring to their family relationships.

Thompson adapted and applied the Care Perspective to marriage, emphasizing women's sense of fairness and morality, which is based within relationship definitions rather than on abstract principles. The focus of her theoretical development is different from traditional theories of power and equity. Fairness and justice are defined as relational morality based on meeting one's own and other's needs. Thompson's theory of marital responsibility is described below.

MARITAL RESPONSIBILITY: CONTEXTUAL AND RELATIONAL MORALITY

Thompson (1989) pointed out that responsibility is a neglected moral concern in the marriage and family literature. She argued for a new conceptualization based on the Care Perspective and emphasizing relational concepts and responsiveness to one's own and others' needs. She drew from the work of Bernard (1981), Bellah, Madsen, Sullivan, Swidler, and Tipton (1985), Gilligan (1982), and Noddings (1984) to define the core concept of the theory of relational morality, marital responsibility, as follows:

Responsibility is the activity of receiving and responding to another. Each partner should be sensitive to the suffering, desires, and needs of the other partner. Marital partners strive to meet everyone's needs, prevent harm, and take positive action to protect and promote each other's welfare. Responsibility does not mean that marital partners must be servile or self-sacrificing in order to be sensitive to the needs of others. Striving to meet everyone's needs includes both one's own and other's needs. Indeed, the moral dilemma of marital responsibility is the accommodation of the needs of all family members and relationships. (Thompson, 1989, p. 2)

Thompson's (1989) model is based on the everyday interactional experiences of family members in their own contextual relationships rather than on social structural distinctions (e.g., gender, income, family position, or other social status indicators). As such, this model has many applications for understanding remarriage and stepfamily life. One example of this is a shift to study the meaning of ordinary life events in a stepfamily, not just assessments of family cohesion, or divorce rates, or the adjustment of children. An important aspect of Thompson's model is the primacy of studying interaction within the immediate and the larger sociohistorical context. Following is a descripton of these two contexts.

The Immediate and the Broader Sociohistorical Contexts

Thompson (1989) described the importance of both the *immediate* and the *broader sociohistorical contexts* to the understanding of fairness. The immediate context includes mundane day-to-day events and the symbolic meanings attributed to those events in the immediate situation. For example, in ordinary, day-to-day interaction, stepfamily members either do or do not respond to each other's needs, develop patterns of attachment or remain alone, and do or do not take responsibility for each other through their behaviors and the meanings associated with those behaviors. This emphasis on the symbolic meanings of day-to-day interactions suggests that research using this perspective would focus on how all members of a family interpret the meanings of each other's actions and reactions.

The broader sociohistorical context includes differences in socioeconomic status, norms about family roles, distribution of resources, and other influences imbedded in the culture in which the family lives. Applied to remarriage and stepfamilies, this would include various stepfamily norms, legal rights and responsibilities, and myths and stereotypes that exist across time and across economic, racial, and ethnic groups. Stepfamilies exist in a culture that labels them negatively (Coleman & Ganong, 1987a), discriminates between biological parents and stepparents in legal rights of custody and parental authority (see Chapter 13 of this volume), provides ambiguous legal definitions of economic and caretaking obligations (Fine, 1989; Ramsey, 1986), and generally mistrusts motives and commitments (Visher & Visher, 1980, 1988). If marital responsibility means striving to meet every family member's needs, we must understand how sociohistorical factors influence stepfamily interaction and individual family members' interpretations of their own needs and responsiblities, as well as those of other family members. Studying the historical context and changes in that context provides meaning to day-to-day interactions and also may lead to suggestions for changes in policies and services or to interventions that may improve the well-being of all family members.

This perspective deemphasizes the pursuit of discrete cause-and-effect relationships. It also emphasizes the continuity of context and patterns of responsibility. Applying this theory to our understanding of remarriage or stepfamilies means that the processes of action and reaction can be examined as a continuous causal chain with each new interaction serving as a precedent for new patterns to develop. Using this conceptualization, particular stepfamilies can be examined as case studies by clinicians or researchers to find periods of high or low enactment of family responsibility and to identify the individual or interactional processes related to variation in perceptions of fairness. Relational morality exists when all family members perceive fairness.

Many systems theorists working on stepfamily issues share the basic assumptions of the Care Perspective and emphasize context, the whole family system, and interactional patterns, as Thompson (1989, 1991) has suggested is fundamental to the theory of relational morality. For example, Clingempeel and colleagues (1987), Keshet (1980), Sager and colleagues, (1983) and Visher and Visher (1989) have emphasized the entire family system within a particular context and the inter-actional patterns that produce change and stability over time. Systems theory, as applied to remarriages and stepfamilies, often emphasizes family boundaries as a particular aspects of the immediate family context. Family boundaries indicate where the family begins and ends, define who is included or excluded, and define what is acceptable interaction: all aspects of the immediate contextual relationship. The concept of family boundaries are also useful for cases in which defining family members seek to get their own needs met and expect to meet the needs of others. Stepfamilies usually include complex subsystems, each with their own boundaries (Keshet, 1980) and, perhaps, their own definitions of responsibility and relational morality. Both researchers and clinicians agree that the stepfamily system tends to have more loosely defined or ambiguous boundaries than the first-marriage family system (Pasley, 1987), a phenomenom that may confuse stepfamily members as they assess the relational morality.

The type of stepfamily also influences the definition of stepfamily system boundaries and, thus, patterns of interaction and responsibility. When compared to other types of remarried families, stepmother families have more loosely defined or ambiguous boundaries (Pasley & Ihinger-Tallman, 1989). This influences patterns of responsibility. For example, a stepmother with children from a prior marriage may be so busy meeting her husband's and her own children's needs that she fails to define the needs of a child of her husband, living in another household, as her responsibility. On the other hand, she may be confused about her responsibility to the stepchild. In this case, it would be important to understand how she and other family members define the system boundaries and their responsibility to meet each other's needs.

Aspects of the larger sociohistorical context also may create boundary confusion in stepfamilies. For example, the norms of society that define a family as a house-hold including only parents and children confuse stepfamilies wishing to include children or adults living in other households in their definition of family. Generally, the norms of society that define family boundaries also define patterns of parental or mutual responsibility for care giving. With the recent increase in the number of family members living in different households, it might be useful to employ a criteria of responsibility as the indicator of family boundaries rather than the residence of the household itself.

Other roles or norms from the larger sociohistorical context also influence boundary definition in stepfamilies and, thus, affect patterns of responsibility. For example, gender appears to influence how family system boundaries are main-tained across households, with women more able to maintain responsible patterns of meeting children's needs across different households than men (Furstenberg, Nord, Peterson, & Zill, 1983). It also has been suggested that shared rituals, routines, and habits help clarify boundaries (Boss, 1987; Boss, Pearce-McCall, & Greenberg, 1987). Many of the actual behaviors that are part of these rituals, routines, and habits are caregiving activities (e.g., feeding people or responding to needs through celebrating and providing support). Stepfamilies with a history of shared rituals probably do have clearer boundaries because they participate more in relational patterns of responsibility. Also within the sociohistorical context, legal rights and obligations influence how family system boundaries evolve and how responsibility is defined. An explicit definition of legal rights and obligations of stepparents might help clarify stepfamily boundaries and help maintain patterns of relational responsibility. When nonresidential parents fail to support or stay involved with their children, legal obligations of stepparents and parents become confused. Who is viewed as the parent in the family? Is it the missing, nonresidential biological parent or the stepparent who is *in-loco parentis*? It is possible that legal remedies that support or sanction parental rights and responsibilities for all parental figures in a stepfamily could alleviate some of this boundary confusion and reduce the family conflicts about moral and fiscal responsibility.

In stepfamilies particularly, parental responsibility is distinct from marital responsibility. Thus, research on remarriage and stepfamilies must clearly distinguish the influence of boundary ambiguity and conflicts about responsibility within one subsystem from those in another. Clinicians report negative consequences of boundary ambiguity on marital responsibility. However, findings from at least one pair of researchers (Pasley & Ihinger-Tallman, 1989) appear to conflict with clinical reports. Thompson's (1989) theory of marital responsibility, which emphasizes case study analyses, could distinguish between different types of boundary ambiguity with their different patterns of responsibility and, thus, help sort out the competing evidence in this and other controversies that arise between clinicians and researchers. It also may be that the association of marital problems with boundary issues is related to other, unacknowledged problems in the marital relationship in some stepfamilies. Other stepfamilies with boundary problems may be more able to separate the responsibility to the spouse from the responsibility to the children. These differences can only be determined by studying through case study comparisons or other appropriate methods how family members do or do not meet their own and each other's needs.

Recently, scholars of remarriage and the stepfamily have cited the need for a heuristic, shared paradigm that provides implications for policy, clinical interventions, and direction for future research (Giles-Sims & Crosbie-Burnett, 1989a). Thompson's (1989) theory of marital responsibility as based on relational morality provides a central concept, responsibility to meet one's own and other's needs within specific contexts, that may provide the focus for integrating clinical and research efforts with remarrieds and stepfamilies. The lack of an integrated, shared theory is a fundamental issue in the ambivalent, and sometimes conflictual, relationship between researchers and clinicians. Clinicians often find research-based theories useless for their purposes, while policymakers find it difficult to design programs and evaluate interventions without a basic theoretical consensus. In addition, there are questions about how to use knowledge that was accumulated through clinical work and program evaluation in the further development of theory. This is because the conceptual focus or the methodologies are not consistent with a well-developed theoretical framework. If researchers, clinicians, and policymakers could agree that for family members to meet their own and each other's needs is fundamental to all their interests, then theory could be developed to explain key issues. These issues are (a) when the meeting of needs is likely to happen, (b) how clinicians can intervene to make this happen, and (c) what policies facilitate or block the development of responsibility and relational morality.

The theory of marital responsibility differs from other existing perspectives and may add insight to the search for a shared, heuristic framework. The following sections suggest additional ways for this perspective to be integrated with existing and future research on stepfamilies. These suggestions will enrich our shared theoretical understandings and help bridge the gap between researchers and practitioners. This discussion includes the conceptual ideas, the value and contribution of the perspective to researchers and practitioners, and the methodological feasibility of research and theory development using concepts associated with the theory of marital responsibility.

Marital Responsibility: Conceptual Issues

The theory of marital responsibility (Thompson, 1989) emphasizes that morality is based on relational processes and evolving definitions of fairness. Conceptually, this is called *relational morality* to distinguish it from more abstract principles of morality. Relational morality in a remarriage between spouses or between stepfamily members is theoretically linked to the success of the marriage and the quality of relationships between all family members because marital (of family) responsibility depends on meeting one's own and others' needs. In stepfamilies ranging from the most simple to the most complex, this would be conceptually linked to interaction patterns and dynamics in relationships that influence how partners balance the needs of various members. In marriages, Thompson says that:

Partners must have a way to strike a balance between the needs of self and others when all are deserving, affect and need one another, and have a future together. Responsibility is not simply mulled over in the solitary minds of individual family members; it is something that is struggled over together in order to shape a shared understanding about what is right and wrong, good and bad. Relationship morality acknowledges that bonds between people have histories and futures. Responsibility is never fully resolved; it is episodic and changeable; it is an ongoing social accomplishment for wives and husbands. Relational morality means that the tension between self and other, as well as the tension between one self-other relationship and another, creates moral dilemmas. Our moral selves evolve through our relations with others. Morality is evident in how we treat each other day by day, and we construct morality through dialogue. (1989, p. 7)

In stepfamilies, responsibility would depend on balancing the needs of individuals, marriages, and children from different marriages, and possibly those of nonresidential family members as well.

Furthering theoretical work in this area requires a greater specification of the processes that lead marital partners or family members to define their relationships as fair and moral. Thompson (1989) identified four interactional concepts that influence patterns of relational morality: attributions, disclosure, empathy, and cooperativeness. Each of these critical concepts needs further definition and explanation here. The following paragraphs provide summaries of Thompson's ideas.

Attribution. Attribution is the process of judging the meaning or intentions of others in order to interpret their behavior and uncover reasons for it. Family members attribute intentions to, and reasons for, each other's behavior. Thus, they build meaning about the nature of their relationships. Behavior can be attributed to either internal/personal factors or situational factors.

Disclosure. Disclosure is the process of verbally or nonverbally revealing one's thoughts, beliefs, and feelings to others. Family members either may or may not disclose their needs to one another. Relational morality requires members to understand and respond to each other's needs, and disclosure appears necessary for this kind of understanding and response.

Empathy. Showing empathy is the process of listening, understanding, and actively responding with care for another. Empathy includes family members recognizing each others' signs of needs, listening for meaning, understanding what another is disclosing, and responding to those needs.

Cooperation. Cooperation is the social process in which individuals work together to meet their own or each other's needs. The benefits of cooperation outweigh those that are available through individual effort. Dialogue can lead to a mutual understanding of needs, and a willingness to act together on those needs equals cooperation.

Family members influence the thoughts, feelings, and behaviors of one another through attributions, disclosure, empathy, and cooperation. Remarried partners and stepfamily members help or hurt each other through the day-to-day, common experiences of living. Usually, family members take this interaction for granted unless strong emotional reactions such as feeling hurt, angry, or dominated occur frequently. These are "moral lapses" on the part of the family member acting unjustly, insensitively, or pressing for unwanted change in another. Tension from these lapses often occurs in stepfamilies because of the difficulty of balancing the needs of all members, particularly given the fact that the family members often lack shared histories and may experience divided loyalties. Tension occurs early in remarriages, and particularly in stepfamilies with adolescents because of the added stresses associated with adolescent development (Giles-Sims & Crosbie-Burnett, 1989b).

Not all the needs of stepfamily members can, or should be, met exclusively within the stepfamily. Other outside sources of support are, or should be, available to meet these needs. Conceptually, relational morality would require each family member to identify and disclose which needs he or she wishes to have met within the family and where (and if) they have other support systems that can meet those needs if they are not met within the stepfamily. This allows a family member to clarify his or her own needs and allows others the opportunity to meet (or not meet) relationship responsibilities.

Members of stepfamilies may define relational responsibility differently from first-married families. A comparison of definitions across individual families, and between different members of the same family, will provide a basis for distinguishing processes in stepfamilies of varying complexity without simply comparing them with first-married families.

Stepfamily members often cross household boundaries. Consequently, patterns of care and responsibility need to be taken into consideration as family members identify their attempts to get their needs met. Some clinicians claim benefits from interventions with the total remarried family system (Sager et al., 1983). However, Visher and Visher (1988) and Browning (Chapter 10 of this volume) have argued that the early inclusion of stepfamily members living outside the residential family household impedes the development of a strong marital unit. Again, the different views of family members may reflect differences in individual contexts or in definitions of inclusion based on patterns of responsibility. The subjective definition of needs in marital responsibility theory provides a framework for including stepfamily members' identification, disclosure, and responses to needs of other members even if they do not reside within the primary household. Relational morality could subjectively be based on behavior in one household. However, this conceptualization also may be useful for understanding how members in different households meet each other's needs, particularly biological parents and their children who live separately.

Cooperation is a particularly critical concept to the theory of relational morality for stepfamilies of one household or across households. Cooperation between family members requires shared understandings and a willingness to discuss, negotiate, and compromise about personal needs and responses to the needs of others. People decide how to meet each other's needs (to what level and according to what priorities). In stepfamilies, members have different, and often competing, needs. The children's needs may compete with the needs of the couple to form a stable marital bond. Stepsiblings may compete with each other for their parents' attention. Former spouses may compete for the time and attention of children. Stepfamily members also sometimes find that their needs do not receive an adequate response. This is because the bases of empathy and cooperation have either (a) never been established or (b) broken down in the turmoil of family transitions (e.g., from preseparation to divorce, courtship, and finally remarriage). Further transitions (e.g., the birth of a new sibling or a transfer of custody) often disrupt new patterns that were beginning to develop.

Thompson (1989) emphasized that cooperation differs from conflict resolution. "The emphasis is on collective interpretation and fulfillment of needs rather than individuals pursuing their own *interests* in a collective" (p. 12). The distinction occurs not so much here between individual needs and interests as between the collective understanding and the pursuit of goals. Cooperation results from collective dialogue: the discovery of what is needed in a particular context, and subsequent understanding. Relational morality emphasizes grounds for understanding rather than grounds for agreement (Gilligan, 1987, 1988) and trustworthiness rather than power (Boszormenyi-Nagy & Krasner, 1986, as cited in Thompson, 1989, p. 13). In this approach, morality is judged on the individual's perceptions of fairness that result from attributing, disclosing, empathic responses, and cooperation.

Achieving high levels of relational morality within the stepfamily would ideally involve all stepfamily members in the processes through which it develops. If members withdraw, withhold themselves, or insist on an individualistic orientation, relational morality will not develop. Relational morality also is not likely to develop without dialogue that is free from rigid definitions of roles. Risman and Schwartz (1989) and Thompson (1989, 1991) have emphasized that stereotypical gender roles or assumptions of gender differences inhibit relational morality.

Rigid ideas about stepfamily roles also would be likely to hinder relational morality. Theoretically, stereotypical stepfamily roles or assumptions about the commitment or predispositions of stepparents would inhibit this process. Thompson (1989) argued that relational morality will be more likely to develop when partners allow the meaning of their family roles to emerge without predefined assumptions. It is easy to advise people not to be influenced by gender roles, stepfamily roles, or other indicators of position in society, such as race or the control of resources. However, it is more difficult for anybody to actually avoid being influenced, given the impact of specific roles, scripts, and differences in resources between people. Thus, it is shortsighted to eliminate all aspects of social-structural influences from this theoretical model. In the relational morality perspective, those influences are analyzed as part of the sociohistorical context for individual family processes.

Other theories more consistent with the Justice Perspective (as outlined in the beginning of this chapter) posit structural influences as independent causes that affect outcomes related to justice and equity in families. The theory of marital responsibility, as based on relational morality, conceptually treats gender, race, socioeconomic status, and other structural factors as part of a context in which individuals work to define and mutually influence their own roles and statuses in relationships. This is in opposition to looking at structural factors as primary causes of power or equity, independent of the subjective definition. The Justice Perspective focuses more on the importance of abstract principles of fairness and justice rather than on definitions of fairness derived through relational processes.

The next section briefly discusses the methodological issues associated with research on marital responsibility. Following that is a discussion of the continuing benefits and relevance of resource theories of power and social exchange theory, which share many of the assumptions of the Justice Perspective.

Marital Responsibility: Methodological Issues

To assess marital responsibility, researchers need both more sophisticated conceptual definitions of relational morality and new assessments of stepfamily members' interactions. Thompson's (1989) theory of marital responsibility strongly suggests using behavioral observation to measure relational morality. Measuring morality within this perspective also requires studying the interactional processes of all family members and/or subsets of two or more members. An assessment instrument would have to go beyond the level of most existing stepfamily instruments. The existing instruments use individual or multiple respondents to report on the whole family. A new instrument would actually assess interaction between multiple family members: ideally, between all family members as a group and as subsets of the larger group. This type of research has problems. It is not easy to gain the cooperation of all family members, mobilize the necessary resources to gather the needed data, and analyze the data gathered using the statistical methods available to most researchers. Many available instruments (e.g., The Stepfamily Adjustment Scale; see Crosbie-Burnett, 1989c) include measures of the quality of relationships, perceived fairness, and mutual suitability gathered from each member's perspective. However, the aggregate measures assess agreement or difference between individuals' reports rather than the actual interaction.

Some studies have used observational techniques to examine behavioral interaction between stepfamily members. Brand and Clingempeel (1987) used a structured interaction task to gather data on quality of the marital relationship in stepfamilies by measuring positive versus negative communication behaviors in videotaped interactions. Hetherington, Cox, and Cox (1985) also video-recorded and analyzed stepfamily interaction in the home using three different family members as targets of observation (two parents and a child). The researchers coded children's behaviors for coping style and degree of social competence. They also coded each family members' affect in the interaction as positive, negative, or neutral. Hetherington and colleagues (1985) used a structured family problem-solving task to stimulate interaction and assess individual family problem-solving processes.

Santrock, Warshak, and Elliott (1982) and Santrock and Sitterle (1987) also used behavioral observations of the interactions of children with their parents and stepparents. The coding categories for the child included warmth, self-esteem, anxiety, anger, demandingness, maturity, and sociability. The coding categories for the parent or stepparent's behavior included control, encouraging emotional independence, engaging in verbal interactions, attentiveness to the child, directive versus facilitative behavior, and authoritarian, authoritative, and/or permissive parenting (Santrock & Sitterle, 1987). This type of interactional analysis could be extended or adapted to measure concepts of attribution, disclosure, empathy, and cooperation, which are central to the theory of marital responsibility based on relational morality.

Existing observational studies may guide the development of new techniques for gathering interactional data, but the existing coding schemes focus on individual behaviors of parents and children separately rather than on relationship processes. Assessing relational morality requires time series observations of disclosure, attributions, degree of empathy in response to needs, and cooperative definition of needs and action to meet those needs. An assessment could use structured tasks that provide opportunities to engage in each of these four relational behaviors. For example, stepfamily members' attributions could be assessed by asking each member to describe what they expect to do for each other and what they expect the others to do for them in a context that allows other family members to respond and discuss their own understandings. In stepfamilies, members are often unclear about what is expected of them. Having them discuss this topic would allow a researcher to identify specific patterns of misunderstanding between family members' attributions of meaning. Transcripts could be analyzed for the presence (or absence) and degree of each different type of attribution. They also could be examined for the interactional consequences of those attributions.

Observing interaction also can reveal the degree of reciprocity in patterns of disclosure and empathic response. Observing intimate behavior would allow researchers to assess how family members meet each other's needs for care and respond to each other's disclosed thoughts, feelings, or beliefs. It also would provide data to analyze what interactional patterns lead to a withholding of needs or response or to a refusal to acknowledge or meet the needs of another. For relational morality to develop, each stepfamily member must first identify his or her own needs. Then the other members must respond with empathy. At a minimum, these initiations and responses must be subjectively defined as reciprocal if all members are to perceive moral fairness. Individual, subjective definitions of degree of fairness could be compared to objective assessments of expressed behavior. The theory of marital responsibility emphasizes the subjective meaning rather than the more objective process of observation and assessment based on an abstract standard.

Methods also could be devised to ask stepfamilies or subsets of stepfamily members to discuss and come to an agreement, if possible, on the nature of the individual and family needs. Then, the opportunity for family members to agree (or not) on priorities for meeting competing and/or conflicting needs could be provided. Methods of assessment must be based on the interactional processes and the family members' own perceptions of fairness in outcomes that result from those processes.

Perceptions of fairness in any family depend on how cultural norms for behavior (e.g., gender roles and stepfamily members' roles, as noted above) influence family members' expectations and behaviors. Thus, any assessment of relational morality will require attention to how interactional patterns have emerged from role expectations and from previous dialogue and interaction. Both gender issues and stepfamily role issues need to be investigated in all research on stepfamily responsibility.

Ideally, observational data will be gathered on normal behavior in normal settings. However, to do so requires enormous amounts of time, and data quality depends on chances of observing a particular behavior and the likelihood of other factors influencing a particular observation. Repeat observations and reliability checks over time do reduce these problems somewhat, but they remain a concern in natural settings. In contrast, laboratory research restricts the number of outside influences on the interaction. However, it raises questions about the validity of data gathered in an artificial setting. New strategies that optimize the benefits and minimize the drawbacks of each method of data gathering will be welcome.

Clinicians have a great deal to contribute to the search for new data-gathering methods. They often use collective discussion and other techniques to identify stepfamily members' problems with attributions, disclosure, empathy, and cooperation. Such clinical techniques help stepfamily members clarify their own and each others' needs and misunderstandings. Techniques that elicit information about these processes in clinical families could be systematized and adapted for use in gathering observational data. Ideally, research teams would combine clinicians and researchers who have computer and statistical knowledge to conceptualize projects, gather and analyze data, and further theory development. This would occur through an explanation of patterns of findings within and across different stepfamilies. The emphasis on the importance of care in the family and the interactional patterns of behavior that are combined in the marital responsibility theory do provide a collective focus for collaborative research and theory development on remarriage and stepfamilies. However, no one approach is likely to answer every question. The development of science depends on the contributions of multiple theories and methodological approaches. The next section discusses the continuing benefits and relevance of social exchange theory and provides some comparison with the theory of marital responsibility based on relational morality.

THE JUSTICE PERSPECTIVE: SOCIAL EXCHANGE THEORY REEVALUATED

Scholars of remarriage and the stepfamily often emphasize social exchange, equity, and power relations in the family as aspects of social justice. Equity theory and resource theories of power borrow heavily from rational models of fairness that are based on assumptions of economic self-interest. This is compared to the assumption of the theory of marital responsibility (Thompson, 1989) that family members try to meet others' needs as well as their own. The Justice Perspective focuses on the benefits that each person receives as outcomes in a relationship as a measure of distributive justice. The Care Perspective focuses on fairness in the emotional processes which is inherent in the relational morality perspective.

Social exchange, equity, and resource theories of power direct attention to outcomes that occur as a result of bargaining, negotiation, and structural variables. These theories seek to explain the nature of the exchange relationship as based on the value of costs and rewards exchanged, the effect of alternative sources of rewards, the effects of a balance or imbalance in power and dependency on a relationship, and how exchange rules develop over time to govern the social exchange process (Giles-Sims, 1987b). Usually, researchers accept the normative definitions of costs, rewards, values, and alternatives rather than rely on subjective evaluations. For example, cultural norms define increased amounts of time, money, and attention as benefits. On the contrary, advancing age and certain sexual orientations are defined as costs. In accepting such cultural norms, researchers fail to consider that a family could perceive these factors differently in different family situations.

Social exchange theory emphasizes abstract principles of justice rather than subjective definitions. This theory tends to emphasize the rational pursuit of self-interest and to discount the presence and importance of care in families. The basic assumptions of social exchange theory consistently fit within the Justice Perspective. Social exchange theory makes several assumptions: (a) individuals seek their own goals, (b) their ability to achieve those goals is highly contingent on power derived from the socioeconomic system, (c) increased power in exchange relationships is related to individual satisfaction, and (d) balance or equity is related to mutual satisfaction and stability in relationships. There is considerable empirical support in the remarriage and stepfamily literature for theoretically derived hypotheses based on these four assumptions (Crosbie-Burnett & Giles-Sims, 1991; Giles-Sims, 1987; Giles-Sims & Crosbie-Burnett, 1989b). Despite the existing research on social exchange and normative resource theories of power, the arguments from the Care Perspective need to be integrated into future research and theory development on remarriage and stepfamilies. People's motivations can, and often do (particularly for women), include care and the desire to meet others' needs in addition to furthering one's own goals. Clearly, subjective assessments of costs and benefits can, and often do, differ from normative assumptions of value.

Future work should focus on the question: Is there any way to integrate the theory of marital responsibility derived from the Care Perspective and theories derived from the Justice Perspective? I can only provide a few suggestions here for such future efforts. However, it is my hope that they will stimulate others to continue this effort.

Social exchange theory is useful for understanding how social-structural variables, particularly gender and racial differences in opportunities, distribution of resources in society, and social class hierarchy, influence social relationships. The theory of marital responsibility based on relational morality includes these concepts as influences within the dimension of the sociocultural context. However, it places an increased emphasis on how race, class, and gender norms from the larger society are defined and adapted within a specific context through family interaction. In addition, it emphasizes individual family definitions rather than normative definitions. This theory assumes that normative definitions influence how families define their own roles, but that the family members make independent contributions to those definitions. The equity and power theories neglect this process of individual adaptation and modification of societal norms and values.

The equity and power theories address other issues that are important to the field of remarriage and stepfamilies and that do not fit easily into the conceptual paradigm suggested by the relational morality theory. For example, structural factors such as age, gender, race, and resource allocation influence whether there will even be a relationship in which to interact. For example, interracial relationships are still rare; people tend to marry within homogamous groups; men have higher chances of remarriage than women (Glick, 1992); age influences the chances of remarriage, as does the presence of children (Sweet & Bumpass, 1988). Focusing on relational morality limits the discussion of fairness to relationships that have already been achieved and omits opportunities for achieving relationships. In contrast, social exchange theory and theories of power include the opportunities to establish relationships and examine the effects of alternatives to current relationships on relationship outcomes. For example, norms suggest that as men age, the value associated with their success and status increases the opportunities available to them for other potential marriage relationships. This is compared to women's value in the marriage market which is traditionally based on fleeting characteristics of youth and beauty. In additon, children in stepfamilies often have the opportunity to choose an alternative home with a nonresidential parent, which influences relationships within the current residential home.

Power and equity theories define alternatives as social structural conditions that independently influence outcomes. It is possible to integrate the emphasis of power and equity theory on opportunities and alternatives into interactional assessments of fairness or equity in relationships by specifically addressing family members' perceptions of their own alternatives. Thus, these concerns from power and equity theory could be integrated with those in the theory of marital responsibility without loosing the benefits of either.

If researchers focus too narrowly on what happens within the couple or family relationship to determine if relational morality exists, they may miss the importance of structural factors. The theory of marital responsibility based on relational morality emphasizes the meaning of exchanges that emerge through dialogue when individuals attribute intentions or motivations to each other, when they disclose, when they empathize, and when they cooperate. The task of integrating the strong points of social exchange theory with this relational morality theory involves including both the individual value of what is exchanged in relationships and the collective meaning that develops through the interactional processes in the family. These are two, quite distinct, analyses, but any integration of the perspectives would need to take both into account.

A more fundamental difference between the assumptions of social exchange theory and those of the theory of marital responsibility based on relational morality may hinder integration. Social exchange theories emphasize negotiation based on self-interest rather than emphasizing cooperation and attempts to meet both one's own needs and those of others. However, social exchange theory does emphasize that commitment in relationships tends to modify self-interest (Cook & Emerson, 1978) and that exchange rules emerge in long-term relationships to govern interaction (Emerson, 1976). These changes that take place over time are assumed to be related to the benefits of security and predictable behavior. There is still little room in this perspective for other-directed behaviors, such as care, empathy, and cooperation unless they produce observable benefits. This fundamental emphasis on care distinguishes the theory of marital responsibility based on relational morality from all theories consistent with the Justice Perspective. At this time, theory to explain remarriage and stepfamily phenomena would benefit from including more emphases from the care perspective in models of family processes, given all the family research already generated by social exchange, equity, and power theories. An integration of the two perspectives allows the theorist to be more inclusive of the perspectives of women, various racial and ethnic groups, children and adults, and older adults.

Overall, the theory of marital responsibility based on relational morality provides a model for understanding many of the same processes identified in social exchange theory. However, the approach uniquely focuses on (a) disclosure rather than benefits contributed to the relationship, (b) identification of needs through dialogue that allows the formation of correct attributions, (c) empathy rather than costs of relating, and (d) cooperation rather than negotiation. The assumptions of these two perspectives differ considerably, and the assumption of self-interest in social exchange theory has been widely accepted. With the emergence of the Care Perspective, we can be more inclusive when examining social relations and developing theoretical models. The theory of marital responsibility based on relational morality challenges theorists to see the world through different lenses and to ask if this alternative perspective is more reflective of social behavior because the assumptions are more consistent with reality.

CONCLUSIONS

This chapter presented a theory of marital responsibility based on relational morality that contrasts with the assumptions of the Justice Perspective and provides an impetus for new theoretical developments to explain remarriage and stepfamily phenomena. It emphasizes that family members try to help each other, meet each other's needs, and protect each other from harm, although they may not always succeed in these efforts. Using this perspective, research is needed to identify the kinds of processes that promote this caring orientation as opposed to those factors that encourage self-interest, as outlined by social exchange theory. Stepfamilies often face conflicting loyalties, competing needs, ungenerous attributions, and undeveloped patterns of empathic response. Most existing theories that explain the influences of these conflicting and competing pressures assume that family members are motivated primarily by self-interest. However, stepfamily members may not necessarily be motivated by self-interest, even when they act to maximize their own rewards. It may be that the characteristics of dialogue between family members do not allow them to accurately disclose their own feelings of care for others's needs or that unsatisfying responses occur because of motivations other than self-interest. These complex interactional problems need to be addressed by both researchers and clinicians.

The theory of marital responsibility based on relational morality challenges the assumption and emphasis of social exchange models on the rational assessment of costs and rewards as the primary motivators in family relationships. The Care Perspective elevates responsibility, commitment, and care to a stronger, more valued position in the analysis of relationship stability, change, or dissolution. Feminists have argued that emotional issues of caring have been devalued compared to rational assessments of justice because females have the traditionally assigned family tasks (Risman & Schwartz, 1989). Being a lower status group, women's unique contributions are tainted by their position in society. This low status influences the relative neglect of women's perspectives within the family theory literature.

Motivations of some women and men toward their partners and children rest largely on commitments to try to give to others, meet their needs, and make continued efforts to promote another's welfare and protect loved ones from harm. Remarrieds may be hesitant and careful about new commitments, trying to avoid past mistakes. However, remarrieds also show significant efforts to make things work out in the remarriage and to try to prevent redivorce. The relational morality perspective and the modification of existing models of fairness in marriage and family relationships allows these patterns of care and responsibility to be considered in more inclusive theories to explain remarriage and stepfamily phenomena. Theoretical models will be more valid by including this new perspective, clinical interventions will be more effective, and research will produce more useful results.

KEY CHAPTER POINTS

1. A redefinition of justice based on care and mutual responsibility is compared to theories of power and equity and applied to remarriage and stepfamily life. Most theories of power and equity assume that people are motivated primarily by self-interest. The theory of relational morality emphasizes that family members try to help each other, meet needs, and protect each other.

2. The immediate and sociohistorical contexts influence the processes that lead to relational morality. Thus, stepfamily resarch must continue to assess factors related to age, gender, socioeconomic hierarchy, role definitions, myths, and so on. Research also must assess how stepfamilies accept, reject, redefine, and respond to the contextual influences through their everyday interaction.

3. Conceptually, this theory emphasizes attribution, disclosure, empathy, and cooperation in interactions that are aimed at attaining marital responsibility.

4. Methods of assessment must be interactional rather than rely on one, or even multiple, family member or members to describe family experience.

5. The theory of marital responsibility based on relational morality and its appropriate methodology allows for greater focus on processes within individual families. Thus, it would be more useful to clinicians than to researchers who use structural theories that emphasize immutable factors.

Chapter 4

MARITAL QUALITY AND MARITAL STABILITY IN REMARRIAGE AND MULTIPLE REMARRIAGES: A TEST OF LEWIS AND SPANIER'S HYPOTHESIS

Kay Pasley and Eric Sandras

For most researchers in the field of family studies, the statistics regarding divorce and remarriage have become all too familiar: About 60% of all first marriages end in divorce (Martin & Bumpass, 1989; Bumpass, Martin, & Sweet, 1991). Cherlin and McCarthy (1985) and Glick (1989b) indicated that more than one out of five households with a married couple is a remarried-couple household. Moreover, the divorce rate for these couples has been predicted to be about equal to that of first marriages, at 61% (Glick, 1984). While research on remarried couples is more common (Pasley & Ihinger-Tallman, 1992; Coleman & Ganong, 1990), little is known about those who marry three or more times. These people are sometimes called *serial marriers* or *serial divorcers* (Brody et al., 1988). Little is known about the differences or similarities between first remarriers and multiple marriers, so it is difficult to predict the marital outcome of those who marry several times. Most research on remarried couples has not distinguished between these groups, although it has been assumed intuitively that there are differences (Brody et al., 1988; Vemer et al., 1989).

Intuitively, such remarriages may differ on two important dimensions: marital quality and marital stability. Lewis and Spanier (1979) proposed that these two dimensions were important to understanding marital relationships. They defined marital quality as the "subjective evaluation of a married couple's relationship" (p. 269), whereas they saw marital stability as determined by the state of intactness of the relationship; those who were currently married were designated as having a stable relationship, while those who divorced had an unstable relationship. Booth, Johnson, and Edwards (1983) refined Lewis and Spanier's definition of marital stability to mean "the propensity to dissolve an existing marriage" (p. 388) because intactness was believed to be a measure of the result, or lack thereof, of stability (Bitter, 1986; Booth et al., 1983; Kelley & Conley, 1987). Lewis and Spanier asserted that quality has a positive influence on marital stability. In short, if a spouse's subjective feelings about the overall satisfaction with the relationship were high, chances were that marital stability would be high as well. Intuitively, one might assume that the two dimensions are not independent. However, Lewis and Spanier hypothesized that it was possible to be high on one dimension and low on the other because of external influences of alternative attractions and external pressures to remain married. For example, a couple might be unsatisfied (low quality), but due to religious convictions, they might choose to remain married (high stability). On the other hand, a couple might be content being married (high quality) but decide to divorce because of financial opportunities (low stability).

Studies have examined the relation between quality and stability as influenced by alternative attractions and external pressure to stay married (e.g., Green, 1983; Schumm & Bugaighis, 1985; White & Booth, 1985). The majority of these studies supported Lewis and Spanier's hypothesis that the quality and stability of marriage are the dominant influences in predicting marital outcome, while alternative attractions and external pressures act as mediating variables.

A majority of the research on married couples that tested Lewis and Spanier's (1979) theory has focused on first-married couples. Some research has reported differences in the quality and/or stability of remarriages as well (Aguirre & Kirwan, 1986; Vemer et al., 1989; White & Booth, 1985). In general, it was found that people in first marriages report about the same level of marital satisfaction as do people in remarriages. Until recently, the stability (as measured by the intactness of the relationship) of first marriages was reported to be slightly higher than that in second or subsequent marriages. However, no study could be found that examined systematically such differences between second marriages and multiple remarriages. Thus, it is not known whether Lewis and Spanier's theoretical predictions hold for multiple-remarried couples.

Using Lewis and Spanier's conceptualization, the purpose of this research is to determine whether marriage order in remarrieds is predictive of marital quality and stability. If this hypothesis is *not* supported, and if marriage order proves not to predict marital quality and stability, the study will attempt to determine whether other factors affect marital quality and stability (e.g., church attendance, number of children, external alternatives, and frequency of agreement). These factors were hypothesized to differentiate marital outcome in remarrieds (Aguirre & Parr, 1982; Brody et al., 1988).

RELATED LITERATURE

Lewis and Spanier's (1979) model was developed to help understand the forces that hold marriages together (or encourage their dissolution). These authors argued that stability is indicated by whether a marriage is intact. Given this conceptualization, those currently married are labeled as having a stable marriage, while those currently divorced are considered unstable. However, a close examination of the theory raises questions about construct validity. Several scholars have pointed out that having a marriage that is legally intact is not a true measure of stability

(Bitter, 1986; Booth et al., 1983; Kelley & Conley, 1987). Instead, it has been argued that "low marital quality does not necessarily signify a high propensity toward divorce, permanent separation or desertion" (Booth et al., 1983, p. 387). It is generally recognized that many spouses whose marriage is of low quality remain married, while some whose marriage is of high quality end the marriage. Thus, propensity to dissolve an existing marriage is the more common conceptualization of marital instability (Bitter, 1986; Booth et al., 1983; Kelly & Conley, 1987).

Numerous influences have been identified that serve to increase or decrease the propensity toward marital dissolution. Among the most common influences noted in the research literature are variables that define the psychological makeup of the relationship (Albrecht, 1979; Kaslow, 1981; Kelley & Conley, 1987), religiosity (Booth et al., 1983; Heaton & Pratt, 1990), the number of attractive or unattractive alternatives to marriage (Aguirre & Kirwan, 1986; Galligan & Bahr, 1978; Udry, 1983), and in remarriage, the presence of children (Ganong & Coleman, 1989; White & Booth, 1985). It has been suggested that the type and number of constraints against divorce affect the probability of not terminating the marriage. Findings suggest that the more resources available that increase the attractive alternatives to marriage (resources may include level of education, income, and other assets), the greater the chance of dissolution. Conversely, the fewer resources one has, the more attractive the marriage, which increases marital stability.

According to Lewis and Spanier (1979), quality is conceived as a combination of many related concepts. The present study employed their concept of *marital quality*, which encompasses a range of terms (i.e., marital "satisfaction," "happiness," "communication," "integration," "adjustment," etc.). The concept of marital quality is the traditional dependent variable in most marriage research. This term represents qualitative dimensions or evaluations of the marital relationship, and at the empirical level, the different terms are highly correlated. These several concepts (e.g., good judgment, adequate communication, and high levels of integration) are all attributes of marital quality, serving to strengthen or diminish the overall marital relationship. The research findings are consistent and support Lewis and Spanier's assertion that these characteristics give an accurate picture of marital quality (Green, 1983; Kelley & Conley, 1987; White & Booth, 1985).

Tests of Lewis and Spanier's Theory: Remarriage

Aguirre and Kirwan (1986) used the model proposed by Lewis and Spanier to examine the effects of marriage order on dimensions of marital quality and stability. The results of their study showed that the model was applicable to both remarried and first-married couples. They classified over 2,000 respondents into one of four categories: husband and wife in first marriage (H1W1); husband and wife in second or higher marriage (H2W2); husband in second or higher marriage and wife in first (H2W1); and husband in first and wife in second or higher marriage

(H1W2). They found a positive relationship between marital quality and stability for couples when both were in a first marriage, consistent with Lewis and Spanier's assertion. For the small number of H2W2 couples, marital stability appeared to be related to quality in a curvilinear fashion, with low stability at both extremes of the marital quality dimension. That is, contrary to what was expected, marital stability declined if the quality was either very high or very low. They also found that there were higher levels of verbal conflict among couples when both were in second marriages. The authors speculated that this finding might stem from different communication patterns being used in these remarriages than had been learned and used in prior marriages. They further speculated that communication may increase constructive arguing and, thus, enhance the subjective evaluation of the marriage while decreasing marital stability because of dissensus. Finally, for both H1W2 and H2W1 couples, two factors were found to influence quality and stability: the presence of children from a prior marriage and the religiosity of the couple. The presence of children had a negative effect on quality and stability, while the amount of time in church had a positive effect on stability (but not quality). The findings regarding the effects of children on marital quality in remarriage are consistent with those of White and Booth (1985).

One study compared the findings from a number of studies to identify correlates of marital satisfaction (Vemer et al., 1989). Using meta-analytic techniques, 34 studies of remarriage that assessed marital satisfaction were examined. The comparison group for most of these studies consisted of first-married respondents. Findings suggested that those in first marriages reported greater satisfaction, but the difference was not substantial. This finding is important because it demonstrates the applicability of measures of marital satisfaction to remarried couples. Given the similar reports of marital quality in first marriages and remarriages, Vemer and her associates suggested that one way to explain the lower stability of remarriages was the fact that "most researchers have not distinguished second marriages from multiple remarriages" (p. 721).[1]

Multiple Remarriers

Information about multiple marriers is scarce, and empirical comparisons of remarrieds and multiple-remarrieds were not found. Some data are available, however, on the prevalence of persons in a second or subsequent marriage. U.S. Census Bureau data from 1975 indicate that 2,318,000 people, or 2.1% of the married population, had been married three or more times (Cherlin, 1978; Spanier & Glick, 1980). Brody and colleagues (1988) suggested that with each successive marriage, the probability of future marital stability decreases. They proposed some of the possible contributing factors to serial marriages: distinct personality characteristics of one or both spouses (e.g., impulsivity, immaturity, social nonconformity, and an individualistic orientation), repetition of maladaptive behaviors across marriages (e.g., selecting incompatible mates), holding low expectations for marital success, perception of marriage as a conditional commitment, and unrealistic expectations (e.g., overromanticism or a view of marriage as a panacea for the problems of life). However, Brody and his associates failed to empirically test their propositions by comparing remarriers with serial marriers or to offer ways of predicting the probability of dissolution.

While Lewis and Spanier's (1979) model has been useful in comparing first-married with remarried couples, it has yet to be applied to multiple-remarried couples. If the conceptual model should hold for multiple-remarrieds, it would follow that they would more likely fall into the low-stability quadrants of the model, and possibly, in the low-quality quadrants as well (when compared with remarriers). Moreover, if the hypothesized typology is supported, determining which remarried persons fall into the four quadrants allows us to identify those more prone to becoming serial marriers or serial divorcers. While a true test of this prediction requires longitudinal research, some insights can be gleaned from a cross-sectional study.

To summarize, the study presented here will first determine whether marriage order in remarrieds is predictive of marital quality and stability. If this hypothesis is *not* supported and marriage order proves not to predict marital quality and stability, the study will attempt to determine whether other factors affect marital quality and stability (e.g., church attendance, number of children, external alternatives, and frequency of agreement).

METHODS

Subjects

Data used for this study came from the National Survey of Families and Households (NSFH; Bumpass & Call, 1988). The NSFH called for a national probability sample of 10,000 households in the United States. It oversampled 3,000 households from a variety of family types, some of which included remarried and minority households. The sampling design yielded a total of 13,017 interviews. For this analysis, only primary respondents who reported that their current marriage was a second or subsequent marriage were included ($n = 1,572$).

The demographic data on this subsample showed that 82% of the respondents were in a second marriage, while 18% were in a third or subsequent marriage. The subsample contained 46% males and 54% females, whose median age was 40-44 years; median household earnings were $30,000-$40,000 annually; and median education was 12 years. Of the subsample, 83% were Anglo, 11% were African-American, and the remaining 6% were Hispanic, Asian, American Indian, or some other ethnic origin.

Measures

Dependent variables. The NSFH included questions ascertaining marital quality and stability, the two dependent variables examined here. The question used to assess quality was a single-item measure that asked, "Taking all things together, how would you describe your marriage?" Responses on a 7-point scale ranged from *very happy* to *very unhappy*, with high scores indicating greater marital quality. The strongest measure of marital quality is said to be a global measure similar to this question (Green, 1983).

The second dependent variable was stability which was measured via scores from two questions. One question asked, "It is always difficult to predict what will happen in a marriage, but realistically, what do you think the chances are that you and your husband/wife will eventually separate or divorce?" Responses on a 5-point scale ranged from *very low* to *very high*. Scores were reversed, so high scores indicated greater stability or less likelihood of separation or divorce. A second item asked respondents, "During the past year, have you ever thought that your marriage might be in trouble?" Responses included *yes* (1) and *no* (2); therefore, a higher score indicated more stability. These items significantly correlated in the expected way. An alpha reliability was calculated with a summed score from these two items at .56.

Independent variables. Factors believed to affect marital quality and stability were also included. These included perceived alternatives (e.g., the perception that certain aspects of life would be better if the respondent were not married), number of children, church attendance, age, sex, income and education levels, duration of marriage, perceived fairness regarding household chores, working for pay and spending money, level of agreement regarding money, spending time together, household tasks, sex, children, in-laws, and beliefs about the permanency of marriage. Recall that Lewis and Spanier (1979) argued that alternatives to marriage were hypothesized to increase the possibility of dissolution, while barriers were posited to work in the opposite fashion. To measure the external alternatives to marriage, respondents were asked the question, "For each of the following areas, how do you think things would change" (if they separated): standard of living, social life, career opportunities, overall happiness, and sex life. The responses on a 5-point scale ranged from *much worse* to *much better*. A summed score was calculated; therefore, lower scores represented a perception that things would be better if they were not married, suggesting that dissolution would be more attractive. An alpha reliability was calculated at .62. Higher levels of income and education also were considered as assets that enhanced one's ability to perceive alternatives to marriage.

Barriers to dissolutions included the presence of biological children and stepchildren, age of respondent, agreement on issues, perceived fairness, attitude toward marriage, church attendance, duration of the relationship, and marital history of spouse. Research has found that: (a) the presence of children increases the propensity for marital stability (Heaton, 1990); (b) older adults are less likely to perceive divorce as a viable alternative (Booth, Johnson, White, & Edwards, 1986; Glick, 1988); (c) agreement on issues is likely to foster marital stability (Lewis & Spanier, 1979; Pasley, Ihinger-Tallman, & Coleman, 1984); (d) the perception of fairness in the relationship enhances the quality and stability of the union (Thompson, 1991); (e) holding certain traditional beliefs about marriage serves as a barrier to dissolution (Booth et al., 1986); (f) church attendance fosters marital stability (Booth et al., 1986; Heaton & Pratt, 1990); (g) relationships of longer duration are less likely to dissolve (Booth, et al., 1986); and (h) the prior marital status of a spouse increases the likelihood of dissolution (Aguirre & Kirwan, 1986).

An assessment of these eight variables was possible using the demographic information provided by respondents and several survey items. Agreement on issues was measured with a series of items that asked how often in the last year the respondent and his or her spouse had had disagreements about money, spending time together, household tasks, sex, and in-laws. Responses ranged from *never* (1) to *almost every day* (7). A summed score was calculated; therefore, higher scores indicated higher levels of agreement. The alpha reliability was calculated at .74. Additional items asked about perceptions of fairness in the relationship in three areas (household chores, working for pay, and spending money). The question asked, "How do you feel about the fairness in your relationship in each of the following areas?" Responses on a 5-point scale ranged from *very unfair to me* to *fair to both* and then to *very unfair to her/him*. The assumption was that the less fair the person perceived the relationship to be to both spouses, the greater likelihood that divorce would be seen as a viable option. These items were scored; therefore, high scores indicated a perception of more fairness to both spouses and low scores indicated fairness to only one of the spouses. These three items were examined separately because the calculated alpha reliability was too low (.08) to permit using a summed score.

An attitude measure asked respondents to indicate their level of agreement with the statement, "Marriage is a lifetime relationship and should never be ended except under extreme circumstances." Responses to a 5-point scale ranged from *strongly agree* to *strongly disagree*. High scores on this item represent a strong commitment to the institution of marriage.

Data Analysis

Of the respondents, 82% reported being in a second marriage, 15% in a third, and 3% in a fourth or subsequent marriage. Thus, 82% of the respondents were considered remarrieds, while 18% were designated as multiple-remarrieds. Subjects were then categorized into four groups in the marital quality and marital stability typology of Lewis and Spanier (1979), depending on their scores on both the quality and stability measures. This reduced the number of respondents to 1,343 because of missing data on at least one of the items assessing the dependent variables. The mean scores from the quality and stability measures were used to designate respondents into four categories. Those scoring 5 or lower on the stability and quality measures were categorized in the low-stability and low-quality quadrant of the model (Group 1, $n = 178$ or 13.3%). Those scoring 6 or higher on the stability measure and 5 or lower on the quality measure were classified into the high-stability and low-quality quadrant (Group 2, $n = 166$ or 12.4%). Those scoring 5 or lower on the stability measure and 6 or higher on the quality measure were categorized in the low-stability and high-quality quadrant (Group 3, $n = 78$ or 5.6%). Last, those scoring 6 or higher on both the stability and quality measures were classified into the high-stability and high-quality quadrant (Group 4, $n = 921$ or 68.6%). Figure 4.1 shows the number and percent of male and female respondents appearing in each of the four quadrants of the model.

FIGURE 4.1

Number and Percent of the Male and Female Respondents Classified in the Four Quadrants of Lewis and Spanier's (1979) Model

	STABILITY	
	LOW	HIGH
LOW	**GROUP 1** Men: 73 (12.1) Women: 105 (14.2)	**GROUP 2** Men: 73 (12.1) Women: 93 (12.6)
HIGH	**GROUP 3** Men: 42 (6.9) Women: 36 (4.9)	**GROUP 4** Men: 417 (68.9) Women: 504 (68.3)

(QUALITY shown at left, with LOW for the top row and HIGH for the bottom row.)

Next a series of analyses of variance tests was calculated separately for men and women to identify differences between the four groups on the variables, with particular attention paid first to differences in the marriage order of those classified into one of the four quadrants of the model. On the basis of these results, only those variables that differed significantly by group were included in a discriminant function analysis to discover which variable or variables most strongly differentiated respondents in each of the four groups and how accurately the variables would predict group membership. All analyses were performed separately for men and women because the literature suggests that men and women experience marriage differently (Thompson & Walker, 1989).

RESULTS

Remarrieds and Multiple-Remarrieds

The results presented in row 1 of Tables 4.1 and 4.2 suggest that the marriage order of the respondent (remarrieds versus multiple-remarrieds) did not significantly differentiate the marital stability and marital quality of respondents in any of the four groups shown in Figure 4.1 for either men or women. The marriage order of respondents' spouses significantly differentiated between Groups 2 and 4 for men only (row 2 of the same Table 4.1). The spouses of men characterized by high marital stability and low marital quality (Group 2) were more likely married for a second time than spouses of men in Group 4 (high stability and high quality).

Table 4.1

Means, Standard Deviations (*SD*), and *F*-Statistics for Marital Stability/Marital Quality Groups for Men

Variables	Group 1 Mean (SD)	Group 2 Mean (SD)	Group 3 Mean (SD)	Group 4 Mean (SD)	F
Number of marriages	2.22 (.48)	2.26 (.44)	2.36 (.58)	2.26 (.55)	1.072
Spouse's marriage order	2.59 (1.89)	2.28 (1.11)	1.95 (.85)	1.89 (.94)	10.113***
Number of children	1.30 (1.29)	1.04 (1.23)	1.14 (.95)	1.03 (1.24)	1.011
Length of marriage[a]	127.76 (70.47)	171.26 (138.01)	113.14 (74.89)	168.47 (140.55)	4.001**
Age[b]	4.84 (2.18)	7.63 (2.98)	6.41 (2.17)	7.24 (3.02)	3.333*
Income	$36,223.12 ($22,977.89)	$31,280.88 ($64,455.95)	$35,831.79 ($36,752.96)	$35,747.36 ($41,042.47)	.867
Education	12.99 (2.42)	12.29 (3.44)	14.55 (15.79)	12.60 (5.40)	.447
Church attendance	1.25 (1.46)	2.13 (2.81)	2.40 (5.95)	2.95 (4.88)	1.627

Table 4.1 (continued)

Variables	Group 1 Mean (SD)	Group 2 Mean (SD)	Group 3 Mean (SD)	Group 4 Mean (SD)	F
Perceived alternatives	13.59 (3.12)	17.39 (3.26)	16.83 (3.32)	18.60 (2.99)	55.715***
Agreement	29.04 (5.13)	31.69 (3.90)	30.62 (3.51)	33.47 (2.66)	25.107***
Fairness-chores	2.53 (.67)	2.63 (.62)	2.71 (.63)	2.77 (.47)	2.725*
Fairness-pay	2.68 (.60)	2.77 (.52)	2.79 (.47)	2.87 (.41)	4.901**
Fairness-spending	2.54 (.65)	2.79 (.48)	2.69 (.56)	2.90 (.33)	16.113***
Attitude toward marriage	3.41 (1.09)	4.04 (.98)	3.90 (.96)	3.99 (1.03)	4.129**

[a] Calculated in months.
[b] Categorized into 4-year groups; for example, 4 = 30-34 yrs., 5 = 35-39 yrs., 6 = 40-44 yrs., and so on.
*$p \leq .05$, **$p \leq .01$, ***$p \leq .001$.

Table 4.2

Means, Standard Deviations (*SD*), and *F*-Statistics for Marital Stability/Marital Quality Groups for Women

Variables	Group 1 Mean (SD)	Group 2 Mean (SD)	Group 3 Mean (SD)	Group 4 Mean (SD)	F
Number of marriages	2.22 (.52)	2.18 (.44)	2.22 (.42)	2.15 (.39)	1.427
Spouse's marriage order	2.78 (1.27)	2.65 (1.20)	2.19 (1.09)	2.36 (1.09)	5.684***
Number of children	1.30 (1.46)	1.20 (1.22)	1.61 (1.27)	1.16 (1.28)	2.189

Table 4.2 (continued)

Variables	Group 1 Mean (SD)	Group 2 Mean (SD)	Group 3 Mean (SD)	Group 4 Mean (SD)	F
Length of marriage[a]	151.95 (99.17)	177.67 (125.87)	129.11 (87.33)	163.62 (134.99)	1.700
Age[b]	5.74 (1.98)	6.69 (2.72)	5.14 (1.90)	6.55 (4.92)	
Income	$34,460.12 ($32,324.03)	$35,169.65 ($33,120.89)	$36,247.47 ($26,806.14)	$38,276.46 ($44,709.35)	1.265
Education	12.26 (2.85)	12.28 (3.23)	12.86 (1.92)	12.35 (2.55)	1.933
Church attendance	2.37 (2.58)	3.47 (4.57)	2.38 (2.36)	3.41 (4.55)	1.978
Perceived alternatives	14.76 (3.66)	16.61 (3.26)	17.77 (2.81)	19.35 (2.92)	67.748***
Agreement	29.04 (5.13)	31.69 (3.90)	30.62 (3.51)	33.45 (2.66)	51.911***
Fairness-chores	2.22 (.73)	2.56 (.60)	2.53 (.61)	2.77 (.49)	25.482***
Fairness-pay	2.63 (.63)	2.77 (.48)	2.53 (.70)	2.83 (.44)	4.569***
Fairness-spending	2.49 (.74)	2.71 (.51)	2.61 (.65)	2.92 (.32)	24.265***
Attitude toward marriage	3.39 (1.29)	3.74 (1.17)	3.25 (1.36)	3.85 (1.19)	5.550***

[a] Calculated in months.
[b] Categorized into 4-year groups; for example, 4 = 30-34 yrs., 5 = 35-39 yrs., 6 = 40-44 yrs., and so on.
*$p \leq .05$, **$p \leq .01$, ***$p \leq .001$.

For the most part, however, marriage order did not differentiate between those categorized into the four quadrants of the marital stability and marital quality model. As a result, further analysis to compare the remarried and multiple-remarried individuals was not undertaken. Therefore, the primary research question was answered by concluding that the marriage order of the respondent does not predict marital quality and stability (except for men in Groups 2 and 4).

Characteristics of the Marital Quality and Marital Stability Groups

Since marriage order was less salient for differentiating marital stability and marital quality in remarriage, attention was directed next to identifying the similarities and differences between those classified into the low and high marital-stability and marital-quality categories. The results of the analyses of variance tests to determine differences between the four groups on the variables (e.g., alternatives and education) found nine of the variables significantly differentiated between groups for men (see Table 4.1). Similar results were found for women, with eight of the variables differentiating the groups (see Table 4.2). The mean scores on each of the independent variables allow us to offer a brief descriptive summary of the men and women who fall into these categories, reporting only those results where significant differences between groups were found.

Group 1 (low stability and low quality). The men ($n = 73$) in this group are best described as (a) the youngest when compared to men in Groups 2 and 4; (b) being married fewer months than men in Group 4; (c) most likely to perceive that their life would be better if they were not married than men in other groups; (d) more likely to report a higher level of disagreement over issues in their marriage than men in Groups 2 and 4; (e) most likely to perceive working for pay as unfair to one spouse than men in Groups 2 and 4; (f) more likely to perceive household tasks and spending money as unfair to one spouse than men in Group 4; (g) most likely to believe that marriage was *not* a lifetime relationship than men in other groups; and (h) less likely to attend church than men in Group 4.

The women ($n = 105$) in this group are best described as younger than women in Groups 2 and 4 and more likely to perceive that their life would be different if they were not married than women in other groups. They reported the least agreement, and they were more likely to perceive household tasks and spending money as unfair to one spouse than women in the other groups. When compared to women in Group 4, these women (like the men) were less likely to attend church and see marriage as a lifetime commitment and more likely to report that working for pay was unfair to one spouse.

Group 2 (high stability and low quality). Men ($n = 73$) in this group were more likely than men in Group 4 to be married to a women with prior marital experience. They had been married longer than men in the other groups. They also perceived significantly fewer alternatives to marriage and more fairness to both spouses in spending money and seeing marriage as a lifetime commitment than men in Group 1. Moreover, these men showed more agreement on issues than men in Groups 2 and 3, but less agreement than men in Group 4. They were older than the men in Groups 1 and 3.

The women ($n = 93$) in this group were older than those in Group 3, and compared with Group 1, they saw more alternatives to their marriage (but fewer than those in Group 4). They reported less agreement on issues than women in Group 4 but more agreement than women in Groups 1 and 3. These women perceived more fairness to both spouses in household tasks than women in Group 1 and less fairness than women in Group 1. Similarly, they perceived more fairness to both spouses regarding working for pay than women in Group 3 and less fairness in spending money than women in Group 4 (but more fairness than women in Group 1).

Group 3 (low stability and high quality). The men ($n = 42$) in this group were younger than those in Group 2 (the oldest) and had been married fewer months than the men in other groups. These men reported fewer alternatives to marriage than those in Group 1 and more than those in Group 4. They had less agreement on issues than men in either Groups 2 and 4, and a stronger belief in the lifetime commitment of marriage than men in Group 1, who were the least committed.

The women in Group 3 ($n = 36$) were the youngest, and were significantly younger than women in Groups 2 (oldest) and 4 (next oldest). They were more likely than women in Group 4, and less likely than women in Group 1, to see alternatives to marriage. These women were more likely than those in Group 1, and less likely than those in Group 4, to perceive that household tasks were more unfair to one spouse; they were less likely to see working for pay as fair to both spouses than were women in Groups 2 and 4; and they were more likely than women in Group 4 to perceive spending money as unfair to one spouse. They were less likely to agree that marriage was a lifetime commitment than women in Group 2 (most likely) and Group 4.

Group 4 (high stability and high quality). The men in Group 4 ($n = 417$) were next to the oldest and significantly older than men in Group 1. They were the least likely to be married to a spouse with prior marital experience, had been married longer than men in either Groups 1 or 3, and were the most likely to attend church. These men were the most likely to (a) perceive few alternatives to their marriage, (b) report agreement on issues, and (c) perceive that spending money was fair to both spouses. In addition, they perceived that household tasks and working for pay were fair to both spouses to a greater degree than men in Group 1. They were less likely to believe that marriage was a lifetime commitment than men in Group 2, but more likely to believe this than men in Group 1.

The women in this group ($n = 504$) were younger than the women in Group 2 and older than the women in Groups 1 and 3. They were more likely to attend church than the women in Group 1. In addition, they perceived the fewest alternatives to marriage, agreed on issues the most, and felt most strongly that household tasks and spending money were fair to both spouses, when compared to women in the other groups. Last, these women were more likely to perceive working for pay as fair to both spouses and that marriage was a lifetime commitment than women in Groups 1 or 3.

Predicting Group Membership

A discriminant function analysis was performed to determine the accuracy with which these variables could predict group membership for men and women. The results of these analyses are presented in Table 4.3. The findings suggest that for men, nine characteristics included in the analysis accurately predicted membership in Group 1 and Group 4 (64.3% and 56.6%, respectively). Only 31.9% of the men categorized in Group 2 (high stability, low quality) were classified accurately. Fewer men (34.3%) were accurately classified into Group 3 (low stability, high quality). The overall predictive accuracy of the equation was about 53%.

The eight characteristics entered in the equation for women were only slightly more successful in accurately predicting group membership. That is, 55.6% of the women were accurately predicted to be in Group 1 (low stability, low quality) and 63.9% were classified into Group 4 (high stability, high quality). Fewer women were successfully predicted into either Group 2 (37.1%) or Group 3 (46.9%). The combined variables resulted in a predictive accuracy of about 59%, slightly better than group placement by chance.

The standardized canonical correlation coefficients are presented in Table 4.4.

Table 4.3

Results of the Discriminant Function Analysis Showing Frequency (Percent) of Group Classification

		Men			
		Predicted Group			
Actual Group	*n*	Group 1	Group 2	Group 3	Group 4
Group 1	42	27 (64.3)	3 (7.1)	6 (14.3)	6 (14.3)
Group 2	47	8 (17.0)	15 (31.9)	9 (19.9)	15 (31.9)
Group 3	35	7 (20.0)	8 (22.9)	12 (34.3)	8 (22.9)
Group 4	302	32 (10.6)	59 (19.5)	40 (13.2)	171 (56.6)
Ungrouped	21	7 (33.3)	5 (23.8)	3 (14.3)	6 (28.6)

Table 4.3 (continued)

Actual Group	n	\multicolumn{4}{c}{Women — Predicted Group}			
		Group 1	Group 2	Group 3	Group 4
Group 1	81	45 (55.6)	16 (19.8)	9 (11.1)	11 (13.6)
Group 2	70	13 (18.6)	26 (37.1)	12 (17.1)	19 (27.1)
Group 3	32	9 (28.1)	0 (0.0)	15 (46.7)	8 (25.0)
Group 4	404	11 (2.7)	67 (16.7)	68 (16.8)	285 (63.9)
Ungrouped	26	5 (19.2)	7 (26.9)	4 (15.4)	10 (38.5)

These were examined to determined which variable or variables were the strongest predictors of group membership. For men, the perception of alternatives (e.g., how much better or worse they would be if separated) was the strongest predictor of group membership (canonical correlation of .668). The next strongest predictor was the agreement over issues, followed by perceived fairness in spending money (canonical correlations of .358 and .291, respectively). For women, agreement about issues was the strongest predictor, with a standardized canonical correlation of .543. The next strongest predictor was alternatives to marriage (.523), followed by perceived fairness regarding household chores and spending money (canonical correlations of .300 and .279, respectively).

Table 4.4

Standardized Canonical Discriminant Function Coefficients

Variable	Men	Women
Spouse's marriage order	-.278	-.141
Length of marriage	.037	--
Age	.075	-.038

Table 4.4 (continued)

Variable	Men	Women
Perceived alternatives	.669	.523
Agreement	.358	.540
Fairness-chores	.220	.300
Fairness-pay	.035	.100
Fairness-spending	.291	.279
Attitude toward marriage	.158	.100

DISCUSSION AND CONCLUSIONS

The prediction that multiple remarriers would be lower in marital quality and marital stability generally was not supported. This finding suggests that being remarried more than two times does not necessarily mean that a person perceives his or her relationship as unstable or of low quality. The one exception was that marriage order of spouse differentiated men in Group 2 from men in Group 4 (both groups had high stability and varied in the level of marital quality). For men, it may be that having a spouse with more marital experience places him at greater risk for variation in relationship quality while not affecting marital stability. There is some evidence to suggest that when a remarriage involves a man with no prior parenting experience, the new stepfather has more difficulty with marital adjustment (Roberts & Price, 1987). When a man's spouse has more prior marital experience, he may be less willing to acknowledge the possibility of divorce, believing that the "second time around" guarantees marital success. These same men may be less willing to admit having thoughts of separation. It may be more acceptable to admit some degree of marital dissatisfaction and less acceptable to admit that the marriage might be in trouble. In other words, it may be easier for such a man to say that the relationship is not as satisfying as he wishes it were than to admit to having serious problems and thoughts of ending the relationship. We tested this interpretation with additional data analysis to determine whether a particular combination of marriage orders was characteristic of a marital-stability and marital-quality group. The findings support our interpretation: we found no significant differences in marital stability between remarried men whose spouse had been married three or more times (H2W3) and those in any other combination of marriages. Examples of other combinations of marriages are a man in a second marriage whose spouse had no prior marriage (H2W1), or man in a third or subsequent marriage whose spouse had three or more marriages (H3W3). However, differences were found between men of various combinations of marriage order on the measure of marital quality, with H1W3 men reporting less marital quality. The combination of marriage order of the spouses (e.g., H2W3, H3W1) may be more salient to understanding these dimensions of the marital relationship for men.

An important question addressed in this study was how persons categorized into the various quadrants of the model differed. The findings suggest consistent differences between Group 1 (low marital stability and low marital quality) and Group 4 (high marital stability and high marital quality). Having high marital stability and quality is associated with increasing age, fewer alternatives, more agreement, and more fairness. Perceiving more alternatives to one's marriage was the strongest predictor of membership in the low stability and low quality group (Group 1 in Table 4.4). According to Lewis and Spanier (1979), Group 1 would be expected to be at the greatest risk for marital dissolution.

When comparisons were made across other groups, several patterns become evident. For example, we compared Group 1 and Group 2 (which share the characteristics of low marital quality but have different levels of marital stability). Commonly, men and women in these groups are more similar in perceiving more alternatives to the marriage, less fairness, and less commitment to the institution of marriage. Regarding Group 3 and Group 4 (which share the characteristic of high marital quality but have different levels of marital stability), fewer alternatives to marriage were reported. Groups 3 and 4 also were dissimilar in other aspects. Those individuals denoted by less marital stability (Group 3) were younger, had less agreement on issues, reported less fairness, and were less committed to the institution of marriage.

Importantly, the nature and quality of interaction (as measured by frequency of agreement and the perception of fairness) were more predictive of the levels of marital stability and marital quality than were any of the demographic characteristics (e.g., income, education, or age). As such, it may be that indicators of processes in a remarriage are more important to understanding marital outcome than is knowledge about the demographic qualities of the spouses or the marriage itself. We make this statement with caution, since the predictive capability of the variables was very low.

Overall, the findings from this study suggest that the variables examined here are stronger predictors of membership in certain marital stability and marital quality groups than in other groups. Because of the poor predictive accuracy of the variables, any attempt to interpret why certain individuals were classified as they were in the quadrants of the model must be done so cautiously. From these findings we can conclude that there are variables that were not identified here that influence marital stability and marital quality. For example, Lewis and Spanier (1979) suggested that role strain, role conflict, and integration processes may be components of marital quality. However, these potentially influential variables were not assessed as part of the study. In addition, personal traits, such as impulsivity, may influence marital stability (Brody et al., 1988). Assessing personal traits was beyond the scope of this study. Additional research is warranted to further delineate the factors that are associated with marital quality and stability.

KEY CHAPTER POINTS

1. A test of Lewis and Spanier's (1979) typology of marital stability and marital quality found that marriage order is not predictive of marital stability or marital quality. The one exception was the difference between men in Group 2 and men in Group 4 (both groups had high stability and varied in level of marital quality).

2. Process variables, such as perceived alternatives to the marriage, agreement on issues, and perceived fairness, were the strongest predictors of two groups: low marital stability and low marital quality (Group 1) and high marital stability and high marital quality (Group 4).

3. However, the variables examined here (demographic, structural, and process) failed to result in predicting group membership with greater accuracy than could be expected by chance.

NOTE

1. The studies used in the meta-analysis were all published before 1988. The most recent figures for divorce and remarriage at that time indicated that 50% of all first marriages were expected to end in divorce, while 60% of all remarriages were expected to do so. These are not the most recent figures available to us now, which suggested instead that first marriages and remarriages have the same likelihood of terminating.

Chapter 5

ROLE INTEGRATION AND MARITAL ADJUSTMENT IN STEPFATHER FAMILIES

James H. Bray, Sandra H. Berger, and Carol L. Boethel

Forming a stepfamily entails many challenges and changes in family relationships. One of the central tasks is to integrate the stepparent into the new family system. This requires that existing family members adapt to the new member as he or she assumes the dual roles of spouse and parent in the remarried family. Given the general lack of socially and legally prescribed roles for stepparents, this task is often fraught with stress and uncertainty. Despite these potential problems, thousands of stepfamilies are formed each year, and many create successful relationships that promote the development and welfare of family members. A few researchers have turned their attention to these families to determine the characteristics of marital and family relationships that contribute to the successful integration of the stepparent into the family.

This chapter presents results from the Developmental Issues in StepFamilies (DIS) Research Project. This cross-sectional research project studied family process in divorce-engendered stepfather families across the first 7 years after remarriage by examining the effects of family formation on children and adults in newly formed and established stepfamilies. The focus here is on the role integration of the stepparent and its relationship to marital adjustment.

THEORETICAL BACKGROUND

Initially, the DIS Research Project used family systems theory as a basis for examining the remarriage process. From this perspective, each family member is viewed as part of an interdependent emotional and relational system that mutually influences other parts of the family system. Thus, change within one component of the system is believed to produce change in other parts. However, it quickly became apparent that examining only the interactional and relational aspects of the stepfamilies was not sufficient to explicate the process of divorce and remarriage.

The stepfamily is a developing and changing system that is continually influenced by the individual developmental trajectories of each family member. Therefore, the developmental aspects of the stepfamily and individual members were integrated with a family systems approach which resulted in a developmental family systems model (Bray et al., 1987).

A central proposal of this approach is that there are developmental stages through which families grow. The stages reflect common stresses and tasks that prompt changes in family structure and functioning. Divorce and remarriage were not originally conceptualized as stages of the family life cycle. However, the prevalence of these family transitions has resulted in their integration into a model of family development (Bray, Berger, & Pollack, 1986; Carter & McGoldrick, 1980; Ransom, Schlesinger, & Derdeyn, 1979).

The application of the model requires the identification of predictable changes and stresses for the family as it progresses through the remarriage process. Several researchers and clinicians offer preliminary ideas on the early phases of stepfamily formation (Bray et al., 1986, 1987; Goetting, 1982; McGoldrick & Carter, 1980; Ransom et al., 1979; Whiteside, 1982). After remarriage, an adult can instantaneously become both spouse and stepparent, meaning that there is no gradual progression during which the marital bond is solidified and consensus is developed in regard to the parenting of children. Consequently, two central tasks confronting the spouses in early remarriage are the development of the marital bond and the integration of the stepparent into a coparental role. These tasks may necessitate changes in roles established in the postdivorce family as well as in family boundaries, which delineate family membership and rules governing interaction of its members (Boss, 1980; Boss & Greenberg, 1984). The related tasks of integration of the noncustodial biological parent and the kinship system of the stepparent, possibly including the stepparents' children from a previous marriage, may require further alterations in roles and boundaries of the postdivorce family.

Little knowledge is available about family life and roles within stepfamilies that have progressed beyond the early stage of remarriage. Whiteside (1982) suggested that progression beyond this early stage includes stability and clarity in family role relationships. The results of research studies, however, are inconclusive. In a longitudinal study of stepfamilies, Furstenberg (1987) found that the amount of time spent living in a stepfamily was not related to changes in the alignment of family boundaries. Of the stepchildren studied, 31% did not perceive that their residential stepparents were members of their families, while 15% of stepparents of residential stepchildren excluded them as a part of their families. Furstenberg concluded that families appear to reconstitute shortly after remarriage and develop stable patterns that are continued later in remarriage. Pasley (1987) also found that boundaries of remarried families were unclear, as spouses frequently omitted nonresidential stepchildren from the list of members in the stepfamily.

In conjunction with children's individual developmental needs, the tasks of later remarriage may contribute to the continuation of more permeable and ambiguous psychological and physical family boundaries and to unclear family roles. For example, the onset of adolescence may be accompanied by a child's need to develop a relationship with a nonresidential parent or to work out unresolved issues with him or her. For adults, this may require renegotiation of coparental relationships among as many as four parental figures, alteration of custody and financial obligations, and changes in family boundaries to include nonresidential adolescent children (Bray, 1991; Whiteside, 1982). However, few empirical studies have examined changes in stepparent roles and child-rearing arrangements during the later years of remarriage.

THE STEPFAMILY IN FORMATION

There are many structural types of stepfamilies, and many names for them. The names given to stepfamilies do not always accurately convey the membership of the residential family. The most common type of stepfamily is a stepfather family in which a man (who either may or may not have been previously married) marries a woman who has residential children from a previous marriage. If the stepfather has no children from a previous relationship, the family is considered a *simple* stepfamily. If the stepfather has children from a previous stepfamily, the family is considered a *complex* stepfamily. A *blended* stepfamily exists when biological children from the previous marriages of each parent reside in the stepfamily. In this case, both remarried parents are simultaneously biological parents and stepparents (Clingempeel, 1981). There is no term designating stepfamilies with children from the current marriage.

The stepfamily also may be *binuclear* in structure, if it remains interdependent, with the family headed by the nonresidential biological parent (Ahrons, 1979; McGoldrick & Carter, 1980; Walker & Messinger, 1979). Static terms classifying stepfamilies according to their structure inadequately convey the complex emotional, interpersonal, and pragmatic changes in a stepfamily that can be effected by children's membership in a binuclear family system (Vemer et al., 1989). Binuclear stepfamilies often need semipermeable boundaries because the membership expands and contracts because of children's periodic visitations (McGoldrick & Carter, 1980; Walker & Messinger, 1979). The complexity of the stepfamily and the rapidity of changes leads to the view that divorce and remarriage constitute a dynamic process.

While some authors feel that the stepfamily operates in a context of chronic system overload (Whiteside, 1982), others suggest that the greater complexity of the stepfamily is not necessarily more problematic than that of other types of families (Cherlin, 1978). Nonetheless, the lack of normative guidelines surrounding instrumental and affective role relationships and family boundaries is often considered a major stressor for stepfamily members (Bohannon, 1970b; Cherlin, 1978, 1981; Fast & Cain, 1966; Goetting, 1982; Pasley, 1987). Potential difficulties generated by a normative vacuum include establishing appropriate authority and disciplinary roles for the stepfather, affection between the stepparent and stepchildren, financial support of the stepchildren, and the exclusion of noncustodial parents or nonresidential children of former marriages from the family. Additionally, the continued participation of the noncustodial father in an active coparenting role may contribute to the further marital and parental role ambiguity of the stepfather and to unclear family boundaries (Ahrons & Wallisch, 1987; Boss, 1980; Roberts & Price, 1989). However, these issues need to be examined by additional research to determine their effects on individual and family adjustment.

Role Integration and Marital Adjustment in Stepfather Families

Visher and Visher (1988a) stated that a secure marital bond is the critical foundation on which the stepfamily is built. With a secure and strong marital bond, a couple will be better able to cope with stresses and issues that may arise in other areas of family life. Additionally, Cherlin (1978) theorized that marital stress in stepfamilies is influenced by the ambiguous and complex role relationships in remarriage. In support of these views, White and Booth (1985) reported that the presence of stepchildren in the home contributes to poorer marital adjustment in second marriages. Similarly, Ambert (1986) found that a larger percentage of stepfathers felt that after an average of 2 years of remarriage, their marital satisfaction would be higher without the presence of either residential or nonresidential stepchildren. However, Furstenberg and Spanier (1984/1987) found no disparity in marital satisfaction of remarried couples with children from a former marriage and those couples without children from a former marriage. In a meta-analysis of studies of marital satisfaction in remarriage, Vemer and colleagues (1989) found no differences in marital satisfaction between remarried couples who had residential stepchildren and those who did not. As half the studies included stepfamilies in the earliest months of remarriage, these authors suggested that the effects of children on the remarriage may become more clear over time.

Conflict over differing coparental role expectations and child-rearing practices has been observed both in clinical stepfamilies (Bray, 1991; Stern, 1978; Visher & Visher, 1979) and in nonclinical stepfamilies (Fast & Cain, 1966; Messinger, 1976; Perkins & Kahan, 1979). While Roberts and Price (1989) found no direct relationship between satisfaction with parental roles and marital adjustment in stepfather families, several cross-sectional studies support the relationship between a lack of clarity and consensus surrounding the stepfather's role, on the one hand, and marital conflict and adjustment, on the other. Schwebel, Fine, and Renner (1991) found a lack of consensus in the attitudes of college students (from predominantly white, nuclear-family backgrounds) on how stepparents should act to meet the needs of stepchildren as compared to how they thought parents from nuclear and adoptive families should act in the same situations. There also were gender differences in respondents' attitudes concerning stepparents' obligations and predictable behaviors. The authors speculated that these differences may create marital conflict. Keshet (1990) reported low consensus between spouses in stepfamilies (remarried an average of 2 years) on attitudes describing family relationships which reflected their expectations of roles and relationships. Gender differences also were apparent. Men indicated that stepfamily relationships were more difficult than biological relationships. Keshet proposed that conflict between remarried couples may focus on the appropriate parental role of the stepfather.

Bray and colleagues (1987) suggested that the absence of a "honeymoon effect" in stepfamilies couples remarried 6 months may be linked to greater stress associated with the complexities of coparenting in the newly formed stepfather family. Other clinicians have proposed that the preexistent mother-child relationship and a vulnerable marital bond can permit an inappropriate triangulation of biological parents in stepparent-child disputes or of children in marital disputes. This dysfunctional interactional pattern is perpetuated by a lack of support for the stepparent's authority in the role of disciplinarian (Messinger, Walker, & Freeman, 1978; Pasley, 1987; Stern, 1978).

Hetherington (1987) and Bray (1988a) noted that in the formative years of the stepfamily, children's negative responses to stepfathers' premature assumptions of closeness and parental roles replicating that of a biological parent have indirect effects on marital adjustment. In concurrence, Keshet (1990) found that higher evaluations of their marriages by remarried spouses were related to attitudes reflecting less rigid adherence to a nuclear family model. She suggested that marital and/or individual distress in stepfamilies from stepparent-child conflicts and issues of family loyalty and boundaries may be linked to inappropriate expectations for stepfamily life derived from an inflexible family model, which is normally associated with a first-marriage family system. While these studies examined attitudes and role expectations for stepfamilies, there was no comparison of stepfamilies at various times after remarriage. Consequently, there were no means of evaluating whether the lack of consensus among remarried couples was a reflection of the complexities of stepfamily formation or indigenous to the stepfamily structure itself.

Another aspect of stepfamily life that may be related to ambiguous roles and boundaries is the relationship with the nonresidential father. Although this relationship is associated with positive outcomes for children and residential mothers in the post-divorce family (Guidubaldi, Cleminshaw, Perry, & McLoughlin, 1983; Hetherington, Cox, & Cox, 1982), research on the effects on the remarriage of the relationship between former spouses reveals conflicting findings (Bray & Berger, 1990). Marital satisfaction in stepfamilies also has been related to both the extent and the quality of this continuing involvement between ex-spouses. Clingempeel (1981) reported that both too frequent and infrequent contact between former spouses were associated with poorer marital adjustment. He proposed that contact at either extreme may be indicative of unresolved emotional issues from the former marriage, while moderate involvement reflects completed emotional divorce (as contrasted with legal divorce). Roberts and Price (1989) found that the maintenance of a friendly relationship between ex-spouses, excluding residual feelings of love, contributed to poorer marital adjustment in remarriage. The maintenance of reciprocal roles and boundaries between former spouses may preclude the establishment of boundaries within the new marriage and effect marital distress (Ahrons & Wallisch, 1987; Boss, 1980; Roberts & Price, 1989).

Gender and Family Roles

A brief mention of the persistent nature of traditional gender roles in the family seems warranted due to the effect of gender role identity on daily role performance in all families. Historically, a mother's child-rearing role has been highly valued (Hareven, 1987). Despite diverse and changing life-styles and family composition, most research indicates that women continue to assume the traditionally feminine responsibilities of child rearing and housework (Teachman, Polonko, & Scanzoni, 1987). Concurrently, few marriages are described as having the spouses equally share child care responsibilities (Teachman et al., 1987). Studies of various ethnic and socioeconomic groups within the United States reveal a strong adherence to traditional, stereotyped child-rearing roles in which the mother dominates in instrumental care and the father lends expressive support (Langman, 1987; Wilkinson, 1987). Although attitudes about gender roles may be more flexible, since 1940, little change has taken place in the actual practice of child rearing (Losh-Hesselbart, 1987).

Questions concerning the enactment of child-rearing roles after remarriage are still unanswered. For example, which parent is in charge of child rearing? What roles and responsibilities does each parent carry out ? What roles and responsibilities does the stepparent assume? How much time does each spouse spend in child rearing? The role and responsibilities of the stepparent in child rearing are unclear.

Ahrons and Wallisch (1987) addressed some of these questions concerning the child-rearing roles that stepparents perform. They found that stepfathers were more involved with stepchildren when their wives had custody of the children. The stepparent's involvement was most often affective (involving such things as celebrations, discipline, and discussions of problems and social activities) and least often instrumental (tasks suchs as dressing and grooming, attending school- or church-related functions, helping children with school work, and religious or moral training). They found that 73 % of mother-stepfather couples usually shared coparental responsibilities. Most stepfathers (78%) said that they themselves handled problems with stepchildren; however, the types of problems that the stepfathers handled were not identified. About 54% of stepfathers felt that the stepchildren had an effect on their marital relationship, but the effect was described as neutral or positive. Still unanswered was the question of the amount of time spent by either parent or stepparent in child care.

THE DEVELOPMENTAL ISSUES IN STEPFAMILIES RESEARCH PROJECT

The DIS Research Project investigated the relationship of family structure, family process, family organization, and adult/child psychosocial variables in stepfather families and nondivorced first-marriage families across the first 7 years of remarriage. To determine developmental differences in family organization and process during this period, stepfather families at 6 months, 2.5 years, and 5-7 years after remarriage were studied.

This chapter reports the findings from the DIS Research Project of the influences of stepfamily roles and child-rearing arrangements on marital adjustment in stepfather families. We focus on the following four issues regarding stepfamily attitudes, roles, and child-rearing arrangements. First, attitudes of parents and stepparents in stepfamilies concerning stepfamily roles are compared with those attitudes of parents in first-marriage families. We examine the differences between men and women in those families, and we also evaluate the consensus between spouses about those roles. Previous research has indicated a lack of consensus; however, most of this research used data collected during the 1970s and early 1980s, and there may be time-related biases. Second, the types of child-rearing arrangements in stepfamilies are examined. Third, since most studies examined stepfamily roles at only one time after remarriage, we examine whether attitudes about stepfamily roles and child-rearing arrangements in stepfather families vary across remarriages of different length. Fourth, the influence of stepfamily attitudes, roles, and child-rearing arrangements on marital adjustment in stepfamilies is examined at three different periods following remarriage. We hypothesized that roles and child rearing are important predictors of marital adjustment, although these relationships might change over time.

THE STUDY

Participants

A total of 196 children and their families participated in this study. There were 98 first-marriage families and 98 stepfather families. The 44 target children were divided about equally by sex. Families were selected to form the following groups:

1. Stepfather families at 6 months post-remarriage ($\pm$ 2 months) with a child between 6 and 9 years old;

2. First-marriage families with children comparable in age to those of Group 1;

3. Stepfather families remarried for 2.5 years ($\pm$ 2 months) with a child between 8.5 and 11.5 years old;

4. First-marriage families with children comparable in age to those of Group 3;

5. Stepfather families remarried between 5 and 7 years with a child between 11 and 14 years old;

6. First-marriage families with children comparable in age to those of Group 5.

The ages of the children in stepfamilies were staggered to control for the length of time in a remarried family. The families were recruited from schools, parent groups, athletic teams, referrals from local clergy and media (c.f., Bray, 1988a, 1988b; Bray et al., 1987). The majority of families came from six suburban school districts in the Houston and Harris County, Texas, metropolitan area. Those who were selected met our criteria of a white, middle-class sample, with parents less than 54 years of age, no more than four children living in the home, at least a high school education for the parents, and no history of psychological or psychiatric problems for the target child before or during the first 6 months of the remarriage. Only stepfather families were studied because they are the most common type of stepfamily (Glick, 1989) and because of differences in various forms of step-families (Clingempeel, 1981; Hetherington et al., 1982). First-marriage children and their families were selected to match the demographic characteristics of the stepfamilies.

First-marriage families had the following demographic characteristics. The mothers' average age was 34.0, and they had an average of 14.6 years of education. The fathers' average age was 36.8, with an average of 15.9 years of education. Children in these families had an average age of 9.6. The average annual family income was $39,000.

Stepfamilies had the following demographic characteristics. The mothers' average age was 33.8, and they had an average of 14.7 years of education. The fathers' average age was 35.3, with an average of 15.5 years of education. Children in stepfamilies had an average age of 9.8. The average annual family income was $40,000. There were no significant differences between the groups on the demographic variables.

Instruments

Family Roles were measured by two self-report questionnaires that were completed independently by each parent or stepparent. The Stepparent Role Questionnaire (SRQ) (Hetherington & Clingempeel, 1992) includes 12 items answered on a 4-point scale from 1 = *strongly disagree* to 4 = *strongly agree*. A factor analysis with varimax rotation of the items indicated three factors. Each scale has four items. The scales are:

1. *Communications with Ex-Spouse* measures the degree to which it is considered appropriate for ex-spouses to talk and meet together to discuss issues about their children (e.g., "It is appropriate for a remarried person to have lunch with a former spouse to discuss the children").

2. *Relationship with Children* is the degree to which family members believe it is appropriate and important for stepparents to have a close relationship with their stepchildren (e.g., "It should take only a few months after the remarriage for the stepparent and stepchild to develop a close relationship").

3. *Parental Role* is the degree to which family members believe it is appropriate for stepparents to assume the role of the parent (e.g., "Stepparents should think of themselves more as a friend to their stepchildren than as a parent").

The scales are formed by averaging the responses to the relevant items. The average of the responses keeps the scale scores in the same metric as the original items. Higher scores indicate more agreement with that scale.

Child Rearing Roles is a self-report questionnaire taken from Baumrind (1979) and modified by Hetherington and Clingempeel (1992). Three items concerning which spouse performs child-rearing tasks in the home and amount of time spent performing child-rearing duties were used. The first question is a categorical item that includes the following child-rearing arrangements: mother almost entirely responsible for child rearing; mother mostly responsible and father helps; equal sharing of responsibilities between parents; father mostly responsible and mother helps; father almost entirely responsible; and some one other than parents is primarily responsible. Each adult indicates the arrangement that best describes their situation. Each parent or stepparent also indicates the number of hours each week that he or she spent on child care and the number of hours each week that the spouse spent performing child care.

Marital Adjustment was measured by the Dyadic Adjustment Scale (DAS; Spanier, 1976). This is a 32-item self-report scale which was completed by each adult. Higher scores indicate better marital adjustment. The DAS has good reliability and validity as a global measure of marital adjustment and satisfaction.

Procedures

All families completed a structured interview, self-report measures about individual functioning and family relationships, and questionnaires designed by Hetherington and Clingempeel (1992). Each participating family member was given an informed consent form before beginning the project. The interview contained the above mentioned scales and others that are not reported here. The data were collected in the family's home during two home visits, each lasting about 3 to 3.5 hours. The home visits were usually 7 to 14 days apart. The adults were interviewed by one research assistant, while the target child was interviewed separately by a second research assistant. Additional questionnaires were self-administered by the adults during the period between home visits.

RESULTS

Multivariate analysis of variance (MANOVA) was conducted to evaluate family type differences and parent differences on the SRQ and on time performing child care variables. A two-way MANOVA comparing family type and parents' sex indicated a significant interaction, multivariate $F(5, 376) = 3.81, p < .002$. Examination of the means, simple effects tests, and univariate F tests indicated that the interaction was significant only for the time performing child care. The results were similar for both variables (see Table 5.1).

Mothers in first-marriage families reported spending more hours performing child care duties each week than did fathers in such families, stepfathers, or mothers in stepfather families. In addition, mothers in stepfather families spent more time on child care than did fathers or stepfathers. There were no differences in the amount of time that fathers or stepfathers spent performing child care duties. In addition, there were significant differences between family types, multivariate $F(5, 376) = 11.04, p < .001$. An examination of the means and univariate F tests indicated that parents in first-marriage families felt it was more acceptable for ex-spouses in stepfamilies to communicate about their children than did parents or stepparents in stepfamilies. Parents and stepparents in stepfamilies felt it was more acceptable for stepparents to assume a parental role than did parents in first-marriage families. Both mothers and fathers in first-marriage families reported that mothers in those families spent more time performing child care duties than did mothers or stepfathers in remarried families. There also were significant differences between parents' reports, multivariate $F(5, 376) = 76.82, p < .001$. Univariate analyses indicated that mothers spent more time performing child care duties than did fathers or stepfathers. Later analyses indicated that the differences on the SRQ variables were found within first-marriage families and not stepfamilies; therefore, differences on these scales will be discussed with the later analyses.

A MANOVA was conducted to examine differences between the stepfamily groups as a function of length of remarriage and parents' sex on the SRQ, on the one hand, and time performing child care, on the other. There were no significant interactions or main effects for length of remarriage. Mothers in stepfamilies reported spending more time performing child care duties than did stepfathers at each point after remarriage, multivariate $F(5, 181) = 26.38, p < .001$. There were no differences between parents or stepparents on the SRQ scales.

A MANOVA was conducted to examine differences between the comparable first-marriage groups and parents' sex on the SRQ and time performing child care. There were no significant interactions or main effects for these groups. However, parents in first-marriage families differed in their attitudes and amount of time spent performing child care duties, multivariate $F(5, 183) = 54.62, p < .001$. Fathers in first-marriage families felt that it was more acceptable than did mothers in these families for stepparents to establish a close relationship with children, while mothers felt that it was more acceptable than did fathers for stepparents to play a parental role with children.

A series of chi-square analyses were conducted to evaluate child-rearing arrangements in stepfamilies and first-marriage families at each period of remarriage as well as differences across remarriage periods. The analyses also were separated by sex of parent. Overall, the most common arrangements for both types of families were for mothers to be in charge of child rearing with fathers or stepfathers assisting or else for the parents to share duties equally. In only one case (a first-marriage family) was a father reported to be mostly in charge of child rearing. The only significant differences between family types were between fathers and stepfathers in the 6-month stepfamilies and first-marriage families, $\chi^2(2) = 13.85, p < .001$. Stepfathers reported more often than fathers in first-marriage families that mothers were completely in charge of child rearing. Interestingly, the differences in child-rearing arrangements reported by males were not reported by mothers in either family type. There was a similar level of agreement between parents in both family types concerning child-rearing arrangements. In stepfamilies, 63.3% of parents and stepparents agreed on the arrangement, while in first-marriage families, 64.7% agreed on the arrangement. In addition, there were no differences in reports of child-rearing arrangements for parents or stepparents in stepfamilies at each period after remarriage.

Correlates of Marital Adjustment in Stepfather Families

To investigate the associations between marital adjustment and family roles, Pearson correlations were generated between the SRQ variables, time performing child care, and reports of marital adjustment in stepfamilies. The correlations are reported by family type and length of remarriage to evaluate the different influences of roles and child care duties at different points after remarriage (see Table 5.2). The self-reports and spouse reports of time spent performing child care duties were averaged because of the lack of differences between parents' reports and in order to increase the reliability of the measure.

Overall, there were few significant relationships between stepparent roles and marital adjustment, and the relationships decreased after longer periods of remarriage. For 6-month stepfamilies, better marital adjustment for stepfathers was associated with the mothers' belief that stepfathers should not play a parental role with the children $(r = -.43)$. Better marital adjustment for mothers was related to stepfathers' views that stepparents should not form a relationship with the children too quickly $(r = -.29)$. For stepfamilies remarried 2.5 years, better marital adjustment for stepfathers was associated with them spending more time performing child care $(r = .34)$ and with mothers' $(r = .32)$ and stepfathers' $(r = .38)$ agree-

Table 5.1

Means, Standard Deviations (SD), and F-Statistics for Stepfamily and First-Marriage Family Step Roles and Time Performing Child Care Duties

	Family Type				F Statistics (1,191)		
	First-Marriage Family Sex of Parent		Stepfamily Sex of Parent				
	Male	Female	Male	Female			
Variable	Mean (SD)	Mean (SD)	Mean (SD)	Mean (SD)	Group x Sex	Sex	Group
Communication with ex-spouse	3.1 (0.51)	3.2 (0.46)	2.9 (0.53)	3.0 (0.54)	0.0	1.9	16.2***
Relationship with children	2.9 (0.42)	2.7 (0.39)	2.9 (0.56)	2.8 (0.53)	2.3	16.1***	1.2
Parental role	2.5 (0.35)	2.6 (0.32)	2.7 (0.34)	2.7 (0.34)	0.5	7.7**	16.4***
Hours in child care (self)	21.9 (15.80)	55.3 (29.30)	18.4 (17.50)	41.9 (25.60)	4.6*	151.2***	13.3***
Hours in child care (spouse)	49.5 (27.30)	24.7 (21.40)	36.1 (24.80)	21.9 (18.80)	5.0*	66.6***	11.4***

*$p < .05$, **$p < .01$, ***$p < .001$

ment that stepparents should form a relationship with stepchildren. Better marital adjustment for mothers was related only to stepfathers' agreement that stepparents should form a relationship with stepchildren ($r = .31$). For 5 to 7-year stepfamilies, there were no significant correlates of marital adjustment for stepfathers or mothers.

A two-way MANOVA was conducted to compare family type and differences in the child-rearing role on marital adjustment. There were no significant interactions with or main effects for family type or child-rearing roles in regard to marital adjustment on the part of mothers, fathers, or stepfathers.

Table 5.2

Correlations Between Family Step Roles, Time Performing Child Care Duties, and Marital Adjustment in Stepfather Families

| | Marital Adjustment | | | | | |
| | 6-Month Families | | 2.5 Year Families | | 5-7 Year Families | |
Variable	Mothers	Stepfathers	Mothers	Stepfathers	Mothers	Stepfathers
Mother Report:						
Communication with ex-spouse	.01	.02	.07	-.08	.05	.08
Relationship with children	-.02	.02	.14	.32*	-.08	.08
Parental role	-.16	-.43**	.05	-.08	-.06	-.24
Hours in child care	.05	.07	.07	.22	-.14	.03
Father Report:						
Communication with ex-spouse	-.23	-.23	.01	-.16	.12	.07
Relationship with children	-.29*	.06	.31*	.38*	-.17	.03
Parental role	-.11	-.11	-.27	-.09	.12	.12
Hours in child care	-.04	.16	.03	.34*	-.10	.14

*$p < .05$, **$p < .01$

DISCUSSION

Parents in stepfather and first-marriage families had different views concerning appropriate roles for members of stepfamilies. However, parents' and stepparents' views about roles did not differ at various times after remarriage, and child-rearing arrangements were generally similar in the two family types. Mothers in both types of families were primarily in charge of child rearing and spent substantially more time performing related tasks. In contrast to parents in first-marriage families, adults in stepfamilies agreed on stepfamily roles, and they also had considerable consensus on child care arrangements. Overall, stepfamily roles and child-rearing arrangements were neither consistent nor strong correlates of the marital adjustment of remarried couples.

Stepfamily and Child Rearing Roles

Parents in remarried families felt that it was more appropriate for a stepparent to assume a parental role than did parents in first-marriage families. Parents in the latter families were more in agreement than parents in stepfamilies that it was appropriate for former spouses to communicate about their children. These differences probably reflect the effects of experiencing a divorce and the ensuing pressures in forming a remarried family. Parents in first-marriage families are less likely to understand the multitude of emotional reactions that can occur between former spouses. Common reactions include anger and hostility from the divorce as well as jealousy and insecurity about the previous marriage on the part of the new spouse. In addition, the realities and demands of caring for children may directly influence parents in remarried families to agree that it is appropriate for stepparents to play a parental role with the children. This process would not necessarily be understood by parents in first-marriage families.

One of the developmental issues for stepfamilies is to change their image of a family from a first-marriage family model to a remarried family model. The lack of a relationship with the former spouse, while the stepparents play a parental role, may reflect the tendency of some stepfamilies to model their family after a first-marriage family. It is noteworthy that during early remarriage, husbands and wives were more satisfied with their relationships when stepfathers were *not* expected to play a parental role and *not* expected to quickly form a close relationship with the children.

Child Care Arrangements

Consistent with previous research on parenting and child rearing (Teachman et al., 1987), mothers were primarily in charge of child rearing and spent considerably more time performing child care duties than did fathers or stepfathers.

Almost 90% of stepfathers reported involvement in child rearing with their spouses, even during early remarriage. In addition, more than 40% of spouses reported an equally shared arrangement of child rearing. However, even in families that reported an equal arrangement, mothers spent significantly more time performing child-rearing tasks than did fathers or stepfathers. While these findings seem contradictory, parents may differentiate between the responsibility for child care and the time required to accomplish the related duties.

Overall, parents in first-marriage families spent more time fulfilling child care duties than did either parent in stepfamilies. There are several possible explanations for these differences. A common complaint of divorced mothers is that they experience role overload, not experiencing enough time for all the demands of supporting and raising a family (Bray & Anderson, 1984; Hetherington, Cox, & Cox, 1978). Thus, the experience of divorce may require parents to become more efficient in child-rearing duties, compelling them to spend less time in performing the necessary child-related tasks. In addition, researchers report that children "grow up faster" after experiencing a divorce (Hetherington et al., 1982; Weiss, 1975). Therefore, children in remarried families engendered by divorce may require less time from parents for help with child-related tasks because they can independently perform more of these tasks. Alternatively, both the parent and the stepparent in stepfamilies are more likely to be employed outside the home than are parents in first-marriage families (Moorman & Hernandez, 1989). Consequently, there may not be as much time available to spend on child-rearing duties in remarried families. In addition, when children visit their nonresidential parents, this may decrease the time spent on child care duties, especially in stepfamilies where there are no biological or adopted children from the remarriage or visiting stepchildren from the stepfather's previous marriage.

Role Consensus

Adults in stepfamilies did not differ in their views concerning stepfamily roles. They also reported considerable consensus in child-rearing arrangements. This suggests that, at least *within* stepfamilies, some type of normative model is beginning to develop. The norms may not be commonly held by all types of families, as indicated by the lack of consensus between first-marriage spouses. The level of consensus found in this study is in contrast to a recent report by Keshet (1990). She analyzed data from a 1978 survey of divorced and remarried families and found little consensus between remarried partners concerning roles for parents in stepfamilies. She concluded that there is not a normative model for remarriage. However, the data that Keshet used are more than 10 years old and may not accurately reflect the attitudes of present-day stepfamilies.

We found it was somewhat surprising that attitudes about stepfamily roles and child care arrangements did not differ for stepfamilies remarried for different periods. This suggests that attitudes about stepfamily roles may form early in remarriage and remain stable over time. Similarly, Furstenberg (1987) found that stepfamilies tend to organize early during remarriage and maintain stable patterns after this period. Because this was a cross-sectional study, the lack of differences between stepfamily groups does not mean that attitudes do not change across time. Rather, the lack of differences may reflect a sampling bias in that successful stepfamilies (i.e., the ones that stay together) are likely to hold similar attitudes from the beginning of remarriage. The current longitudinal follow-up of these families will allow us to directly address whether such changes in attitudes occur.

Stepfamily Roles and Marital Adjustment

Stepfamily roles and child-rearing duties were not strong correlates of marital adjustment for remarried couples. It was hypothesized that the marital subsystem functions somewhat independently from the parent-child subsystem in stepfamilies (Bray, 1992; Visher & Visher, 1988), and these findings are generally supportive of that point of view. Consistent with research and clinical views on the formation of stepfamilies (Bray, 1988a; Hetherington et al., 1982; Visher & Visher, 1988), marital adjustment during early remarriage was associated with beliefs that step-parents should not quickly form a relationship with children nor immediately parent them. This pattern was different after 2.5 years of remarriage, when marital adjustment was linked with the tendancy of stepparents to perform more child care duties and form a closer relationship with the children. In contrast, after 5 years of remarriage, marital adjustment was not associated with stepfamily roles and child rearing. It may be that these parents have resolved the issues concerning parenting and roles. In addition, since their children are adolescents at this piont, child-rearing roles and duties may require less attention and, therefore, may have less impact on the marriage. Many of the stepfamilies in which remarriage had occurred more than 5 years indicated in anecdotal comments that after 4 or 5 years, they stopped thinking of themselves as a stepfamily. Thus, issues about special roles for step-parents became less important to them. They indicated that this had not been the case during the early years of their stepfamily.

Limitations of the Study

It is important to remember several limitations of this study. First, this is a cross-sectional study that used a sample of convenience consisting of white, middle-class, stepfather families. Only a longitudinal study of a randomly selected group of families can assess the actual impact and change in roles, child care arrangements and marital adjustment across time. Second, it is important to remember that all the stepfamilies were formed when the children were between the ages of 6 and 8 years. Stepfamilies with different developmental paths (e.g., those with younger, adolescent, or adult children) may respond to family transitions with varying outcomes (Hetherington et al., 1982). Third, the study included only stepfather families and, therefore, may not generalize to stepmother families or other types of custodial arrangements. Many clinicians and researchers have speculated that it may be more difficult for a stepmother than for a stepfather to integrate into a stepfamily because of the added social pressures on women to take on a parental role. The current longitudinal study of these families will address more directly issues of causality and will be able to examine the possible confounds associated with stepfathering compared with stepmothering.

IMPLICATIONS AND CONCLUSIONS

Although attitudes about stepfamily roles and child care arrangements appear to remain constant over the course of remarriage, the relationship of these variables to marital adjustment does differ after longer periods of remarriage. However, an unexpected finding was that stepfamily roles and child-rearing arrangements had relatively little influence on marital adjustment. This may be due to the lack of linkage in stepfamilies between parent-child relations and marital relations. Thus, the commonly held view that concerns about parenting or child care arrangements are a reflection of marital problems may not always hold true in stepfamilies.

The consensus between adults in stepfamilies regarding stepparent roles may indicate that normative models develop *within* stepfamilies. The development of a consensus model regarding stepfamily roles may require the experience of divorce and remarriage. Adults in first-marriage families may not understand the issues of forming a stepfamily and stepparenting because of their lack of experience with the context of remarriage. Many writers have argued for the need to educate stepfamilies about the stresses and expectations of remarriage. The development of a consensus about stepfamily roles may be due to the proliferation of information about the unique aspects of stepfamilies and may signal the success of education efforts on the part of professionals and lay persons alike directed to stepfamily members.

Finally, this study raises many questions that need to be addressed in future research. The roles of stepparents in other areas of family life, such as decision making, financial arrangements, and housekeeping, are additional areas that may influence the adjustment of the remarried couple. In particular, research needs to focus on the factors that contribute to the long-term success of stepfamilies and that promote the well-being of individual family members as they develop across their life cycles.

KEY CHAPTER POINTS

1. Parents in first-marriage families compared to parents in stepfamilies have different views of appropriate role behaviors for adults in stepfamilies.

Those in stepfamilies believe more strongly that it is appropriate for a stepparent to assume a parental role.

2.   Amount of time in remarriage did not affect parents' or stepparents' views of appropriate role behaviors, and adults in stepfamilies agreed on stepfamily roles.

3.   The perceptions of stepfamily roles and child care arrangements are neither consistent nor strongly associated with marital ajustment in remarried couples.

   a.   Early in remarriage, marital adjustment is associated with the expectation that stepfathers should not play a parental role nor quicly form close relationships with stepchildren.

   b.   By 2.5 years, this expectation changes; marital quality is then associated with stepparents performing more child care and forming a close relationship with stepchildren.

   c.   After 5 years, marital adjustment is not associated with stepfamily roles and child rearing.

4.   Regardless of family type, mothers assume more responsibility for child care than fathers or stepfathers.

ACKNOWLEDGMENTS

This research was supported by NIH grants R01 HD18025 and R01 HD22642 from the National Institute of Child Health and Human Development and by a grant from the Harris and Eliza Kempner Fund of Galveston, Texas, to James H. Bray. The hard work of the Developmental Issues in StepFamilies Research Project staff made this endeavor possible. Special thanks are extended to E. Mavis Hetherington and her research team for their consultation and help throughout this project.

Chapter 6

ADOLESCENT STEPCHILD-STEPPARENT RELATIONSHIPS: CHANGES OVER TIME

Lawrence H. Ganong and Marilyn Coleman

One of the most important relationships within stepfamilies is that between step-parents and stepchildren (Crosbie-Burnett, 1984). Recognizing the central nature of this relationship within stepfamilies, in recent years considerable attention has focused on this bond (Coleman & Ganong, 1990). Despite this increased scrutiny, much is still unknown about these relationships. This is unfortunate, since the quality of stepparent-stepchild ties is a powerful predictor of the quality of family life (White & Booth, 1985), family happiness (Crosbie-Burnett, 1984), and levels of family stress (Visher & Visher, 1988).

Although the couple's relationship is often identified as the key to stepfamily success (Mills, 1984; Visher & Visher, 1988), there is evidence that the quality of the stepparent-child relationship is more predictive of overall family satisfaction than the quality of the couple's relationship (Crosbie-Burnett, 1984; White & Booth, 1985). White and Booth (1985) found that adults in remarriages in which at least one partner had children from a prior relationship consistently reported that they were less satisfied with their family life than those in remarriages that did not involve stepchildren. However, marital satisfaction for couples with stepchildren was only modestly lower than for couples without stepchildren. It was concluded that "stepchildren do not appear to effect a substantial reduction in the quality of marital relations, but they do reduce the quality of family life and decrease the quality of parent-child relationships" (p. 697).

Crosbie-Burnett (1984) found that 59% of the variance in overall family happiness in her sample of stepfather families with an adolescent stepchild was explained by the quality of the stepfather-stepchild relationship; marital satisfaction explained only 10% of the variance in family happiness. She concluded that the unsatisfactory relationships between adolescent stepchildren and their stepparents caused stress in the entire family.

It is commonly believed that the stepparent-stepchild relationship is especially problematic when the stepchild is an adolescent. Clinicians have identified adolescence as a particularly difficult age at which adapt to stepparents (Visher & Visher,

1988), and studies of the perceptions of adults in stepfamilies have supported this belief (Duberman, 1975; Smith, 1953). It should be noted that virtually all the attention on adolescent stepchildren has focused on newly formed stepfamilies and the problems of "adjustment," whereas little is known about adolescent stepchildren in long-term stepfamily relationships. In this chapter we describe some of the results of an in-depth longitudinal study of stepfamily relationships, with particular attention to changes in the relationships between stepparents and their adolescent stepchildren.

DEVELOPMENTAL ISSUES

Parent-adolescent conflict is typically considered to be a developmental phenomenon. According to Roehling and Robin (1986), developmental changes associated with early adolescence set in motion intraindividual, interpersonal, and systemic transformations. For example, biological changes in adolescents appear to augment problems in the mother-adolescent relationship as well as temporarily increase efforts by fathers to dominate their children (Steinberg, 1981; Steinberg & Hill, 1978).

Adolescence is a period of life in which several significant developmental transitions are experienced: physically, the child becomes an adult, cognitively children can now think and reason abstractly, and psychologically, self-identity develops and autonomy-seeking behaviors increase (Elkind, 1967; Erikson, 1968; Pasley, 1988). These changes often alter interaction patterns within the family, requiring adjustment by parents and adolescents alike. Sometimes these adjustments are accompanied by increased conflict and tension between the parents and adolescents. It should be noted, however, that few cases of parent-adolescent conflict are serious enough to reach clinical significance (Montemayer, 1983).

As adolescents work to develop their unique identity as people, they typically become increasingly self-focused (Elkind, 1967). This egocentrism can be irritating to parents and other adults. Every request from an adult for assistance from the adolescent is filtered through the perspective of, "What does it do for me?" The heightened self-awareness of the adolescent can contribute to rapid mood swings and the trying out of new identities. Adolescents in stepfamilies are not developmentally different from other adolescents, but these changes may be manifested and interpreted differently for stepchildren. For example, adolescents who are stepchildren may threaten stepfamily equilibrium as they "withdraw" and/or engage in new behaviors as part of trying out different roles. In first-marriage families, these behaviors may not be appreciated, but nonetheless, there will be a great deal of good will built up through a long, shared history. These feelings will enable the family to weather this developmental stage. However, stepfamilies lack this shared history. Therefore, normal adolescent behaviors may be seen by remarried parents and stepparents as a rejection of the stepfamily life style that the adults work hard to achieve. On the positive side, however, stepfamilies provide adolescents with multiple models of parenting and relating interpersonally as husband and wife. Thus, adolescent stepchildren have more choices and may be encouraged to experiment with more new identities than children of first-marriage families.

Consider also that as part of the quest for identity, adolescents are expected to begin establishing some independence from their families (Pasley & Healow, 1988). This normative autonomy seeking by adolescent stepchildren may be at odds with a newly remarried parent's desire to create a sense of family cohesion and family identity (Pasley & Healow, 1988; Visher & Visher, 1988). On the other hand, stepfamilies generally are less cohesive than first-marriage families (Pink & Wampler, 1985), and thus may facilitate independent behavior on the part of adolescents. In fact, there is some evidence that adolescent stepchildren attain some of the markers of adulthood sooner than do other adolescents. Stepchildren may leave home sooner (Mitchell, Wister, & Burch, 1989; White & Booth, 1985) and engage in sexual behaviors at younger ages (Flewelling & Bauman, 1990).

Cognitive changes in adolescents are important developmental considerations when attempting to understand adolescent-family relationships. For example, as stepchildren attain formal-operational thought, they may begin hypothesizing about how different their life would have been had their parents not divorced and remarried. This may cause new conflicts and a "rehashing" of divorce and stepfamily issues that the parents thought had been long resolved. On the other hand, adolescents who are moving from concrete to formal-operational thought may be better able to understand the multiple contributors to divorce, motives their parents might have for remarrying, and their own motives and feelings regarding divorce and remarriage.

Regardless of the level of abstract thought, cognitive distortions and unreasonable beliefs are often held by parents and adolescents alike (Roehling & Robin, 1986) which may further exacerbate stepfamily problems. Roehling and Robin (1986) identified seven common themes that underlie unreasonable beliefs, undermine family system goals, and create dysfunction in parent-adolescent relationships. Some of these themes are adhered to by parents and others, by children, while some are shared. These beliefs are summarized briefly below.

Parents

1. Ruination: If teenagers are given too much freedom, they will ruin their lives by engaging in dangerous behavior.

2. Obedience, perfectionism: Teenagers should always obey their parents and instinctively behave in a flawless manner.

3. Malicious intent: Teenagers purposely misbehave to hurt, anger, or annoy

their parents.

4. Self-blame: Parents are at fault for their teenagers' mistakes and misbehavior.

Adolescents

5. Unfairness, ruination: Parental restrictions are intrinsically unfair and will ruin teenagers' lives or spoil their fun.

6. Autonomy: Teenagers should have as much freedom from parental rules and restrictions as they desire.

Parents and Adolescents

7. Love, approval: Family members should always approve of each other's actions and motives. Disapproval is a sign of lack of love and affection, which is catastrophic.

According to Roehling and Robin, distressed fathers (i.e., those in therapy for parent-adolescent relationship problems) display the most unrealistic thinking regarding demands for flawless, obedient behavior; worry about the adverse consequences of too much adolescent autonomy; and personalize the adolescent's motives for rebellious behavior. This unrealistic thinking may be even more exaggerated in distressed stepfathers, especially those who have had little previous experience with children.

Roehling and Robin also found that distressed adolescents were most concerned about the injustice and adverse consequences of too much parental restriction of their freedoms. Once again, this behavior may be exacerbated in adolescent stepchildren, who often believe that the stepparent has no right to discipline or restrict them in any way. As it is nearly impossible to live with an adolescent without imposing some sort of rules or behavioral guidelines, acrimony can result.

Biological parents tend to take a more benign view of their children's behavior than do stepparents (Ganong & Coleman, 1986b). For example, adolescent behaviors that are positive are more likely to be perceived by biological parents as intentional and reflective of dispositional characteristics than are negative behaviors, which are more often attributed to situational or environmental influences (Dix, Ruble, Grusec, & Nixon, 1986). Parents also tend to hold a positive view of their role in the child's behavior. In a stepfamily, negative child behaviors are often attributed to the nonresidential parent (e.g., "He acts like that because his mother never taught him to behave properly"). A positive bias in the interpretations that parents make of their children's behavior undoubtedly helps children maintain a positive self-image. If stepparents hold less positive views of their stepchildren's behavior and are more likely to perceive negative stepchild behaviors as intentional and reflective of dispositional characteristics, family stress can escalate.

Stressful relationships between stepparent and stepchild can have a variety of outcomes. Some evidence suggests that stepfamilies "eject" children from the home at an earlier age than nuclear families (White & Booth, 1985).

Because many people remarry when their children are nearing puberty or are in adolescence (Sweet, 1991), an important question becomes: How much family turmoil can be attributed to normative problems of adolescence and how much is due to the specific dynamics of stepfamily relationships? Considering the potential of stepparent-stepchild relationships to affect the marital relationship and stepfamily satisfaction, it is important to examine these relationships more fully.

In this chapter we describe some of the results of an in-depth longitudinal study of stepfamily relationships. In 1985, we interviewed members of 105 Missouri stepfamilies in an effort to determine if childbearing in remarriage has an effect on family affect and satisfaction (Ganong & Coleman, 1986a). In addition, we collected data on family process factors, expectations about role behaviors, and perceptions of family functioning.

In 1989 we attempted to obtain additional information from as many of these families as could be located. We wanted to see how they had changed over time. We were interested particularly in whether and how the relationship between stepparents and their adolescent stepchildren had changed. Our previous work on adolescent stepchildren's relationships with their stepparents (Ganong & Coleman, 1987), as well as that of most other stepfamily researchers (cf. Crosbie-Burnett, 1984; Pasley & Healow, 1988), utilized cross-sectional designs that are ill-suited to answer questions about change over time. The data reported here are from the families that had adolescent stepchildren at the time of the follow-up study (Time 2).

METHODS

Initial Sample

A detailed description of the original sample is found in Ganong and Coleman (1986b). There were 100 men, 105 women, and 172 children in this sample. To be included in the initial study at least one of the adults had to have at least one child from a previous relationship who was between the ages of 6 and 18 and who resided in the household. Moreover, the women had to have been younger than age 45 at the time of the remarriage.

Represented were 66 stepfather-mother households, 19 stepmother-father households, and 20 households in which both adults were stepparents to children residing in the home. The number of years married ranged from 1 to 16, with an average of 4 years together. Based on Hollingshead's (1975) four-factor classification of social status, 31% of the families were in the unskilled category, 15% were in the semiskilled category, 22% were in skilled crafts and sales category, and 21% were classified as owning or administering medium-sized business, working in technical positions, or being "minor professionals."

This sample was obtained in several ways: (a) names were obtained from marriage license records of one Missouri county, (b) participating families identified other stepfamilies at the conclusion of the interview, and (c) media notices about the study were placed in several area newspapers. Families were contacted initially by a letter describing the study. Then a few days later they were contacted by phone. Those families that met the criteria and wished to participate were included in the study.

Sample at Time 2

In 1989 attempts were made to contact all the 105 families in the original sample. Of the original 105 families, 5 could not be located, 41 families in which there were still children in the household were interviewed, and 3 refused to be interviewed. Additionally, in 1 family, the father had died and the rest of the family had moved overseas, and in 14 families, the couples had divorced. Questionnaires were sent to 41 families that either had moved out of the area or whose children were grown; in 28 of these families, at least 1 member returned a set of questionnaires. Of these, 14 were from households containing married couples only, 12 were from couples with at least one child in the household, 1 was returned by the mother only, and 1 was returned by an adult and a child.

The data reported in this chapter were from the 53 families that still had at least one child residing in the household. Data were gathered from parents, stepparents, and the stepchildren still residing in the household.

We compared the families that participated in the follow-up study with those that did not participate on a number of demographic characteristics. They did not differ on type of stepfamily (i.e., stepmother, stepfather, or complex), socioeconomic status, wife's age, husband's age, years living together, years married, or total number of children. The families did differ, however, on number of children residing in the household, but this difference disappeared when couples whose children were adults at Time 2 were excluded from the comparison. We can safely conclude that families that remained in the sample over time were structurally and demographically similar to those that dropped out.

At Time 2, the couples had been living together for an average of 9.38 years ($SD = 3.04$) and had been married for a mean of 8.65 years ($SD = 3.06$). They had an average of 3.4 children ($SD = 1.52$), with a mean of 1.62 children still living at home ($SD = .99$). The mean age for men was 41.22 years ($SD = 7.79$); for women, 40.53 ($SD = 6.86$); and for the oldest stepchild, 15.

Procedure

The data reported here came from interviews and questionnaires administered or mailed to the families. A letter was sent to the local families, and appointments were made in follow-up phone calls for them to be interviewed on our campus. With the exception of a brief introductory interview with the whole family, all data were collected from family members individually.

The families who had left the area since the initial data collection also were contacted by mail or phone, and questionnaires and standardized instruments were mailed to them. Each person in the family was mailed a separate packet and received separate return envelopes. Families who received questionnaires in the mail were instructed to fill out the instruments individually and not to consult with other family members.

RESULTS

Since the focus of this chapter is on the adolescent stepchild-stepparent relationship, most of the results reported are limited to areas identified by researchers and clinicians as representing important issues in these relationships (Lutz, 1983; Visher & Visher, 1988). We examined the following issues: closeness of the stepparent-stepchild relationship, names and labels, loyalty conflicts, stepparent role ambiguity, and discipline.

Stepparent-Stepchild Relationship

Stepparent's views. During interviews at Time 1 and Time 2, stepparents were asked to compare their current relationship with each of their stepchildren to how it was before they remarried. They also were asked to rate the closeness of their relationship with each stepchild currently. We report perceptions of the relationships between each stepparent and his or her oldest stepchild still residing in the household.

At Time 1, 80% of the stepparents said that their relationship with the target stepchild was better than before the remarriage. By Time 2, only 64% perceived this relationship as better now than before the remarriage. Thus, it appears that in several families, the relationship of the stepparent and stepchildren had deteriorated over time, at least from the stepparent's view.

These findings are not congruent with what might be expected from a sample of stepfamilies that have been together for several years. In some of the clinical literature on the development of stepfamily relationships, for example, there is the suggestion that step-relationships become more positive and closer in a linear fashion over time; stepfamilies are advised that "integration" may occur after 2 years, 4 years, or longer. Family therapist David Mills (1984) speculated that the number of years that it takes for a stepparent and child to bond roughly equals the child's age when he or she entered into a relationship with the stepparent. Therefore, if a person becomes a stepparent to an 8-year-old child, Mills would estimate that it might take 8 years for a strong relationship to form. What is not taken into account, however, are developmental changes in children. Because the stepchildren in our sample at Time 2 were adolescents (the average age of the oldest child in the household was 15), the changes in perceptions may be partly due to developmental changes in the child. Adolescents developmentally withdraw from their families as they begin to seek independence and self-identities that separate them somewhat from their family members. The withdrawal is manifested in many ways: spending more time with friends away from home; spending time alone; becoming more critical of parents, teachers, and other authority figures; and resisting attempts by adults to control their actions. Consequently, communication with adolescents may be difficult. The stepparents may have perceived the relationships at Time 2 more negatively because the child was now engaging in "adolescentlike" behaviors that had not yet begun at Time 1.

Stepparents also were asked to indicate on a 5-point scale how close they were during the last 6 weeks to each of their stepchildren. The responses were nearly identical at Time 1 and Time 2. A substantial minority (40%) of stepparents felt emotionally close to their oldest stepchild at both times, and results across all responses (*not at all close* to *extremely close*) were relatively consistent.

Parent's views. We also asked biological parents to rate the closeness between their spouse and their children. More so than stepparents, biological parents perceived a slight reduction in closeness over time. This reduction may represent a disappointment in how they perceive current family bonds. Parents might have hoped that the stepparent would get along well with their children (42% reported this) for various reasons (e.g., to relieve guilt over possible divorce effects or to redevelop a feeling of family). The parents may have believed to such an extent that the remarriage was a good thing for all parties concerned that their desired level of closeness between stepparent and children was unrealistic. It is difficult to maintain illusory beliefs over time, which could account for the change in parents' perceptions.

Stepchildren's views. Data regarding the children's perception of closeness to the stepparent were collected only at Time 2. About 80% perceived themselves as at least moderately close to their stepfather, as compared to 61% who perceived themselves to be at least moderately close to their biological father. Sixty-four percent indicated that they were at least moderately close to their stepmother, and 93% felt at least moderately close to their mother. However, the *moderately* close category was the midpoint on the scale of choices. This was the modal category chosen when rating stepfathers and stepmothers. At the positive ends of the scale (*quite close* and *extremely close*), the percentages dropped to 37% for stepfathers, 28% for stepmothers, 42% for fathers, and 71% for mothers.

The views held by stepparents, biological parents, and stepchildren about the closeness of the stepparent-stepchild relationship were quite similar. Indeed, we were surprised by the level of agreement of perceptions. Such intrafamily agreement in perceptions is relatively rare. However, if the stepparent-stepchild relationship is as important to overall family well-being as some researchers have claimed, it is logical to expect that attention is paid to these relationships by the stepfamily members. These results may indicate that the members of these stable stepfamily systems have focused on the stepparent-stepchild relationship, at least to the extent that they hold similar views about the degree of closeness between stepparents and stepchildren.

Another reason for our surprise at these results was that the data did not fit the overall impressions that we formed during the initial interview period. That is, our subjective impressions suggested that stepparents thought that their stepchildren were more negative about them than we perceived the stepchildren to be. We speculated that at Time 2, stepparents who had believed for a number of years that their stepchildren found them aversive would see the relationships as less close than their stepchildren. However, this obviously was not the case.

We can think of one explanation that would fit both our initial impressions and the Time 2 responses. If the stepchildren were the main force in defining the nature of the stepparent-stepchild relationship, then early in the relationship, stepparents may feel more pessimistic and frustrated than the stepchildren. This would be particularly true if the stepparents wanted more closeness than did the stepchildren, or if they wanted the relationship to be more like a parent-child bond than the stepchildren would accept. Stepparents may interpret the children's desire for more emotional distance in the relationship as bad, and as reflective of negative feelings toward them on the part of the child, when actually it simply could have reflected different expectations for the stepparentstepchild relationship.

Evidence for this is found in some of the other questions that we asked of stepchildren. For example, when asked to indicate how frequently they wished their stepparent to express more affection toward them, the majority at both Time 1 (63%) and Time 2 (59%) responded by choosing *rarely* or *never*. Thus, the majority of stepchildren were satisfied with the amount of affection in the stepparent-stepchild relationship. The percentage who *always* or *fairly often* wanted more affection decreased over time from 12% to 2%.

Approximately 78% of the adolescent stepchildren at both Times 1 and 2 said that they got along with their stepparents at least some of the time, and 65% at Time 1 and 66% at Time 2 indicated that they got along with them always or fairly often. A relatively high percentage of these stepchildren reported fairly good relationships with their stepparents (65% at Time 1 and 66% at Time 2).

Names and Labels

The names that stepchildren use in referring to their stepparents may be indicative of emotional closeness (i.e., children who feel close to their stepparent would be more likely to refer to them as "Mom" or "Dad"). In stepfamilies trying to recreate a first-marriage family model, children also may be more likely to call their stepparent "Mom" or "Dad." The assumptions, clinical impressions, and informal observations about names or labels that stepchildren use for stepparents have seldom been empirically tested.

We asked the stepchildren in our sample what they called their stepparent when directly interacting with him or her. At Time 1, the majority (61%) called their stepparent by a first name, 32% referred to the stepparent as "Mom" or "Dad," and 7% used a nickname. Time 2 responses were similar, with 57% using the stepparent's first name, 37% using the terms "Mom" or "Dad," and 6% using a nickname.

We also asked the adolescent stepchildren how they introduced their stepparent to others. At Time 1, 41% used the label "parent" to introduce their stepparent, 22% used their stepparent's first name, and 37% used another term (e.g., a nickname or "my mother's husband"). At Time 2, 45% introduced the stepparent as a parent, 39% used the first name, and 16% used another label.

These results suggest that terms of address are fairly stable over time, at least on the part of stepchildren who are adolescents. It should be noted that terms of address were also relatively constant across children in a family; 83% of the stepchildren in families with more than one stepchild called their stepparent by the same label.

There was no statistically significant relationship between what stepchildren called their stepparents and feelings of closeness. Instead, stepchildren began early in the relationship to call their stepparents by a certain name, which was chosen usually by the child but sometimes by the parent or stepparent. The stepchildren continued to call the stepparent by this name over time, at least in conversation with the stepparent. Stepparents did gradually receive the "parent" label in conversations with nonfamily members, but this was not necessarily related to closer feelings toward the stepparent.

Let us offer one final comment about labels. In nearly one-fifth of these stepfamilies, siblings used different forms of address when talking to their stepparents. While the norm may be for all stepchildren to use the same term, diversity of address was practiced in almost 20% of the families.

Loyalty Conflicts

Loyalty conflicts occur when stepchildren feel emotionally drawn toward adults in their family that do not get along with each other (e.g., mother and father, mother and stepmother) and who may compete with each other for affection from the child. Loyalty conflicts are more likely to occur when there is interparental hostility and/or when stepparent role expectations overlap greatly with what is typically expected from biological parents.

We found that loyalty conflicts between parents were more frequently experienced than those between parent and stepparent. A majority of the adolescents (60%) felt the pressure of loyalty conflicts ("I feel like I have to choose between my mother and father") at least occasionally at both Time 1 and Time 2. This perceived pressure to choose between parents increased over time for these adolescents from 60% to 88%. We do not know why this is so. It could be due to cognitive and emotional changes within the adolescents, changes in family relationships, or increased pressure from the biological parents. The data from this study do not allow us to select which of these hypotheses is most plausible. We can conclude, however, that for some adolescent stepchildren, loyalty conflicts between biological parents do not decrease over time and, thus, serve as a chronic stressor.

On the other hand, feeling unfaithful to a parent when having fun with a step-parent, which was not identified as being a frequent problem Time 1, had become even less so by Time 2 (26% compared to 19% noting *at least sometimes*). This may be related to the fact that a slight majority of these adolescents perceived that their parent and stepparent of the same sex got along well most of the time (52% at Time 1 and 57% at Time 2), thereby reducing the probability of the adults consciously putting the adolescents in a position where they feel divided loyalty. Alternatively, it may be that these adolescents have reduced loyalty conflicts by developing unique and specific relationships with each stepparent and biological parent, or maturation itself may have aided their ability to handle the relationship between two parents of the same sex.

Another way of viewing the loyalty issue is to explore children's wishes or fantasies regarding the reuniting of their parents. At Time 1, almost half (47%) of the children responded *sometimes*, *fairly often*, or *always* to the statement, "I wish my parents were still married." At Time 2, this proportion diminished to 32%. Conversely, the majority of adolescents at Time 2 continued to hold fairly positive views of their parents' marriage to their stepparent, with 56% responding favorably (*always* or *fairly often*) to the item, "Remarriage was a good thing."

Role Ambiguity

Role confusion has been identified as a major stressor for all stepfamily members. Cherlin (1978) argued that role confusion is related to the lack of institutionalized norms for stepfamilies. In particular, the role of the stepparent is one in which ambiguity predominates (Crosbie-Burnett, 1989c; Giles-Sims, 1987a; Pasley, 1987). Pink and Wampler (1985) suggested that stepparents are confronted with a choice between a parent or a nonparent role. Fast and Cain (1966) found that most stepparents alternate between three roles (i.e., parent, stepparent, and nonparent), all of which were described as vulnerable to dysfunction. When stepparents choose the parent role, they must deal with issues of how much and when to parent in the absence of legal or social sanctions and guidelines (Giles-Sims, 1984; Lutz, 1983). Developmental issues also are salient when choosing to enact a parenting role in the stepfamily; younger stepchildren may be more willing than an adolescent stepchild to accept a stepparent who assumes a parent role.

Stepparent's views. We asked the stepparents a number of questions designed to elicit perceptions of their stepparenting role. The most direct question asked if they thought of themselves as a stepparent. There was a dramatic change over time in responses to this question. At Time 1, 47% thought of themselves as a stepparent, while 53% did not. However, at Time 2, 86% indicated that they thought of themselves as a stepparent. Those who did not think of themselves as a stepparent thought of themselves either as a parent or as playing a nonparent role (e.g., as a friend).

Both stepparents and parents responded to questions about the amount of involvement and responsibility that the stepparents had in raising their stepchildren and their influence regarding decisions about the stepchild. Most parents (63%) thought that their partners had *about the right amount* of involvement with their children, and this perception did not change over time. The stepparents, on the other hand, were nearly as likely to think that they had *somewhat more* involvement than they wanted (34%) as they were to think they had *about the right amount* of involvement with their stepchildren (38%). This latter figure increased to 52% at Time 2. There were indications that over time, the amount of involvement was gradually becoming more in line with what the stepparent wanted. In contrast, both stepparents and parents tended to agree about the amount of responsibility assumed by the stepparent in raising the stepchild. Moreover, their views did not change much over time. Both stepparents and parents thought that the stepparents had a great deal of influence in decisions that were made about the stepchildren. Few thought that the stepparent had little or no influence (2% of parents and 6% of stepparents at Time 1). Over time, parents tended to perceive that the influence of their partner had increased (from 69% to 76% reporting that it had increased *a great deal*), while stepparents perceived a decrease in their influence over decisions regarding the children (from 62% to 53%). Therefore, the perceptions of stepparents and parents were more similar at Time 1 than at Time 2.

Stepchildren's views. The stepchildren agreed with their stepparents that the stepparent had *some* degree of influence over decisions regarding the stepchildren, at least at Time 2. We did not ask stepchildren about this influence during the initial interview, so we cannot see to what extent these perceptions may have changed. However, at Time 2, the percentages of choosing each response were about the same for stepchildren and stepparents. One exception was that more stepparents saw themselves having *a great deal* of influence (53%), while fewer stepchildren (41%) held the same perception.

We did ask children some similar questions about their stepparents' behavior at both Times 1 and 2. We asked: Who makes most of the decisions around your house? Who makes the rules around your house? When you get in trouble or do things you are not supposed to do, who usually gets after you about it? By the second data collection period, the majority of adolescent stepchildren saw both adults in the household as sharing in discipline (64%), rule making (85%), and decision making (70%). From the adolescents' perspective the parents increasingly shared discipline over time (from 6% at Time 1 to 64% at Time 2). Stepparents less often were seen as the primary decision maker, providing some evidence that overzealous stepparents may have backed off from the role of primary disciplinarian (from 25% at Time 1 to 17% at Time 2).

These responses are not surprising. Indeed, they are consistent with what clinicians advise stepparents to do (Visher & Visher, 1988a). Over time, we might expect stepfamilies to come to engage in at least some of the behaviors and interactional patterns that are recommended by clinicians. Moreover, these results are not surprising insofar as adolescent stepchildren may negatively respond to a stepparent attempting to act like a parent, at least in the arena of discipline and rules for children. Of course, we cannot determine from these data whether the changes in disciplining are a consequence of developmental changes in the stepchild, developmental changes in the stepparent-stepchild relationship, or adaptations occurring in the family as a whole over time.

As a final note, we want to point out that stepsons and stepdaughters had somewhat different patterns of responses to items on discipline. At Time 1, girls were consistently more likely than boys to identify the stepparent as the primary disciplinarian and rule maker. Although both boys and girls saw an increase in shared decision making over time, at Time 1 boys tended to perceive their residential parent (usually the mother) as doing more disciplining than the stepparent. The only sex difference at Time 2 was in rule making; more girls than boys said that their stepparent made the rules in their households.

Discipline

An issue that is clearly related to role ambiguity in stepfamilies is stepparent discipline of the stepchildren. Along with financial issues, discipline is one of the major problems facing stepfamilies, according to clinicians (Visher & Visher, 1988).

In Lutz's (1983) study, adolescents identified "Adjusting to living with a new set of rules from your stepparent," "Accepting discipline from a stepparent," and "Dealing with the expectations of your stepparent" to be contributors to stress. These are certainly cogent examples of discipline problems related to stepparent role ambiguity or role confusion. These adolescents especially seemed to resent stepparents who donned parent roles in the realm of discipline.

Evidence of stepparent role ambiguity regarding discipline was evident in our study as well. Despite having lived with a stepparent for a number of years, a substantial percentage of these adolescents did not approve of the stepparent acting in the role of disciplinarian. For example, at Time 1 32% of the stepchildren preferred that their parent do more disciplining than their stepparent. By Time 2, the percentage that preferred the parent to do more disciplining had risen to 44%. Most of this increase was due to changes in the stepdaughters' responses; stepsons' preferences for parents to discipline did not change over time, while for stepdaughters, there was a large shift from preferring their parent to discipline *rarely* or *never* (54% at Time 1) to preferring it *always* (42% at Time 2).

This was evidently not due to excessive friction in the relationship, because 65% of the stepchildren at Time 1 and 60% at Time 2 agreed that they got along fine with their stepparent. It may be that there are other reasons why stepchildren did not want their stepparents to discipline them. Perhaps adolescent stepchildren simply want the stepparent to make fewer efforts to control them. There was evidence, however, that stepparents do engage in disciplining their stepchildren, at least from the perception of the stepchild. A minority of respondents at both Times 1 and 2 indicated that their stepparent rarely or never told them what to do (19% and 24% respectively). Approximately 40% of children at both Times 1 and 2 indicated that the stepparent told them what to do *always* or *fairly often*. The percentage of stepsons who said that their stepparent "tells me what to do" decreased over time, while there was no corresponding decrease in the percentage of stepdaughters who responded in this way. These findings are compatible with those of Hetherington (1991), who indicated that negativity between stepdaughters and stepfathers tends to increase rather than decrease over time. Vuchinich and colleagues (1991) reported that the stepdaughters withdrew from their stepfathers, and Hetherington (1989) found more sullen, withdrawn behavior and negative problem-solving behavior directed toward stepfathers on the part of stepdaughters than stepsons. This is interesting, considering that the stepfathers in these observational studies were less involved with discipline and control and more involved in positive social behavior with children than were fathers in first-marriage families. It may be that girls are more resentful than boys of the intrusion of a stepfather into the mother-child relationship and, therefore, interpret the stepfather's behavior less positively, or at least differently. Hetherington (1991) hypothesized that because daughters in one-parent families have played more responsible, powerful roles and have more positive relations with their divorced mothers than have sons, the introduction of a stepfather may more strongly threaten both their independence and their relationship with their mother, compared to those of stepsons. This resentment may continue to build and color a stepdaughter's perceptions of her stepfather's behavior over time, including her perception of the amount of discipline.

Stepparents also may be harsher in handing out punishments. For this reason, their discipline is rejected. In our initial interviews with parents and stepparents, we noted that stepparents were almost universally described by themselves and their partners as being "more strict" than parents (Ganong & Coleman, 1986b). Of course, being more strict could mean holding higher standards for acceptable behavior and tolerating fewer transgressions against household rules. This may not be related to levying harsher punishments for violating the rules. However, the "mean and wicked stepparent" is part of our culture's folklore, so this hypothesis could be relevant. Nonetheless, the adolescents in this sample tended to disagree with the statement that stepparents were meaner than biological parents. Even at Time 2, only 20% felt that step-parents were more mean even *fairly often*, so the evidence does not strongly support the "mean stepparent" hypothesis as a source of discontent with stepparents' discipline.

It may be that stepparents tried to assume a disciplinarian role too soon in the stepparent-child relationship, a behavior that has been identified by clinicians as causing problems in stepfamilies (Visher & Visher, 1988). In our sample, the majority of stepparents did not do so, at least from their stepchild's perspective. Similarly, approximately 70% of stepchildren did not see the stepparent as trying to take over *most of the time.*

We asked several other questions about discipline, using the statments: "Other children in the family get less discipline than I do," "Whenever anything goes wrong around my house I get blamed," and "I have fewer privileges now than before my parent remarried." On all three items, the percentage indicating *always* and *fairly often* increased at Time 2. There were no sex differences in the pattern of responses over time. Overall, these adolescent stepchildren perceived that their home discipline environments were somewhat more restrictive than when they were younger. They also perceived that they were targeted for more frequent punishments than other children in the household/family. This may be true. However, these perceptions also could be attributed to adolescent egocentrism.

DISCUSSION

Before we discuss the possible meanings and implications of these results, the limitations of this study should be noted. First, the sample is small. This limits our ability to examine various aspects of adolescent stepchild-stepparent relationships, such as the differences in stepchildren's relationships with stepmothers compared to stepfathers. The sample size also precludes an examination of the influences of various stepfamily structural configurations on stepparent-stepchild ties. A second limitation is the volunteer, nonrandom nature of the sample. Although the original sample was roughly representative of U.S. stepfamilies in terms of socioeconomic status, it consisted of volunteers from one geographic area, was predominantly white, and basically lower-middle to middle class. The sample reported here consisted of families from the original study that agreed to be interviewed or receive questionnaires a second time, and we do not know how different these families may be from those who never volunteered. It may be that the stepparent-stepchild ties reported here involve less functional stepfamilies than average, or conversely, they may be from the most adaptive stepfamilies. A third limitation is that we did not have comparison groups of other family structures (e.g., first-marriage or single-parent), thus limiting our ability to know if changes observed in stepparent-stepchild relationships were unique to step relationships in stepfamilies or were characteristic of adolescent-adult dyads in general.

This study had several strengths that should be noted as well. First, the stepfamilies were long-lasting and presumably stable family systems. The study affords us a look at family processes in stepfamilies that have experienced the early transition period following remarriage and reached some level of equilibrium as a group. Second, the longitudinal design allows an examination of changes over time. Such longitudinal investigations of stepfamilies are still relatively rare. Finally, the data were obtained from whole stepfamilies; biological parents, stepparents, and stepchildren were respondents in this study. Differences between stepfamily members as well as differences between stepfamilies can therefore be assessed.

Having identified the strengths and weaknesses of the design, what can be said from these data about adolescent stepchild-stepparent relationships? The following are several conclusions that seem reasonable. On the whole, it appears that the intimacy and closeness in these adolescent stepchild-stepparent relationships grew less than when the stepchildren were younger. This could be due to a general reduction in family closeness over time as a result of conflict or a gradual deterioration of family intimacy. However, the greater distance between stepparents and stepchildren may be due to developmental changes in the adolescent (e.g, autonomy seeking, a search for a unique self-identity, and shifts in his or her cognitive perspective).

Increased emotional distance between adolescents and their parents is normative in our culture. It should not be surprising, therefore, to find that as children reach adolescence, relationships with stepparents also become less intimate. After all, stepparents are the relative newcomers to the adolescent's family, so there may be less "emotional glue" to bond the stepparent and child. The more tenuous nature of these relationships may make stepparents easier targets for rebellious behavior as adolescent stepchildren attempt to assert some autonomy from their families.

The development of adolescent stepchild-stepparent relationships is not a smooth, linear trajectory. Some relationships become closer over time, some attained a level of functioning that remained fairly constant and some deteriorated. Some relationships improved, but then worsened. Unfortunately, we cannot determine from these data what causes some relationships to grow closer while others become more distant.

Perhaps the most important point is for remarried parents and stepparents to be aware that step-relationships do not automatically become gradually closer over time, to culminate in an approximation of a biological parent-child relationship. While this no doubt happens in some step-relationships, the evidence from the families studied here indicates that there is wide variation in the developmental course of adolescent stepchild-stepparent ties. It also may be more helpful to remind stepparents to expect some pulling away by their stepchild as the child reaches early adolescence.

It should be emphasized that most of these adolescent stepchild-stepparent relationships are close rather than conflictual. We mention this because the prevailing cultural perspective on these relationships is that they will be primarily conflictual and negative, which is not the case for many stepfamilies.

In many stepfamilies, stepchildren continue to prefer that their biological parents do most of the disciplining. From the stepchild's perspective, stepparents may be too strict, or have unrealistically high standards for behavior, or their punishments may be too harsh. It also may be that adolescents are more comfortable in dealing with rules levied by their parents because of their shared history.

In most of the families in this study, parents took the lead in disciplining their children. Over time, however, there was a trend toward more shared discipline. This change may have resulted from increased familiarity between stepchild and stepparent and the evolution of the stepfamily's own rules for conduct. Stepparents may be socialized into the role of backup disciplinarian in stable, long-term stepfamilies such as the ones participating in this investigation.

Adolescent stepchild-stepparent relationships are more difficult for girls than for boys. This finding is consistent with a growing body of literature on gender differences in stepchildren's adjustment (Clingempeel, Brand, & Ievoli, 1984; Hetherington, 1989; Lutz, 1983; Peterson & Zill, 1986; Vuchinich et al., 1991).

One possible explanation is that stepparents interact differently with stepdaughters than with stepsons, resulting in more difficult adjustments for girls. There was evidence in our study that stepparents seemed to "back off" in disciplining their stepsons as they become adolescents, but did not do so with their stepdaughters. Vuchinich and associates (1991) also found that both fathers and stepfathers tended to oppose daughters more than sons. Of course, it could be that girls perceive more restrictions than boys and only feel that stepparents maintain harsher rules for them. For example, girls may have different standards for family relationships, expecting more closeness, warmth, and understanding than do boys. When these expectations are not met, then they will be more disappointed and upset than stepsons.

In this sample, girls also reported poorer relationships with both biological parents than did boys; 65% of the girls had a positive relationship with their mothers, and 51% had a positive relationship with their fathers. The perception of boys was virtually equal, with 70% and 71% having a positive relationship with their mothers and fathers, respectively. This finding is consistent with that of Peterson and Zill (1986), who reported that in both first-marriage and so-called disrupted families, fewer girls than boys had positive relationships with both parents.

If girls are more sensitive to family transitions, and if this sensitivity is displayed indirectly through withdrawal, depression, and other internalizing behaviors (Vuchinich et al., 1991), they may be at greater risk than boys, even in well-functioning, stable stepfamilies. It is important that future studies of stepchildren follow them into young adulthood and beyond to examine how these gender differences play out over time.

This study is only a "tease." It provides provocative glimpses of changes in stepparent-adolescent stepchild relationships over time, without a thorough and comprehensive view of those interactions. Obviously, more in-depth longitudinal studies of stepparents and stepchildren are warranted, but the need remains for qualitative studies and for research that includes data gathered from parents, stepparents, and stepchildren. Considerably more attention needs to be paid to communication and other family process variables when studying stepfamilies with adolescents. Intuition about these relationships based on first-marriage family models has not served us well. However, we feel confident that in the future, more investigators will examine the important connections between stepparents and their adolescent stepchildren.

KEY CHAPTER POINTS

1. Intimacy and closeness with the stepparent decreases over time as stepchildren become adolescents.

2. There is variability in the ways in which the relationship between adolescent stepchildren and stepparents develops over time. To expect it to become closer may be unrealistic, as some relationships deteriorate, some improve and then deteriorate, and some gradually improve.

3. Conflict is *not* the overriding characteristic of adolescent stepchild-step-parent relationships.

4. Adolescents typically prefer that their biological parent assume responsibility for limit setting, although over time, stepparents and parents come to share in the children's discipline.

5. Girls in stepfamilies have more difficulty with stepparents *and* parents than do boys.

Chapter 7

STEPMOTHERS AND THEIR ADOLESCENT CHILDREN: ADJUSTMENT TO NEW FAMILY ROLES

Donna S. Quick, Patrick C. McKenry, and Barbara M. Newman

One virtually unexplored stepfamily relationship is that of the stepmother and adolescent child (Coleman & Ganong, 1990). Research assessing the adjustments and effectiveness of stepmothers indicates that they do not fare as well as stepfathers. Findings suggest that compared to stepfathers, stepmothers are more anxious, depressed, and angry about family relationships (Ihinger-Tallman & Pasley, 1987; Sauer & Fine, 1988). In addition, stepparent role adjustment may be more difficult for stepmothers since our society usually expects the woman to be the more loving, nurturant parent and, thus, to be more involved than the man with parenting their stepchildren. Furthermore, the role of the stepmother is ambiguous. Consequently, stepmothers may feel frustrated, depressed, and dismayed at attempting to fit a largely undefined role for which they may have had no prior training.

The general writings on stepfamilies indicate that adolescent stepchildren have the most significant adjustment problems of children of any age (Chilman, 1983; Lutz, 1983). By extrapolation, the literature suggests that the stepmother-adolescent relationship is potentially the most problematic of all stepparent-stepchild combinations. However, few research findings are available to support this claim. What does seem clear is that the nature of parent-child relationships affects the relative ease with which a young person adjusts to the changed roles and new demands of adolescence (Leigh & Peterson, 1986). In turn, the adolescent's adjustment influences the ease of the stepmother's transition to the marital and parental roles (Santrock & Sitterle, 1987). How the special nature and circumstances of the stepfamily influence these transitions is a critical question.

This chapter reviews the literature on the stepmother-stepchild relationship, with a special focus on adolescent stepchildren. In addition, we present the preliminary findings from a research study examining selected psychosocial factors related to the adjustment of stepmothers and their adolescent stepchildren. We conclude with recommendations for future research and theory development.

THE STATE OF CURRENT RESEARCH ON STEPMOTHER-STEPCHILD FAMILIES

Adolescence is a time of transition and developmental change. The formation of a stepfamily also produces change and adjustment for adolescents and may generate added stress. Combined, the dual adjustment demands of adolescence and stepfamily formation can pose significant challenges to the entire stepfamily. Studies that focus on adolescent adjustment in stepfamilies are summarized in Table 7.1. Surprisingly, this small body of research suggests that there may be no significant difference between adolescent well-being in stepfamilies compared to first-marriage families. Nye (1957) found no difference in school adjustment and delinquency rates between adolescents in first-marriage families and those in stepfamilies. He reported that stepchildren displayed better adjustment to parents, had fewer psychomotor complaints, and had fewer delinquent behaviors than did children from intact but unhappy first-marriage families. Burchinal (1964) investigated the effects of divorce and remarriage on the behavior of adolescent children in Grades 7 and 11. He concluded that the data did not show detrimental effects of divorce and remarriage on children: "There is no question that in terms of the variables measured, family dissolution and, for some families, reconstitution, was not the overwhelming influential factor in the children's lives that many have thought it to be" (p. 50).

Other studies have indicated that step relationships are more likely to be characterized by stress, ambivalence and low cohesiveness than relationships in first-marriage settings (Bowerman & Irish, 1962). The work of Rosenberg (1965) also suggests that adolescents in stepfamilies have lower self-esteem and more psychosomatic complaints than adolescents in first-marriage families.

More recently, an investigation of what adolescents between the ages of 12 and 18 perceived to be the most stressful aspects of stepfamily living found "issues pertaining to divided loyalties and discipline" to be the most stressful (Lutz, 1983, p. 367). Children who had lived in stepfamilies less than 2 years also reported greater stress than those who had lived in a stepfamily for a longer period. One other study discovered a positive relationship between the length of time in remarriage and preadolescent adjustment. Clingempeel and Segal (1986) reported that the quality of the stepparent-stepdaughter relationship and child outcomes were related positively to the total time for which the biological father and the stepmother had lived together. The longer the stepdaughters lived with their stepmothers, the more positive they perceived the relationship to be.

These few studies provide little direction for further research into the adjustment of stepmothers and adolescent stepchildren. While several studies have suggested that the perceived stress of adolescence played a role in the child's ultimate adjustment (Furstenberg, 1987; Lutz, 1983), no studies examined the coping strategies employed by adolescents that affect the nature of their relationship with their stepmothers. Do adolescents who (a) use coping behaviors and (b) have lived longer in the stepfamily adapt more readily to life in stepmother families? Do

Table 7.1

Research on Adolescents in Stepfamilies

Study	Sample Size and Characteristics	Method	Major Findings
Bernard (1956)	2,000 total college students, 112 college students from SM* and SF* families (nonprobability sample)	Questionnaires and interviews with stepchildren and informants	1) stepchildren had positive attitudes toward parents who had remarried
Nye (1957)	789 students, grades 9-12 (nonprobability sample)	questionnaire developed by researcher	1) no differences in adjustment to school, church attendance, delinquent companions 2) stepchildren better adjusted to parents, had fewer psychosomatic complaints, less delinquent behavior than children from unbroken, unhappy families
Bowerman & Irish (1962)	29,000 total students grades 7-12 2,145 stepchildren from both SF and SM families (nonprobability sample)	questionnaire	1) stepchildren were not as close to parents as nuclear family children 2) stepchildren experienced more rejection and discrimination 3) stepmothers fared worse than stepfathers

Table 7.1 (continued)

Burchinal (1964)	1,566 total students grades, 7 & 11 210 from both SF and SM families (nonprobability sample: junior and senior high school students from one community)	questionnaire	1) no difference in personality characteristics, grades, school and community activities, number of friends, school attitudes, days absent
Lutz (1983)	103 total stepchildren 12-18 years of age from SF and SM families (nonprobability sample)	questionnaire	1) issues of divided loyalty and discipline were more stressful 2) stepfamily life may not be as stressful as literature suggests
Brand & Clingempeel (1987)	40 stepfather families 22 stepmother families 62 children ages 9-12 (recruited from marriage license records in Philadelphia, PA)	observation	1) in SM families, higher marital quality was associated with more positive stepmother-stepson relationships and better stepson adjustment, but less positive stepmother-stepdaughter relationships and poorer stepdaughter adjustment

Table 7.1 (continued)

Sauer & Fine (1988)	130 college students from intact families, 47 students from stepfamilies, 16 students from stepmother families (nonprobability sample)	questionnaire	1)	now adult children from stepfamilies perceived their relationships with their noncustodial biological mothers and stepmothers less positively than now adult children from intact families perceived their relationships with their biological mothers to be

Note: SM = stepmother; SF = stepfather

Table 7.2

Research on Stepmothers

Study	Sample Size and Characteristics	Method	Major Findings
Duberman (1973)	88 random sample of parents who had remarried from 1965-1968, drawn from county marriage records (included both stepmother and stepfather families)	interviews and researcher ratings	1) relationships between SM* and children were generally positive 2) younger SM more likely to have excellent relations with their stepchildren than the older SM
Nadler (1976)	24 part-time stepmothers 24 full-time stepmothers 24 biological mothers 72 total families (nonprobability sample)	questionnaire	1) both types SM indicated more depressed, angry than biological mothers 2) part-time SM less involved in family interactions, more conflict with family, parent role, etc 3) full-time SM with older children--more conflict over child-rearing, less marital satisfaction than biological mothers with older children 4) part-time SM with older children--more conflict with child than biological mothers with older children

Table 7.2 (continued)

Santrock, Warshak, & Elliot (1982)	64 total families (stepmother, nuclear, single parent), 12 stepmother families (stepchildren ages 6-11), and informants (nonprobability sample)	observation	1) boys showed less competent social behavior in SM families than girls in SM families or boys in nuclear families 2) no differences for stepdaughters
Brown (1984)	51 stepmothers (nonprobability sample)	questionnaire and interview	1) most difficult aspects of stepmothering were: relating to the biological mother of one's stepchildren, being a stepmother without being a biological mother, discipline of children, and handling "unacceptable" feelings toward stepchildren
Clingempeel & Segal (1986)	60 total stepfamilies 40 SF families 20 SM families (half of each structural type had a male and half had a female 9-12 target child) (sample gathered from marriage license records and newspaper ads)	questionnaire and observation	1) few significant findings for those with stepfathers 2) for girls with stepmothers, less frequent visits with mother and longer time in stepfamily were related to positive relations with stepmother

Table 7.2 (continued)

Brand & Clingempeel (1987)	40 stepfather families, 22 stepmothers families, 62 children ages 9-12 (recruited from marriage license records in Philadelphia, PA)	questionnaire and interview	1) stepmothers reported generally positive relations with their stepchildren 2) the stepmother-stepchild relationship correlated with partner's satisfaction with marriage 3) many stepmothers did, however, acknowledge during this interview that the stepmother role was particularly difficult
Guisinger, Cowan, & Schuldberg (1989)	62 remarried fathers and their new wives (cross-sectional and longitudinal participants)	questionnaire and interview	1) stepmothers reported generally positive relations with their stepchildren 2) the stepmother-stepchild relationship correlated with partner's satisfaction with marriage 3) many stepmothers did, however, acknowledge during this interview that the stepmother role was particularly difficult

Note: SM = stepmother; SF = stepfather

stepmothers who (a) feel positive about themselves and their marriage and (b) agree with their spouse on how to raise adolescent stepchildren adapt more successfully to living in a stepfamily? These are the questions examined in the study that we report in this chapter.

RESEARCH FINDINGS ON STEPMOTHERS

We present a summary of the studies focusing on stepmothers in Table 7.2. The compiled results present a fairly consistent picture. There is more confusion, more problematic interaction, and a greater risk for poor adjustment among family members in stepmother families compared to members of first-marriage, biological mother families or stepfather families (Clingempeel, Brand & Ievoli, 1984; Clingempeel & Segal, 1986; Duberman, 1973; Santrock et al., 1982).

Parent-Child Relationships and Role Satisfaction for Stepmothers

In one of the first studies of stepfamilies, Duberman (1973) found that stepmothers were less satisfied in their role than were stepfathers. Nadler (1976) provided insight into the role of stepmother by comparing part-time and full-time stepmothers with a matched set of biological mothers. Both types of stepmothers reported more depression and anger regarding family relationships than did biological mothers.

Santrock and Sitterle (1987) examined parent-child relationships in stepfather, stepmother, and first-marriage family structures. They concluded that although the group of stepmothers was attempting to establish a good relationship with their stepchildren, they felt they were less involved with their stepchildren compared to mothers from first-marriage or stepfather families. Stepmothers reported sharing many of the parental and child-rearing responsibilities and persistently tried to involve themselves with their stepchildren. However, the children continued to view them as somewhat detached, unsupportive, and uninvolved in their lives.

Brown (1984) provided further insight into the role of the stepmother and how role enactment potentially influences the quality of the parent-child relationship in stepfamilies. Fifty-one stepmothers were interviewed in a nonclinical, exploratory study addressing the questions: What satisfactions and strains do women experience as they assume this role, and what methods have they developed to become "effective" stepmothers? This study revealed that the "cruel stepmother" image had a negative influence on the participants' self-concepts and on their stepchildren. The most difficult aspects of stepmothering to be identified were: (a) relating to the biological mother of the stepchild; (b) being a stepmother without being a biological mother; (c) dealing with negative feelings toward stepchildren; and (d) handling discipline.

Sauer and Fine (1988) studied college students' memories of their upbringing. Students' perceptions of parent-child relationships in stepfamilies were more negative than perceptions of parent-child relationships in first-marriage families. The researchers reasoned that the remarriage of a custodial father and the entrance of a stepmother into the family creates a new role in the family. The children may view the stepmother role as a threat to the family roles that had already been established. This is especially true for children who continue to remain close to the nonresidential parent (Lutz, 1983).

Characteristics of the Stepmother's Remarriage and the Parent-Child Relationships

Researchers who study stepmothers are beginning to examine the marital system to identify factors that influence the quality of stepfamily adjustment and parent-child relationships. Two studies looked at the relationship between the stepmother's perceived marital quality and the stepparent-stepchild relationship (Brand & Clingempeel, 1987; Guisinger, Cowan, & Schuldberg, 1989). In contrast to first-marriage families, Brand and Clingempeel (1987) found that marital quality in stepmother families differentially affected male and female stepchildren. For stepdaughters, a more positive marital relationship was associated with lower levels of psychological adjustment and a less positive stepmother-stepdaughter relationship. On the other hand, for stepmother families with boys, the reverse was true. A more general finding was reported by Guisinger et al. (1989), who found that the quality of the stepmother-stepchild relationship related positively to marital satisfaction.

Limitations of the Research

Unfortunately, most research on stepmother families to date has focused heavily on problems of stepfamilies. This is the result of the frequent use of the deficit comparison model in which researchers perceive stepfamilies as deviant from the traditional family milieul, which consists of biological parents and one or more children (Coleman & Ganong, 1990). Most investigators studied stepfamilies from this perspective which assumes that members are lacking in some social or psychological aspect. Therapists perpetuate this damaging perceptual bias in clinical settings when they indiscriminately compare stepfamily functioning with functioning in first-marriage families.

We believe that research is needed to identify strengths and resources that contribute to high-quality stepfamily relationships, especially for stepmothers (Coleman, Ganong, & Gingrich; 1985; Knaub, Hanna, & Stinnett, 1984). Little is known about factors contributing to positive adjustment in stepmother families in which adolescent children reside.

Other weaknesses in stepmother-stepchild research include generalizing the results from small, nonrandom samples to the general stepfamily population

(Coleman & Ganong, 1990; Ganong & Coleman, 1984). In addition, researchers typically gather data using information from only one source (usually the child or mother). Reliance on a single source may be the major weakness of this body of literature. Finally, few studies adequately employ a multimethod, multisource approach. These limitations need to be addressed to provide a holistic, logically integrated picture of stepmothers and their adolescent stepchildren.

In the following study we employ a multisource approach to the study of adolescents growing up in stepmother families. We also identify social and psychological factors that relate to the adjustment of stepfamily members.

AN EXPLORATORY STUDY OF THE STEPMOTHER-ADOLESCENT RELATIONSHIP

Because research and theory have indicated that the stepmother-adolescent relationship may be inherently stressful (e.g., Chilman, 1983; Lutz, 1983; Sauer & Fine, 1988), the study reported here investigated the social and psychological influences that affect this relationship. According to role theory, whether the stepmother and the stepchild adjust to the stress associated with the formation of a stepfamily depends, in part, on resources that each individual brings to the situation, as well as to characteristics of the new family structure (Clingempeel, Brand, & Segal, 1987). Several such resources were identified in the stepmother-stepchild literature that is related to adjustment. Based on a role adjustment perspective and related stepfamily literature, the following independent variables were predicted to be related to the quality of the stepmother-adolescent relationship: (a) age of stepmother at the time of the remarriage (Duberman, 1975); (b) adolescent's time in the current stepfamily (Papernow, 1980); (c) adolescent's perception of family coping patterns (McCubbin, Larsen, & Olson, 1981); (d) self-esteem of stepmother (Pearlin & Schooler, 1978); (e) marital quality (Brand & Clingempeel, 1987); and (f) frequency of agreement between the stepmother and the father on how to raise the stepchild (Messinger, 1976). We indicated earlier that a major methodological weakness in the study of families has been the reliance on a signle source of information regarding the entire family; this is usually the wife/mother (McKenry, Price-Bonham, & O'Bryant, 1981). Assessing the perceptions of multiple family members has "the potential of gaining much valuable insight into the family as a unit of interacting personalities" (Ball, McKenry, & Price-Bonham, 1983, p. 895). The present study was unique in two ways. First, the dependent variable of adjustment, as conceptualized in terms of the quality of the stepparent-stepchild relationship, took into account the perceptions of both the stepmother and the adolescent child. Responses from the stepmother and the adolescent were analyzed separately. Second, the study combined quantitative and qualitative data on stepfamily relationships and focused on the adolescent stepchild.

METHODS

Sample Selection

The sample used in this study was obtained in 1987-1988 and consisted of 50 stepmothers and their adolescent stepchildren (legally custodial and noncustodial) who resided in two large metropolitan areas of Ohio and Kentucky. For inclusion in this study, the children had to be between 12 and 18 years of age, have divorced parents, and either live with the stepmother and biological or adoptive father or visit at least once a month. The stepmother, father, and adolescent stepchild were surveyed, although the father's responses are not reported here. Where there was more than one adolescent stepchild in the home, only the eldest eligible stepchild participated in the survey.

This sample was obtained using a reputational sampling technique that drew on stepfamily support groups as well as suggestions from colleagues and study participants. Stepfamily groups were first contacted, followed by subjects whose names were generated by professionals. Participants were interviewed, and they were asked to give the names of other stepfamilies that met the study criteria.

It should be noted that althought at 50, the number of stepmother-adolescent dyads is relatively small statistically, this sample is one of the larger stepmother-stepchild samples to have been gathered. Only 5-10% of fathers in the general population obtain custody of their children following divorce, and in 1-2 years after a divorce, a child's regular visitation with the father substantially decreases (Furstenberg & Nord, 1985). These facts suggest that the population of stepmothers who have regular contact with their adolescent stepchildren is small. Identifying and obtaining a sample was further limited by the geographical constraint of using only two metropolitan areas. To obtain the sample size of 50 stepmothers and their adolescent stepchildren, 75 stepmother families were originally contacted and agreed to participate. Twenty-five of these later declined to participate for the following reasons: (a) the child moved back with the mother and therefore, the stepmother family no longer saw the child on a regular basis; (b) one or more family members decided not to participate; (c) the stepmother or father feared that discussing the divorce and remarriage in a survey would be too painful; (d) it was impossible to schedule a time when the stepmother, adolescent, and father would all be at home to complete the questionnaires; or (e) the stepmother felt the family had too many problems to assess relationship quality at this time.

Subjects

The sample consisted of 50 stepmother families with a biological or adoptive father, his oldest adolescent child living with the family (82%) or visiting regularly (18%), and a stepmother. The father and stepmother had no biological or adoptive children between them. It is difficult to divide these families into traditional categories of father custody, mother custody, split custody, and joint custody. Because the stepchildren were adolescents, they often could determine to some extent their physical custody arrangement. There appeared to be many combinations, and these were constantly in flux.

The all-white sample consisted of 21 female and 29 male adolescents. The mean age of the children was 15.26 years (SD = 1.71). The mean age of the stepmothers was 41.31 years (SD = 1.93). The number of years the stepmothers had been married to their spouses ranged from 1 to 12 years with a mean of 4.4 years (SD = 2.78). Twenty-four percent (n = 17) had been married less than 3 years, whereas 42% had been married between 3 and 6 years.

The sample is best described as highly educated and middle to upper-middle income. The level of education for both husbands and wives ranged from not completing high school through completing graduate degrees. Seventy-four percent of fathers had completed at least 4 years of college, and 48% had graduate degrees. Seventy-six percent of the stepmothers had completed 4 years of college, and 34% had graduate degrees.

Additional demographic information indicated that all the fathers were employed full-time and 98% of the stepmothers were employed. Using Hollingshead's (1957) criteria, 32% were higher executives, proprietors of large concerns, and highly skilled professionals; 34% were business managers, proprietors of medium-sized businesses, and less skilled professionals; 22% were administrative personnel of smaller businesses and minor professionals; 6% were clerical/sales workers, technical workers, and owners of small businesses; and 4% were skilled manual employees. Total family income ranged from $20,000 to more than $100,000, with 44% of the families falling within the interval of $40,000-$75,000; 22% earned more than $100,000 per year. The religious affiliation of the families reflected national averages: approximately 50% were Protestant, 25% were Roman Catholic, and 8% were Jewish.

Procedures

Stepmothers and their oldest adolescent stepchildren were mailed a letter of introduction inviting them to participate in the study. This letter was followed by a telephone call to give families the opportunity to ask further questions and to schedule an appointment for the administration of the survey. Data were collected by either the principal investigator or other trained personnel.

During the visit in the home, questionnaires were administered by the investigator to the adolescent, his or her father, and the stepmother. The questionnaire took an average of 1 hour to complete. Family members were requested to keep their written answers confidential, and the investigator's presence assured that an inappropriate sharing of responses between family members did not confound the results.

Measures

The adolescent and stepparent versions of the questionnaire used in the study were composed of various standardized instruments which were chosen for their psychometric properties and relevance to understanding stepfamily role adjustment. Demographic and family background questions were included. In addition, three open-ended questions were posed to the respondents. The survey materials were pretested with several stepmothers and stepchildren who were not members of the sample to identify and correct inappropriate or ambiguous items.

The dependent measure, which was conceptualized as the *quality of the adolescent-stepmother relationship*, was assessed with the Parent-Adolescent Communication Scale (Barnes & Olson, 1982). This instrument describes parent-child communication in a variety of family types and captures some of the diversity of communication experiences. Pink and Wampler (1985) also used this instrument as an indicator of the quality of the stepparent-child relationship. The measure is designed to assess the perceptions of both the parent and the child. Although the stepmother and adolescent scores were treated independently, the two responses were highly correlated ($r = .91$). The reliability of the instrument was established at .88; it tested at .91 in this study.

The Family Crisis Oriented Personal Evaluation Scale (F-COPES; McCubbin et al., 1981) was used to measure the *adolescent's perception of family coping*. This measure was designed to identify effective problem solving and behavioral strategies utilized by families in difficult or problematic situations. Three subscales were used: *family passivity* (the ability to accept problematic issues thus minimizing reactivity), *reframing family problems* (the capability to redefine stressful events in order to make them more manageable), and *acquiring social support* (the ability to actively engage in acquiring support from relatives, friends, neighbors, and extended family). Alpha coefficients of reliability range from .63 to .83 and were .54 to .62 for this study.

Stepmother's self-esteem was measured with the Rosenberg (1965) Self-Esteem Scale. This scale measures the self-acceptance aspect of self-esteem using 10 items. Responses range from *strongly agree* to *strongly disagree* and are scored so that high scores represent more positive self-esteem. The scale has been used with a variety of samples, including adolescents. Cronbach alpha reliability was established at .85; it was .85 in this study as well.

The *stepmother's marital quality* was assessed using the Marital Comparison Level Index (MCLI; Sabatelli, 1984). Theoretically grounded in exchange theory, the MCLI was designed to assess an individual's current perceived marital outcomes in comparison to what he or she originally expected in various marital domains. The MCLI consists of 32 items with a 7-point Likert-type response pattern. For each item, respondents are asked how their experience within their relationship compares with their expectations. Responses range from *worse than I expect* to *better than I expect* and were scored from -3 to +3. Cronbach alpha reliability was established at .93; it was .92 in this study.

Frequency of agreement between stepmother and the father was assessed with a single, fixed-response question. The stepmother was asked how often she and her husband agreed in decisions regarding his child. The response set ranged from *never* (1) to *always* (5).

Raw scores were used to assess the independent variables, *age of stepmother at the time of the remarriage* and *adolescent's time in the current stepfamily* (in months). In addition, three open-ended questions were asked: (a) Is there any additional information you would like to share that you feel might be helpful in trying to understand your particular experience with divorce, remarriage, and living in a stepfamily? (b) What are the most positive aspects of living in a stepfamily? and (c) How do you feel you could improve relationships with your adolescent stepchild (or stepmother)? These questions were designed to elicit additional factors that might explain the process of adjusting to these new family roles.

RESULTS

Quantitative Findings

The relationship between the dependent variables (the quality of the stepmother-adolescent relationship, as perceived by the stepmother and the adolescent) and the independent predictor variables was assessed by Pearson product moment correlation and multiple regression analysis. The results of correlational analysis indicated significant relationships between the adolescent's perception of the quality of the stepmother-adolescent relationship and (a) frequency of reframing family problems by the adolescent ($r = .22, p < .05$) and (b) acquiring social support, as perceived by the adolescent ($r = .43, p < .01$). Neither the length of time for which the adolescents had been in this family structure nor the use of passivity as a coping strategy were significantly associated with the perceived quality of the stepmother-adolescent relationship ($r = -.09$ and $-.16$, respectively).

In terms of the stepmother's perception, three factors were significantly correlated to the quality of the stepmother-adolescent relationship: her self-esteem ($r = .25, p < .05$), her marital quality ($r = .36, p < .05$), and frequency of agreement between the stepmother and father on how to raise the stepchild ($r = .54, p < .01$). The age of the stepmother at the time of the remarriage was not significantly associated with the perceived quality of the stepmother-adolescent relationship ($r = -.08$).

A stepwise multiple regression procedure was used to determine the strongest predictors of relationship quality. Only those independent variables that were found to be significantly associated with the quality of the stepmother-adolescent relationship as perceived by the stepmother or adolescent were entered into the equations. Two independent variables were entered into the regression equation to determine which factor was the strongest predictor of the quality of the step-mother-adolescent relationship as perceived by the adolescent. The analysis yielded a significant adjusted R^2 of .23 ($F = 8.16$, $p < .001$), with "acquiring social support" as the strongest predictor (beta = .47). Reframing family problems also was a significant, albeit less effective, predictor of the quality of the stepmother-stepchild relationship (beta = .27).

Using the three independent variables, which were significantly associated with stepmother's perception of the quality of the stepmother-adolescent relationship, the multiple regression analysis yielded a significant adjusted R^2 of .32 ($F = 6.12$, $p < .001$), with "frequency of agreement on how to raise the stepchild" as the sole predictor (beta = .50).

Qualitative Findings

An examination of responses to three open-ended questions was conducted to determine themes that might enhance the interpretation of the study's findings. In response to the question asking the stepmothers to share any additional infor-mation that they felt might be helpful in trying to understand their particular experiences with divorce, remarriage, and stepfamily living, many stepmothers indicated that time was the major factor in facilitating the development of their relationship with their stepchildren. These women seemed to be saying that they could not identify any specific effective coping mechanisms, but with time, the relationship had improved. Moreover, the vast majority of the stepmothers indicated strong support from their husbands regarding their parenting and generally high levels of agreement regarding child rearing issues. Other stepmothers indicated that individual support groups to which they belonged were an important source of help. Lack of privacy was a common complaint, and almost half the stepmothers noted that adolescent development issues accentuated the problems of stepfamily living. Some of the mothers (14%) indicated that the transition inot remarriage was made more difficult than expected because they had not expected to assume a major parental role with their stepchildren. Almost one-third complained about some aspect of the custody arrangements.

Interestingly, the adolescents wrote little in response to this question. What was written tended to be more positive than negative. The adolescents, like their stepmothers, typically indicated that initial adjustment was difficult, but said that in time, it had improved. Ten percent of adolescents commented on the fact that their fathers were much happier since remarrying. However, 24% seemed disillus-ioned about marriage and family life.

In response to the question asking about the most positive aspects of stepfamily living, almost 40% of stepmothers stated that being a stepmother gave them the opportunity to engage in a maternal role, either for the first time or in a new situation (e.g., "makes holidays more meaningful" or "feels good to add stability to the lives of these children"). Approximately one-third expressed enjoyment of the challenge of living in a stepfamily or the personal growth resulting from this transition. Comments included, "[This experience] has given me the opportunity to grow" and "I like the diversity."

In response to this same question, adolescents most frequently (42%) mentioned a sense of having a "complete" or "real" family again. Several adolescents (32%) mentioned having more material things, as well as more time and money with which to pursue leisure activities. Girls (76%) were more likely to mention the sense of having a family again, whereas boys (69%) were more likely to mention material things. Some children (16%) indicated the absence of parental conflict as a positive factor.

When asked how they might improve their relationship with their stepchildren, the most frequent response of the stepmothers (44%) was by improving communication (e.g., "work on communication skills," "spend more time one to one"). A similar number (36%) stressed the need for greater patience and more time (e.g., "it takes time to develop trust"). Spending more time together was also frequently mentioned (30%). It should be noted that a few stepmothers (8%) indicated that they knew of little they could do personally to improve the situation. Compared to other stepmothers, these women were more likely to feel that they had tried and failed in their role, and more likely to have resisted assuming the role from the beginning.

In response to this question, the majority of adolescents (72%) also mentioned communication (e.g., "being more open," "listening more"). A few adolescents (16%) indicated that the relationship was already good and they could think of now ways to improve it. However, 22% stated that they were in a hopeless situation; these adolescents tended to be older and to have shorter terms of membership in the stepfamily when compared to other adolescents.

DISCUSSION

Consistent with other research (e.g., Clingempeel et al., 1987), the findings from this study indicated the utility of viewing the quality of the stepmother-adolescent relationship as a component of the characteristics of the new family. For both the adolescent and the stepmother, family factors were far more predictive of relationship quality than were structural and/or individual factors such as age and time in the stepfamily. The qualitative findings also underscore the importance of family members having adequate time together in our understanding of the adjustment process. In addition, the qualitative findings suggest that stepfamily members have different perspectives on what affects adjustment: in this case, the perspectives of the adolescent and his or her stepmother. The difference noted here indicates the importance of studying stepfamily processes from a systemic perspective in which multiple respondents are queried.

An examination of the normed scores developed for the dependent measure indicates that both the stepmother (65.17) and adolescent (60.22) mean scores were slightly below the means established for the Parent-Adolescent Communication Scale (mother mean = 75.47 and adolescent mean = 66.56; Barnes & Olson, 1982). It is not surprising that the study sample had a somewhat lower mean score. The families used in the Barnes and Olson study were first-married families with adolescents, whereas the sample in this study was comprised of stepfamilies, including adolescents which had been together for an average of only 4 years. Many of the families in this study still may be in the process of integrating the stepmother into the family system. In the qualitative responses, both the adolescents and the stepmothers noted the importance of time in enhancing the quality of their relationship.

While no studies to date have examined coping strategies within the stepfamily as perceived by the adolescent, the family's ability to reframe or redefine a stressful event may be an important coping dimension for predicting the quality of the step-mother-stepchild relationship from the perspective of the adolescent. Because the roles of stepmother and stepchild are not clearly defined and society offers no clear guidelines as to what can be expected in those roles, family members must work out their own definition of how to behave. This process can pose particular challenges for some stepfamilies, especially those with stepmothers.

These data also suggest that the family's ability to acquire social support from relatives, friends, and neighbors is an important predictor of the steprelationship, particularly from the adolescents' perspective. Clinical literature suggests that many adolescents and their families turn to friends for support during marital transitions (Visher & Visher, 1982a). While social support was an important predictor of adjustment for adolescents in stepmother families, these same adolescents are likely to have already gained *and* lost support during the transitions of divorce and remarriage. For example, those who lived with their mothers may have gained support from teachers while having lost some support from the biological father, since he may be less available to them on a daily basis due to the divorce. This may be reflected in the adolescents' statements regarding the importance of having a "complete" family again. Moreover, the adolescent's parents may not be as emotionally available during these transitions as they were earlier, during the predivorce period, because of the energy required for their own adjustments (Hetherington, Stanley-Hagan, & Anderson, 1989; Wallerstein & Kelly, 1980).

The relationship between the stepmother's satisfaction with the remarriage and the quality of the steprelationship is partially consistent with the findings of Brand and Clingempeel (1987), which indicated that marital quality was associated with more positive stepmother relationships for boys, but not for girls. In the present study, the stepmothers' mean score on the Marital Comparison Index was 144.56. The normative score indicating that expectations are being met is 128. Thus, the stepmothers in the current study indicated that the marital relationship more than met their expectations. A quality marital relationship was found to be related to the quality of the stepmother-adolescent relationship and can serve as a resource to the family. The qualitative data also reflected this in that the stepmothers felt that the strong support from their husbands and lack of disagreement with them regarding child rearing were important in successfully carrying out the stepmother role. Importantly, based on the correlational findings, these relationships can be interpreted conversely, such that a quality parent-child relationship also could enhance the parent's marriage.

Studies of first-marriage families emphasize the potential importance of the marital relationship as a source of help to individuals in times of stress (e.g., Coombs, 1991). In stepfamilies, the strength and health of the marital bond may be particularly important as these stepfamily members (who are often from different backgrounds) find themselves suddenly living together in the intimacy of a family. Furthermore, there are typically former spouses, assorted relatives, and friends who continue to have input into, and influence on, the family unit. A positive marital atmosphere also may send a clearer message to the children that reconciliation between the child's biological parents is no longer likely. This, in turn, may promote the children's ability to accept the reality of the marriage and help them focus on the positive aspects of their current family situation.

While self-esteem and marital quality were significant correlates of the quality of the stepmother-stepchild relationship, only stepmother-father agreement on how to raise the child was predictive. This is consistent with the stepfamily literature (see, as examples, Albrecht et al., 1983; Duberman, 1975; Messinger, 1976; Visher & Visher, 1982a). The importance of consensus in child rearing was reiterated in the qualitative findings. Although studies regarding the stepmother's disciplinary role are practically nonexistent, the clinical literature on stepfathers indicates that disagreements related to the enforcement of rules and discipline strategies are a source of stress for parents and children alike (Lutz, 1983). Because of the salient role of the mother as parent, stepmothers are often expected to be more involved in parenting than stepfathers. As the stepmother and father experience more cooperation and agreement on issues related to child rearing, the role strain associated with the unclear nature of how the stepmother is supposed to function in regard to discipline may be reduced. A "united front" presented by both the father and the stepmother regarding discipline and child guidance may contribute to a quality relationship between the stepmother and stepchild.

The findings of this study indicate that self-esteem may play a role in the step-mother's relationship satisfaction, albeit a minor one. Although several studies have assessed the child's self-esteem in terms of adjustment to stepfamily living, no studies heretofore have examined self-esteem of the stepmother as a component of family functioning. In addition the qualitative findings indicating the desire of many of these stepmothers to nurture the children and to take on a known challenge also may reflect the role of self-esteem in adjusting to the stepmother role. The tendency of these mothers to note that time was a major factor in their adjustment and, thus, to avoid blaming themselves for disappointments, indicates the role of self-esteem in coping with this transition. Small (1988) found that in first-married families, the mother's self-esteem was highly related to better communication with her adolescent child. Such may be the case with stepmothers.

Stepmother often are depicted in the media as self-centered, uncaring, and even evil. Nonetheless, there are societal expectations that stepmothers should participate in child rearing duties. A strong sense of self-worth may allow these women to effectively and realistically cope with the ambiguity and negative connotations of their role.

IMPLICATIONS AND FUTURE DIRECTIONS

The study described here provides an example of research that begins to address some of the significant weaknesses in the extant literature. It focuses on within-group differences. The sample was purposefully restricted to families in which fathers either had legal custody of their adolescent children or the children visited at least once a month, and in which the stepmothers had no children of their own. The families were all white, and all were middle- or upper-middle class. Although our restricted approach to sample selection limits generalizability, as a pilot study, it establishes a strategy for future studies in which each structural element can be varied systematically.

Further, the study included data from two partners in the relationship, the stepmother and the adolescent child. This permitted us to examine relationship quality from the points of view of both adult and child. The study helps to identify those factors that serve as sources of support for the stepmother-stepchild relationship, suggesting that from these families we can learn ways to make the relationship work to the mutual advantage of adults and children alike. The most important finding for adolescent children was that their ability to draw on friends, neighbors, and other relatives and to reframe or reappraise stressful situations were predictive of their adjustment. For stepmothers, the most important finding was that their husbands contributed significantly to their positive evaluation of the stepparent-stepchild relationship.

The study of stepmothers is plagued by the changing social context in which these families are being formed. Historically, fathers have been far less likely than mothers to be awarded custody of their children (Glick, 1989b). In many stepmother families in which the father has custody, the custodial arrangement is the result of unusual circumstances in which the child's mother abandoned the family, became emotionally and/or physically dysfunctional, or abused (or threatened to abuse) the children. In these cases, the stepmother enters a context in which the prior mother-child relationship was disorganized and/or dysfunctional. Without casting the entire study of stepmother families into the perspective of the deficit model, we need to be mindful of the potential context of disruption that is likely to have preceded the formation of stepmother families. Thus, a common finding that stepmothers perceive as difficult the establishment of parent-child relationships is due to more than just the lack of clarity of roles and role boundaries and the strain associated with facing conflicting role demands.

KEY CHAPTER POINTS

1.   From the perspective of the adolescent stepchild, the family's ability to reframe and to acquire social support from relatives, friends, and neighbors may be important coping behaviors in predicting and explaining the quality of the stepmother-stepchild relationship (measure of adjustment).

2.   While quality of the marital relationship and self-esteem were related to a stepmother's adjustment, neither proved to be significant predictors of the stepmother-stepchild relationship. Instead stepmother-father agreement on how to raise the child was the only predictor of a stepmother's adjustment.

3.   Qualitative data also supported the quantitative finding that stepmothers believed that strong support from their spouse and lack of disagreement with him regarding child rearing were important to their adjustment.

4.   The qualitative findings also underscore the importance of current aspects of stepfamily functioning (e.g., having adequate time together) in our under-standing of the adjustment process.

5.   The findings suggest that stepfamily members (the stepmother and the adolescent stepchild) have different perspectives on what factors affect adjustment.

Chapter 8

FORMER-SPOUSE RELATIONS AND NONCUSTODIAL FATHER INVOLVEMENT DURING MARITAL AND FAMILY TRANSITIONS: A CLOSER LOOK AT REMARRIAGE FOLLOWING DIVORCE

Cheryl Buehler and Catherine Ryan

One does not need to be a family scholar to recognize the increasing, and sometimes overwhelming, complexity of today's marital and family life. This complexity arises from various family scenarios and circumstances. In particular, the relatively high divorce and subsequent remarriage rates have created a challenging, complex set of circumstances for families (Glick, 1989b). Scholars have begun to theorize about the family changes created by marriage, divorce, and remarriage by developing new descriptive concepts such as "remarriage chain" (Bohannon, 1970a), "linked household" (Jacobson, 1979), "binuclear family" (Ahrons, 1981), and "conjugal succession" (Furstenberg & Spanier, 1984/1987).

Changing demographic patterns, a recognition of the complexity involved in remarriage following divorce, and the development of new concepts to describe complex family systems have stimulated research on remarriage and stepfamilies. (See Coleman and Ganong, 1990, for review of remarriage and stepfamily research from the 1980s.) Some researchers have begun to describe the patterning of family relationships following divorce and remarriage, concluding that part of the complexity in stepfamily life stems from the need to redefine various existing family relationships (Ahrons & Wallisch, 1987). In families with children, one such relationship requiring redefinition following the remarriage of either or both parents is the relationship between former spouses (Guisinger, Cowan, & Schuldberg, 1989). This process of renegotiating parental expectations, responsibilities, and rights is important because the residential parent often serves as the "gatekeeper" between the nonresidential parent and his or her children (Ahrons, 1983). Because the gatekeeper role functions within the context of the coparental relationship, the nature and quality of former spouse relations is one of the major factors determining the degree to which the residential parent (usually the mother) facilitates or inhibits continued involvement by the nonresidential parent (usually the father) in child rearing and socialization.

Although existing research on the effects of father involvement on child well-being postdivorce is equivocal, most scholars agree that fathers' continued emotional, social, and economic committment to their children is important (e.g., Furstenberg et al., 1987; Seltzer & Bianchi, 1988; Visher & Visher, 1990). Thus, it is important to study how former-spouse relations influence the father's involvement postdivorce and how this connection is influenced by the remarriage of either parent. That is the purpose of this chapter.

Specifically, the interrelationships among former-spouse relations, father involvement, and remarriage status are examined through three sets of analyses. First, divorced, single, nonresidential fathers' reports of several aspects of former-spouse relations were compared to reports by remarried, nonresidential fathers. Second, divorced, nonresidential fathers' reports of their involvement with their biological children were compared to reports by remarried, nonresidential fathers. Third, the moderating effects of remarriage (of either former spouse) on the relationship between former-spouse relations and father involvement were examined.

The first two analyses address the *direct effect* of remarriage status on (a) former-spouse relations and (b) nonresidential father involvement, whereas the third analysis addresses *moderating effects* of remarriage status on the relationship between these two important components of the binuclear family system. (In this chapter, the binuclear family system is conceptualized as a family *structure* that consists of a biological mother and biological father living in separate households and at least one child who lives with one of the biological parents. *Binuclear* is a structural concept and does not imply a specific process, e.g., that parents share certain parenting responsibilities at any given level.) Moderating effects differ from direct effects. Variables exhibiting direct effects influence the level of a dependent variable, whereas a moderating variable changes either the *strength* or *direction* of a *relationship between variables* (James & Brett, 1984). For example, the question of whether remarriage effects the frequency of paternal visitation involves testing the direct effect of remarriage status on visitation frequency. The question of whether the relationship between coparental conflict and visitation frequency is stronger for nonremarrieds than remarrieds, however, involves testing the moderating effect of remarriage status on the *relationship between* conflict and visitation. Both direct and moderating effects are tested in this study with the purpose of increasing our understanding of how family members negotiate the remarriage transition.

LITERATURE REVIEW

Former-Spouse Relations

Social conflict theory suggests that there are important differences between the level of conflict (or disagreements) and the way in which people choose to address these disagreements (Deutsch, 1973; Horowitz, 1967; Sprey, 1979). Conflict theorists assume that disagreement between spouses/parents is inevitable and inherently neutral (Farrington & Foss, 1977; Sprey, 1979; Straus, 1979). However, the conflict behaviors used to manage or resolve disagreement are not inherently neutral. Cooperative conflict behaviors theoretically and functionally differ from competitive conflict behaviors (Sprey, 1979). Thus, for this study, coparental conflict, competition, and cooperation are defined as distinct components (although they are moderately correlated empirically; see Buehler & Trotter, 1990; Trotter, 1989). *Conflict* is defined as disagreements about goals, issues, resources, status, and privilege, whereas cooperation and competition are patterns of behaviors that people enact when faced with disagreements (Camara & Resnick, 1988; Deutsch, 1973; Sprey, 1979). *Cooperation* is defined as behaviors that allow for continued interaction in spite of differences and, even, fundamental disagreements (Horowitz, 1967). When parents cooperate, it implies that they are willing to place their children's needs above their own individual interests and emotions (e.g., revenge, dominance, or jealousy). According to conflict theory, without cooperation, the management of conflict remains primarily competitive. *Competition* is defined as a state of negative interdependence between family members such that gains for one member mean losses for others (Sprey, 1979). Research with divorcing parents suggests two major types of coparental competition: *direct* and *indirect* (Ryan, 1991). Direct competition is represented by overt behaviors that express the negative interdependence between former spouses, such as yelling, threatening, and attacking. Indirect competition is represented by passive-aggressive attempts to triangulate children in parental conflict, such as by using them as spies or allies or by denigrating the other parent in front of the children.

Given this conceptualization from Trotter's (1989) review, what is known about former-spouse relations postseparation? It seems that high levels of disagreement and conflict are normative during the first year of separation, with arguments occurring during the majority of contacts between parents (Bloom & Hodges, 1981; Hetherington et al., 1982; Isaacs, 1988; Kressel, Jaffe, Tuckman, Watson, & Deutsch, 1980; Wallerstein & Kelly, 1980). Typically, conflict escalates during initial discussions of the nature and future of the marriage, reaches a peak around the point of separation, and then gradually decreases (Hetherington et al., 1982; Ponzetti & Cate, 1986; Spanier & Thompson, 1984). However, fairly high levels of conflict typically occur well into the postdivorce period. Although normative, frequent conflict is not inevitable, even during early separation. What distinguishes couples who cooperate (called "perfect pals" by Ahrons and Rodgers, 1987), from other couples is not the absence of conflict but rather their ability to disagree in a civilized manner (Luepnitz, 1982).

However, relatively few couples achieve this civility during the first few months of separation. During this time, most spouses exhibit open hostility and indirect competitive behavior which includes character assassination and using the children as spies, allies, weapons, and hostages (Ahrons & Rodgers, 1987; Hetherington et al., 1982; Maccoby, Depner, & Mnookin, 1990; Oppawsky, 1988/1989; Sandler, Wolchik, & Braver, 1989). Although most coparenting relationships become less acrimonious over time (Ahrons & Rodgers, 1987; Hetherington et al., 1982;

Johnston, Gonzalez, & Campbell, 1987), somewhere between 20 and 35% continue to exhibit a style that has been labeled "bitter enemies" or "fiery foes" (Ahrons & Rodgers, 1987; Maccoby et al., 1990). The relationship between couples who relate as enemies appear to be strikingly impervious to the passage of time (Maccoby et al., 1990; Spanier & Thompson, 1984).

Although their coparental relationships typically are conflictual, about a third of divorced parents do cooperate and act as primary child care supports for one another (Clingempeel & Reppucci, 1982; Maccoby et al., 1990; Wallerstein & Kelly, 1980). The ability to cooperate seems to increase with time *and* also with determined effort (Ahrons & Rodgers, 1987; Kressel et al., 1980).

How are relations between former spouses affected by remarriage? Although little empirical study of this issue has been conducted, some scholars suggest that remarriage by either former spouse creates stress in the former-spouse relationship (Ahrons & Wallisch, 1987; Wallerstein & Blakeslee, 1989). It seems that remarried spouses hold more hostile feelings and negative opinions about their former spouses than nonremarried spouses (Masheter, 1991; Schuldberg & Guisinger, 1991). Whether or not these hostile feelings translate into competitive behaviors has not been examined empirically. Conflict theory would suggest that competitive behavior may predominate postdivorce and remarriage with potentially negative effects on the functioning of the binuclear family (Trotter, 1989). In addition, clinical and educational experience suggests that spouses who can negotiate a cooperative coparental relationship during the transition of remarriage construct more satisfying, functional stepfamilies than those coparents who remain primarily competitive (Visher & Visher, 1989, 1990). Thus, based on theory and clinical documentation, we hypothesize that remarried spouses will report more competition and less cooperation than nonremarried former spouses.

Father Involvement

Following marital separation, father involvement can be conceptualized as father-child contact, participation in child-rearing decisions, and the provision of financial support for the child's care. Seltzer (1991) has shown that these components are interrelated empirically and that together they comprise the fathering role post-separation.

Data from longitudinal and large-scale surveys indicate that although father-child contact may increase immediately following marital separation, such contact greatly decreases during the first year or two (Furstenberg et al., 1983). Using data from the National Survey of Families and Households (NSFH), Seltzer (1991) reported that 18% of the children surveyed had not seen their nonresidential father during the past year, 36% had seen their father several times that year, but not as often as monthly, and 46% had seen their father at least once a month during the past year. (In reporting these figures, we choose to aggregate the data using monthly contact rather than weekly contact as in the original study, because most divorcing couples and judges define every other weekend as a "reasonable" visitation schedule; see Buehler, Betz, Ryan, Legg, & Trotter, 1992. Thus, describing visitation frequency in terms of weekly contact counterindicates what most parents establish in their divorce settlements.)

Is father-child contact affected by the remarriage of either parent? Most existing data seem to indicate that it is and that contact decreases after either parent remarries, especially when it is the residential mother who does so (Furstenberg et al., 1983; Hetherington, Arnett, & Hollier, 1988; Seltzer, Schaeffer, & Charng, 1989; Tropf, 1984).

Fathers' participation in child-rearing decisions is an aspect of father involvement that has received much less attention than the frequency of father-child contact. However, recent research reported by Seltzer (1991) indicated that most fathers have little authority in child-rearing decisions. Of the 73% of formerly married parents who even discussed the children's welfare, 17% of the fathers had "a great deal" of authority, 31% had "some," and 52% had "none" (as reported by mothers). Fathers who visited *and* paid child support were reported by mothers to have more decision-making authority (Seltzer, 1991).

Although the relationship between remarriage status and nonresidential fathers' child-rearing authority has received little attention, there is some indication that remarriage decreases a father's authority (Hetherington et al., 1988). Although remarriage and authority were not examined specifically, Seltzer (1991) reported that remarriage by either parent decreases the frequency of child-related discussions between former spouses.

Fathers' economic involvement postseparation has received much attention because of the great number of children living in poverty postdivorce (U.S. Bureau of the Census, 1990). Recent census data indicate that only 74% of eligible divorced or separated mothers were awarded child support. Of those due support, 50% received the full amount, 25% received a partial payment, and 25% received no payment. Of those who received at least partial payments, the mean amount received annually was $3,073. Using NSFH data, Seltzer (1991) reported that 64% of mothers had received at least some child support in the past year; the annual mean amount received was $2,640. Although the data on economics postdivorce are relatively detailed and clear, the relationship between remarriage status and father's economic involvement is less so. Some researchers have found no relationship (Furstenberg & Nord, 1985; Peterson, 1987; Wallerstein & Huntington, 1983), whereas others have found that payments decline when one or both of the former spouses remarry (Buehler, Hogan, Robinson, & Levy, 1986; Cassetty, 1978; J. Dudley, personal communication, August 3, 1991; Seltzer, 1991; Seltzer et al., 1989). This pattern of findings is further complicated by the fact that the effect of remarriage on child support compliance seems to depend both on which parent remarries and on the length of time since the separation.

In sum, the literature suggests that remarriage by either parent creates a situation in which fathers' continued involvement with their children declines. We hypothesize that remarriage by either parent will be associated with lower levels of father involvement (i.e., less frequent visitation, shorter visits, and more infrequent payment of child support). This relationship between remarriage and father involvement postdivorce was tested in this study using a multidimensional conceptualization of father involvement, fathers' reports of involvement, and statistical controls for time since separation.

Former-Spouse Relations and Father Involvement

Conflicting evidence exists concerning the empirical relationship between former-spouse relations and child-rearing involvement by nonresidential fathers. Many researchers report *no relationships* between certain aspects of former-spouse relations and father involvement (Coysh, Johnston, Tschann, Wallerstein, & Kline, 1989; Kurdek, 1986; Kurdek & Blisk, 1983; Spanier & Thompson, 1984; Tschann, Johnston, Kline, & Wallerstein, 1989), some report *slight relationships* (Bowman & Ahrons, 1985; Kurdek, 1986; Peterson, 1987; Tschann et al., 1989), and others report *strong relationships* (Ahrons, 1983; Isaacs, 1988; Koch & Lowery, 1984; Pearson & Thoennes, 1988; Wright & Price, 1986). Without using systematic meta-analysis, it is difficult to identify patterns with any certainty; however, one pattern is fairly evident. The researchers finding slight and strong relationships measured specific conflict strategies (i.e., coparental competition and cooperation) rather than level of conflict. Researchers finding no relationship measured coparental conflict (i.e., level of disagreement). Thus, it seems reasonable to hypothesize that it is *how* former spouses manage their disagreements that influences father involvement rather than the actual level of disagreement in the relationship.

How does remarriage influence the relationship between former-spouse relations and father involvement? To our knowledge, this question has not been examined in previous research. We can speculate about the effect by comparing correlation coefficients (representing a former-spouse variable and a father involvement variable) between divorced samples and remarried samples, but we were unable to find data from remarried samples. Most of the remarriage literature that we examined focused on stepfamily relationships or descriptive aspects of former-spouse relations. Although we could speculate about possible relationship patterns, the effect of remarriage status on the relationship between former-spouse relations and father involvement is examined in this chapter from an exploratory rather than a hypothesis-generating stance.

To summarize, the focus of this chapter is on the influence of remarriage on several aspects of former-spouse relations and father involvement 3 to 4 years following marital separation. The existing literature suggested that remarriage may create problems and difficulties in former-spouse relations such that ex-partners may become more conflicted, more competitive, and less cooperative. The literature also has suggested that remarriage may make it more difficult for nonresidential fathers and their children to stay involved with one another. Finally, we did not find literature to suggest how remarriage may affect the empirical connections between former spouse relations and father involvement. Thus, potential moderating effects of remarriage following divorce are examined in this chapter with the goal of better understanding the interrelationships between the divorce and remarriage transitions.

METHODS

Data Collection and Sampling

Data for this study were collected using telephone interviews with 109 nonresidential fathers. The sample was drawn from 1986 court records, and fathers who met the following criteria were asked to participate: (a) the divorce was decreed rather than dismissed because of reconciliation, (b) the mother had physical custody of at least one of the children, and (c) the father was designated the payer of child support. Of the 264 eligible fathers, 65 were untraceable, 36 did not respond to letters or phone calls, 54 refused to be interviewed, and 109 were interviewed. Thus, the response rate was 41%. In addition to the data collected from interviews, court records of all fathers (respondents and nonrespondents) in the sampling frame were coded.

Sample characteristics. The sample consisted of 106 white and 3 black divorced fathers. Ages ranged from 24 to 54 years ($M = 36$, $SD = 5.81$). Educational level ranged from grade school (1%) to completion of a graduate degree (11%), with 29% having received a college degree. Modal occupational status was skilled laborer. Median 1990 net income was $21,010, ranging from $10,000 or less to $100,000 or more ($SD = $10,000-$20,000$).

Ninety-two percent of the fathers had one or two children, and 8% had three children. The duration of marriage ranged from 1 to 26 years ($M = 9$, $SD = 5.28$), and time since divorce ranged from 19 to 46 months ($M = 38.97$, $SD = 5.40$). Forty-four percent of the fathers had remarried, and the mean length of remarriage was 20 months ($SD = 11.39$). Of those who had remarried, 23% had mutual children from the remarriage.

Sample representativeness. Two different procedures were used to evaluate the representativeness of this sample. First, survey respondents and nonrespondents were compared using data from court records. There were no group differences on fathers' age, income, duration of marriage, number of children, or age of oldest child. Group differences existed for educational and occupational status. Respondents were better educated, $t(61) = 3.18, p = .002$, and held more prestigious occupations than did nonrespondents, $t(36) = 2.12, p = .04$.

Second, 10% ($n = 20$) of the former wives of respondents and nonrespondents were selected randomly and interviewed. Responses from these former wives were compared on measures of the quality of former-spouse relations and child support compliance. There were no group differences on coparental conflict, cooperation, and direct competition. Group differences existed for indirect competition and the number of full child support payments. The former wives of nonrespondents described their relationships with their former husbands as more covertly competitive than did former wives of respondents, $t(16) = 2.67, p = .02$. The former wives of nonrespondents also reported that their former husbands had made more complete child support payments in the preceding 12 months than did the former wives of respondents, $t(15) = 2.17, p = .05$.

Thus, respondents and nonrespondents were comparable on age, income, duration of marriage, number of children, and age of oldest child, despite a slight bias in education and occupational status. Respondents also seemed to have slightly higher rates of child support noncompliance than the nonrespondents.

Measurement

Father involvement. Three aspects of father involvement were measured: frequency of visits, duration of visits, and child support compliance. Frequency of visits was measured using a 7-point scale that ranged from *never* (1) to *daily* (7). Duration of visits was measured using a 7-point scale that ranged from *a few minutes* (1) to *a week or more* (7) (no visitation was coded 0).[1] Child support compliance was measured by combining data collected from fathers' self-reports and court records. Using a series of decision rules developed to handle discrepancies between fathers' reports and court records, 24 divorced fathers (22%) were coded as noncompliant and 8 (78%) as compliant (see Ryan, 1991, for decision rules). Braver, Fitzpatrick, and Bay (1991) have suggested that it is important to include father's reports of child support payment when measuring compliance. They argued that support data should be collected using mother report, father report, and court records. Although Braver and collegues found that fathers' reports of support compliance were higher than those of mothers, we did not find reporting differences in our validity checks.

Former-spouse relations. *Coparental conflict* was measured by averaging five items with scale responses ranging from *never* (1) to *always* (5). Divorced fathers assessed the frequency of disagreements regarding daily decisions, major decisions, planning events, children's school or medical problems, and children's personal problems. This measure was adapted from Ahrons (1981, 1983) and Berg and Kurdek (1983). Cronbach's alpha was .81. *Direct coparental competition* was measured using five items adapted from Jacobson (1978) and Ahrons (1981): the frequency of stressful, tense conversations, a hostile atmosphere, verbal attacks, yelling and screaming, and name-calling. Responses were scaled from *never* (1) to *always* (5) and were averaged. Cronbach's alpha was .86. *Indirect coparental competition* was measured by a scale developed by Kurdek (1987) and used by Buehler and Trotter (1990). It includes six items that ask the frequency of using the children to get personal information about the other parent, trying to get the children to side with one parent, and denigrating the other parent in front of the children. Responses were scaled from *never* (1) to *always* (5) and were summed. The internal consistency of the index was determined by correlating the individual items with the total score (Babbie, 1986). Zero-order correlation coefficients among items ranged from .36 to .77 ($p < .001$). *Coparental cooperation* was measured using five items adapted from the coparental support subscale of Ahrons' (1983) Quality of Coparental Communication Scale. The items assess the frequency with which each former spouse provides emotional support and acts as a resource for the other, accommodates the other's needs for changed plans, and encourages the children to maintain active involvement with the other parent. Cronbach's alpha was .82.

Remarriage. Two operational definitions of remarriage status were used. The first included two dummy variables: (1) former husband remarried ($n = 48$), former husband not remarried ($n = 61$), and (2) former wife remarried ($n = 42$), former wife not remarried ($n = 63$). This was labeled a *simple remarriage structure.* The second was a categorical variable with four categories: both remarried ($n = 22$), former husband remarried/former wife not remarried ($n = 23$), former wife remarried/former husband not remarried ($n = 20$), and neither remarried ($n = 40$). This was labeled a *complex remarriage structure.* These different operational definitions were used because it is important to distinguish between two possible patterns associated with remarriage postdivorce. The first definition facilitates the examination of the role of remarriage by either spouse, *regardless* of the other spouse's marital status. The second definition allows for the examination of the role of remarriage, given a specific marital status of the former spouse. The implication of this distinction can be illustrated by an example. It may be that remarriage, in and of itself, does not moderate the relationship between former spouse relations and father involvement. Rather, remarriage by one former-spouse when the other has not remarried may be an important moderator variables. Thus, the two operational definitions are needed to examine thoroughly the effects of remarriage as a moderating variable between the former-spouse relationship and father involvement postdivorce.

Control Variables

Based on suggestions in the literature, the following variables were included in preliminary analyses as potential control variables: father's educational level, geographical distance between mother and father households, number of months since divorce, and father's level of psychological attachment toward his former wife (measured using Boss's scale of psychological presence; see Boss, Greenberg, & Pearce-McCall, 1986). Cronbach's alpha was .85.

Analytic Strategy

After determining the adequacy of psychometric properties for each measure, zero-order correlations among variables were examined for the entire sample. Next, the direct effects of remarriage status on former-spouse relations and father involvement were estimated. *T* tests for independent samples were calculated using the simple structure measures of remarriage status. One-way ANOVAS with follow-up *t* tests (Fisher's LSD) were calculated using the complex structure measure of remarriage. Then, as a preliminary examination, the zero-order correlations among the former spouse and father involvement variables were examined for subsamples identified by individual remarriage structure. Finally, the moderating effects of remarriage on the relationship between former-spouse variables and father involvement were tested using hierarchial regression with interaction terms when visitation frequency and duration were the dependent variables, and logistic regression with interaction terms when child support compliance was the dependent variable. To prevent multicollinearity problems associated with the use of interaction terms in regression, each variable was centered using the mean before calculating interaction terms (Jaccard, Turrisi, & Wan, 1990; Smith & Sasaki, 1979).

RESULTS

Correlations among Variables

Correlations among variables based on the entire sample of fathers were examined with two purposes in mind. First, correlations among the four indicators of former-spouse relations were studied to assess the validity of the conceptualization of former-spouse relations. As expected, the different dimensions were only moderately correlated, providing some evidence that these measures represent different, but related, aspects of the former-spouse relationship (see Table 8.1). Second, correlations among the three dependent variables were examined for redundancy. This examination revealed only a modest correlation between visitation frequency and duration; and therefore, both indicators were included as dependent variables in subsequent analyses.

Former-Spouse Relations and Remarriage

The first hypothesis was that remarried former spouses are more conflicted, more competitive, and less cooperative with one another than nonremarried former spouses. This hypothesis was supported, for the most part, when using the individual definition of remarriage (see the former-spouse variables in the top panel of Table 8.2). Compared to nonremarried former husbands, remarried husbands reported more conflicted, more indirectly competitive, and less cooperative relationships with their former spouses. Compared to nonremarried former wives, remarried wives had less cooperative relationships with their former husbands (based on men's reports). Thus, the hypothesis was supported more strongly for former husband's remarriage than for former wife's remarriage.

Using the former-spouse couple definition of remarriage status, group differences were evident only for former-spouse cooperation. The group in which both parents had remarried was less cooperative than the group in which neither had remarried. (See the former-spouse variables in the bottom panel of Table 2.) There was a trend for former-spouse conflict ($p = .07$) such that the *former husband remarried/former wife not remarried* group was more conflicted than the *former wife remarried/former husband not remarried* group.

Noncustodial Father Involvement and Remarriage

The second hypothesis was that remarriage is associated with lower levels of father involvement. Using the individual definition of remarriage, paternal visits were less frequent when the former wife had remarried than when she had not (see visitation variables in the top panel of Table 8.2). The duration of paternal visits was not related to the former wife's remarriage status. The former husband's remarriage was unrelated to either frequency or duration of visitation, although the means for remarried fathers were lower than those for nonremarried fathers. Using the former spouses couple definition of remarriage status, frequency of father visits was related to remarriage status, whereas duration was not (see visitation variables in the bottom panel of Table 8.2). Visitation was most frequent when neither former spouse had remarried and when the father had remarried but his former wife had not. Visitation was least frequent when the former wife had remarried and the father had not.

Shifting from visitation to child support compliance, former wife's remarriage status was related to compliance such that a greater proportion of noncompliance existed when mothers had remarried than when they had not re-married, $\chi^2(1, N = 109) = 3.62, p = .06$; Phi $= .19$. As with visitation, former husband's remarriage status was unrelated to child support compliance. Using the former couple structure definition of remarriage status, compliance and remarriage were unrelated, $\chi^2(3, N = 109) = 4.31, p = .23$.

Former-Spouse Relations and Father Involvement Moderated by Remarriage

Correlations disaggregated by simple remarriage structure. The third objective of this study was to examine the moderating effects of remarriage on the relationship between former-spouse relations and father involvement. As a preliminary step,

Table 8.1

Means, Standard Deviations, and Zero-Order Correlations Among Independent and Dependent Variables

Variables	1	2	3	4	5	6	7	8	9
1. F.h. remarried[a]		.16	.23	-.22	-.08	.20	-.08	-.04	-.06
2. F.w. remarried[a]			-.11	-.23	-.03	-.02	-.37	-.07	-.18
3. F.s. conflict				.07	.39	.42	.14	.01	.02
4. F.s. cooperation					-.05	-.18	.37	.19	.32
5. F.s. direct competition						.45	.07	.05	-.07
6. F.s. indirect competition							.06	-.06	-.11
7. Visitation frequency								.24	.23
8. Visitation duration									.28
9. Child support compliance[a]									
Mean	48[b]	42[b]	2.11	3.17	1.83	12.01	4.25	4.08	85[b]
Standard deviation	---	---	0.75	0.99	0.77	3.37	1.86	1.70	---
Alpha	---	---	.81	.82	.86	---	---	---	---

Note: $N = 109$. F.h. indicates former husband; F.w. indicates former wife; F.s. indicates former spouse. Variables were measured on a 1-5 point scale, except visitation frequency and duration, which used an 8-point scale, and indirect competition, which ranged from 6 to 30. Any coefficient greater than .19 was significant at .05 p value.

[a] Biserial correlations were calculated.

[b] Represents frequency rather than mean.

Table 8.2

Former Spouse Relations and Father Involvement by Remarriage Status

	Simple Structure					
	Former Husbands			Former Wives		
	Remarried	Not Remarried		Remarried	Not Remarried	
Variables	M (SD)	M (SD)	t	M (SD)	M (SD)	t
F.s. conflict	2.30 (0.83)	1.96 (0.64)	2.42*	2.02 (0.84)	2.18 (0.65)	1.08
F.s. cooperation	2.93 (0.97)	3.36 (0.97)	2.31*	2.91 (1.03)	3.37 (0.87)	2.43*
F.s. direct competition	1.76 (0.77)	1.88 (0.77)	0.78	1.81 (0.95)	1.86 (0.64)	0.31
F.s. indirect competition	12.77 (3.42)	11.40 (3.24)	-2.13*	11.93 (3.58)	12.07 (3.30)	0.21
Visitation frequency	4.08 (1.83)	4.38 (1.88)	0.82	3.45 (1.80)	4.81 (1.65)	3.99*
Visitation duration	4.00 (1.87)	4.15 (1.56)	0.45	4.00 (1.93)	4.11 (1.49)	0.67
n	48	61		42	63	

Table 8.2 (continued)

	Complex Structure								
	Both Rem		F.H. Rem/ F.W. Not		F.W. Rem/ F.H Not		Neither Rem		
Variables	M	(SD)	M	(SD)	M	(SD)	M	(SD)	F
F.s. conflict	2.21	(0.91)	2.39	(0.72)	1.82	(0.73)	2.06	(0.57)	2.48
F.s. cooperation	2.88	(1.07)	3.07	(0.82)	2.94	(1.02)	3.54	(0.86)	3.24*
F.s. direct competition	1.75	(0.98)	1.79	(0.54)	1.87	(0.93)	1.91	(0.69)	.22
F.s. indirect competition	12.41	(3.55)	13.09	(3.52)	11.40	(3.62)	11.49	(3.07)	1.41
Visitation frequency	3.81	(1.82)	4.48	(1.68)	3.05	(1.73)	5.00	(1.62)	6.57**
Visitation duration	3.86	(1.93)	4.30	(1.72)	4.15	(1.95)	4.18	(1.36)	.27
n	22		23		20		40		

Note: Rem indicates remarried; F.s. indicates former spouse; F.w. indicates former wife; F.h. indicates former husband.

$*p < .05$, $**p < .01$.

the correlations between former-spouse relations and father involvement were calculated separately for the simple remarriage groups. The correlations, disaggregated by former husbands' remarriage status, are shown in the top panel of Table 8.3 and indicate that some of the correlations for the remarried fathers compared to nonremarried fathers may be significantly different in magnitude. Most dramatically, the biserial correlation between former-spouse cooperation and child support compliance was .51 for remarried fathers but only .15 for nonremarried ones. Correlations for remarried and nonremarried mothers are shown in the lower panel of Table 8.3. The differences among correlations seem to be even stronger when former wife's remarriage status is considered. Also, some of the correlations produce a disordinal pattern (opposite-direction correlations). Specifically, the correlation between former-spouse conflict and frequency of visitation was .38 for remarried mothers and -.19 for nonremarried ones. The biserial correlation between former-spouse cooperation and child support compliance was .57 for remarried mothers and -.03 for those who had not remarried. Other differences are identified below in a subsequent result section based on the statistical tests of the remarriage interaction effects (moderator analyses).

Moderating effects. The statistical examination of moderating effects involved several sets of analyses. The first analysis for each dependent variable used the individual definition of remarriage and focused on the remarriage status of former husbands. In the analysis of *frequency of visitation*, none of the *former-spouse relationship* by *former husband's remarriage* interaction terms were significant, block $F(13, 91) = .68, p = .61$.[2] (The significant direct effects of former-spouse and control variables are in notes 2 and 3. By design, these variables were significant in each regression equation using visitation frequency as a dependent variable, regardless of the specific interaction terms entered into the equation.)

The second analysis again used the individual definition of remarriage and focused on the remarriage status of the former wife. Two (out of four) of the *former spouse* by *wife's remarriage* interaction terms were significant, block $F(13, 91) = 4.15$, $p = .004$, total $R^2 = .48$: conflict over parenting and direct competition.[3] The correlation between former-spouse conflict and paternal visitation frequency was -.19 for nonremarried wives and .38 for those who had remarried. This disordinal interaction suggests that remarriage changes the *pattern* of relationships, and not just the strength. Similarly, the correlation between direct competition and visitation frequency was -.26 for nonremarried wives and .32 for those who had remarried.

Using the former-spouse couple definition of remarriage status, the analysis of remarriage effects involved calculating three equations: the *neither remarried* group compared to (a) the *former husband remarried/former wife not remarried* group, (b) the *former wife remarried/former husband not remarried* group, and (c) the *both remarried* group. The interaction terms for the comparisons between the *former husband remarried/former wife not remarried* group and the *neither remarried* group were not significant, block $F(13, 49) = 0.60, p = .66$.[4] In contrast, the relationship between direct competition and visitation frequency differed for the *neither remarried* group and the group in which the former wife had re-

Table 8.3

Zero-Order Correlations Among Independent and Dependent Variables by Marital Status of Former Husband and Former Wife

Variables	Former Husbands						
	1	2	3	4	5	6	7
1. F.s. conflict		.16	.37**	.41**	.23	-.08	-.08
2. F.s. cooperation	.06		.01	.01	.38**	-.01	.15
3. F.s. direct competition	.48**	-.14		.46**	-.01	.08-	.06
4. F.s. indirect competition	.37**	-.33*	.50**		.19	.14	-.21
5. Visitation frequency	.09	.33*	.14	-.06		.17	.28*
6. Visitation duration	.11	.40**	.01	-.25	.32*		.29
7. Child support compliance[a]	.13	.51**	-.10	.02	.16	.26	

Table 8.3 (continued)

Former Wives

Variables	1	2	3	4	5	6	7
1. F.s. conflict		-.10	.25*	.46**	-.19	-.18	-.09
2. F.s. cooperation	.16		-.08	-.11	.24	-.02	-.03
3. F.s. direct competition	.47**	-.06		.40**	-.26*	-.23	-.16
4. F.s. indirect competition	.40**	-.23	.52**		-.01	-.04	-.11
5. Visitation frequency	.38*	.29	.32*	.22		-.11**	-.05
6. Visitation duration	.10	.35*	.22	.15	.56**		.30
7. Child support compliance[a]	-.03	.57**	-.05	-.09	.34*	.19	

Note: Correlations for nonremarried former spouses are in the upper triangle and for remarried former spouses in the lower triangle; F.s. indicates former spouse.

$p \leq .05$, ** $p \leq .01$.

[a] Biserial correlations were calculated.

remarried but the former husband had not, block $F(13, 46) = 3.31, p = .02$. For the *neither remarried* group, the correlation between direct competition and visitation frequency was -.34, whereas it was .49 for the *former wife remarried/former husband not remarried* group. Finally, the interaction terms for the comparisons between the *both remarried* and *neither remarried* groups were nonsignificant, block $F(13, 48) = 2.02, p = .11$.

The analyses of *duration of visitation* followed the same strategy as that used for frequency. In the first analysis, none of the interaction terms using husband's remarriage status were significant, block $F(13, 91) = 1.40, p = .24$. On the contrary, however, some of the interaction terms were significant when former wife's remarriage status was analyzed, block $F(13, 91) = 4.16, p = 004$. Specifically, the correlation between direct competition and visitation duration was -.23 for the *nonremarried former wife* group and .22 for the *remarried former wife* group. Again, this disordinal interaction indicated that the pattern of relationship was influenced by the former wife's remarriage. The correlation between indirect competition and visitation duration was -.04 for the *former wife nonremarried* group and .15 for the *former wife remarried* group.

Using the former-spouse couple definition of remarriage status, the comparisons between the *neither remarried* group and the *former husband remarried/former wife not remarried* group indicated no differences in the pattern of relationships between former-spouse variables and visitation duration, block $F(13, 49) = .66$, $p = .62$. Differences did exist for the other two comparisons. The comparisons between the *neither remarried* group and the *former wife remarried/former husband not remarried* group indicated differences for cooperation and direct competition, block $F(13, 46) = 2.96, p = .03$. The correlation between cooperation and visitation duration was -.21 for the *neither remarried* group and .28 for the *former wife remarried/former husband not remarried* group. The correlation between direct competition and visitation duration was -.22 for the *neither remarried* group and .37 for the other group. The third comparison using the former-spouse couple definition of remarriage indicated that the *neither remarried* and *both remarried* groups differed on the relationships examining former-spouse conflict, direct competition, and indirect competition, block $F(13, 48) = 5.26, p = .001$. The correlation between conflict and visitation duration was -.28 for the *neither remarried* group and .15 for the *both remarried* group. The correlation between direct competition and duration was -.22 for the *neither remarried* group and .07 for the *both remarried* group. The correlation between indirect competition and duration was -.04 for the neither remarried group and -.58 for the both remarried group.

The analyses of child support compliance followed the same analytic strategy as that used for paternal visitation except that logistic regression was used rather than ordinary least-squares regression. The first analysis examined former husband's remarriage status using the individual definition of remarriage. There were two significant interaction terms: former-spouse cooperation and indirect competition. The correlation between cooperation and child support compliance was .15 for nonremarried husbands and .51 for remarrieds. The correlation between indirect competition and compliance was -.21 for nonremarried husbands and .02 for remar-rieds.[5]

The second analysis of child support compliance examined associations with former wife's remarriage status. The only significant interaction term was for cooperation. The correlation between cooperation and child support compliance was -.03 for nonremarried former wives and .57 for remarried former wives.

Using the former-spouse couple definition of remarriage, the first comparison was made between the *neither remarried* group and the group in which the former husband had remarried but the former wife had not. None of the interaction terms were significant. The second comparison was between the *neither remarried* group and the group in which the former wife had remarried but the former husband had not. None of the interaction terms were significant at the level of $p < .05$, but there was a trend for cooperation ($p < .10$). Follow-up analyses indicated that the correlation between former-spouse cooperation and child support compliance was -.16 for the *neither remarried* group and .55 for the *former wife remarried/former husband not remarried* group. The last comparison was between the *neither remarried* group and the *both remarried* group. There was one significant interaction term (cooperation) and one trend (indirect competition, $p = .063$). The correlation between cooperation and compliance was -.16 for the *neither remarried* group and .58 for the *both remarried* group. The correlation between indirect competition and compliance was -.25 for the *neither remarried* group and -.02 (nonsignificant) for the *both remarried* group.

DISCUSSION AND CONCLUSIONS

This chapter commenced by acknowledging the complexity of life in stepfamilies. In this discussion, we build on this idea by delineating some of the elements of complexity. Systems theory suggests that complexity consists of at least two major components: structural and interactional. Structural complexity was analyzed in this study by examining different configurations of former spouses' current remarriage status. Interactional complexity was examined by correlating measures of former-spouse relations and nonresidential father involvement. The result of these examinations indicated that interactional complexity is associated with structural complexity. However, the association does not suggest a linear relationship such that interactional complexity increases as structural complexity increases. Rather, the findings indicated that the *pattern* of relationships between former-spouse relations and father involvement differ among various remarriage configurations.

The results of this study support the proposition that some of the complexity of the remarriage family system results from the need to integrate children from a previous marriage and the redefined relationship between former spouses into a new marital and family structure. However, the nature of complexity that arises is somewhat dependent on which former spouse has remarried and which relationship is being considered. Binuclear family systems in which the former husband has remarried seem to have more difficulty with former-spouse conflict, competition, and cooperation than those systems in which this spouse has not remarried. The reasons for relationship problems were not measured in this study, so it is difficult to explain with certainty why former-spouse interaction is threatened more by the husband's remarriage than by the wife's. However, theory can be used to offer some plausible explanations. Social conflict theory suggests that conflicted relationships will remain primarily competitive in nature unless the interested parties are motivated and able to negotiate cooperative patterns of conflict management. What is it about family systems in which former husbands have remarried that is different from systems in which they have not, and how might these differences influence patterns of conflict management? The major difference is the addition of a new wife. Does this addition change the motivation of the former spouses or their investment in previous relationships? Perhaps the men have begun to invest their time and psychosocial energy in the new marital relationship. This may be particularly true if the men become residential stepfathers to their wives' children and interact with them daily. As a result, they may become less invested or motivated to "work things out" with their former wives. Former wives also may be less willing to negotiate for several reasons, including fear of interference, hostility from a new wife, or jealousy and envy. A third explanatory factor may be that new wives encourage more involvement with the husband's children, thus potentially creating more conflict and competition.

Conflict theory suggests that cooperation in the context of divorce requires attention, motivation, and investment. Neither of the former spouses may maintain this level of motivation when the former husband remarries. This may be especially true in the situations in which neither former spouse fears losing something if the relationship becomes less cooperative (e.g., financial support or access to children).

Although former-spouse relations were more vulnerable to deterioration when former husbands remarried, the findings from this study indicate that nonresidential father involvement (i.e., visitation frequency and child support compliance) was more vulnerable to discontinuation when former wives remarried. The wife's remarriage, rather than that of the husband, served as a barrier or disincentive to continued involvement. The addition of a new husband (and, possibly, a new father figure) increased the complexity of the binuclear family system in such a way that former husbands found it either unnecessary or too difficult to maintain premarriage levels of involvement with their children. The former wife may attempt to "close ranks" around the new family and may advertently or inadvertently block the nonresidential father's attempts to participate in child rearing. In addition, biological fathers may begin to believe that stepfathers should share child-rearing responsibilities (Tropf, 1984). These interpretations are offered to facilitate the additional research that is needed to identify underlying causes and explanations for reduced involvement by the father when their former wives remarry.

Before discussing the results of the moderating effects of remarriage, it is important to recognize that many statistical tests were calculated in this part of the analysis, increasing the chances of committing a Type I error (i.e., accepting statistical significance as representing a true difference in the population when the findings actually occurred by chance). Although more interaction terms were significant than would be expected to occur by chance, given the small group sample sizes and general concerns related to Type I error, it is important to interpret these findings cautiously. We do this by suggesting and discussing patterns of findings rather than examining isolated significance.

One of the most important findings from the tests of moderating effects of re-marriage was that the significant differences reflected disordinal rather than ordinal interaction effects. This means that remarriage by one of the former spouses changed the *direction* of the relationship between a former spouse variable and a father involvement variable. (An ordinal interaction effect would change the strength of the relationship, but not the direction.) Specifically, former-spouse relations and nonresidential father involvement are related differently when one of the former spouses remarries compared to families in which remarriage has not occurred. One interpretation of this pattern of findings is that remarriage dramatically changes the structure of the binuclear family system such that interactional changes occur in some of the preexisting patterns of postdivorce relations. Boundaries, rules, and roles must consequently be redefined.

What is the nature of these differences? Does any one pattern of remarriage create more difficulties than another? In general, the findings suggest that when no remarriage has occurred, the negative aspects of former-spouse relations and father involvement are inversely related (e.g., direct competition as through hostile yelling and arguing leads to less frequent visitation). Although the causal direction is not clear, one interpretation of this pattern is that one of the consequences of former-spouse conflict and hostility will be reduced visitation. This avoidance or resigned behavior by fathers reduces the chance of confrontation with their former wives. On the contrary, when the former wife has remarried, the empirical relationship between former-spouse relations and father involvement is different such that the two covary positively. Higher levels of former-spouse conflict and competition are related to more frequent and longer paternal visits, and vice versa. One explanation for this pattern is that a nonresidential father may react to his former wife's remarriage by firmly enacting his commitment to his children. One of the concomitant realities to nonresidential father visitation is the increased opportunity for former-spouse conflict and competition (Seltzer, 1991). Herein lies one of the complexities of remarriage in binuclear family systems. The data from this study indicate that former-spouse competition and visitation frequency are related negatively and that remarriage by the former wife tends to reduce father involvement. However, when remarried and nonremarried samples are analyzed separately, the relationship between competition and visitation differs such that more competitive behavior accompanies more frequent visitation. The causal direction of the association needs to be examined longitudinally in future research.

The second striking pattern of results from the interactional analysis centers around former-spouse cooperation. Cooperation and child support compliance are related positively and strongly in the remarried sample but are unrelated in the nonremarried group. This provides some support for the conclusion that cooperation may help address the complexity that is inherent in remarried binuclear family systems. Although the exact role of cooperation needs further study, possible explanations for the findings may be that cooperation eases the ambiguity of the system by reducing uncertainty and increasing predictability. Over time, it also may facilitate better communication and reduce the occurrence of power struggles.

The findings from this study support the conclusion that the transitions of divorce and remarriage are inextricably linked. Movement through these marital and resultant family transitions involves an interplay between structural and interactional complexity. We believe that the specific implications for practice and further research of this interplay center around the concepts of individual and family beliefs and goals. This complexity of beliefs and goals is a fundamental motivator of behavior postdivorce and in remarriage. Choices of specific former-spouse-related conflict behaviors and father involvement behaviors are based, to a great extent, on beliefs and goals.

In terms of practice, we suggest that clinicians work with their divorced and remarried clients by trying to identify beliefs and parenting goals that are shared between former spouses (e.g., children have a right to be loved by both biological parents). Identification and commitment to shared beliefs and goals postdivorce may help encourage coparental cooperation rather than competition. Coser (1964) has suggested that if a group (i.e., a family) can try to resolve a conflict by referring to basic shared beliefs, the results of the conflict will be increased cohesion. Ideally, this process also would include the stepparent, when applicable. A commitment to a few shared beliefs and goals regarding the children may induce parents to make behavioral choices that over time will check coparental hostility and antagonism and help to keep children out of the middle of parental (whether coparental or stepparent) conflict.

In terms of research, we have two suggestions for further study based on the findings from this project. The first is for a qualitative study that examines why former spouse relationships are more vulnerable to deterioration when former husbands remarry than when former wives remarry, and why nonresidential father involvement is more vulnerable to deterioration when former wives remarry. The second is for a longitudinal study that examines the causal ordering between coparental competition/cooperation and aspects of father involvement. Generally, does former-spouse competition reduce father involvement over time, or does continued father involvement increase former-spouse competition over time? How are these patterns influenced by remarriage by either or both former spouse? These questions will need to be addressed using a longitudinal research design with data collected from time of separation to approximately 3 years following remarriage, employing multiple family informants, and using measures that acknowledge the distinction between conflict and conflict behavior.

KEY CHAPTER POINTS

1. When both former spouses had remarried, there was less cooperation than when neither had remarried. There was more difficulty regarding former-spouse conflict, competition, and cooperation when the former husband had remarried than when he had not.

2. Nonresidential father involvement (i.e., visitation frequency and payment of child support) was more vulnerable to discontinuation when former wives remarried.

3. When no remarriage occurred, conflict and direct competition in the form er-spouse relationship was inversely related to father involvement. For example, as hostile yelling and arguing increased, less frequent visitation occurred.

4. When the former wife had remarried, the relationship between former-spouse relations and father involvement was different than noted in (3). That is, higher levels of former-spouse conflict and cooperation were associated with more frequent and longer paternal visits.

5. When remarriage occurred, cooperation and child support compliance were related positively and strongly; however, they were unrelated in the nonremarried group.

ACKNOWLEDGMENT

Support for data collection was provided by a grant to the first author from the University of Tennessee Faculty Research Program. We appreciate this support.

NOTES

1. A preliminary study of approximately 60 formerly married couples indicated no differences in mothers' and fathers' reports of either frequency or duration of visits (using the items reported in this study).

2. Predictors of visitation frequency in this analysis were geographic distance (beta = -.43) and former spouse cooperation (beta = .26); R^2 = .33.

3. In addition to distance and former-spouse cooperation, former wife's re-marriage status also predicted visitation frequency (beta = -.30); R^2 = .48.

4. The introduction of the set of interaction terms created multicollinearity, despite efforts to prevent the problem. Multicollinearity does not affect estimates of F and R^2, but it does bias individual parameter estimates for the independent

variables (Smith & Saski, 1979).

5. Child support was related directly and negatively to indirect competition between former spouses. In other words, high competition was associated with lower compliance, and vice versa.

Chapter 9

TOWARD A COGNITIVE DISSONANCE CONCEPTUALIZATION OF STEPCHILDREN AND BIOLOGICAL CHILDREN LOYALTY CONFLICTS: A CONSTRUCT VALIDITY STUDY

W. Glenn Clingempeel, John J. Colyar, and E. Mavis Hetherington

Family therapists and clinicians who work with stepfamilies have often described the "loyalty conflicts" of stepfamily members (Sager et al., 1983; Visher & Visher, 1988a). Custodial biological parents are reported to be torn between loyalty to biological children and to new spouses. Children are described as having difficulty relating positively to a new stepparent because they view it as disloyal to the nonresident biological parent.

During the early years of stepfamily formation, a particularly enigmatic type of loyalty conflict for adults involves decisions about the proportion of personal resources including time, money, gifts, and affection to be allocated to stepchildren from current marriages and biological children from prior marriages. Residential stepparents attempting to develop positive marital relationships usually want to commit personal resources to their stepchild and, by doing so, to please the current spouse. They also have a history of emotional ties to their biological children and usually want to commit personal resources to them as well. However, personal resources (e.g., time and money) are finite. As such, stepparents may perceive that giving resources to one set of children (thus demonstrating loyalty) is taking away resources from the other set (and hence showing disloyalty). Moreover, this perception may be reinforced by competition between stepchildren and biological children for the stepparents' limited personal resources. Stepparents who spend too much time with biological children may become the subject of accusations of favoritism from stepchildren and current spouses. On the other hand, stepparents who spend too much time with stepchildren may engender complaints of disloyalty from their biological children as well.

Stepchildren-biological children loyalty conflicts may be especially problematic for stepparents who live with stepchildren and have biological children living with former spouses. In these *complex stepfamilies*, stepparents may encounter barriers to across-household distributions of personal resources, including: (a) pressure from the current spouse to "close ranks" and make a primary commitment to the stepfamily household; (b) anticipated conflicts with current and former spouses associated with contacts with biological children, and (c) jealousy of the new spouse regarding contacts with ex-spouse. Visher and Visher (1988a) reported that stepparents in complex stepfamilies frequently "feel guilty and resentful about giving of themselves to stepchildren when they feel deprived of the same opportunity to give to their own children" (p. 167). Thus, these stepparents may be caught in the middle of intra- and interpersonal cross fire in which giving resources to one household is viewed as being disloyal and unsupportive toward the other.

Stepfamily clinicians have reported that stepchildren-biological children loyalty conflicts are a significant obstacle to developing a cohesive stepfamily. However, stepfamily researchers have not generated a clear theoretical definition of this construct, and psychometrically sound measures are nonexistent. The extant stepfamily literature also lacks theory-driven, testable hypotheses that link loyalty conflicts to other constructs (e.g., marital quality) within a theoretical system.

Given these deficiencies in the stepfamily literature, the overarching goal of this chapter is to describe a process of construct validation of a measure of stepparents' stepchildren-biological children loyalty conflicts. Consistent with extensive discussions of construct validity (e.g., Campbell & Fiske, 1959; Cronbach & Meehl, 1955; Nunnally, 1978), this chapter has four interrelated goals:

1. To propose a theoretical definition of stepparents' loyalty conflicts;

2. To develop an operational definition of this construct derived from the theoretical definition;

3. To provide evidence of convergent validity of the loyalty conflicts measure; and

4. To assess the measure's nomological validity, or the extent to which it correlates in expected ways with measures of another construct, the marital quality of remarried couples.

COGNITIVE DISSONANCE THEORY AND LOYALTY CONFLICTS

Cognitive dissonance theory (Festinger, 1957) and its revisions (Cooper & Fazio, 1984) may provide a theoretical definition of stepchildren-biological children loyalty conflicts. In the original theory, Festinger (1957) proposed that persons who behave in ways that are inconsistent with their beliefs will experience uncomfortable physiological arousal (cognitive dissonance) which motivates them to change either their beliefs or their behavior so as to render the two synchronous with each other. In summarizing recent revisions of the theory, Cooper and Fazio (1984) proposed that cognitive inconsistency is especially likely to lead to *dissonance arousal* and *dissonance motivation* when people perceive the inconsistent behavior as having produced an aversive event for which they accept personal responsibility.

Loyalty conflicts for residential stepparents who also are parents to biological children living with former spouses may be conceptualized as perceived inconsistency between the proportion of four personal resources (time, money, gifts, and affection) that they *actually give* to biological children and stepchildren (resource allocation behavior) and the proportion of these resources that they believe they *ideally should give* (resource allocation beliefs). Extrapolating from the revised cognitive dissonance theory, actual-ideal disparities may cause the individual to experience an uncomfortable intrapersonal state because stepparents may view their behavior (failing to give enough resources to either stepchildren or biological children) as being under their control and as potentially having adverse consequences. Thus, according to this theoretical orientation, stepparents will be motivated to reduce the perceived disparity between resource allocation beliefs and behavior. Furthermore, the greater the disparity, the greater the intensity of the loyalty conflict, and the more motivated stepparents will be to resolve it.

The development of an operational definition of stepchildren-biological children loyalty conflicts should derive from the theoretical definition of the construct. Consequently, the construction of the Loyalty Conflicts Assessment Questionnaire (LCAQ; Clingempeel, Segal, & Hetherington, 1981) was based on two interrelated assumptions. First, the intensity of stepparents' loyalty conflicts may be measured by assessing perceived discrepancies between the actual and ideal proportions of time, money, gifts, and affection given to stepchildren and biological children. The LCAQ includes a total discrepancy score which was computed by summing the absolute value of actual-ideal discrepancies across the four personal resources. Second, the intensity of loyalty conflicts may be measured by assessing the degree to which stepparents are dissatisfied with the proportions of personal resources given to stepchildren and biological children. The LCAQ includes a total dissatisfaction score which was computed by summing dissatisfaction ratings across the four personal resources. The score for the total intensity of loyalty conflicts was obtained by summing the total discrepancy and total dissatisfaction scores. The LCAQ is described in detail in the Methods section of this chapter.

The process of convergent validation involves assessing the extent to which multiple indicators of a construct correlate with each other as expected. Since no alternative measure of stepchildren-biological children loyalty conflicts was available, the strategy for establishing convergent validity of the LCAQ focused on assessing the relations between the LCAQ and measures of peripheral components of the same construct, and also between the LCAQ and measures of closely related constructs. Although our theoretical definition delineates intrapersonal cognitive conflict as the *core* component of loyalty conflicts, both cognitive dissonance theory and the clinical literature on stepfamilies suggests that loyalty conflicts have emotional concomitants (such as guilt and sadness). In addition, loyalty conflicts may be affected by interpersonal processes, including the quality of relationships with biological children and the frequency of accusations of favoritism from stepchildren and current spouses. Consequently, we assessed the relationships between the LCAQ and measures of both emotional and interpersonal processes. (A detailed description of convergent validation procedures and results of analyses are provided in the Results sections of this chapter.)

Nomological validity refers to the extent to which the measure of a construct correlates in expected ways with measures of other constructs and to which it behaves as predicted over time and in response to experimental manipulations. In this chapter, we assess the nomological validity of the LCAQ by testing predictions derived from cognitive dissonance theory pertaining to three questions heretofore unaddressed by stepfamily researchers. Those three questions are:

1. Do stepchildren-biological children loyalty conflicts change over time?

2. How does the intensity of stepparents' loyalty conflicts affect the marital quality of remarried couples?

3. How does the marital quality of remarried couples affect the intensity of stepparents' loyalty conflicts?

We will discuss these three questions in light of cognitive dissonance theory and the literature currently available on stepfamilies.

Do Loyalty Conflicts Change over Time?

Borrowing from cognitive dissonance theory, we expect that the greater the perceived actual-ideal disparities in stepparents' distribution of personal resources to biological children and stepchildren, the more aversive their intrapersonal state will be. Moreover, the greater this disparity, the more motivated stepparents will be to reduce it. Thus, the intensity of stepparents' loyalty conflicts is expected to dissipate over time. The theory suggests that stepparents may reduce the discrepancy in a least two ways. First, they may change their resource allocation beliefs (what they believe is ideal) to more closely approximate their resource allocation behavior (what they actually do). For example, they might lower their expectations regarding what they believe is the ideal amount of time that they should spend with biological children. Second, they may alter their resource allocation behavior to more closely match their resource allocation beliefs. Since stepparents are likely have high levels of emotional investment in the various resource distribution outcomes (e.g., spending more time with biological children), they may first attempt to alter resource allocation behaviors via negotiation with the spouse. If they fail to negotiate successfully, they may resort to altering resource allocation beliefs.

How Do Stepparents' Loyalty Conflicts Affect the Marital Quality of Remarried Couples?

The extant clinical literature characterizes loyalty conflicts as negative processes which may engender adjustment difficulties for stepfamily members (Sager et al., 1986; Visher & Visher, 1988a). Thus, according to this "negative effects hypothesis," more intense loyalty conflicts are expected to be associated with lower quality marital relationships. However, cognitive dissonance theory suggests that, at early stages of stepfamily formation, the effects of stepparents' loyalty conflicts on marital quality may vary, depending on both the intensity of the conflict and the dimension of marital quality being assessed (perceptual or behavioral). During the first 24 months of the remarriage, stepfamily clinicians report that remarried couples often deny problems and are unassertive with regard to the expression of negative emotions pertaining to stepfamily-related problems (Papernow, 1984; Visher & Visher, 1978). This "fantasy" stage of stepfamily development (Papernow, 1984) is motivated ostensibly by fear of a second divorce and the belief that "love will conquer all."

Thus, denial proclivities may be stronger than the intrapersonal discomfort (dissonance arousal) engendered by loyalty conflicts of low to moderate intensity. Consequently, the resulting motivation to resolve these conflicts (dissonance motivation) via self-disclosures and assertive communications with the spouse may be overshadowed by tendencies to keep loyalty conflicts a primarily intrapersonal problem. Increases in the intensity of loyalty conflicts from low to moderate levels may be associated with increases in intrapersonal distress and concomitant decreases in perceived marital satisfaction. However, rates of positive communication behaviors (assertiveness and self-disclosures) may remain at uniformly low levels (or evidence only slight increases) and may be associated with increases in loyalty conflicts from low to moderate intensities.

As stepparents' loyalty conflicts increase from moderate to high intensities, the intrapersonal discomfort (dissonance arousal) will reach a threshold in which the motivation to reduce the conflict via self-disclosure and assertive interactions with the spouse will be greater than the countervailing denial proclivities. At this point of maximum ambivalence (the dissonance motivation and denial forces are equal), perceived marital satisfaction may be at its lowest level. Increases in the intensity of loyalty conflicts beyond this threshold (which should occur at the midpoint of loyalty conflicts scores) may be associated with increases in positive communication behaviors (as stepparents attempt to resolve the conflicts via interactions with the spouse) and corresponding increases in perceived marital satisfaction.

Thus, during early stages of stepfamily development, stepparents' loyalty conflicts may have a curvilinear effect on the perceived marital satisfaction of stepparents and a moderate positive linear effect on positive marital behaviors of stepparent couples. Increases in loyalty conflicts from low to moderate intensities may be associated with decreases in marital satisfaction; however, increases from moderate to high intensities may be associated with rising marital satisfaction. Positive communication behaviors (self-disclosure, assertiveness) may be uncorrelated (or may exhibit a low positive correlation) with loyalty conflicts ranging from low to moderate intensity, but they may be significantly and positively correlated with loyalty conflicts ranging from moderate to high intensity.

How Does the Marital Quality of Remarried Couples Affect the Intensity of Stepfathers' Loyalty Conflicts?

Causal processes in families may be reciprocal. As such, marital satisfaction and positive marital behaviors also may affect the intensity of stepfathers' loyalty conflicts. Moreover, the pattern of effects may differ from the curvilinear relations predicted for the reverse direction. Recently remarried stepparents who exhibit lower rates of positive marital behaviors and experience lower marital satisfaction may be more likely to deny, and thus less likely to resolve, biological children-step-children loyalty conflicts. Stepparents in more positive marital relationships (e.g., married to a spouse with better communication skills and problem-solving abilities) may be more likely to self-disclose negative emotions pertaining to actual-ideal disparities and to reach compromises with the new spouse regarding changes in resource allocation patterns. Over time, higher quality marriages should be associated with a reduction in the intensity of stepparents' loyalty conflicts.

In the current study, longitudinal relations between the intensity of stepfathers' loyalty conflicts and marital quality were examined in a sample of 26 complex stepfather families (residential stepfathers who had biological children living with ex-spouses). From the above general propositions, three major hypotheses were derived and tested:

1. The intensity of stepfathers' loyalty conflicts will decrease between 4 and 17 months after remarriage.

2. The intensity of stepfathers' loyalty conflicts at 4 months after remarriage will be curvilinearly related to stepfathers' marital satisfaction and positively correlated with both stepfathers' and spouses' positive marital behaviors at 17 months after remarriage.

3. Stepfathers' and spouses' marital satisfaction and positive marital behaviors at 4 months after remarriage will be negatively associated with the intensity of stepfathers' loyalty conflicts at 17 months after remarriage.

METHOD

Family Recruitment and Sample Description

The sample for this research included 26 Caucasian, middle-class stepfather families. The respondents had completed the first two waves of interviews in Hetherington and Clingempeel's (1992) longitudinal study of divorce and remarriage. The families were recruited from the marriage license records of Philadelphia, Pennsylvania, and surrounding counties. The families were mailed a cover letter (describing the criteria for participation and goals of the research) and Demographic Information Questionnaires, which they were asked to complete and to return in self-addressed, stamped envelopes. Approximately 40% of the stepfamilies that returned questionnaires and met all participation criteria agreed to participate in the study.

Thirty-one complex stepfather families completed the first wave of interviews, but five families dropped out of the study and did not complete the Wave 2 interviews. Dropouts did not differ from families that completed both waves on measures of loyalty conflicts or marital quality.

Demographic Characteristics of Stepfather Families

All stepfathers and spouses had been previously married and divorced. No adults had more than one previous marriage. All stepfathers had at least one child from a prior marriage, and former wives had custody of all children. All wives were custodial, biological mothers and had at least one child between 9 and 13 years of age.

All adults had a minimum of a high school education. Husbands averaged 16 years of formal education (*SD* = 2.6) and wives averaged 14 years (*SD* = 2.4). The mean age of wives was 35.5 (*SD* = 4.1), and the mean age of husbands was 38 (*SD* = 6.4). The average duration of the first marriage was 9.8 years (*SD* = 4.8 years) for wives and 12.3 years (*SD* = 6.5 years) for husbands. The mean interval between final separation from the first spouse and remarriage was 5 years (*SD* = 2.7 years) for wives and 4.4 years (*SD* = 3 years) for husbands. The couples had been remarried an average of 4 months at Wave 1 and 17 months at Wave 2.

Procedure and Measures

The current study focuses on a subset of the data collected during Hetherington and Clingempeel's (1992) larger longitudinal study. Remarried couples were interviewed in their homes at 4 months and 17 months following their remarriage (on the average). During home visits, stepfathers and their spouses independently completed several questionnaires and participated in structured and unstructured family interaction tasks which were videotaped. The measures of loyalty conflicts and marital quality used in this research are described below.

Loyalty Conflicts Assessment Questionnaire (LCAQ, Clingempeel et al., 1981). The LCAQ consisted of four items that assessed separately the magnitude of perceived discrepancies between the actual and ideal proportions of time, money, gifts, and affection given to stepchildren and biological children. These items were derived using the following procedure. First, stepfathers rated separately for time, money, gifts, and affection the *actual* proportion of each resource given to biological children and stepchildren during the last 2 months. Second, stepfathers rated separately for the same four personal resources the proportion they believed *ideally* should be given to biological children and stepchildren. Both ratings were recorded on the following 7-point scale: 1 = *all to biological children*, 2 = *much more to biological children*, 3 = *more to biological children*, 4 = *same to both*, 5 = *more to stepchildren*, 6 = *much more to stepchildren*, and 7 = *all to stepchildren*. Finally, a total discrepancy score was computed by summing the absolute value of the difference between actual and ideal ratings across the four personal resources.

The LCAQ also contained four items that focused on the extent to which stepfathers were dissatisfied with the allocation of personal resources between biological children and stepchildren. Thus, stepfathers rated separately for time, money, gifts and affection their degree of dissatisfaction on a 5 point scale with response alternatives ranging from 1 = *very satisfied* to 5 = *very dissatisfied*. The sum of dissatisfaction ratings across four personal resources yielded a total dissatisfaction score.

The intensity of loyalty conflicts total score, which was used in subsequent analyses, was derived by summing the 4-item total discrepancy score and the 4-item total dissatisfaction score. The range of potential total scores on this 8-item scale was 4 to 44.

Internal consistency reliabilities (Cronbach alphas) were computed separately for stepfathers' loyalty conflict scores obtained 4 months after remarriage (Wave 1) and 17 months after remarriage (Wave 2). The Cronbach alpha was .80 for Wave 1 scores and .76 for Wave 2 scores.

Dyadic Adjustment Scale (DAS; Spanier, 1976). Husbands and wives' total scores on the DAS were used as measures of perceived marital satisfaction. The widely used DAS has exhibited high reliability and adequate validity coefficients across numerous studies detailing its psychometric properties (Crane, Allgood, Larson, & Griffin, 1990).

Behavioral coding of videotaped couples interactions. During both waves of interviews, stepparent couples were videotaped during 10-minute, structured, problem-solving interactions including a dyadic task (husband and wife) and a triadic task (mother, stepfather, and child). For both tasks, family members were asked to discuss and try to reach agreement on solutions to two problem areas (e.g., curfew and table manners) that, according to questionnaire responses, had been the focus of frequent conflict during the previous 2 weeks. At both waves, 30- to 45-minute observations of unstructured family interactions during dinner were videotaped as well. The interviewers left the room during all videotaping in an effort to minimize reactivity effects.

Using a global behavioral coding system developed specifically for this research, trained observers rated husbands' behaviors toward wives and wives' behaviors toward husbands on nine dimensions, including hostility, warmth, dominance, assertiveness, coercion, communication skills, self-disclosure, mood, and trans- actional conflict using 5-point scales (5 = *mainly characteristic* to 1 = *not at all characteristic*). Coders first rated each person's behavior toward the other separately during the dyad, triad, and dinner videotapes. Coders then reexamined each person-to-person interaction across all tasks (dyad, triad, and dinner) and generated the cross-task ratings that were used in this research.

Thirty-seven percent of the tapes at each wave of assessment were randomly selected to be rated by a second coder. Weighted kappas for codes of wives' behaviors toward husbands ranged from .61 (mood) to .96 (hostility) at Wave 1 ($M = .72$) and .50 (warmth) to .75 (self-disclosure) at Wave 2 ($M = .66$). Weighted kappas for codes of husbands' behaviors toward wives ranged from .45 (self-disclosure) to .86 (hostility) at Wave 1 ($M = .73$) and .57 (mood) to .74 (hostility) at Wave 2 ($M = .65$).

Factor analyses of the nine behavioral codes yielded two factors: (a) *positivity*, which included the warmth, assertiveness, communication skills, self-disclosure, and mood codes; and (b) *negativity*, which included the hostility, coercion, and transactional conflict codes. These two factors, with the same scales loading on each factor, were essentially replicated for husbands' behaviors toward wives and wives' behaviors toward husbands.

The major hypotheses linking the intensity of loyalty conflicts to marital quality focus on behavioral codes from the Positivity Scale. Three of the Positivity codes including assertiveness, communication skills, and self-disclosure are specified directly in our hypotheses. One interpretation of low ratings on these codes is that this may be an indirect measure of stepfathers' "denial" (keeping the intra- personal conflict to themselves), and systematic increases in ratings on these codes may reflect stepfathers' attempts to resolve loyalty conflicts via communication with spouses. While our hypotheses do not relate directly to the mood and warmth codes, these codes may reflect important dimensions of marital communication. Consequently, two measures of Positivity were used in this research including a 3-code scale (the sum of ratings on self-disclosure, assertiveness, and communication skills) and the full 5-code scale.

A detailed description of the global coding system training of coders, reliabilities of individual codes, and scale construction procedures is provided in Hetherington and Clingempeel (1992).

RESULTS

The results are organized into four sections. In the first section, evidence for convergent validity of the LCAQ is provided. The remaining sections focus on nomological validity and address three research questions:

1. How do resident stepfathers' stepchildren-biological children loyalty conflicts change from 4 to 17 months after remarriage?

2. What are the relationships between the intensity of stepfathers' loyalty conflicts at 4 months after remarriage and perceived marital satisfaction and positive marital behaviors of stepfathers and spouses at 17 months after remarriage?

3. What are the relationships between the perceived marital satisfaction and positive marital behaviors of stepfathers and spouses at 4 months after remarriage and the intensity of stepfathers' loyalty conflicts at 17 months after remarriage?

Convergent Validation of the Loyalty Conflicts Assessment Questionnaire

Evidence for convergent validation of the LCAQ was obtained via assessment of the relations between stepfathers' intensity of loyalty conflict scores and four related variables: (a) spouses' ratings of stepfathers' dissatisfaction with proportions of resources given to stepchildren and biological children; (b) stepfathers' self-reports of concomitant negative emotions (e.g., guilt or sadness) associated with loyalty conflicts; (c) stepfathers' ratings of their degree of dissatisfaction with relationships with biological children; and (d) spouses' ratings of the frequency of accusations of favoritism expressed by themselves and their children toward stepfathers.

Spouses' ratings of stepfathers' loyalty conflicts. Spouses rated the stepfathers' level of dissatisfaction with the proportion of time, money, gifts and affection given to stepchildren and biological children on 5-point scales with response alternatives ranging from 1 = *very satisfied* to 5 = *very dissatisfied*. Wives' ratings were summed across the four personal resources to yield a spouses' rating of stepfathers' dissatisfaction score. The correlation between wives' ratings and stepfathers' self-reported dissatisfaction was positive and statistically significant, $r = .45$, $p < .01$. Wives' ratings of stepfathers' total dissatisfaction also correlated significantly with stepfathers' total loyalty conflict scores, $r = .45, p < .01$, and with stepfathers' total actual-ideal discrepancy scores, $r = .39, p < .05$.

Stepfathers' self-reports of expected negative emotions. According to the clinical literature (Sager et al., 1983; Visher & Visher, 1988a), stepfathers who experience more intense loyalty conflicts are also more likely to experience guilt and sadness stemming from these conflicts. Stepfathers who spend much less time with biological children than they believe they should may be more likely to feel both guilty and sad regarding their personal resource distribution than stepfathers whose perceived actual time spent with stepchildren and biological children more closely matched their perceived ideal time.

To test this proposition, stepfathers were asked to indicate separately for two emotions (sadness and guilt) whether they had experienced that emotion in the last month as a result of thinking about the proportion of resources given to biological children and stepchildren. Cross-tabulations of the intensity of loyalty conflict scores, trichotomized into high, moderate, and low groups by two emotions groups, including "both emotions experienced" and "both emotions not experienced," were conducted separately for stepfathers remarried 4 months, on average, and 13 months later, when stepfathers had been remarried 17 months, on average.

The chi-square for data obtained four months after remarriage was marginally significant, $\chi^2_{(2)} = 4.46, p = .10$, and the chi-square for data obtained 17 months after remarriage was statistically significant, $\chi^2_{(2)} = 8.68, p < .01$. At both waves of interviews, stepfathers who reported more intense loyalty conflicts also were more likely to report having experienced both guilt and sadness in the last month related to thinking about these conflicts.

Stepfathers' ratings of dissatisfaction with relationships with biological children. Stepfathers may experience greater loyalty conflicts to the extent that they are dissatisfied with the quality of relationships with nonresident biological children. Dissatisfaction also may stem from stepfathers' perceptions that they are giving less time, money, gifts and affection than they ideally should.

To assess this assumption, stepfathers were asked to indicate the extent to which they were satisfied with the quality of their relationships with biological children on a 5-point scale, ranging from 1 = *very satisfied* to 5 = *very dissatisfied*. Two data-analytic strategies were used to assess the relations between loyalty conflict scores and dissatisfaction ratings. First, a cross-tabulation of the intensity of loyalty conflict scores at Wave 1, trichotomized into high, moderate, and low groups by ratings of relationship satisfaction and dichotomized into satisfied and dissatisfied groups, yielded a statistically significant chi-square value, $\chi^2_{(2)} = 12.31, p < .01$. The measures covaried in expected ways. Only 1 of 12 stepfathers in the *"low"* loyalty conflicts group reported that he was dissatisfied with the quality of his relationship with his biological children. In contrast, 9 of 10 stepfathers in the *"high"* loyalty conflicts group reported that they were dissatisfied with the quality of relationships with their nonresident biological children.

A second data-analytic strategy involved using a *t*-test to determine whether stepfathers who were satisfied differed from those who were dissatisfied with the quality of relationships with biological children on the continuous measures of loyalty conflicts. The results were statistically significant, $t_{(29)} = 3.61, p < .01$. Dissatisfied stepfathers experienced more intense loyalty conflicts ($M = 18.07$, $SD = 5.36$) than did satisfied stepfathers ($M = 12.44; SD = 3.08$).

Spouses' ratings of the frequency of accusations of favoritism. The intensity of stepfathers' loyalty conflicts may be exacerbated by accusations of favoritism from stepchildren and current spouses. To assess this possibility, residential biological mothers indicated the frequency with which their biological children had complained to them during the last 2 months that their stepfathers had shown favoritism. Mothers recorded their responses to both items on 7-point scales, with responses ranging from *not at all* to *once a day*. A cross-tabulation of loyalty conflict scores trichotomized into three groups (high, moderate, and low) and accusations of favoritism scores dichotomized into two groups (accused by mother or children versus not accused by mother or children) at 4 months after remarriage yielded a marginally significant chi-square value, $\chi^2_{(2)} = 5.06$, $p = .08$. The data suggested that stepfathers who reported more intense loyalty conflicts also were more likely to have been accused of favoritism by spouses or stepchildren.

How Do Stepfathers' Loyalty Conflicts Change over Time?

Loyalty conflicts may change from 4 to 17 months after remarriage in both *intensity* (including total scores and their discrepancy and dissatisfaction components), in *structural characteristics*, including the type of personal resource discrepancies (e.g., money, affection) and the direction of discrepancies (e.g., actual, "more to stepchildren," but ideal, "more to biological children"). Consequently, possible changes on both dimensions were assessed.

To assess whether the intensity of stepfathers' loyalty conflicts changed over time, the *t* test of dependent samples were used to test for differences across waves for the total loyalty conflict scores and their two components (discrepancy scores and dissatisfaction scores). These analyses revealed no time-related differences in the intensity of stepfathers' loyalty conflicts.

Pearson correlations also indicated that the intensity of stepfathers' loyalty conflicts were stable across waves. Across waves, total loyalty conflict scores were correlated, .54, $p < .01$; discrepancy scores were correlated, .53, $p < .01$; and dissatisfaction scores were correlated, .37, $p < .05$.

To assess whether the type and direction of resource discrepancies changeg across waves, stepfathers' Wave 1 and Wave 2 responses on the LCAQ, separated by each personal resource (time, money, affection, and gifts), were categorized into three groups ("more to biological children," "same to both," and "more to stepchil-dren") for both "actually gave" and "ideally should give" items. The percentages of stepfathers at 4 and 17 months after remarriage who reported that they "actually gave" and "ideally should give" more personal resources to biological children, more to stepchildren, and the same to both biological children and stepchildren are presented in Table 9.1. An examination of 3 x 3 crosstabulations and associated chi-square analyses (three groups at Wave 1 by three groups at Wave 2) suggested two overarching conclusions. First, the type and direction of personal resource discrepancies remained remarkably stable across waves of assessment. At both 4 and 17 months after remarriage, most stepfathers "actually gave" more time and money to stepchildren and more affection to biological children but believed that ideally they should give the same amount of these personal

Table 9.1

Stepfathers' Reports of Actual and Ideal Proportions of Time, Money, Gifts, and Affection Given to Biological Children and Stepchildren at 4 Months and 17 Months After Remarriage

Personal Resources	Percentage (and Number) of Stepfathers Reporting at 4 months after remarriage (N = 31)			Percentage (and Number) of Stepfathers Reporting at 17 months after remarriage (N = 26)		
	More to Children	Same to Both	More to Stepchildren	More to Children	Same to Both	More to Stepchildren
1. Time						
Actual	16% (5)	19% (6)	65% (20)	19% (5)	15% (4)	66% (17)
Ideal	26% (8)	52% (16)	22% (7)	23% (6)	54% (14)	23% (6)
2. Money						
Actual	19% (6)	43% (13)	38% (12)	27% (7)	35% (9)	38% (10)
Ideal	13% (4)	77% (24)	10% (3)	27% (7)	65% (17)	8% (2)
3. Gifts						
Actual	10% (3)	71% (22)	19% (6)	31% (8)	54% (14)	15% (4)
Ideal	16% (5)	77% (24)	7% (2)	19% (5)	77% (20)	4% (1)

Table 9.1 (continued)

Personal Resources	Percentage (and Number) of Stepfathers Reporting at 4 months after remarriage (N = 31)			Percentage (and Number) of Stepfathers Reporting at 17 months after remarriage (N = 26)		
	More to Children	Same to Both	More to Stepchildren	More to Children	Same to Both	More to Stepchildren
4. Affection						
Actual	35% (11)	42% (13)	23% (7)	50% (13)	38% (10)	12% (3)
Ideal	29% (9)	68% (21)	3% (1)	38% (10)	62% (16)	0% (0)

resources to both sets of children. At both waves, most stepfathers reported that they actually gave and ideally should give the same amount of gifts to biological children and stepchildren. Thus, perceived actual and ideal allocations of gifts were less discrepant than allocations of the other three personal resources. Second, the majority of stepfathers subscribed to an *equity principle* in regard to the ideal proportion of personal resources that they believed should be allocated to stepchildren and biological children. At both 4 and 17 months after remarriage, the majority of stepfathers indicated that ideally they should give the same amount to biological children and stepchildren for all four personal resources (*time*: 52% at Wave 1, 54% at Wave 2; *affection*: 68% at Wave 1, 62% at Wave 2; *money*: 77% at Wave 1, 77% at Wave 2; *gifts*: 77% at Wave 1, 77% at Wave 2).

What Are the Effects of the Intensity of Stepfathers' Loyalty Conflicts on the Marital Satisfaction and Positive Marital Behaviors of Stepparent Couples?

The bidirectional problem associated with interpreting correlational analyses can be remedied if measures of "presumed causes" are obtained temporally prior to measures of "expected effects." Capitalizing on the longitudinal design, multiple regressions were used to predict the two marital relationship measures obtained 17 months after remarriage from the loyalty conflict measures obtained 4 months after remarriage.

In all regression equations, the autoregressive effect, or the effect of a variable on itself over time (e.g., stepfathers' DAS scores at 4 months after remarriage as a predictor of stepfathers' DAS scores at 17 months after remarriage) was controlled by entering it first into the equation. Gollob and Reichardt (1987) demonstrated that longitudinal predictions can yield biased estimates of effects unless the autoregressive term is either controlled or assumed to be zero.

Since curvilinear effects of loyalty conflicts on stepfathers' DAS scores were hypothesized, hierarchical polynomial regressions with, the autoregressive term entered first (DAS scores at Wave 1), the linear loyalty conflicts term at Wave 1 entered second, and the quadratic loyalty conflicts term at Wave 1 entered third, were performed on both stepfathers' and spouses' DAS scores at Wave 2. In all analyses, a significant quadratic effect was reported only if the quadratic term contributed significantly more variance after the autoregressive effect and the linear terms were controlled.

Positive linear relations between loyalty conflict scores at Wave 1 and Positivity scores at Wave 2 were hypothesized. Consequently, two-predictor hierarchical regressions, with the Positivity scores at Wave 1 entered first and the linear loyalty conflicts term at Wave 1 entered second, were performed on both stepfathers' and spouses' Positivity scores at Wave 2.

All regressions were performed twice with total Positivity scores (the sum of ratings across all five positive behavior codes) used in one equation and abbreviated Positivity scores (the sum of ratings across the self-disclosure, communication skill, and assertiveness codes) used in the second equation. The abbreviated Positivity scores permitted more precise analyses relevant to our specific hypotheses. Thus, for example, stepfathers' "denial" (which was not assessed directly) may be inferred from low ratings on self-disclosure, assertiveness, and communication skills. Positive linear relations were hypothesized for a restricted range of loyalty conflict scores (moderate to high), and these regressions have an elevated probability of Type II error. Consequently, across-wave zero-order correlations between loyalty conflict scores and Positivity scores also were examined.

Hierarchical regressions predicting stepfathers' scores on both 3-code and 5-code Positivity scales yielded nonsignificant increases in R^2 for the linear term of stepfathers' loyalty conflict scores (after controlling for autoregressive effects). The zero-order correlation between stepfathers' loyalty conflict scores at Wave 1 and 3-code Positivity scores at Wave 2 was positive as hypothesized but not statistically significant ($r = .29$, ns). Separate correlations for the restricted ranges of loyalty conflict scores (low to moderate and moderate to high) were not performed due to the small sample sizes involved in such analyses.

The longitudinal prediction of stepfathers' DAS total scores resulted in a marginally significant quadratic effect. The autocorrelation of stepfathers' total DAS scores obtained 4 months and 17 months after remarriage was significant, with 34% of the variance of Wave 2 scores accounted for by Wave 1 scores ($F = 11.22$, $p < .01$). After controlling for this autoregressive effect, the linear term for Wave 1 loyalty conflict scores accounted for a negligible and nonsignificant amount of additional variance in husbands' Wave 2 DAS scores. However, the quadratic term for the Wave 1 loyalty conflict scores added 9% additional variance to that accounted for by both the autoregressive term and the linear term for Wave 1 loyalty conflict scores. The R^2 change was marginally significant ($F = 3.26$, $p = .08$). The full model accounted for 43% of the variance of husbands' DAS scores 17 months after remarriage.

A plotting of the regression equation revealed a modified U-shaped or concave-upward relationship between stepfathers' intensity of loyalty conflict scores 4 months after remarriage and their total DAS scores 17 months after remarriage. Increasing loyalty conflict scores were associated with decreases in DAS scores up to approximately one-half standard deviation below the mean of the loyalty conflict scores. At this point, the pattern reverses and begins an upward, linear accelerating trend, with further increases in loyalty conflict scores associated with increases in DAS scores.

Hierarchical regressions predicting wives' scores on both 3-code and 5-code Positivity scales at 17 months after remarriage from the linear term of stepfathers' loyalty conflict scores at 4 months after remarriage yielded nonsignificant results. However, in analyses involving the 3-code Positivity scores, the linear loyalty conflicts term at Wave 1 accounted for 20% additional variance in Wave 2 Positivity scores after controlling for the variance accounted for by Wave 1 Positivity scores.

The zero-order correlation between stepfathers' loyalty conflict scores at Wave 1 and wives' Positivity scores at Wave 2 was positive as hypothesized ($r = .41$, $p = .10$).

Consistent with results for husbands, predictions of wives' DAS total scores yielded a marginally significant quadratic effect. The autocorrelation between wives' total DAS scores obtained 4 months after remarriage and 17 months after remarriage was significant with 43% of the variance of Wave 2 scores accounted for by Wave 1 scores ($F = 15.54, p = .001$). After controlling for this autoregressive effect, the linear term for husbands' loyalty conflict scores 4 months after remarriage contributed no additional variance to wives' Wave 2 DAS scores. However, the quadratic term for stepfathers' Wave 1 loyalty conflict scores accounted for 9% additional variance, and the R^2 change was marginally significant ($F = 3.60, p = .07$). The full model accounted for 52% of the variance of wives DAS scores 17 months after remarriage.

A plotting of the regression equation revealed a concave-upward, U-shaped function similar to the pattern obtained for husbands. Increases in stepfathers' loyalty conflict scores were associated with decreases in wives' DAS scores for the low range of loyalty conflict scores. However, as was the case for husbands, the pattern changed directions at about one-half standard deviation below the mean of the loyalty conflict scores. At this point, further increases in husbands' loyalty conflict scores were associated with increases in wives' DAS scores.

What Are the Effects of the Marital Satisfaction and Positive Marital Behaviors of Stepparent Couples on the Intensity of Stepfathers' Loyalty Conflicts?

While loyalty conflicts may affect the marital satisfaction and positive marital behaviors of stepparent couples, the bidirectional path is also plausible. Thus, dimensions of the marital relationship may attenuate or exacerbate the intensity of stepfathers' loyalty conflicts. Consequently, hierarchical regressions were used to predict stepfathers' loyalty conflict scores at 17 months after remarriage from linear terms of husbands and wives marital relationship scores (DAS total scores and Positivity ratings) at 4 months after remarriage. In all regression equations, the effect of loyalty conflicts on itself over time was controlled by first entering the autoregressive term into the regression equation.

Hierarchical regressions predicting stepfathers' loyalty conflict scores at 17 months after remarriage from stepfathers' Positivity ratings at 4 months after remarriage yielded nonsignificant results. However, predictions of loyalty conflict scores from DAS total scores yielded a marginally significant effect. The autocorrelation between stepfather's loyalty conflict scores obtained 4 months and 17 months after remarriage was significant ($F = 9.36, p < .01$) with 29% of the variance of Wave 2 loyalty conflict scores accounted for by Wave 1 scores. After controlling for this autoregressive effect, the linear term for husbands' DAS scores 4 months after remarriage accounted for an additional 9% of the variance of stepfathers' loyalty conflict scores 17 months after remarriage, and the R^2 change was marginally significant ($F = 3.27, p = .08$). The zero-order correlation between stepfathers' DAS scores at Wave 1 and loyalty conflict scores at Wave 2 was -.43, $p < .05$.

Hierarchical regressions predicting stepfathers' loyalty conflict scores at 17 months after remarriage from wives' DAS scores and Positivity ratings at 4 months after remarriage yielded nonsignificant increases in R^2. However the zero-order correlation between wives' 3-code Positivity scores at Wave 1 and stepfathers' loyalty conflict scores at Wave 2 was negative, as hypothesized, and was marginally significant ($r = -.51, p = .07$).

DISCUSSION

This research suggests that the Loyalty Conflicts Assessment Questionnaire (LCAQ; Clingempeel et al., 1981) is a reliable and valid measure of stepfathers' loyalty conflicts. Derived from principles of cognitive dissonance theory, the LCAQ exhibited high internal consistency reliabilities at both 4 and 17 months after remarriage. In addition, the convergent validity of the LCAQ was supported by several analyses. Correlations between stepfathers' ratings of their level of dissatisfaction with resource allocation behavior and spouses' ratings of stepfathers' dissatisfaction were positive and statistically significant. In addition, more intense loyalty conflicts were associated with a greater likelihood of stepfathers experiencing negative emotions (both guilt and sadness) and accusations of favoritism, and with higher levels of self-reported dissatisfaction with relationships with their biological children. These results corroborate both the clinical literature on stepfamilies and cognitive dissonance theory in regard to the expected relations between loyalty conflicts and emotional and interpersonal processes.

The findings pertaining to nomological validity provide partial support for our conceptualization of loyalty conflicts. The results that are relevant to each of the three major research questions are discussed below.

Do Stepfathers' Loyalty Conflicts Change in Intensity or Structure during the First 1.5 Years of the Remarriage?

The results did not support our prediction that the intensity of stepfathers' loyalty conflicts would dissipate over time. The means of total scores on the LCAQ at 4 and 17 months post-remarriage did not differ significantly; and Pearson correlations between Wave 1 and Wave 2 scores were positive and statistically significant.

The structural characteristics of stepfathers' loyalty conflicts also were remarkably similar across waves of interviews. The majority of stepfathers at both 4 and 17 months after remarriage subscribed to an *equity principle*, or the proposition that stepchildren and biological children should receive the same amount of their time, money, affection, and gifts.

Moreover, a majority of stepfathers at both waves of interviews reported that they *actually* gave more time and money to residential stepchildren but gave more affection to nonresidential biological children. Thus, at both waves, most actual-ideal discrepancies involved actually giving more time and money to stepchildren and more affection to biological children but believing ideally that equal amounts of these resources should be given to both groups.

Cognitive inconsistency may not engender the necessary level of dissonance arousal and motivation to produce alterations in stepfathers' resource allocation beliefs and behavior. Revised cognitive dissonance theory (Cooper & Fazio, 1984) suggests that cognitive inconsistency does not lead to behavioral or attitudinal change in two situations: (a) when personal responsibility is abrogated and (b) when the consequences of behavior are perceived as benign rather than harmful. Thus, stepfathers who attribute responsibility for their resource allocation behavior to external sources (e.g., current or former spouses) or who believe that their behavior is not harmful to stepchildren or biological children may not be motivated sufficiently to reduce the inconsistency between resource allocation beliefs and behavior.

What Are the Effects of the Intensity of Stepfathers' Loyalty Conflicts on the Marital Satisfaction and Positive Marital Behaviors of Stepparent Couples?

Our results provided support for predictions derived from cognitive dissonance (Cooper & Fazio, 1984; Festinger, 1957) and stepfamily development theories (Papernow, 1984). For both husbands and wives, the intensity of stepfathers' loyalty conflicts at 4 months after remarriage was related in a curvilinear fashion to DAS scores at 17 months after remarriage. Consequently, the negative effects hypothesis, or the assumption that loyalty conflicts will have adverse effects on marital quality throughout the full range of loyalty conflict scores, was not supported. Instead, throughout a low-to-moderate range of loyalty conflict scores, increasingly intense loyalty conflicts were associated with lower DAS scores. However, as the intensity of loyalty conflicts increased from moderate to high levels, DAS total scores increased rather than decreased.

The results from regressions involving behavioral observation measures provided some, albeit limited, support for our hypothesized links between stepfathers' loyalty conflicts and positive marital behaviors of stepparent couples. Although longitudinal hierarchical regressions yielded nonsignificant results (after controlling for shared variability among Wave 1 and Wave 2 Positivity scores), zero-order correlations between stepfathers' loyalty conflict scores at Wave 1 and both stepfathers' and spouses' 3-code Positivity scores (consisting of the sum of assertiveness, self-disclosure, and communication skills codes) at Wave 2 were positive ($r = .29$ for stepfathers' scores and $r = .42$ for spouses' scores), as hypothesized. Given that significant positive relations were expected only for a restricted range of loyalty conflict scores (moderate-to-high intensity), positive correlations of this magnitude for the full range of scores are not inconsistent with our predictions. Conducting across-wave correlations separately within the restricted ranges of loyalty conflict scores was not feasible, given the small sample sizes and associated high probability of Type II error. However, comparisons of stepfathers who had low-to-moderately-intense loyalty conflicts at Wave 1 with those who had loyalty conflicts in the moderate-to-high range revealed a lower mean on the 3-code Positivity score at Wave 2 for the low-to-moderate group. These results provide indirect and limited support for our proposed "denial" process.

According to cognitive dissonance theory (Festinger, 1957), stepfathers' perceived actual-ideal disparities in the personal resources (e.g., time and money) given to biological children and stepchildren should produce an aversive intrapersonal state that the stepfathers will be motivated to reduce by either changing their resource allocation beliefs (what they believe is ideal) or their resource allocation behaviors (what they actually do). Moreover, in accordance with recent theoretical revisions (Cooper & Fazio, 1984), perceived inconsistency between beliefs and behavior is especially likely to produce a negative emotional state if stepfathers view their resource allocation behavior as being under their control and as having potentially negative effects on stepchildren and/or biological children. One strategy that stepfathers likely use to reduce this dissonance-related aversive intrapersonal state is to negotiate with the current spouse for changes in resource allocation behavior (e.g., spending more time with biological children). Thus, intrapersonal conflict may lead to marital communication.

During early stages of stepfamily formation, the motivation to reduce the unpleasant emotions engendered by loyalty conflicts or the open discussion of conflicts with spouses is in direct opposition to strong proclivities to deny problems (stemming from fears of another divorce) and preserve the honeymoon period. At low-to-moderate levels of loyalty conflicts, there may be increasing intrapersonal discomfort, which translates into decreasing marital satisfaction. However, the intensity is not sufficiently strong to overcome the forces of denial. As a result, stepfathers may not make their intrapersonal conflict a marital issue. However, at moderate-to-high levels of loyalty conflicts, the intrapersonal discomfort is sufficient to overcome denial. Hence, stepfathers may attempt to resolve loyalty conflicts via negotiation with their spouses. Moreover, these efforts manifest themselves in greater self-disclosure, assertiveness, and communication within the marital dyad. The more intense the loyalty conflicts, the more effort stepfathers will expend in attempting to reach a compromise solution to problems related to their across-household allocation of personal resources. At moderate to high levels of loyalty conflicts, increasingly intense loyalty conflicts are associated with increases in marital satisfaction.

Why was the same curvilinear pattern obtained for the wives' DAS scores? As the intensity of the stepfather's loyalty conflicts increases from low to moderate levels, the wife may become increasingly aware of their husband's dissatisfaction. She also may experience increasing dissatisfaction herself regarding her husband's resource allocation behavior. However, as for the husband, the tendency to avoid discussion of the issues leads to increases in negative emotions and concomitant reductions in marital satisfaction. As the intensity of the stepfather's loyalty conflicts increases from moderate to high levels, the associated increases in the husband's self-disclosures and negotiating behavior will lead to increases in the wife's marital satisfaction.

A caveat is in order: These curvilinear findings involved the interpretation of marginally significant results. The F values for the R^2 change associated with the entry of the loyalty conflicts quadratic term reached probability levels of .08 for husbands and .09 for wives, and thus did not fall within the conventional .05 range. Nevertheless, we believe that these results are important for at least three reasons: First, they supported, and were derived from, an explicit theoretical framework. Second, they were obtained using an extremely conservative data-analytic strategy that mitigated against finding significant results. In analyses of both husbands' and wives' data, the variance in Wave 2 DAS scores accounted for by Wave 1 DAS scores was substantial and greatly limited the remaining variability to be predicted by the loyalty conflict scores. Furthermore, there was a 13-month interval of prediction, on the average (loyalty conflict scores at 4 months after remarriage were used to predict DAS scores at 17 months after remarriage), and "effects" of earlier loyalty conflicts on marital satisfaction may dissipate over time. With a shorter "interval of prediction," the results may have been more salient. Given these factors, we believe that the additional variance accounted for by the quadratic term is quite remarkable.

What Are the Effects of the Perceived Marital Satisfaction and Positive Marital Behaviors of Stepparent Couples on the Intensity of Stepfathers' Loyalty Conflicts?

For stepfathers, the results provided support for our prediction from cognitive dissonance theory. A significant negative linear association was obtained between stepfathers' DAS scores at 4 months after remarriage and the intensity of stepfathers' loyalty conflicts at 17 months after remarriage. Over time, greater marital satisfaction may result in a reduction of stepfathers' loyalty conflicts. Stepfathers who are happier in their marriages may be more likely to discuss even low-intensity loyalty conflicts with spouses, and thus, may be more likely to arrive at solutions that reduce the magnitude of perceived actual-ideal disparities in resource allocation. Greater communication and problem-solving skills associated with higher marital satisfaction may translate into solutions that alter either stepfathers' behavior (so that the actual more closely matches the ideal) or expectations (so that the ideal more closely matches the actual).

Although hierarchical regressions yielded nonsignificant R^2 changes for the Positivity scores, the zero-order correlation between wives' 3-code Positivity scores at Wave 1 and stepfathers' loyalty conflict scores at Wave 2 was negative as hypothesized and marginally significant ($p = .07$). The equivalent correlation for stepfathers' Positivity scores also was negative but was not significant. Wives' positive communication behaviors during the early months of their remarriage may facilitate the resolution of their husbands' stepchildren-biological children loyalty conflicts.

No hierarchical regressions assessing the relations between stepfathers' loyalty conflicts and the behavioral observation measures of marital quality were statistically significant. It is possible that the global behavioral codes were not sensitive enough to detect variability in marital behavior attributable to stepfathers' loyalty conflicts. The reactivity of the videotaped problem-solving tasks may have been unrepresentative of the daily communication and problem-solving behaviors of remarried couples.

Limitations. This research has limitations that suggest possible foci of future research. First, this study did not assess several components of the revised cognitive dissonance theory. For example, we did not examine (a) the extent to which stepfathers believed that their resource allocation behavior would have a negative impact on their step- or biological children, nor (b) the extent to which stepfathers believed that they controlled their resource allocation behaviors. Numerous studies in experimental social psychology have demonstrated that these factors influence the likelihood that cognitive inconsistency will engender dissonance arousal and dissonance motivation (Cooper & Fazio, 1984). Future studies that assess these components and examine their influence on stepparents' resource allocation beliefs and behavior would add to our knowledge of stepchildren-biological children loyalty conflicts. Second, this research did not provide evidence for the discriminant validity of the LCAQ. While evidence of convergent validity was provided, measures of constructs can be invalidated because they correlate too highly with measures of different and theoretically unrelated constructs (Campbell & Fiske, 1959; Nunnally, 1978). Consequently, future studies should assess both the discriminant validity and the convergent validity of loyalty conflict measures. Multitrait-multimethod studies that assess at least two different constructs via two different methods would be especially informative. Third, our interpretations of the interdependencies of loyalty conflicts and marital quality, while theory-driven, are still speculative. A direct assessment of the extent to which stepfathers with low-to-moderately intense loyalty conflicts kept these conflicts to themselves was not conducted. Instead, denial was indirectly assessed via behavioral ratings of assertiveness and self-disclosure. Future studies that directly assess the denial process and include larger samples permitting statistical analyses within the restricted ranges of loyalty conflict scores (e.g., assessing relations between loyalty conflicts and positive marital behaviors within the moderate-to-high range of loyalty conflict scores) would shed additional light on hypothesized family dynamics. Fourth, this research provided only partial support for the nomological validity of the LCAQ. The relations between stepchildren-biological children loyalty conflicts and only one construct (marital quality) was assessed in the current study. Future studies should examine the relations between LCAQ scores and other constructs within the theoretical system (e.g., stepparent warmth toward the stepchild).

KEY CHAPTER POINTS

1. The development and validation of the Loyalty Conflicts Assessment Question-naire (LCAQ, a measure of stepchild-biological children loyalty conflicts among stepparents who live with the stepchild but who also have biological children living with former spouses) is described through extrapolation from revised cognitive dissonance theory.

2. The LCAQ assesses the intensity of stepparents' loyalty conflicts, operation-alized as the magnitude of perceived discrepancies between the proportion of four personal resources (time, money, gifts, and affection) that stepparents actually give to children and stepchildren (resource allocation behaviors) and the proportion that they believe they ideally should give (resource allo-cation beliefs).

3. The study reported here includes data from 26 remarried couples (mother-step-father families) who completed both the LCAQ and several measures of marital quality at 4 and 17 months after remarriage, providing data for assessing both convergent and nomological validity.

4. More intense loyalty conflicts were associated with greater dissatisfaction with relationships with biological children, accusations of favoritism by spouses or stepchildren, and a greater likelihood of stepfathers experiencing conflict-related negative emotions during the previous months at both times of data collection.

5. The intensity of stepfathers' loyalty conflicts did not change significantly between 4 and 17 months after remarriage.

6. A both times, most stepfathers subscribed to an equity principle: a belief that equal amounts of personal resources should be given to stepchildren and biological children. However, they reported that they actually gave more time and money to stepchildren and more affection to biological children.

7. The intensity of stepfathers' loyalty conflicts at 4 months after remarriage was related in a curvilinear fashion to stepfathers' and wives' marital satisfaction at 17 months.

8. Greater marital satisfaction of stepfathers and a higher rating of positive communication behaviors of wives at 4 months were associated with less intense loyalty conflicts of stepfathers at 17 months after remarriage.

Chapter 10

TREATING STEPFAMILIES: ALTERNATIVES TO TRADITIONAL FAMILY THERAPY

Scott Browning

Why does stepfamily therapy seem more challenging than therapy with the traditional first-marriage family? If one asks a family therapist how many stepfamilies he or she is seeing, it is likely that most at first will not be sure. They will then begin thinking about the different families with which they work, remembering which ones are remarried and which ones are not. Unlike the gay family, the alcoholic family, or the single-parent family, the stepfamily is hidden within the general rubric of family more than families that are recognized as falling within a distinct and acknowledged type. In this chapter, I argue that a clinical approach that instead perceives the stepfamily as a distinct type of family offers many advantages.

Problems presented clinically by stepfamilies frequently seem to match, in tone and nature, problems from traditional, first-marriage families. However, attempting to address these problems by incorporating a traditional family therapy approach only reminds the clinician of the unique dilemmas experienced by most stepfamilies. Therapeutic impasse is not uncommon when the distinction between the stepfamily and traditional first-marriage family is ignored. This impasse arises from the position in which the therapist might put the family by following traditional tenets of family therapy.

From the emergence of the field of family therapy, many individuals have supported the idea that the therapist's ability to understand the systemic functioning of a family may be a necessary and sufficient foundation for family therapy (Haley, 1976). This notion, which established the entirely unique view that the family, and not the individual, was the patient, may have created precedents that are not optimal for treating stepfamilies.

Theoretical models embracing all living systems (Bertalanffy, 1968) and research on schizophrenia and the family gave family therapists a vocabulary that dramatically shifted the way in which they understood how clinical change could occur. In understanding a family as a system, clinicians recognized that they could intervene at a variety of levels. Thus, clinicians and researchers began shifting their ideas of the therapeutic process. The ideas that were central to this movement involved accepting a new epistemology which accepted the belief that the client could be a family rather than an individual. Such ideas were seen as an assault on the established doctrine (Bowen, 1972). Thus, the notion of family therapy energized a substantial subsection of the mental health field. Today's acceptance and popularity of family therapy suggest that the idea of treating an entire family and understanding problems in light of its systemic functioning can be intrinsically useful to clinicians.

The divergent schools of thought that defined this early family therapy movement have been well chronicled (Hoffman, 1981). One is struck by the fundamental shift that was necessary in order to open clinicians to the belief that therapeutic goals could be achieved with all family members present. Previously, the assumption had been that including all family members in a session would be harmful to the therapeutic process because their presence might "contaminate" therapy. What began with research into the role of families with a schizophrenic member (Jackson, 1957) soon shifted to a fascination with the role of family dynamics (Bowen, 1960) and then evolved into viewing the family in its systemic totality and believing that clinical work could occur with all family members present. Once a clinician had accepted the family as a system, seeing the family together became a useful and, some thought, a necessary requirement for clinical change.

The commitment to family therapy made it difficult to utilize the traditional diagnostic methods that had been created for individuals. The traditional diagnostic agenda included examining the patient's strengths, weaknesses, contact with reality, and individual dynamics. Once he or she had been diagnosed, the patient's treatment was determined through an interaction of the clinician's theoretical stance and the assigned diagnosis. Psychoanalysts and psychotherapists developed expertise in treating patients by specializing in a certain age range and specific diagnostic categories. Those who trained in family therapy in the 1960s and 1970s were taught to think of the problem in the family context and dealt with a wider variety of ages, using either a different diagnostic system or none at all.

The family therapy movement represented a radical departure from individual-focused treatment (Haley, 1981). Although some clinicians continued to conceptualize their family cases psychodynamically, a range of clinical theories began to emerge. A unifying factor across models involved the importance of understanding or observing the family's systemic pressures and patterns. As one indication of its acceptance, recent research (Ganong & Coleman, 1987a) has suggested that 78% of family therapists writing about remarriage and stepparenting identify themselves as adhering to systems theory. Family therapy can be understood best as a movement that accepted different theories in regard to the specifics of treatment but was united in conceptualizing the presenting problem in the context of the family.

Given the novelty of the notion of family treatment, it is not surprising that students of this form of therapy needed to follow closely the writings and lectures of established practitioners. When a leader of a new movement creates a model, the initial ideas take on considerable influence for eager students. Even as theorists evolve, change their theories, or adapt to changing clinical needs, their initial writings are only just beginning to be absorbed and understood by those in the field. When adapting to an entirely unique view, the nuances that would represent a significant revision to the theorists might only slightly shift the thinking of the practicing clinician.

One myth that clinicians formerly accepted as true was that all families are similar. However, as Jackson (1967) stated, "There is no such thing as a normal family." Jackson's statement implied that rather than establishing whether a family was normal or pathological, it was more important to understand that families were systems. A system, as defined by Bertalanffy (1968), involved the interaction of elements. When the elements, or component parts, interacted, they influenced each other. Solar systems, corporations, and computer networks were systems, and so, too, the family was viewed as a system, insofar as it included the interaction of elements. Furthermore, the interaction of elements followed specific rules. Given the extraordinary range of relational units that were considered systems, all families were subsumed as equally amenable to the benefits of family therapy.

The pioneers of family therapy established theories based on therapy with a "generic" family in order to gain acceptance and establish credibility. There were good reasons to avoid heading in the direction of addressing family typologies (Hoffman, 1981). It might have been destructive to the nascent field of family therapy to dilute the conception of systems thinking by creating separate rules for stepfamilies, single-parent families, adoptive families, and other nontraditional family types. Different proponents of family therapy did not identify their models as particularly useful for one family type compared to another. In fact, the early general acceptance of "the family" allowed early theorists to focus on the systemic nature of family.

The theories and techniques that were set forth as the basis of family therapy established precedents that ill prepared the family therapist for the great variety of family types. Although they were always aware that families that did not fit any hypothetical norm might seek therapy, the pioneers in the field chose to avoid focusing on generating different treatments for each of the many possible discrete categories of family types (Nichols, 1984). Therefore, in accepting systems thinking, the ideas was also accepted that any and all families could be understood within the framework of family patterns, compositions, and rules. Stepfamilies were no exception: they, like any family type, could be understood as a system. However, while one could understand stepfamilies as a separate system, the therapy imposed on them was based on beliefs about the traditional first-marriage family.

Recent efforts in studying other family types (e.g., single-parent or alcoholic families) have increased the effort to provide sophisticated treatment to these different populations. In recognizing the unique nature of a particular family type, a therapist need not reject his or her systemic theoretical foundation. For example, a deeper understanding of stepfamily development (Papernow, 1984) can serve as an adjunct to utilizing systems thinking in assessing and treating stepfamilies. In combining a fuller understanding of the unique nature of the stepfamily with clinical attention to family rules and patterns, the clinician can increase his or her effectiveness with this population. Although relatively new, there is already a small but significant body of clinical literature on stepfamilies.

EARLY WORK ADDRESSING STEPFAMILIES

Reviewing the major theorists in the field of family therapy, one is struck by the fact that stepfamily therapy is rarely mentioned. Among the pioneers of family therapy, only Virginia Satir (1967) discussed the remarried family at any length. As suggested earlier in this chapter, for many theorists to have made special provisions for each different family composition would have been seen as negating the general applicability of their own theory.

Stepfamily therapy was formed and elucidated by theorists and clinicians who became aware of the glaring void of information that was applicable to this family type. Some had experienced living in stepfamilies and found that they needed to better understand what was happening in their own lives, while others found themselves with a number of stepfamilies in their clinical practice and were unsure how to proceed.

As early as the 1960s, researchers recognized the importance of studying this type of family (Bernard, 1956; Bowerman & Irish, 1962; Fast & Cain, 1966) and those working with stepfamilies described them as an exciting and challenging population (Visher & Visher, 1979). However, several questions have continued to both fascinate and perplex researchers and clinicians: Why is the remarried family so often a clinical challenge? Is it simply the structural complexity of these families, or is there an inherent problem caused by the addition of a new authority figure to an already established family system?

In addition, therapists have attempted to treat this unique family type with therapeutic methods that were not specifically designed to be responsive to their special problems. It was not until the late 1970s, when Visher and Visher authored *Stepfamilies: A Guide to Working with Stepparents and Stepchildren* (1979), that it became clear that therapy with stepfamilies demanded unique skills.

The 1980s produced an explosion of clinical information on stepfamilies. Visher and Visher continued their writings (1982b, 1988a, 1989, 1990, 1991) on stepfamily therapy. The 1988a publication was an excellent compilation of theoretical considerations and clinical intervention strategies. Carter and McGoldrick's 1988 work is another example of clinicians who are dedicated to providing colleagues with an understanding of the process of remarriage and suggests clinical methods of addressing the problems that are unique to stepfamilies (e.g., triangulation). Finally, the systemic aspect of the stepfamily was expanded by Ahrons and Rodgers (1987) in their description of the binuclear family system. Their book created a fuller understanding of the dilemmas facing stepfamilies.

All these authors have done an excellent job in describing the stepfamily system, and they have begun to establish therapy models tailored to the specific needs of stepfamilies. The treatment suggested by different stepfamily therapists establishes certain goals and interventions. This chapter continues the development toward a comprehensive stepfamily therapy by addressing the common mistakes of family therapists working with stepfamilies and proposes positive alternatives to applying uniform interventions with all families.

The honored role played by the early theorists and pioneers of family therapy in the history of psychotherapy is well-deserved. In challenging the status quo of treating the individual patient, they achieved an epistemological shift in the understanding of what therapy is and does. The following critique is not intended to question the tenets or efficacy of the theories postulated by the originators of family therapy. Rather, the critique offered here is meant to examine how established theories set forth precedents that caused confusion and inconsistent clinical results when applied to stepfamilies.

My primary argument is that the generic application of general systems theory to all family types serves the stepfamily only poorly. First, a discussion of specific tenets that are common in traditional family therapies will be offered. This is followed by an examination of how to apply systemic notions to the stepfamily in a manner that respects the unique realities experienced by each of the stepfamily subsystems.

COMMON PRACTICES OF FAMILY THERAPY

Inviting Entire Families into Sessions

Formerly, family therapists were taught that in order to conduct effective therapy, the entire family must be present (Bell, 1975). Any missing member posed a significant problem because the *family* was seen as the patient. Therefore, without the entire family present, the patient was not present. A systems orientation dictates that the clinician must never lose sight of the family system as a whole. In fact, it was not unusual for family therapists to request that a family leave if all the members could not be present, and only return when the family was complete. This approach further reinforced the notion that an initial session required all family members to present an honest picture of family rules and patterns.

Later, as subsystem therapy became more widely accepted, a common pattern was to see the entire family first, and then to concentrate on various subsystems (Haley, 1976). Among the pioneers of systems-based family therapy, only Bowen (1972) suggested that meaningful change could occur without the presence of the entire family. Bowen's acceptance of subgroups and interest in individuation made his approach more applicable to stepfamilies than the approaches of many of his contemporaries.

Throughout the growth of family therapy, theorists have established strong reasons for seeing all members involved early in treatment. Virginia Satir (1967) suggested that this was necessary in some families in order to track the family communication. Although Satir frequently saw the couple first, her public teaching, which was preserved through presentations and videotapes, showed her involving whole families in hearing each other's messages. As they hear these messages, the clinical hope is that family members will begin "to see old situations with new eyes." The process involved having families facilitate here-and-now experiences in order to experience real affect.

When a family is focusing on an intensely felt issue, an important question is whether stepfamilies with no significant history will be best served by direct communication between family members early in treatment. Can the family that may never have experienced any significant period of stability be served by a model suggesting "family reconstruction"? Although the term sounds well-suited to working with stepfamilies, the therapist must remember that frequently, the family is hovering on the edge of deconstruction. The following example is based on a session in which causing direct communication to occur among stepfamily members was a clinical error.

The Johnson family came to therapy as a consequence of tremendous stress being felt by all family members. Phillip, the stepfather, was "glad to do his bit to help Sandy." Sandy, the biological daughter to Lisa and stepdaughter to Phillip, was perceived as a "holy terror" by Phillip and "someone with a big heart and a lot of pain" by Lisa. Before any significant clinical rapport could be established, the family responded to the clinician's opening inquiry with direct, honest communication. Phillip stated that Sandy was headed for a life of crime and that her lack of respect would assure her failure in the business world. He suggested that she was "too disgusting to be able to be loved by a man." Lisa responded quickly and with anger. She stated that Phillip was completely "unsuited to help raise a teenager. In fact," continued Lisa, "if I had been aware of his issues with control, I wouldn't have married him." Sandy, who had been silent to this point finally looked up to her mother and said, "Why did you ever marry this asshole?" Phillip's chair flew back, and he turned to Lisa, saying only, "See?"

After further discussion, it was found that all these statements had been said previously but usually only to a single receiver, and never with a therapist present. Lisa had commented to Sandy that Phillip was not used to dealing with teenage girls, Phillip had expressed his concern for Sandy's future, given her attitudes, and Sandy had certainly suggested to Lisa that Phillip was not the perfect choice. Although the messages discussed in the initial session were not original, they only served to solidify each member's position in the early stages of treatment. Without the buffer of a shared family history, such cataclysmic statements can produce a more rigid clinical impasse than existed prior to the initial session. An alternative that can temper the power, and consequently, the crisis, of an all-inclusive initial session is to select a subgroup for the initial interview.

Establishing a stepfamily involves numerous changes and adjustments. Stress is created by the increased complexity of the family, conflicting loyalties, and the assumption of immediate love (Pasley & Ihinger-Tallman, 1982). An emphasis on seeing the entire family allows a therapist to receive information that was previously left unspoken or that had not been spoken in the presence of all family members. Statements made in the presence of a therapist that are driven by extreme anger and frustration may create an environment that is poorly suited to the development of trust necessary for therapeutic intervention. Clinical experience with stepfamilies results in questions regarding whether including all members of the stepfamily in the initial session or sessions is as useful as it seems to be with first-marriage families.

Although seeing the stepfamily as a series of subsystems may seem logical, it must be recognized that doing so goes against a basic premise of family therapy. The pioneers of family therapy began therapy with entire families and recommended that this was necessary in order to get a true picture of the issues and dynamics of the family. Thus, the precedent was established. More recently, an equally influential school of family therapy also has recommended seeing the members of the entire family in the first session. The Milan Associates, which included Selvini Palazzoli, Boscolo, Checcin, and Prata, made a strong case for the importance of involving all family members in their earliest and most influential treatise, *Paradox and Counterparadox* (1978). The necessity for all or most family members to be present during systemic therapeutic interventions was reinforced and was believed to represent sound clinical practice-and theoretical brilliance. Again, however, stereotyping of the family as the traditional first-marriage family is apparent.

The importance of having all members of the family present in therapy fits with the emphasis of the family therapy model on shared information and the necessity of all persons being privy to it. In support of the concepts espoused by the Milan Associates, Tomm (1984) discussed how family problems occur when an old epistemology come to no longer fit the family's new behavior. In the case of a stepfamily, there is no old epistemology that is shared by all members of the stepfamily. Only relationships that existed prior to the remarriage constitute the one or more "old epistemologies." These relationships represent critical subgroups in stepfamily therapy.

Therefore, in concentrating on the subsystems during the initial therapy session rather than on the entire stepfamily system, the therapist discourages the notion that the stepfamily must be viewed as a single unit. Instead the therapist will more accurately address the stepfamily's true composition. The therapeutic process is meant to parallel the reality of stepfamily life by stabilizing the subsystems with the eventual goal of subsystem integration.

Establishing Hierarchical Boundaries

The Structural school of family therapy is most commonly associated with the concept of establishing hierarchical boundaries. Although Minuchin (1974) dedicated more of his clinical interests to the nontraditional family form than did other theorists (due, in part, to his work in the inner city), he still instructed family therapists to reinforce appropriate boundaries. The boundaries in stepfamilies in which children are brought in from previous marriages are more complex than those of the traditional first-marriage family (Pasley, 1987). Consequently, without an examination of a myriad of contextual variables, any discussion of an appropriate boundary in a stepfamily is unreasonable. This is not to say that stepfamilies never adopt a hierarchical system that is parallel to that of the traditional first-marriage family. In fact, in some stepfamilies, such a system evolves naturally and effectively. For example, in some stepfather families, the new stepfather may, without much discussion or conflict, adopt a role that is indistinguishable from that of a biological father. However, more frequently, stepfathers who attempt to establish such equal parental authority find that neither the parent nor the stepparent see the other as working effectively with the child.

For those therapists who considered themselves Structuralists, a clear agenda existed when dealing with child-related problems in a family context. That agenda includes a commitment to correct dysfunctional hierarchies by putting the parents in charge of the children (Minuchin, 1974). Giles-Sims (1984) discussed the difficulty for a stepparent to become established as a parental figure. Recent work has advocated that stepparents should adopt the role of monitor or supervisor of the stepchildren rather than disciplinarian (Bray et al., 1987; see also Chapter 6 of this volume). Discipline and decision-making actions produce ambiguous results for the stepparent, who is as likely to be censured as to be rewarded for the effort.

Adhering to Structural theory, a therapist might see a stepfamily and correctly diagnose the presence of a coalition between the biological parent and child. The assumption that follows from the diagnosis would normally be that this coalition developed in order to redirect stress away from the couple's relationship. Through family mapping, the usual intervention is to establish the coalitions that exist in the family, and then to work to strengthen the generational boundaries. Although it is frequently well-suited to the traditional first-marriage family, such a move on the part of the therapist can cause a deeper fracture in the structure of the stepfamily.

The following case example examines the experience of a remarried couple and their resulting frustration as they attempted to establish a hierarchical structure compatible with each of their worldviews. The family consists of Jim (the biological father), Sally (the stepmother), and Mark and Shannon (Jim's biological children from his prior marriage). Jim's worldview includes the idea that he wants the very best for Mark. Jim feels guilty that Mark is not happy or successful in high school. Sally believes that she was brought in to be Mark's stepmother and that, as a result, she deserves respect. She also believes that Jim should be willing and capable of supporting her in times of her conflicts with Mark. This segment is from a session to which only Jim and Sally were invited.

Jim: I've been doing my utmost lately, you know, getting Mark ready to go off and live with his mother, natural mother. SJ [Jim's nickname for Sally] has been a real help also.

Therapist: That raises a question for me. I have been wondering, Sally, about your role as stepparent. Are you two clear on what is expected from a stepmom?

[spoken simultaneously]

Jim: Oh yeah, we've worked that out.

Sally: No, I don't think it's clear. *[laughter]* Sometimes I don't think you know what you want me to. . .

Jim: That's not the case, I know, it's just, well, you're hard on him.

Sally: You have no idea how hard it is to ask him to do something, any-thing, and have him just ignore me, or worse.

Therapist: Worse?

Sally: He's really scared me a few times. I thought that he might hit me a couple times I've insisted he do something.

Jim: Come on, he was never going to hit you.

Sally: You have no idea. What does it matter? If I tell, you don't believe me.

Jim: I'm not sure what to do. I feel so guilty. I know he needs more discipline. I love SJ, but I am driven to care for my son.

Therapist: I know you deeply love your son, and this is difficult. I have two questions, however. Is it possible for Sally to give Mark the discipline you feel so uncomfortable providing, and second, why are we only talking about Mark? Shannon is involved in this as well, isn't she?

Sally: *[taking Jim's hand]* Well actually, Shannon does what she is asked, and Jim doesn't seem to feel like he failed with her.

Jim: *[composing himself]* No, with her I was OK, consistent, the whole bit, I don't know why.

The couple represented here works well together, has coped with a difficult child, and remains absolutely committed to staying married. Even with the strength of their strong marital bond, however, the problems of hierarchy defy traditional approaches. The bond between Jim and Mark has ceased to be functional for either person. Mark resents his father's intrusions into his life, and Jim admits to being "overly concerned" about his son. An attempt by the therapist to strengthen the generational boundary by teaching Jim more assertive parenting skills is unlikely to help the situation. Jim's sense that he has "failed" his son causes him to resist forcing Mark to experience fully the outcome of his actions. Indeed, Jim's posture toward Mark will only change if he comes to believe that taking a new tack will benefit both his son and his wife. Given Jim's continued stance, even in the face of logic, it is unlikely that a clinical suggestion aimed at strengthening boundaries will achieve such a goal.

Enactment and Therapeutic Intensity

Two other powerful tools utilized in Structural family therapy are "enactment" and "therapeutic intensity" (Minuchin, 1974). The former tool involves the process of acting out "dysfunctional" familial transactions during the therapy session, while the latter occurs when the therapist delivers a more forceful message or strongly confronts the status quo of the family. A therapist is trained to intervene in the family's process by clearly denoting boundaries or increasing the intensity of the problematic interaction. In doing so, the clinical intention is to solidify or shift boundaries and/or change dysfunctional familial patterns.

In a stepfamily there naturally exists a level of intensity. This intensity is so great that to increase it clinically or to enact a problem situation often will produce a reaction that can be too powerful for the permeable boundaries of the system. In such cases, the members of the stepfamily are likely to retreat from family therapy in uncertainty over whether they can trust that their family is capable of tolerating additional stress.

A disturbing fear that exists for many stepfamilies is the likelihood of redivorce. This fear is made only more real by the fact that it already has been experienced by at least one of the remarried parents. The need for a sense of stability is often paramount in a stepfamily. Any intervention designed to create a crisis in order to restructure it is likely to increase the already present fear of dissolution.

Family Rules

In thinking about a family there is the expectation that rules govern its actions (Jackson & Weakland, 1961). Family rules might include how members speak to each other (e.g., "What mom says is law") or how much should be shared with the therapist (e.g., "Our family's dirty laundry isn't to be openly discussed"). Satir (1972) educated families to recognize the rules of communication organizing the way in which they interact. In doing so, she taught family members to communicate with one another more clearly.

The rules that existed in a previous first-marriage family are often revised or dropped from the remarried family. Even a rule that is retained from one family to the next is no longer the same rule because the family context is more powerful than the content of the actual rule. A change in family membership shifts the rules by which family members live. That is, out of the original context, an old rule will no longer serve the purpose it was intended to achieve.

Stepfamilies also have rules. However, the explication of family rules can undermine the therapeutic agenda. Whereas working to discover the rules of a traditional first-marriage family may lead to some revelations that explain behaviors and communication styles in the home, the stepfamily often lives with a necessary double standard regarding rules. The rule in a previous family that people should immediately discuss an issue when someone bothers them serves the first-marriage stable family better than a stepfamily. When such a rule is put into practice in the remarried family, behavior that previously assisted open communication may come to alienate stepfamily members.

The following example examines how a rule that is supposedly accepted by both parties of a remarried couple serves to alienate rather than unify the two. The family consists of Chris, Mark, Sean, and Patty. Chris is the biological mother of Patty and stepmother to Sean. Mark is the biological father to Sean and stepfather to Patty. In both spouses' first marriages, there had been a standing rule that no one entered the master bedroom if the door was closed. The only exception was that the rule was void in the case of an emergency.

Chris: Well, at least we have private time at night.

Mark: Oh yeah, when the wind blows the door shut.

Chris: Now what? We have the rule, which I have no objection to by the way, but we have the rule, and you open that door as often as I do.

Mark: Patty comes in with a broken nail, and it's an emergency.

Chris: I knew you'd get that one. . .

Mark: OK, I'm listening, how is that one an emergency?

Chris: We're getting off the point. You want privacy, we've got the rule. That's that.

Mark: No, I want to understand this. Patty comes in almost every night. Have I asked her to leave?

Chris: You've done everything but. . .

Mark: But I've never asked her to leave. Sean comes in twice in the
            past 4 months and both times you asked us to talk in the other
            room so you could sleep.

            The rule is that an emergency is necessary to open the door. Sean
            asked to come in, he was crying, I call that an emergency.

Chris: Patty is older than Sean and what is an emergency for her is differ-
            ent than an emergency for him. Patty might be worried about
            what is going to happen the next day, or she's worried about a
            serious problem that a friend is having.

It becomes increasingly clear that neither parent feels that the rule is being
abused by their biological child. However, they do believe that the rule is being
ignored by their stepchild. Their next move is to try to even the playing field
by bringing in other factors.

Chris: Well, at least Sean has Marty [Sean's biological mother]. Walt
            [Patty's biological father] doesn't even call Patty.

Mark: Meaning?

Chris: Meaning that Patty has no one else to go to. Sean can save up
            and talk to Marty, who does Patty have besides me? Plus it's
            even harder for Patty because she sees you with Sean.

Mark: Oh I get it, now I'm really guilty because I'm a better father than
            Walt.

Chris: All I'm saying is that you could be more involved when Patty
            comes in at night to talk.

Mark: When it is an emergency or when it isn't an emergency?

Chris: Dammit Mark, when Patty comes in, for her it's an emergency
            and I'm not about to ask her to leave. If it is something stupid,
            like needing nail polish, I give it to her and she leaves.

In the past, for each spouse, an emergency was something that could not wait
until the next day. As is common in many families, no strict rules defining emergency were needed. It was generally assumed that if a child needed to get in to
see his or her parents at night after the door was closed, something serious was

occurring. If abused, the rule would simply be reinforced by both members of the couple.

In the stepfamily serving as the example here, however, the definition of emergency had been so stretched that in effect the rule no longer existed. Both spouses felt that if their biological child needed to speak to them, no matter what time of day or night, nothing should interfere with assuring the child that he or she remained extremely important in the eyes of the parent. Each adult also believed that his or her biological child presented situations that did, in fact, merit opening the bedroom door.

The rule regarding entrance into the bedroom is not at issue here. The therapist who worked with a stepfamily to determine how this rule could be strengthened or revised would miss the issues that are critical to stepfamily living. Instead, the example demonstrates a typical evolution in which the topic moves from a rule to a deeper question of parental responsibility. The rule only was used as a way to strike out at the other adult. Indeed, Mark discussed what merited an emergency only after Chris had begun to request that Mark be more involved as a stepfather. The rule itself had long since disappeared as a legitimate clinical issue.

The Assumption that Behind All Child-Focused Problems Is a Marital Problem

A familiar axiom for family therapists is that a child's behavior problem serves as a warning signal of marital distress. Minuchin, Rosman, and Baker (1978) discussed their hypothesis that couples mask their difficulties by attending to the needs of a "sick" child. The concept that a child's behavior reflected the needs of the marital dyad was incorporated and made more sophisticated by Selvini Palazzoli (1974). He suggested that all behaviors in a family exist in a mutually supportive manner and that therefore, each action by an individual served to continue the patterns of the system.

Family therapists frequently utilize the concept of symptom functionality by looking at the systemic ramifications of a child's behavior. The concept provides the clinician with a theoretical backdrop that is useful in understanding the systemic nature of problem behavior rather than its linear nature. Common sense suggests that there could be no harm in focusing on the marital subsystem even if a child's problem was the presenting problem. However, research and clinical experience suggest otherwise.

In studying stepfamily relationships, research suggests that the quality of the stepparent-stepchild relationship is more critical than that of the marital relationship in predicting family functioning (see, as examples, Anderson & White, 1986; Crosbie-Burnett, 1984). In addition to supporting these earlier findings, Brown, Green, and Druckman (1990) also postulated that the "family therapy axiom that there is marital distress in families with child-focused problems does not seem to hold true" (p. 565).

It is not uncommon that those who work clinically with stepfamilies misconstrue the concept of the function of the system into a direct correlation between a child's behavior and the quality of the marriage. In so doing, the marriage becomes the focus of treatment rather than the parent-child and stepparent-child relationships. Often, however, the assumption of the marriage's centrality to the resolution of the stepfamily's problems only serves to obstruct necessary clinical interventions required by the more critical subsystems within the stepfamily.

Establishing a Mutually Agreed upon Problem

Therapists who adhere to the strategic models proposed by the Mental Research Institute (MRI; see Fisch, Weakland, & Segal, 1982) and Haley (1976) focus on the problem that brings the client to treatment. Finding a workable and observable problem is frequently considered necessary for therapy to progress. Practicing within the MRI modality, one utilizes a style of questioning aimed at determining which problem most concerns the client. The client must be a customer, meaning someone who wants change. In the case of a child-based problem, the customer would often be the parental subsystem living with the child. In my view, most first-marriage families are able to agree on some problematic behavior of a child. There *is* frequently a problem; it is not necessarily the most important one to either parent, but is nonetheless a problem that both parents want to see changed. A shared concern helps the therapist begin to understand why the problem is identified as such, to track the sequences of interaction, and to determine the attempted solutions employed by the parents. Frequently, the therapist working within this model patiently helps establish one goal shared by the parental subsystem to the point that the parents agree that the removal of or change in some behavior is considered clinical progress.

As efficient and practical as this model may be for a therapist who is treating first-marriage families, difficulties arise when a therapist adapts it to stepfamilies. Although a common reason for stepfamilies to enter treatment is the existence of some child-based problem (Brown et al., 1990), agreement on a mutual focus is generally far more challenging to achieve. The difficulty in establishing a shared goal may be due to the role ambiguity of the stepparent, as described by Fast and Cain (1966) and later elucidated by Visher and Visher (1979).

Sometimes even challenging the parental subsystem to agree on a uniform concern may prevent one or both adults from being honest with the therapist about their real concern. This is not to say that remarried parents never come to therapy with a uniform concern. However, the presentation of a concern regarding a child often represents two separate concerns on the part of the adults. That is, a stepparent and the biological parent will often view a child's behavior from different perspectives. The biological parent may find it to be disturbing because it represents a greater, personality-based concern, such as an indicator of low self-esteem or depression. On the other hand, the stepparent may see the problem behavior as an indication that the child is incapable of becoming properly socialized. The stepparent may suggest that the child's "rude" behavior will damn him or her to a life of inappropriate social interactions, while the biological parent might view the same behavior, label it as shyness, and look to therapy as a means to bolster the child's confidence. In such a case, there is no "right" description of the behavior. In fact, therapists may find themselves silently agreeing with one position over another, yet siding with either adult on a goal will inevitably disrupt the therapeutic alliance. Each person holds his or her own view sincerely, and each is confident that his or her understanding of the situation is more accurate.

Such a situation is exhibited in the following case example involving the Newly family. The family consists of Mary (biological mother), Fred (stepfather), and Raya (Mary's daughter from a previous marriage, who has no contact with her biological father). The content of the first session reinforces the notion that a single or shared presenting problem cannot be established due to the divergent meanings assigned to Raya's behavior. Only the remarried couple is present at this session.

Therapist: So, what is the problem that brings you both to therapy?

Mary: We are both very worried about Raya. She is having a very hard time adjusting to, this. . . our new family. She seems a little depressed and is very angry at Fred.

Fred: She's angry at me because I'm the first person in years to make her do anything. You would, you know, just let her have her way all the time. I think her problem is a very simple, age-old one: she's spoiled.

Mary: She tries so hard; it take two to tango and you just ignore her efforts.

Fred: That doesn't excuse her for her rudeness toward you and me. I can understand her treating me badly, I don't like it, but I understand it. But you, you've given her everything she has ever wanted, you treat her like an equal, and yet she still can't take 5 minutes to do what you ask. Her attitude is so disrespectful; don't you care how she will be able to deal with other people in the future?

Mary: The future? I am worried about right now. She is learning that the most important man in my life can't stand her.

This segment demonstrates the two perspectives taken by parent and stepparent in regard to a child's behavior. The presenting problem is quite different for Mary than it is for Fred. Mary clearly believes that her daughter continues to be wronged and is forced to suffer a difficult relationship with her stepfather, only reinforcing her belief that any real support will come from her mother. This, in turn, reinforces Mary's overindulgence of Raya because she surmises that she is Raya's only ally. Therefore, a cycle begins in which both members of the remarried couple assume correctly that they are doing the best thing for Raya.

Although both positions can be justified, Mary is Raya's unswerving supporter, while Fred sees Raya acting in a way that will hamper her socialization. Each parent needs to see the bind they have created and recognize its overarching negative impact on the family. Each stepparent and parent takes a position on a child. Some expect too much, while others expect too little; generally, however, their stance can be understood. Referring to the actions of either parental figure as dysfunctional obscures the larger issue. The critical issue is that no person enters a remarriage with the intent to see it fail. The actions taken by each party are done out of the needs of that individual within the context of the family.

In Mary's case, she had survived a extremely difficult period during which she and Raya supported each other emotionally. Mary had seen the pain and insecurity caused Raya by the divorce, and she knew that at times, the only thing that had kept her going was her commitment to the child. This intense time of bonding between the child and the single parent is referred to by Betty Carter as "the foxhole period" (1989). The tendency of a biological parent to have a protective attitude toward his or her child during the early postdivorce period is not unusual. Although this style serves to support the child in times of need, it is often an ineffective parenting style when the child reaches adolescence or after a remarriage. However, to discuss this behavior as dysfunctional represents a failure to understand its previous usefulness.

Fred had entered the situation with every intention of winning Raya over. In fact, during the courtship, Raya had enjoyed Fred and had confided to her mother that "this guy seems nice." Fred had made classic mistakes such as accepting the challenge to begin as a disciplinarian shortly after the remarriage and complaining nonstop to Mary about Raya's behavior. Early in the remarriage, Mary had been grateful for Fred's concern, but she had noticed a knot in her stomach every time Fred implied that Raya was somehow abnormal. Fred loved Mary, and although Raya's comments to her mother were not offensive to his wife, Fred found them infuriating. He felt that Raya insulted her mother. In so doing, Raya insulted the woman he loved.

SUGGESTION FOR CLINICAL PRACTICE

Beginning Stepfamily Therapy

The clinical skills necessary to treat first-marriage families are different from those that are most useful for working with stepfamilies. In an initial call to a therapist, stating one's membership in a stepfamily often creates a series of assumptions and questions for the therapist. However, when the therapist prepares to meet with a stepfamily, numerous questions of inclusion, attitudes, shared children, custody, years of remarriage, and the status of the absent biological parent and of that person's family of origin are generated.

Simply based on the fact that a stepfamily is entering the office, a therapist should question (a) the legal custody arrangement, (b) the visitation policy, (c) the developmental stage of the family now and at the time of remarriage, (d) the presence and acceptance of a mutual child, and (e) the style of parenting utilized in the home. Questions about these topics communicate three valuable messages to the stepfamily. First, such questions show respect for the differences in the experience of various stepfamilies. Second, these questions establish a necessary level of understanding about the family. Third, in this way, the therapist avoids perpetuating expectations that these families should function as a intact, first-marriage family.

The stepfamily entering therapy is taking a substantial risk. Unless its members are among those who believe in preventative counseling, the stepfamily has no doubt reached a point in family life at which unpleasant patterns are occurring. Engaging in therapy with someone who is unfamiliar with this family form will be problematic, so the stepfamily should be encouraged to select a therapist intelligently and with great care. The client(s) should be assured by the therapist that he or she is knowledgeable about stepfamilies. Unfortunately, there is little pressure for therapists who do not treat stepfamilies regularly to seek out supervision. Such supervision is as necessary in working with stepfamilies as it would be if a therapist began seeing a family representing an unfamiliar culture or sexual orientation.

Treating stepfamilies requires a different perspective, some specific knowledge, and remarkable mediating skills (Sager et al., 1983; Visher & Visher, 1988a; Wald, 1981). It is questionable whether traditional family therapy training, even augmented with the stepfamily literature, represents adequate training to assure that a therapist can work effectively with a stepfamily. Even a well-trained family therapist may conceive of the family and the presenting problem in such a way that a stepfamily begins treatment at a disadvantage. This warning is not intended to scare therapists away from working with stepfamilies. Rather, it is meant to assure therapists who are unfamiliar with the nuances of these families that in order to be most helpful, a level of understanding serves as an essential foundation for treatment. In fact, supervision and therapy often become parallel processes.

As the therapist gains an understanding of the patterns that are unique to stepfamilies, a degree of safety for the client stepfamily emerges. This sense of security is likely to be reflected in the success of therapy.

Identifying Subsystems for Therapy

When receiving a call for an appointment from an individual in a stepfamily, a therapist must consider a number of factors: Who is making the call? How have the situation and problem been defined? Does it sound as though there is support for therapy from the family or the former spouse? What clues can be picked up regarding the completion of the "emotional divorce" (Carter & McGoldrick, 1988)? Generally, it is helpful to think in terms of the smallest workable subsystem. Others may be added if the problems described do not rest solely in the relationship between stepmembers. To accommodate the special needs of stepfamilies, the kin network can be conceptualized as including five subsystems: three primary subsystems and two secondary subsystems. The distinction between primary and secondary subsystems is based purely on living arrangements rather than on any difference in perceived importance. Members of the primary subsystem live together as a family, which includes the spousal subsystem, the parent-child or stepparent-stepchild subsystem, and the sibling subsystem. In the case of a family in which both adults have stepchildren living within the home, a fourth primary subsystem is constituted of stepsiblings. For clinical reasons, a mutual child is certainly a relevant factor in the home; however, he or she does not constitute another primary subsystem.

The secondary subsystems are composed of one member from the primary subsystems and another member living outside of that home. These subsystems include the remarried couple (legal marriage is not necessarily mandated for this status), the biological parent and his or her child or children, and the stepparent and his or her stepchild or stepchildren. The secondary subsystems also include the former spouse(s) of the remarried couple and any residential biological parent-child(ren) subsystems not already identified (e.g., a nonresidential parent and his or her biological child living with the remarried parent and stepparent). These subsystems are quite important and can be critical to the functioning of the overall kin network. Their inclusion frequently achieves significant results in cases where there is a great deal of miscommunication affecting daily life in the primary home.

In most cases, the caller him- or herself is a sure bet for inclusion in the first clinical session. Additional people will then be added as therapy progresses. Assuming that the caller is the parent or stepparent, a critical question will be to determine whether the spouse is willing to attend. Working in this manner, the therapist can choose not to invite the children to the first session unless the stepparent refuses to attend. In that case, it is best to begin with the biological parent-child subsystem.

The pattern that emerges in following this model is that the various family members are seen by the clinician in clusters, with each cluster involving a different subsystem. As therapy progresses, a combination of subsystems are seen. Frequently, the most common composition in the first session is limited to the first primary subsystem: the remarried couple. The second session can either be a continuation of the first or a meeting with the subsystem that includes the residential biological parent and her or his child(ren). In designing the therapy to involve the participating members in this manner, the emphasis is to address the separate concerns of each subsystem first rather than artificially imposing on the stepfamily an agenda that was designed for a first-marriage family. The time necessary to address the separate concerns of the first two primary subsystems can vary. Several sessions with each subsystem are usually necessary before attending to a combination of or different subsystems. The advantages of forming a therapeutic alliance with two of the primary subsystems far outweighs the disavantage of information not being shared simultaneously among all family members. In fact, an understanding of how information is shared across subsystems is of value when the entire stepfamily is eventually seen together.

When the two primary subsystems have both made clinical progress, regardless of how distinct their goals are from one another, the third primary subsystem should be invited into treatment. This subsystem is extremely important for the success of the stepfamily, as indicated by the research of Brown and colleagues (1990). This third primary subsystem should be brought into treatment as soon as the first two primary subsystems have achieved some degree of stability.

Education as a Necessary Foundation for Treatment

With any of the subsystems it is necessary to encourage adjunct education to coincide with treatment. Education of this sort may take the form of bibliotherapy or attendance in a stepfamily group, and can normalize for clients their own experience as they are exposed to some of the disturbing factors of stepfamily living that are actually relatively common.

The therapist must help each subsystem member feel that his or her concern is worthy of support. Members of a stepfamily frequently fail to support the concerns of other members because for some, such support is tantamount to giving up on the stepfamily. The therapist should help each person see that his or her reality is understandable and that frustration is normal. This support needs to occur in front of other members of the subsystem so that they can begin to hear the other person's reality as well as receive support for their position. The challenge for the clinician is to avoid choosing sides and to remember that each person's position is a natural outgrowth of his or her fear about the possible dissolution of the family.

Once individuals no longer feel blamed for their views and behavior, questioning the usefulness of holding such views becomes important. It may be that imagining that one's stepchild will "never amount to anything" is an unnecessary concern once that same stepparent begins to establish a relationship with the child: a new relationship that is unencumbered by the misperceptions and anger that previously accompanied the relationship. Frequently, individuals know that what they are doing does not work but are unsure that any alternative would be preferable. It is the therapist's job to assist the client in identifying unhelpful assumptions and exploring possible changes in both thoughts and behaviors.

Agreeing upon a Problem

Stepfamily members often approach therapy with different agendas and goals. Due to a desire to avoid strong disagreements, a single goal may be agreed on that does not actually represent the true focus of one of the adult members. Typically, the goal raised by a stepparent for his or her stepchild runs contrary to the convictions of the biological parent, and visa versa. Therefore, some consideration should be made to addressing separate goals for each of the subsystems. Returning now to the Newly family (used as an example earlier), the therapist can intervene in the following manner:

Therapist: Mary, Fred, let me stop you here for a minute and discuss what I'm seeing happen here. Each of you has a separate concern about Raya, and each of you is justified in your concern. I know I sound like I'm trying to pull a rabbit out of a hat here, but I'm not. I'm very serious. Mary, you had years alone with Raya where you knew that she depended almost entirely on you. That sense of responsibility doesn't go away because you fell in love. Fred, you're not used to seeing a daughter being so familiar with her mother, but following a divorce that often happens. You're concerned that her behavior is not only aggravating in the home, but you also worry about her future socialization. Each of you can justify your position, but there is also a flaw in each of your arguments. I'm not interested in having either of you convince the other or convince me, I'm already convinced you're both right.

Mary: If we're both right, what can we do now?

Therapist: You both have to decide what concerns you about Raya's behavior. If in fact it is something that you can influence, then we begin work on that. Where we draw the line is in trying to convince the other person that your goal is the real goal--that runs straight into trouble. Remember, you're both right. Arguing your position only hurts.

Mary: Like I said before, I think she's depressed.

Therapist: What would be one indication that she is not depressed?

This approach is then followed for both members of the couple. Each works on their goal, with the other hearing their progress and concerns but without the couple being asked to work together. In so doing, the therapist takes the position of respecting the systemic interaction of family members while accenting personal control for subsystem members. Taking on a separate goal for her husband in regard to Raya also allows Mary to complain about her daughter and to feel occasional frustration.

In a first-marriage family, the parents often switch positions, being alternately supportive of and frustrated by their child(ren). In other words, the child may feel closer to one parent than the other but then grow to feel closer to the other (Richardson, Galambos, Schulenberg, & Peters, 1984). This switching allows normal frustrations to be vented without increasing the family's overall feeling of stress or alienation. On the other hand, the stepfamily is usually not in a position to enjoy this process, which I call the "alternating advocate." Instead, the stepfamily evolves in such a way that the biological parent becomes the "fixed advocate" of the child(ren), even during those times when he or she is annoyed with the child's behavior. The frustration experienced by biological parents may explain the research findings. Browning (1987) suggested that children in stepfamilies perceive their biological parents to be less supportive than do children in first-marriage families. Brown and associates (1990) similarly reported that stepchildren in therapy perceived their biological parents to be less supportive than did stepchildren not in therapy, who also rated their biological parents.

Clinically it is useful to encourage the biological parent to allow him- or herself to return to acting as an "alternating advocate" for the child. Rather than feeling that he or she must either defend or ignore those aspects of the child's behavior that are not pleasing, the parent can be encouraged to discuss the wide range of feelings that he or she holds for the child(ren). If this can take place in front of a supportive spouse, it makes for a better intervention. If a supportive spouse is not available, however, a group is an effective adjunct treatment. When the biological parent finds her- or himself in the role of a "fixed advocate," a resulting frustration and tendency to pull away from the child can occur. Over an extended period of time, feeling driven to always defend one's offspring can make the parent feel disenchanted and emotionally removed from the child.

Working with the biological parent-child subsystem allows the parent to hear the concerns of his or her child, focus on the well-being of the child without the pressure of being observed by the new spouse, and discuss aspects of the larger kin network, which is frequently left unmentioned. The therapist follows a path similar to what was established with the parental subsystem. That is, each person's concerns are listened to, and the reality of his or her view is explored and supported. This subsystem frequently benefits simply from having time to reconnect.

The stepparent-stepchild subsystem should enter into work having already discussed this particular meeting during other subsystem meetings. The purpose of this meeting is to establish (if none exists elsewhere) a safe environment for members of this subsystem to make contact with one another. Utilizing a technique for conflicted couples, the therapist takes charge, assuring that no interaction will escalate into open conflict. Simply increasing the rapport of those involved in this subsystem is the goal. Eventually, however, the goal expands to include the integration of the stepfamily. Here, the outcome is not to blend these separate families into one but rather recognize that the stepfamily and extended kin network or binuclear family constitutes a system in its own right. Members need to know that there is safety in living as a stepfamily. While each subsystem remains critical to the functioning of the whole, the therapist's role is to reinforce this movement.

Therapy is frequently quite helpful with all types of families, and stepfamilies are no exception. However, there are different rules that must be respected and observed for the sake of both therapist and client when working with stepfamilies rather than first-marriage families. If they feel a sense of safety, a family will frequently feel capable of experimenting with options. Without feeling safe, however, a stepfamily will cling to familiar patterns, no matter how destructive they have become.

CONCLUSIONS

The model advocated in this chapter remains aligned with the basic tenets of systemic thought. However, the model offers specific alterations in clinical practice that are necessary to effectively treat stepfamilies. In addressing the separate stepfamily subsystems, one is more free to accept and understand the experience of each member of the stepfamily. It is not uncommon for a dilemma to exist whereby one member's perception of reality is not shared by other members. It is here that the clinical orientation toward addressing subsystem clusters provides the most workable format to assist all involved parties to gain an empathic understanding of each other's perceptions, as well as to address their own concerns.

KEY CHAPTER POINTS

1. The theories and techniques originally set forth as the basis of family therapy created a series of precedents that hinder effective clinical work with stepfamilies.

2. Six tenets that are common in traditional family therapy were critically evaluated for their utility in clinical work with stepfamilies, including the tradition of inviting the entire family into sessions and the use and enactment of therapeutic intensity.

3. Clinical practice is enhanced when therapists are well educated about the

stepfamily dynamics that set them apart from first-marriage families. Supervision is a necessary part of becoming well educated.

4. Subsystems therapy with different dyads is the recommended starting place for clinical intervention, followed by therapy with different combinations of subsystems in the stepfamily.

5. Educational intervention must accompany therapy.

6. Therapists must encourage stepfamily members to work on separate goals or problems, as shared goals or problems may be more difficult to identify. This allows the biological parent to become an "alternating advocate" for his or her child.

Chapter 11

THE INTERFACE BETWEEN STEPPARENT FAMILIES AND SCHOOLS: RESEARCH, THEORY, POLICY, AND PRACTICE

Margaret Crosbie-Burnett

Our schools are social institutions. As such, their policies and practices are based on ideologies about life in the United States. The policies and practices that relate to students' families usually assume biological, first-marriage families with the husband as breadwinner and the wife as homemaker, because historically, this family structure was the norm, both statistically and culturally (Davis, 1988; Hareven, 1987). However, the demographic character of American family life has been changing rapidly (Teachman et al., 1987), and educational institutions have not adequately adjusted to the changes that currently affect large numbers of students.

The purpose of this chapter is to make a contribution toward improving relations between schools and stepfamilies by identifying areas of needed change. The chapter begins by discussing how the needs of children and adults in stepfamilies often are ignored or misunderstood by school personnel. This is followed by a review of relevant scholarly publications that explores the various aspects of the interface between stepfamilies and schools. Then, a presentation of theoretical approaches through which to examine this interface and promote needed change is offered. The chapter concludes with a series of recommendations for changes in policy and practice based on a broadened conceptualization of the family.

SCHOOLS AND STEPFAMILIES

Demographic Change

One major change in the structure of the American family is an increase in the number and variety of stepfamilies. In 1987, 7.0% of all minor children were stepchildren living with a remarried parent; another 2.4% of minor children were stepchildren living with a cohabiting parent, including both previously married and never-married parents (Bumpass, Sweet, & Cherlin, 1991; Sweet, 1991). However, these figures do not include children who live primarily with a single parent and spend time with a nonresidential, recoupled, or remarried parent. They also do not include college-aged stepchildren, who often are financially and emotionally dependent on parental figures. Also not included in the statistics are children who live in stepfamilies and are born after the remarriage or recoupling. In addition, because the available statistics are based on data collected at only one point in time, they grossly underestimate the number of children who live in stepfamilies at some point during their childhood or adolescence. Despite statistics that suggest that stepfamilies are fast becoming the norm, there has been a reluctance to acknowledge them as an integral part of contemporary life.

Psychosocial Implications of Demographic Change

Becoming a stepchild is often a stressful transition for children (Hetherington et al., 1985; Wallerstein & Kelly, 1980), adolescents (Duberman, 1975; Lutz, 1983; Strother & Jacobs, 1984), and young adults (Crosbie-Burnett, 1987). The remarriage of a parent means an expansion of one's family into a more complex family system, with many concomitant financial, psychological, and emotional adjustments (Crosbie-Burnett, Skyles, & Becker-Haven, 1988; Sager et al., 1983; Visher & Visher, 1979). Making this adjustment more difficult for children is the lack of understanding about, and support for, their concerns in the various microsystems in which they live: schools, religious groups, athletic teams, and even the family. For example, some children do not get permission from parents or other adults to express anxiety or unhappiness about parental remarriage because marriage, by definition, is supposed to be a happy occasion in our culture. Consequently, schools are in a vital position to help support children during such transitions by giving them a safe place to express and explore their feelings, questions, and concerns about parental remarriage.

As a result of our cultural ideology about the family, and despite contemporary family demographics, schools do not usually consider the uniqueness of the structural and psychosocial aspects of stepfamilies in their policies and practices (Crosbie-Burnett, et al., 1988; Crosbie-Burnett & Skyles, 1989; Pasley & Ihinger-Tallman, 1986). For example, stepchildren are often members of two different households and in which they may have three or four parent figures. Some of these children experience loyalty conflicts or must deal with other emotional issues with respect to these parents. Meanwhile, school policies and practices are created that relate only to a single legal mother and father. This becomes problematic in terms of activities ranging from parent-teacher conferences to making cards or gifts for "Mom" for Mother's Day. Furthermore, the student's most important psychological parent may be a stepparent, who may or may not be the legal parent. Other examples of the unique needs of stepfamilies relate to school forms and notices. Too often, school notices are sent home with students on Fridays, the day on which some children go to stay at the nonresidential household. Therefore, the residential household does not receive important information on school matters. Moreover, stepparents are rarely included on official forms that request family information. Without legal adoption, the stepparent has no legal status as a parent and is, therefore, often invalidated as a contributing parent figure by the school system.

A Need for Change in the Schools

It is clear that the time has come for education to take a proactive stance toward acknowledging and responding to stepchildren and their families. The family-school relationship is at risk for stepfamilies because that relationship depends on mutual trust and understanding; too many administrators, teachers, and other school professionals lack knowledge of, and skills in relating to, families other than biological, first-marriage families (Shea, 1982).

At present, one of two rather contradictory processes occurs frequently. One possiblity is that (a) schools perpetuate the invisibility of stepfamilies by relating to all two-parent families as though they were biological, first-marriage families. (This is more likely to be the case when the adults and children in the family have the same surname.) When this happens at the level of school-family relations, the rights and responsibilities of nonresidential, biological parents are ignored and the residential stepparent may be treated as though he or she is the biological parent. This is usually inappropriate. At the level of school staff-student relations, stepchildren are grouped with children in biological, first-marriage families in the minds of school personnel. This can mean that staff members unintentionally speak insensitively to a student about "Mom" or "Dad." It also means that the student will not be identified for special services. For example, students from stepfamilies are often excluded from a support group for children of divorce. Alternatively (b), at both the family-school relations and the school staff-student relations levels, members of stepfamilies are grouped with members of divorced families. In this situation, the school does not acknowledge the contributions of stepparents, and school staff may be insensitive to any additional psychological issues (e.g., competition between the biological father and stepfather or the delicate nature of step relationships) with which stepfamily members cope.

REVIEW OF RELEVANT RESEARCH

Research that addresses the interface between stepfamilies and the schools has not been systematically guided by theory. Empirical research has been conducted in three areas: (a) atheoretical comparisons between children in remarried families and other types of families on a variety of variables that are relevant to success in school (e.g., grades, scores on standardized tests, or relations with peers at school), (b) tests for bias against stepfamilies in educational materials and among school professionals, and (c) evaluations of school-based, psychological interventions with children. (Some of these interventions have been based in psychological theory.) In addition to research, there is a literature on school policy and practice. This consists of position papers written by school-based professionals who have recognized the unique needs of their students from remarried families. Most of this literature calls for change in the educational system but fails to outline specific recommendations. The group of stepchildren living in first-marriage households (children born to unmarried mothers who later marry) has not yet been addressed in the stepfamily literature, let alone the school-family literature. These empirical studies are addressed in greater detail below.

Comparative Studies

Stepchildren and schools. Most of the research on the interface between stepfamilies and schools has focused on comparisons between the school-based social and academic performance of stepchildren in remarried families and children in first-marriage families. However, the results of these studies are inconclusive. Utilizing a representative national sample, one study reported that adolescents in stepfamilies earned lower grades than did adolescents in first-marriage families (Dornbusch et al., 1987). Stepchildren's grades also were found to be significantly lower than grades of children in first-marriage families in two smaller studies of white, middle-class junior high school students (Kurdek & Sinclair, 1988; Mensink & Sawatzky, 1989).

Contrary to these results, a second study using a large, nationally representative sample found *no* difference among children whether residing with two biological parents, a single-parent, or a stepparent, on grades, achievement test scores, absenteeism, aspirations, or discipline problems in school (Marsh, 1990). These findings are supported with findings from smaller studies. For example, Mensink and Sawatzky (1989) reported no differences between the three groups of children on achievement test scores. Similarly, Kurdek and Sinclair (1988) found no differences on verbal achievement test scores, absenteeism, or number of detentions for these groups. However, they did find lower scores for stepchildren on quantitative achievement tests.

Several authors have suggested why these findings are mixed. Family environment, especially parenting style and parent-child relationships, have been identified as factors that covary with school achievement, regardless of family structure. In the Kurdek and Sinclair (1988) study, family structure accounted for only 7% of the variance in academic performance but family environment accounted for 10%. Not surprising, a family environment that emphasized an achievement orientation and encouraged intellectual and cultural pursuits, as measured by two subscales of the Family Environment Scale (Moos & Moos, 1981), was associated with better grades for all groups of children. Similarly, Dornbusch and colleagues (1987) found that adolescents' grades were positively related to an authoritative (as opposed to authoritarian or permissive) parenting style, regardless of family structure. A study of the relationship between high school students' grades and their perceptions of their relationships with parents showed the relationship with the biological mother to be the best predictor of school achievement across all family structures (Crosbie-Burnett & Landfried, 1987).

In summary, psychosocial factors in the family, and especially parent-child relations, appear to be better predictors of children's school success than family structure. However, the results reported above suggest that these psychosocial factors may covary with family structure. In other words, on the average, parent-child relations may be worse in stepfamilies than in first-marriage families. Two possible interpretations of these findings are that the stresses of divorce and remarriage negatively affect psychosocial factors in the family or, alternatively, that those persons who have lower ability for positive family relationships divorce and remarry more frequently than those who are more capable.

In studies of teachers' subjective reports of children's behavior problems, stepchildren were reported to have more behavior problems than children in first-marriage families (Crosbie-Burnett, 1988; Touliatos & Lindholm, 1980). School counselors also reported having more problem-related contact with stepchildren than with children from first-marriage or single-parent families (Crosbie-Burnett, 1988). Children's self-reports are consistent with the reports of teachers and counselors. In a study of white lower- and middle-class 5th to 10th graders, children in first-marriage families reported better school adjustment and better peer relations than did stepchildren (Nunn, Parish, & Worthing, 1983).

Parents, stepparents, and schools. Few studies have directly addressed school-family relations. With respect to school-parent contact, Dornbusch and associates (1987) found that stepparents are less active than biological parents in school affairs. Perhaps this is explained by reports of both stepparents and nonresidential parents that they receive poor treatment by school staff (Lutz, Jacobs, & Masson, 1981, 1988). Similarly, Crosbie-Burnett (1988) found that both remarried biological parents and stepparents reported less face-to-face contact with teachers than did parents in first-marriage or single-parent families.

Biases against Stepfamilies

One source of bias is the invisibility of stepfamilies in school texts. Although images of, and text about, single-parent families are now scattered throughout many books, the mention of stepfamilies is noticeably absent (Crosbie-Burnett, 1988). In one study of schoolbooks, lessons in elementary school texts for English, mathematics, science, and social studies included references to biological family members (e.g., mother, father, grandmother, brother, and even fathers or mothers who lived elsewhere), but no references to stepparents, stepchildren, stepsiblings, or half-siblings were found. The only exceptions were chapters within some social studies books that specifically addressed various family types. This example of the cultural invisibility of stepfamilies could be changed readily.

A more blatant bias against stepfamilies was identified in a study of the attitudes of counselors and social workers (Bryan, Ganong, Coleman, & Bryan, 1985). Rating written descriptions of family members in which family structure was identified as either "intact" or "step," subjects rated stepchildren and stepparents more negatively than children and parents from intact, first-marriage families. In a similar study of teacher ratings of fictitious student records in which only family structure was manipulated, stepchildren were evaluated as worse than children in first-marriage families on academic, social, and emotional functioning (Guttman & Broudo, 1988-1989). In addition, some teachers in a study (Mensink & Sawatsky, 1989) negatively changed their ratings of students when they were told that the student was a stepchild.

These findings have important implications for school-based studies. They *call into question nearly all the results of studies that use school grades and ratings of students by school staff as dependent measures*. School staff who know children well enough to give grades or other ratings often know the family structure of these children, especially in elementary and middle schools. Therefore, all the results of studies using such data may be biased against stepchildren. In order to correct this problem, research subjects reporting on children would have to be blind to family structure; this would eliminate most school staff members who know the students well enough to make subjective ratings of them. Behavioral observations by persons outside the school system could be one answer to this problem.

School-based Interventions for Stepchildren

School-based interventions for children experiencing family change have consisted of small, time-limited, structured support groups conducted by counselors, social workers, or psychologists. Most of these groups have a postdivorce rather than stepfamily emphasis. While researchers continue to refine effective curricula for these groups, studies have documented that they can help children cope with family restructuring. Interventions can modify beliefs and attitudes about family change, teach coping behaviors (Anderson, Kinney & Gerler, 1984), reduce anxiety (Pedro-Carroll & Cowen, 1985), reduce depression (Crosbie-Burnett & Newcomer, 1990), and improve self-concept (Stolberg & Garrison, 1985). Although these groups have focused on children's experiences of parental divorce, there is every reason to believe that such groups could be equally successful in directly addressing children's experiences with parental remarriage or the marriage of a never-married parent. Again, schools are in a powerful position to help. Many children who enter stepfamilies have no other forum in which they feel safe to talk about psychosocial aspects of family life. In addition, reducing anxiety and depression and improving self-esteem should have a positive effect on school performance both academically and socially.

One school-based intervention aimed at increasing the self-esteem of all children, including stepchildren, is the training of teachers. Parish and Philip (1982) intervened with 3rd through 8th grade, midwestern children by teaching their teachers about Maslow's Hierarchy of Needs Model (e.g., the need for belonging is more basic than the need to learn). Then, they were asked to assess their own students' needs and to fulfill them to the best of their ability, over the following weeks. After 1 month, children from first-marriage families reported higher self-esteem. However, the scores for children in single-parent and stepparent families showed no change. The authors offered no explanation for this difference between the groups of children; they concluded only that teachers should have special training about the impact of parental divorce and remarriage on children.

Another school-based study intervened with teachers, counselors, and their students. The assessment of combined didactic and experiential interventions with fifth grade students and their counselors and teachers found that even a 2-hour classroom intervention (Crosbie-Burnett & Pulvino, 1990) and a 4-hour training session with only the teachers and counselors increased family-related communication between teachers and stepchildren more than between teachers and children in other family structures (Crosbie-Burnett, 1988). In addition, after the intervention, teachers and counselors reported feeling more knowledgeable about stepchildren's family experiences and more competent to handle problems and issues that stepchildren might bring to them. Teachers reported anecdotally that the classroom intervention stimulated good feelings and respect among kids from all family types and that there was a lot of giving and sharing of information following the intervention.

Information for School-based Professionals

In addition to the above research, a growing body of practical information for school staff members is now available. This includes information about stepchildren for teachers (Coleman, Ganong, & Henry, 1984; Gray & Pippin, 1984; Skeen, Robinson, & Flake-Hobson, 1984) and counselors (Gardner, 1984; Herlihy, 1984; Kosinski, 1983; Lutz et al., 1981, 1988; Medler, Strother, Dameron, & DeNardo, 1987; Poppen & White, 1984; Strother & Jacobs, 1984; Wilcoxon & Comas, 1987), as well as suggestions for change in school services for stepchildren (Barney, 1990; Pasley & Ihinger-Tallman, 1986). Curriculum for a classroom guidance unit on divorce and remarriage is now available for school-based professionals serving elementary grades through high school (Crosbie-Burnett & Pulvino, 1990). In addition, suggestions for school personnel on how to better relate to stepfamily members were solicited from groups of stepparents and have been summarized by Manning and Wootten (1987).

Clinicians and researchers alike have concluded that school staff members are in a key position to provide continued structure and support for children who are adjusting to the restructuring of their families. Furthermore, school-based counselors, social workers, and psychologists can play a crucial role in helping stepchildren function successfully in school and, to some extent, at home (Appel, 1985; Poppen & White, 1984; Strother & Jacobs, 1984; Wallerstein & Bundy, 1984). Apparently, however, school personnel are not receiving the necessary training: 62% of the school counselors in one statewide study reported that the most critical deficit in their training was knowledge about "changing family structures" (Olson, 1986).

THEORETICAL APPROACHES TO EDUCATIONAL CHANGE

At present, the status of knowledge about the interface between schools and stepfamilies is mainly a collection of results from atheoretical research studies. We do not know *why* some studies found stepchildren to perform worse in school than children in first-marriage families while others did not. We do not know *why* bias against stepchildren exits. We do not understand fully *why* or *how* support groups in schools have been shown to change the self-esteem, depression, anxiety, beliefs, attitudes, and behaviors of postdivorce children, and improve family-related communication between teachers and stepchildren. However, most of the intervention studies are grounded in some variation of social-cognitive-behavioral theory (Crosbie-Burnett & Lewis, 1993) and group psychotherapy theory (Yalom, 1985). We certainly do not understand *why* teacher training about human needs was associated with an increase in self-esteem for children from first-marriage families but not for children in single-parent or stepparent homes, as in the Parish and Philip study (1982). Clearly, theory is useful to help explain the observations reported in the studies described above.

More important, if future research in this area is guided systematically by theory, our understanding will be deepened. Perhaps, various types of theory are needed: sociological theory to explain observations of relations between the family and the school as social institutions, social psychological theory to explain social cognitions and behaviors between individuals (e.g., teachers and parents, or counselors and students), and psychological theories to explain the performance at school (e.g., grades and behavior) of stepchildren as compared to other children.

Family Stress Theory

Although little of the relevant research has been theory-driven, there is some treatment of the interface between schools and stepfamilies in the theoretical writings. The relationship between stepfamilies and education was addressed in an application of Family Stress Theory to the adjustment involved in remarriage (Crosbie-Burnett, 1989a). Family Stress Theory was created originally from Hill's studies of separation and reunion of family members during World War II. Although it has since been developed and improved (Boss, 1987), Hill's (1949, 1958), the basic ABC-X model is still the heart of the theory. In this model, A is the stressor event and the hardships that accompany it, B includes resources that the family can use to cope with the event, and C is the subjective meaning that the family gives to the event. These three factors combine to predict the outcome, X, which is a state of either crisis or relatively successful coping.

In the application of Family Stress Theory to remarriage, remarriage was considered to be a normal developmental stressor, factor A in the Double ABC-X Model, a modification of the original theory. Encompassed within A are hardships associated with the transition to stepfamily living. Biases against stepchildren and the invalidation of stepparents in schools are examples of school-related hardships for stepfamilies. Conversely, schools can function as a resource, factor B, for stepfamilies. For example, school-based support groups for stepchildren could be a resource. If schools help stepchildren perceive parental remarriage positively, either through support groups or education about families, the schools also will be influencing factor C, the subjective meaning associated with remarriage and stepfamily living. Because schools are such an important influence in the lives of children and their families, they are in a strong position to either increase or reduce the stress of stepfamily adjustment.

Family Empowerment Model

An application of theory to the interface between stepfamilies and education has been developed using the Family Empowerment Model, which is embedded within Urie Bronfenbrenner's ecological perspective (Crosbie-Burnett, 1993). According to the Family Empowerment Model of Moncrieff Cochran and the Cornell Empowerment Group, empowerment is defined as "an intentional, ongoing process centered in the local community, involving mutual respect, critical reflection, caring, and group participation, through which people lacking an equal share of valued resources gain greater access to and control over those resources" (Cornell Empowerment Group, 1989, p. 3). They further stated that social institutions (in this case the school) control access to valued resources, such as political power, purchasing power, information, social support, the skills acquired through education, and social status. The Family Empowerment Model is placed within an ecological model (Bronfenbrenner, 1979). In Bronfenbrenner's model a school system and a family system are each considered microsystems. A student lives in both those spheres and possibly in other microsystems as well (e.g., a sports team, religious group, or social club). The relationship between any two microsystems is called a mesosystem. Therefore, the relationship between a family system and a school system is a mesosystem.[1] In a recent paper written for practitioners, Crosbie-Burnett (1992) delineated how educational institutions control access to valued resources and how families can be empowered in the mesosystems that include them. However, in the next section of this chapter, the empowerment model and Family Stress Theory are used to show how educational institutions disempower stepfamilies.

Finally, recommendations for change are addressed.

INCREASED SCHOOL-RELATED STRESS AND THE DISEMPOWERMENT OF STEPFAMILIES THROUGH THE PRESENT CONCEPTUALIZATION OF "PARENT" AND "FAMILY"

Legal Definitions

The most basic source of stepfamily disempowerment lies in another social institution: the law (see Chapter 12). State laws usually define the "legal parent" as the biological or legally adoptive parent unless these parents have been found to be inadequate by the courts (Liss, 1987). Consequently, schools must interact with the legal parent(s) for official business. Because the U.S. legal institutions also assume the traditional American family structure that is inherent in the country's ideology, family laws are written so that there can be only one legal mother and one legal father. This is problematic for stepfamilies, for lesbian and gay families, and for families of cultures in which authority over a child may be shared by, or be in the hands of, a group member other than the legal parent. Consider the following examples: the law, and concomitant school policies, disempower a stepparent who lives with a child, helps that child with homework daily, and may be perceived as a parent by the child. This stepparent is invalidated as a parent within the school system. The situation is equally difficult for lesbian stepfamilies. In these families, the legal parent is the biological mother, and the "other mother" has no legal rights even if (a) she shares equally in the rearing of the child and (b) there is no legal father. Alternatively, the law supports the parental status of a nonresidential biological parent (including those without legal custody). For this parent, a school risks losing federal funds if it fails to allow access to the child's record, unless there is a legal document restricting such access. Furthermore, the federal act states that if that parent lives far away from the school, the school must send copies of important information at his or her parent's request.

Social Norms

Nearly as powerful as the law are social norms and customs. Society's conceptualization of stepfamilies and the language used to define them have an inherent bias that must be changed before new policy strategies can be devised. A revealing example can be found in the use of the term *reconstituted family*, meaning a family in which a single parent has *remarried*. The word *reconstituted* reveals how we conceptualize remarried families as recreating the "real" family again, after being in an incomplete, temporary, single-parent household. This view was somewhat more accurate historically when nearly all stepparents *replaced* a deceased parent;

however, today, 90% of remarried families are formed after the divorce of two living parents (Bumpass, Sweet, & Martin, 1990). Furthermore, the lack of recognition that the first marriages of unwed parents who marry someone other than their child's biological parent create stepfamilies suggests that the label *stepfamily* means "deviant" and is to be avoided. In both cases *this recreation of the myth of the first-marriage family denies the distinct structural and psychological differences between two-biological-parent families and stepfamilies which contain only one biological parent*. Grouping both family types together under "two-parent families" is the basis for inappropriate policy, or, as is more often the case, no policy for stepfamilies. Stepfamilies become invisible when they are not perceived as unique.

Many families that have parental figures who are not legally married to the biological single parent are structurally and psychologically similar to stepfamilies. However, these families are inappropriately categorized as single-parent families. These include single parents who cohabit with a partner in a committed relationship, single parents who share parenting with extended family members (e.g., two divorced brothers rearing their children in one home), and homosexual stepfamilies, in which a homosexual parent recouples but cannot legally marry. In all these family types, the family structure is certainly different from that of a single parent living alone with offspring because the second parental figure may be an important psychological parent to the child.

All this suggests that people seem uncomfortable with the many variant family structures in which children live today. Rather than include them, social norms and behaviors hide them when possible under the label of "real" family (e.g., heterosexual families) and define the others as deviant (e.g., homosexual or single-parent families). In all U.S. social institutions, policy has been developed that is based on this outdated and distorted view of family life in America. It is now necessary to modify policies to reflect the reality of family life in the late twentieth century in a way that demonstrates support for *all* families.

NEW CONCEPTUALIZATIONS

The development of new family-related policy and practice in education requires a fundamental change in the conceptualization of family composition. No longer can *family* be defined for all students as the members of the household of their primary residence. For increasing numbers of students, the "immediate family" is comprised of persons in two or more households that are linked together by primary parent-child relations and/or sibling relations. In the postdivorce situation, these families have been called *binuclear* families (Ahrons, 1984; Ahrons & Wallisch, 1987). This word is designed to describe the reality of a family situation in which a child spends time in households of both biological parents. This term also is applicable to the households of two biological parents who were never married but who share the parenting of their child.

If one or both of the biological parents marries or cohabits with a new partner and thereby brings a stepparent into one of the households, the binuclear family becomes more complicated. The more complicated binuclear family has been labeled an *extended stepfamily network*. This term was created to denote a group of households that are connected to one another through biology or marriage. It is a combination of the traditional extended family of grandparents, aunts, uncles, and cousins and the modern extended family formed by the interrelated households of multiple sets of coparents (Crosbie-Burnett et al., 1988). It is different from the binuclear family in that it includes the extended families of stepparents and the households of their former spouses; the binuclear family is subsumed within, and is a subsystem of, an extended stepfamily network.

While a more expansive view of *family* is necessary, so is the need for an examination of the relationships between schools and stepparents. At present, legally married stepparents are denied the legal rights and responsibilities of biological parents in school policies (e.g., school permission slips, medical emergency release forms, access to school records, and signing report cards) because schools are required by law to relate to the legal parent or parents (Stenger, 1986; see also Chapter 12 of this volume). However, there are many school policies and practices (e.g., invitations to events at school) that could be modified to acknowledge the role of stepparents and other adults who play an important role in a child's extended stepfamily network. School policies usually do not validate stepparents' significant contributions to their stepchildren's development. Instead, schools too often convey a message of the unimportance of stepparents in school-related issues. While stepchildren may be taught to respect a stepparent at home, they learn that stepparents are not respected as parental figures by the schools. This implied message can be detrimental to children, disempowering to stepparents, and erode the already fragile stepparent-stepchild relationship.

Before new policies can be developed, there are four changes in current conceptualizations that must occur:

1. Change from the assumption of hostility between divorced biological coparents' households, which form the binuclear family, to an assumption and encouragement of enduring *cooperative coparenting* by the biological parents and stepparents in those households. Even if this cooperation is not a reality for many sets of coparents and stepparents, the power of the school as a social institution in making the assumption of cooperation may promote this behavior and encourage a norm of cooperative parenting.

2. Change from thinking about the involvement of the parent and residential stepparent and the nonresidential parent and stepparent from the dichotomous categories of "real parent" versus "not a real parent," as well as "involved" versus "uninvolved" to thinking about *parenting involvement* as dimensions on a continuum. Parental involvement occurs in many ways, ranging from having actual behavioral involvement with the child on a daily basis to irregularly communicating by mail. The meaning that a child gives to a relationship with a parental figure can be more important than the frequency of parent-child interactions. Even a physically absent

parent or stepparent may still function psychologically as a primary parent to a child.

3. Letting go of the ideology that "there can be only one mother and one father" and promoting a subsequent change from perceiving the stepparent as a parental replacement to *perceiving the stepparent as an additional parental figure*. Even in the situations in which there is a stepfather who is involved with his stepchild and the biological father is nonresidential, the child may still perceive the stepfather as an additional parent and not a replacement of his or her father.

4. Expansion of our narrow definition of "parent" as the biological parent or parents with whom the student lives to *significant parental figures* in the child's extended stepfamily network. Parental figures can include nonresidential biological parents, residential or nonresidential stepparents or stepsiblings, grandparents, or other relatives. Educators must recognize that a child's most important *psychological parent* or parents may not be synonymous with a residential, biological parent, and that all parental figures have the *potential* to contribute to the child's development in school. Therefore, all significant parental figures should be acknowledged and included formally in family-related policy and practice. These persons are all potential sources of support on whom the school can call when helping children maximize their potential.

RECOMMENDATIONS FOR CHANGES IN POLICY AND PRACTICE

Clearly, translating the above changes in conceptualization about *family* into new school policy and practice might reduce the stress of becoming a stepfamily by eliminating the hardships that schools inadvertently create for stepfamilies. Equally important, schools could become resources for stepfamily members, particularly stepchildren. In the process, stepfamily members could be empowered in their roles of parent, stepparent, and student in the school microsystem. Ideally the changes suggested below will maximize the ability of schools to better serve stepchildren and their families.

Recommendations for State Departments of Education

1. Sponsor educational workshops on stepfamilies for school personnel including: (a) descriptions of children's experiences in stepfamilies, and (b) an experiential self-exploration of the school personnel's own beliefs, attitudes, and feelings about divorce, remarriage, and never-married parents and the effect of these situations on children who live in these families. These workshops should increase our understanding and empathy for the complexities of stepfamily living and reduce the negative bias of school staff.

2. Review existing policy for first-marriage family bias and expand these policies to include the needs of stepfamilies. Policy and practice that invalidate and discour-

age involvement of parental figures decrease the person-power that is available to support a child's success in school. In this way, the school disempowers itself as well.

3. Review existing curricula for bias toward first-marriage families. New curricula that include all family structures in the content needs to be developed. When children are taught with curricula that use the first-marriage family as the only model of *family*, the deviant status of the many children in binuclear families and extended stepfamily networks is promoted. Obvious curricular areas needing change are social studies, family life, and mental health, but all subjects should be examined. For example, English lessons could include terms like *stepfather* or *half sister*, while the complexity of living in extended stepfamily networks lends itself nicely to word problems in arithmetic. These changes help normalize and validate the experiences of a growing proportion of students.

4. Allow for the many variations of family structure (not simply labeling a family as "one-parent" and "two-parent") in the data that are collected by the state on children's family structures. As noted above, grouping first-marriage families with stepfamilies under so-called two-parent families denies the reality of stepchildren and presents an erroneous profile of the student body. This practice also contributes to the invisibility of stepfamilies, which precludes the promotion of an understanding on the part of students and school personnel, as well as any changes that are needed in the school-stepfamily relationship.

5. Include the analysis of student achievement by family structure and socio-economic status in research on student achievement; this would give the state feedback on how well the schools are succeeding in educating children from various family structures and social classes. These two factors need to be analyzed separately because there is a correlation between family structure and social class. In general, households headed by mothers only are poorer than other family structures (Weitzman, 1985).

6. State certification for new school administrators, teachers, school counselors, school psychologists, school social workers, and school nurses should require training in the diversity of family structures. Colleges and universities that prepare school personnel need to be encouraged to integrate this topic into their training.

Recommendations for School District Administrators

1. Workshops on family structures should be made available to *all* school personnel, and incentives for them to attend should be provided. The reason for sensitizing the professional staff to the variability of students' families is obvious. However, it is equally important that *all* school staff who interact with family members under-stand various family structures. For example, bus drivers often have face-to-face interactions with parental figures, while school secretaries are crucial liaisons between parental figures and the school.

2. Discourage the use of negative language like "broken home," "reconstituted

family," "real mother," "natural father," and " having no father." Teachers and other school personnel are powerful models for children regarding their perceptions of the world. When children that are not from first-marriage families hear teachers and others use these terms, they receive negative, nonsupportive messages to the effect that there is something wrong with their family situations: that their families are unacceptable and abnormal. When children in first-marriage families hear adults using these terms, it encourages "I'm better than he [or she]" thinking and makes children from stepfamilies more vulnerable to peer ridicule and rejection.

3. Review local policy, practices, forms, and curricula for first-marriage family bias. Assistance from a committee of parental figures from various family structures is necessary in this endeavor. Examples of potential areas for change include: addressing correspondence from the school to "Parent(s) of: (student's name);" sending important notices home with children on days other than Fridays, when some children go directly to nonresidential parents' homes; modifying school projects that relate to family members to include the variety of family structures (e.g., making Mother's Day cards for two mothers or making Christmas or Hanukkah gifts for two sets of parents or parental figures).

4. Annually update family structure information for each student; include names, addresses and phone numbers of all significant parental figures and any court order related to the student (e.g., concerning child custody or visitation). Encourage parents to notify the school when family changes occur in order to maximize services for their children. Be particularly cognizant of custody dispute cases as a precaution against child snatching.

5. Mail report cards and important announcements to nonresidential parents with information stating that they have the right of access to their biological children's records (unless this right has been legally denied). By doing so, the school validates their parental rights and responsibilities and relates to these parents in a way that invites involvement.

6. Offer separate teacher-parent conferences for coparents and parental figures who will not attend conferences together but still wish to learn about their child's progress.

7. Have at least one single parent, one nonresidential parent, and one stepparent on the Parent-Teachers' Organization board of officers. Since this organization coordinates activities within the school-family mesosystem, it is important that the planning of such activities do not discriminate against children and parents who are not in first-marriage families.

9. Maintain library materials that focus on the experiences of children in stepfamilies. This will normalize the stepfamily within the culture and also will validate the experiences of stepchildren in the schools, helping their peers understand stepfamily living.

10. Ask single-parent mothers if they would like their children placed with male teachers and single-parent fathers if they would like their children placed with female teachers.

11. Sponsor support groups for parental figures in extended stepfamily networks.

Schools are in an excellent position to perform this service. Many potential group members can be identified from school files, and schools also have the space to offer evening or Saturday groups.

12. Provide a list of books and community services for parental figures in stepfamilies to help ease the transition for themselves and their children. This is another example of how schools can serve as a resource for stepfamilies.

13. Direct school-based professionals to be available to all parental figures. The more adults that the school empowers to help a child, the better likelihood of school success for him or her.

14. Write to textbook publishers stating that your district would like to use books that include references to stepfamilies in a normative manner. Schools are in a powerful position to request that publishers expand family images in both pictures and written text to include stepfamilies.

Recommendations for School Boards

1. Obtain input from parental figures of extended stepfamily networks when developing policies. Exploring the consequences of proposed policies should include examination of their impact on students from stepfamilies. A school board is elected to represent the entire community, including the various types of families.

2. Hold school administrators responsible for implementing family-related policy that is generated at the state and local levels. Conduct periodic reviews of relevant policies and the practices of school personnel, including counselors, psychologists, social workers, nurses, and other support services professionals.

Recommendations for Other School-based Professionals

1. Learn about common stepfamily issues and appropriate intervention strategies. Professionals must take into account the structural and psycho-emotional complexities of stepfamilies when serving stepchildren.

2. When working with an individual student, identify the significant parental figures in the student's family and be sensitive to the student's family experience from his or her own perspective. Most theory and concomitant training is based on first-marriage families.

3. Include significant parental figures in the assessment of the student's problem and in any intervention; solicit their support in working with the student. Help facilitate communication and cooperation between adults in different households.

4. Facilitate discussion groups for parental figures that focus on school-related issues and student-focused problem solving.

5. Periodically offer support groups for stepchildren in the schools.

6. Identify local counselors, psychologists, and therapists who have training in stepfamily issues for purposes of referral and consultation. Identify any com-

munity support services, such as support groups, for stepfamily members who are having problems.

CONCLUSIONS

Schools are the most influential institution in the lives of children, second only to the family. The research discussed above has shown that bias against stepchildren and stepparents exists at the various levels of the educational institution. Attitudes, policies, and practices that devalue or ignore stepfamilies have an adverse effect on growing proportions of students. In both subtle and blatant ways, the present situation adds stress and is disempowering to stepfamilies as they interface with schools in the school-family mesosystem. The need for change is crucial because education, as a social institution, controls access to valued resources.

Educational institutions both reflect societal values and, at the same time, are in a powerful position to change them. New policies and practices must be implemented to provide an environment of acceptance and inclusion of stepfamily members within our schools. The time has come to acknowledge and embrace the diversity of America's families in our educational institutions.

KEY CHAPTER POINTS

1. Nearly 10% of all school-aged children live in stepfamilies, yet much of school policy and procedure relates to these families either as single-parent or first-marriage families.

2. Relevant research has been almost entirely atheoretical and has focused on comparisons of children from various family structures, cultural bias against stepfamily members among school-based professionals and students, and evaluations of school-based support groups for children of divorce and remarriage.

3. Disempowerment of stepfamilies occurs in schools indirectly through the narrow legal definitions of *parent* and *family*.

4. The perception of an extended stepfamily network offers a more expansive and inclusive view of *family*.

5. Certain assumptions about the parent held by school-based personnel do a disservice to stepfamilies. Some of these include:

   a. Believing that hostility always exists between divorced parents.

   b. Relying on dichotomous thinking about "real" versus "not real" and "involved" versus "uninvolved" parents.

   c. Believing that there can be only one mother and one father.

   d. Assuming that "parent" always equates to a biological parent.

6. Recommendation for interventions at various levels of school governance (e.g., state departments of education, school district administrators, and school boards) based on new conceptualizations of parent and family are suggested.

NOTE

1. The mesosystems linking together family microsystems and school micro-systems have many faces. They include, not only direct communication between members of both systems, but also beliefs and attitudes that members in each system have about the other system (e.g., some parents believe that "school is a waste of time." Similarly, some teachers believe that "kids with stepparents cannot achieve as well as others.") The mesosystems include formal structures (e.g., the "family information form" that is recorded for each student) and more subtle interfaces between school and family (e.g., family-related images, terms, and descriptions found in books and other teaching materials used in schools).

Chapter 12

STEPPARENTS AND THE LAW: A NEBULOUS STATUS AND A NEED FOR REFORM

Sarah H. Ramsey

Perhaps the most striking aspect of the law relating to stepfamilies is its lack. The empty spaces where the law might be are far more interesting than the law that exists. They tell us, very clearly, that for the most part, stepparents do not have a legally recognized status in relation to their stepchildren. Similarly, the existing law reflects the ambiguous and unclear status of the stepparent in our society. Of course, the complexity and diversity of stepfamilies, coupled with the sometimes competing claims of the noncustodial parents, makes the development of a coherent policy difficult.

In order to regulate family relations, the law first needs to categorize who is to be regulated. Thus, the first step in analyzing the law relating to stepfamilies is to reflect on the legal meaning of *stepparents*. Traditionally, a stepparent is a person who is, or was, married to a person who had a child born of a prior marriage. Now the term typically also includes a person married to the parent of an illegitimate child. Stepparents are created solely by the legal act of marriage, and not through the development of any bond to the stepchild. Thus, an unmarried person who has taken a parental role, such as a long-term cohabitor or a homosexual partner, is not included within the legal meaning of stepparent. However, persons married to noncustodial parents are classified as stepparents even though they may have no relationship to the child. Some law reform proposals would limit the term *stepparents* to those that lived with the custodial parent (Tenenbaum, 1991). A person married to a noncustodial parent might not even see the spouse's child (the person's stepchild by the marriage), much less make any emotional or financial commitment to that child.

Perhaps because no connection between stepparents and their stepchildren is required, the law has tended to treat stepparents as remote from the stepchildren's lives, giving them almost no rights or responsibilities, even when the stepchildren live with them. In analyzing custody and visitation claims of a stepparent, a court may refer to the stepparent as a third party or as a nonparent, the same terms that are used to describe any such claimant who is not a biological parent. Interestingly enough, however, when courts make custody decisions between biological parents, they sometimes take a very different view of the stepparent. Instead of considering the stepparent as a stranger, they look with favor on a parent who has remarried and, thus, provides a two-parent household.

In spite of this general lack of legal status, stepparents have managed to get their claims heard in a number of cases. A major goal of this chapter is to describe the law relating to stepparents during the marriage with the biological parent and to the postmarriage issues of custody, visitation, and child support. A second goal is to consider what the law might become by analyzing the possible objectives of stepfamily law and describing some alternative reforms.

To describe the current state of the law, some specific appellate cases are used to illustrate the complexity of the problems before the courts, demonstrate the approaches courts have used, and make the conflicts real, in an effort to emphasize the costs and benefits of the rules on families. A disadvantage of describing particular cases, however, is that appellate cases represent atypical disputes. Most families settle their differences about such matters as custody and visitation without even a trial (Mnookin, Maccoby, Albiston, & Depner, 1990). Stepparents are even less likely to litigate, since they do not see themselves as having rights. Few families decide to appeal because of the delay, the emotional stress, and the cost involved. To some extent, then, the rules in this area are responsive to the extraordinary case and little is known about the ordinary dispute resolution of stepfamilies.

RIGHTS AND RESPONSIBILITIES OF STEPPARENTS DURING MARRIAGE

What are the rights and responsibilities of a stepparent married to a child's custodial parent? One way to understand the stepparent's status, or lack thereof, is to contrast it to that of the biological parent. Biological parents in an ongoing marriage have the obligation to support, care for, educate, and discipline their child, as well as the right to the custody and control of the child. In contrast, the stepparent (even one who lives with a custodial parent) basically has no legal status in relation to the child: no right to discipline, consent to medical care, or access school records, and no responsibility to support (Clark, 1988).

Even though stepparents have no enforceable rights or responsibilities toward their stepchildren, they frequently do take on parental responsibilities. The stepparent may provide substantial financial support, as well as assistance in child rearing. Practically, the role of the stepparent in matters such as care, discipline, education, and support is whatever the stepparent and custodial parent agree on. However, their private agreement does not empower the stepparent to take the place of the biological parent in legal matters.

In contrast to the stepparent's tenuous and ambiguous relationship, the noncustodial parent usually retains most of the rights and responsibilities of parenthood, even after divorce. These rights and obligations might be explicitly delineated at the time of divorce, either through a separation agreement or by a court order. Typically, the agreement or order would specify the child support, custody, and visitation arrangements. If the custodial arrangement was classified as joint custody, then the time allotments for sharing custody might be specified. The responsibility for major decisions about the child's education, religious training, and medical care also might be specified.

In Loco Parentis

By virtue of the stepparent's day-to-day contact with the children in a parental role, however, some states might apply the common law doctrine of in loco parentis to the stepparent in some instances (Ramsey & Masson, 1985). This doctrine was developed to respond to the problems resulting from any person (not just a stepparent) serving in a parental role without any legal status. The *in loco parentis* doctrine also is used to explain the exercise of parental authority by the state and by private institutions such as schools. The doctrine basically allows a person to be treated legally as a parent in certain circumstances. Whether an *in loco parentis* relationship exists is a factual question that must be determined on a case-by-case basis, with the primary question being whether there was an intentional assumption of parental responsibilities. As one court explained, "In order for one to be regarded as *in loco parentis* he must put himself in the situation of a lawful parent by assuming the obligations incident to the parental relation, with the result that his rights, duties and liabilities are the same as those of a lawful parent" (*Richards v. United States*, 1950, p. 212).

How might the *in loco parentis* doctrine work in practice? Under common law, a parent is entitled to a child's wages. If a stepparent was supporting a stepchild and also kept money that the child earned in a summer job, the stepparent could use the *in loco parentis* doctrine as a defense in a subsequent lawsuit by the child against the stepparent for the child's wages. The stepparent would argue that the fulfillment of a parental role gave him or her the parental right to the wages. The *in loco parentis* doctrine also could be used to the disadvantage of a stepparent, whose claim for reimbursement for support of a stepchild against the estate of the noncustodial parent, for example, could be denied because the stepparent was *in loco parentis*.

Traditionally, the doctrine was primarily used for categorizing past behavior rather than future behavior, because the *in loco parentis* status could be terminated by the parties at any time. For example, if the stepparent was being asked to support the stepchild, the stepparent could simply say that the *in loco parentis* relationship with the child had ceased. The relationship also would typically end if the marriage ended, since the stepparent would no longer be living with the stepchild. Thus, the *in loco parentis* doctrine has been more retrospective than prospective. In some recent cases, however, the *in loco parentis* doctrine has been used as a mechanism for classifying stepparents as parents to provide a justification for considering their prospective "parental" claims. For example, a court considering a stepparent's request for visitation upon divorce from the custodial parent assumed that a stepparent who was *in loco parentis* is like a biological parent and, therefore, should be given rights similar to rights of such a parent (*Carter v. Brodrick*, 1982). This approach would give a new permanence to the *in loco parentis* status, implying that once it was obtained, it could continue indefinitely, even if the stepchild and stepparent no longer lived together. This court's approach is a major change from the common-law view. If accepted by other jurisdictions, it would be a basis for giving stepparents continuing rights and responsibilities for their stepchildren.

Adoption

In contrast to the *in loco parentis* doctrine, adoption provides a relatively clear path to an official parental status for a stepparent. When a stepparent adopts stepchildren, he or she takes the place of the biological parent in the eyes of the law. The family legally would be like the original first-marriage family of two parents plus children. The stepparent would have the same rights and responsibilities as the custodial parent, and the other biological parent usually forfeits any legal status.

Adoption is not always desirable. Although in a few states, the biological parent may be allowed visitation rights based on the best interests of the child, traditionally, adoption by a stepparent results in a permanent break between the noncustodial biological parent and the child. Although the laws in some states favor stepparent adoption by making it relatively easy, questions have been raised about whether adoption by a stepparent is beneficial for the child. The stepparent presumably will continue to provide support and care whether or not the child is adopted; however, upon being adopted the child's access and right to support from the biological parent is lost (Chambers, 1990). Adoption reinforces the norm of the first-marriage family rather than encouraging a more flexible view (Bartlett, 1984; Masson, 1984).

In addition to the problem of desirability, adoption is not always feasible. After an adoption, the noncustodial biological parent will have no legal tie to the children. Thus, a parent with an active interest in the child will be unlikely to consent to adoption. When such parents have paid support or maintained contact, it is unlikely that adoption will be allowed without their consent. However, parental consent usually will not be needed if the parent is considered to have abandoned the child.

RIGHTS AND RESPONSIBILITIES AT THE END OF MARRIAGE

Given the nebulous status of stepparents in the ongoing family, it is not surprising that they are given little recognition if their marriage to the parent ends by either divorce or death. The following section explores the difficulties that stepparents face when they petition for custody or visitation, and describes their limited support obligation.

Custody

Stepparents must overcome barriers that parents do not face in custody disputes. Generally, when a custody dispute is between biological parents, custody is decided based on the best interests of the child. When a nonparent is disputing with a parent, however, the best interest test is not used until the nonparent has overcome the legal barriers that are designed to protect the biological parents from interference in their parental rights by third parties (Clark, 1988). Such barriers can take different forms. Some states (Illinois, for example) limit access to the courts by limiting the categories of persons who are allowed to petition for custody. Persons who are allowed to petition, thus, would fall under one of the designated categories. Others use a more stringent standard for reviewing nonparent claims. New York, for example, does not closely limit the types of claimants, but rather uses a standard for review that makes it difficult for a nonparent to prevail over a parent.

Limits on claimants. In states that limit the categories of claimants, stepparents who have not met certain statutory requirements are not allowed to have their claims heard. Under Illinois law a nonparent is allowed to petition for custody only if the child is in the physical custody of one of his or her parents (Illinois Revised Statutes, 1987). This rule would tend to eliminate stepparents' claims that arose on the divorce of a custodial parent and stepparent. In the typical case, the custodial parent would maintain physical custody of the child rather than leave the child with the stepparent. When a custodial biological parent dies, however, the stepparent with physical custody may petition for custody against the noncustodial biological parent.

The Illinois rule is modeled on section 401 of the Uniform Marriage and Divorce Act, an influential reform proposal first made by the National Conference of Commissioners on Uniform State Laws in 1970. The commentary on section 401 of the present Uniform Act states of the limitation:

[This] makes it clear that if one of the parents has physical custody of the child, a non-parent may not bring an action to contest that parent's right to continuing custody under the "best interest of the child" standard. . . . If a non-parent. . . wants to acquire custody, he must commence proceedings under the far more stringent standard for intervention provided in the typical Juvenile Court Act. In short, this subsection has been devised to protect the "parental rights" of custodial parents and to insure that intrusions upon those rights will occur only when the care the parent is providing the child falls short of the minimum standard imposed by the community at large-the standard incorporated in the neglect or delinquency definitions of the state's Juvenile Court Act (National Conference of Commissioners on Uniform State Laws, 1987, p. 550).

Interestingly enough, this section does not mention stepparents at all. Although the Uniform Act restricts requests for custody, a court nonetheless has wide latitude to allow the views of interested parties to be heard.

Under this approach, if the statutory requirements are met, the stepparent can petition for custody. Custody would be decided based on the child's best interests. Within the best interests test, however, a state may still favor the biological parent. For example, in Illinois "the superior right of a natural parent to custody of his or her child" would be one of the factors considered in determining the child's best interest (*In re Marriage of Carey*, 1989, p. 1297).

The case of *In re custody of Krause* (1982) provides an example of the difficulty of overcoming the preference for a parent when it is incorporated in the best interest test. In that case, the stepfather married the mother when the child was aged 4, but had participated in child care activities since the child was about 16 months old. The biological father maintained regular contact with the child, even though he had remarried and had another child. The child's mother died when the child was age 9. The child's preference was to remain with the stepfather. The only expert witness, a psychiatrist, testified that because of the importance of continuity in the child's life, the child should remain with the stepparent. Nonetheless, the court awarded custody to the biological father, stating that the prior long-term actual custody of the stepfather should not be controlling, although it was a factor to be considered in ascertaining the child's best interests. The court relied heavily on the presumption that placement with a biological parent was in the child's best interests.

Extraordinary circumstances requirement. Other states do not limit the categories of claimants as a barrier, but instead require a stepparent to prove that a parent was unfit or that extraordinary circumstances are present before custody is decided, based on the child's best interest. For example, New York allows anyone who has an interest in the welfare of a child to petition for custody (*Trapp v. Trapp*, 1984). In order to be awarded custody, however, a stepparent must show that extraordinary circumstances exist before custody will be decided based on the child's best interest.

Meeting the test of extraordinary circumstances can be difficult. In the New York case of *Tyrrell v. Tyrrell* (1979), the court refused to grant custody to the stepparent when the mother died, basing its holding on a lack of extraordinary circumstances. The court explained that a father's decision to allow the mother to have custody should not impair the father's rights with regard to a stepparent to whom custody was never surrendered. The court expressed concern that a contrary rule could hinder the settlement of custody disputes "because a parent's voluntary consent to custody in the other parent could mean eventual loss of the child to a stepparent" (*Tyrrell v. Tyrrell*, 1979, p. 250). The court stated:

The circumstances of the family in this case until the custodial parent's death were no different from those of thousands of families where the parents are divorced or separated and where one parent has made the painful decision that under all the circumstances it would be best to agree to give custody of the child to the other. Nor is it unusual for the custodial parent to remarry and have children by the second spouse, or as unfortunately has happened here, to die. To hold that these factors rise to the level of "extraordinary circumstances" after the death of the custodial parent so that the surviving parent has no greater right to custody than a nonparent is, in our opinion, a misreading of [prior case law]. If this were the rule, the requirement of a showing of "extraordinary circumstances" would no longer be a threshold test for the protection of parental rights. The test in all custody cases, whether between parents or between parents and nonparents would be the best interests of the child. (p. 251)

Hence, in deciding similar cases, the New York court, using "extraordinary circumstances," reached the same result as did the Illinois court, using the "best interests" test.

Other restrictions. Other states require a showing that the parent is "unfit" either in addition to, or instead of, a showing of extraordinary circumstances. Some states also have a standard of proof that is higher than is usually required in a civil matter. In a case involving a stepfather's petition for custody of his stepson upon divorce, the Vermont Supreme Court held that if a stepparent stands *in loco parentis* to the child of the marital household, custody may be awarded to the stepparent "if it is shown by clear and convincing evidence that the natural parent is unfit or that extraordinary circumstances exist to warrant such a custodial order and that it is in the best interest of the child for custody to be awarded to the stepparent" (*Paquette v. Paquette*, 1985, p. 30).

The Reasons for Custody Barriers

Before turning to visitation and child support, the two other major legal issues that arise at the end of marriage, it is useful to reflect on the legal structure that protects biological parents from claims to children by stepparents. Why do states have these protective barriers against nonparents? A major reason advanced for these barriers is the need to protect parental autonomy. However, I believe another reason for these barriers is the difficulty of determining and defining what standard could be used in lieu of parental preference. In other words, the strength of the doctrine of parental autonomy is due in part to the indeterminacy of the best interests standard, which is the standard typically used in disputes between parents.

Parental autonomy. Early U.S. Supreme Court cases identified a right to parental autonomy in disputes between the parents and the state in resounding language: "It is cardinal with us that the custody, care and nurture of the child reside first in the parents, whose primary function and freedom include preparation for obligations the state can neither supply nor hinder" (*Prince v. Massachusetts*, 1944, p. 166). Interestingly, the case involved a dispute between the child's guardian (her aunt) and the state. The court considered the guardian as the "parent" in the opinion. However, the protection of this right typically involves a balancing of the degree of interference by the state with the seriousness of the problem that the state is addressing. For example, compulsory education laws are seen as a relatively minimal interference with parental rights. However, much greater infringement would result if the state wanted to remove the child from the parent's custody, and consequently, the justification for the state's interference would have to be stronger. Generally, the state can remove a child if he or she is being abused or neglected, but not if the child might simply be better off somewhere else (Clark, 1988).

The protection of parental autonomy is the traditional reason for limiting the state's power to intervene in an ongoing family. When a family has been disrupted by divorce, the disruption gives the state a basis for asserting some control over parental decisions related to the child. Upon divorce, the state claims the authority to decide which parent should get custody of children, typically using the standard that the custody decision should be made based on the child's best interests. Although the disruption caused by divorce is used to justify the authority of the state to decide between parents, the state usually does not use the divorce alone as a basis for deciding that the child should be placed with an entirely new set of parents.

Where should stepparents' claims be placed in this matrix of rights? When a stepparent and custodial parent divorce, should the stepparent be treated like a parent so that custody can be decided based on the child's best interests? Should the stepparent be classified as a nonparent whose claims are considered equivalent to state interference? Finally, should the stepparent's claim fall somewhere in between these extremes?

To answer these questions we need to focus on what goals we want to achieve through the custody decision and what family relations we want to protect. A narrow focus on the classification of stepparents does not help us identify these goals. If we define the stepparent as a parent, using the *in loco parentis* doctrine or the concept of psychological parent, then it would follow that the best interests standard would be appropriate for decisions between parent and stepparent.[1] However, if we categorize the stepparent as a nonparent, we would use a more stringent test such as parental unfitness. Thus, the classification of the stepparent produces the legal conclusion or outcome. The classification is instrumental, or a means to an end. The question that should be addressed is: Why would we choose to place a stepparent in the category of parent or nonparent, or in some other category? What goal does the classification accomplish?

Indeterminacy of the best interests standard. To begin to answer these questions, it is necessary to consider what would happen if we classified stepparents as parents and used the best interests standard. Unfortunately, the best interests standard does not provide a clear basis for decision making. Indeed, it has been harshly criticized because of its indeterminacy (Mnookin, 1985). Since we have no consensus about the meansing of "best interests," the standard allows for wide variation in decisions. Assume that a court is trying to decide a custody dispute between a stepfather and a biological father in a case with the following facts:

The child is a 10-year-old girl whose mother, the custodial parent, has died. The stepfather was married to the child's mother for 5 years, treats the child as his own, and wants her to stay with him. The stepfather is wealthy, well-educated and capable of taking care of the child. The biological father loves the child, has seen her regularly every month since the divorce, is poorly educated, and has a low income. The child feels close to both men.

Is it in the child's best interests to stay with the stepparent who will provide continuity of care as well as financial and educational advantages, or should the biological tie be given greater weight? Should the court be primarily concerned with the child's immediate emotional needs and desires, or should it be more concerned with long-term emotional satisfaction and other long-term goals such as educational attainment? One critic of the standard wrote, "Deciding what is best for a child often poses a question no less ultimate than the purposes and values of life itself" (Mnookin, 1985).

In addition to the lack of agreement on goals, we also have little ability to predict the effects of a particular decision on a child. In a trial, the court frequently has to make a decision based on little information. Even with extensive information, we simply do not have the ability to predict which choice would produce which results (Mnookin, 1985).

The end result of the use of an indeterminate standard is that it allows for highly discretionary decisions that can be biased and unpredictable. If the standard has no real content, then a judge's decision will have virtually no limits. Because of the complexity of families and the sense that the child's interests should be paramount, courts frequently are instructed to make decisions about custody based on the child's best interests (Clark, 1988). When the choice is between parents, we accept this degree of discretion, although the courts are quick to adopt presumptions, such as the now-outdated maternal preference or the more current gender-neutral preference for the primary caretaker, to guide their decisions. When they see the possibility of the child being removed from a biological parent based on a discretionary standard that has few limits, courts and legislatures feel the need to add restrictions. These restrictions probably are added, not only because of uncertainty about what is truly "best" for a child, but also because of a belief that biological parents have a right to their children.

Parental autonomy or parental right frequently is the rationale for adding these additional restrictions (Clark, 1988; *Sheppard v. Sheppard*, 1981). The doctrine of parental autonomy was developed to protect parents from easy intervention by the state. However, when the dispute is between a stepparent and a biological parent, the concept of parental autonomy is less compelling. The heart of the dispute is that the stepparent should be considered a parent. In other words, the quality of the adult-child relationship is as important as the biological connection. If the stepparent is categorized as a parent, then the use of the parental autonomy doctrine becomes nonsensical: stepparents' claims should be considered because they are parents, but their claims should be denied because they are not parents. A similar problem arises when a preference for parents is incorporated into the best interests test by the assumption that the parent has natural love and affection for the child. Therefore, placement with the parent is presumed to be in the child's best interests.

Policymakers formulating new laws to deal with stepfamilies should be concerned with the tension between having a limited standard that would deny some meritorious claims and accepting instead an open-ended standard such as best interests, with the concomitant problems of bias, unpredictability, and the court's desire for a guiding presumption. In my opinion, focusing on the goals of law reform is the best way to resolve this dilemma. Before addressing these goals, it is useful first to consider two other major legal issues related to the end of the marriage: visitation and support.

Visitation

Problems with the best interests standard and parental autonomy also are evident in disputes between stepparents and biological parents over visitation. Because visitation is considered much less intrusive than custody, the barriers to stepparent visitation are frequently less substantial than those related to custody. Here, the best interest test is more readily employed. Five states have statutes specifically authorizing stepparent visitation in certain situations, including divorce from a custodial parent (Morris, 1989; Victor, Robbins, & Bassett, 1991). Stepparent visitation also is included in more general state statutes that allow any interested party who has a close relationship with the child to make a claim for visitation. A number of state courts have acted without explicit statutory authority and have made visitation orders based on equitable considerations. However, some courts have refused stepparents' petitions for visitation because they feel they have no jurisdiction to issue such orders. They believe they should follow the common law rule that parents have a right to control who has access to their children. In jurisdictions that do allow stepparent visitation, the emphasis more often is on the best interests of the child rather than any rights of the stepparent. Hence, in the typical case, the stepparent has to show a close, personal connection to the stepchild. In contrast, the visitation rights of a biological parent usually could not be denied unless it was shown that the visitation would be harmful to the child. Here, visitation is perceived as a parental right.

Courts have considered a number of factors in deciding whether stepparent visitation is in a child's best interest. Certainly, a major concern is the closeness of the stepparent-stepchild relationship and the question of whether the stepparent took a parental role (*Carter v. Brodrick*, 1982; *Hickenbottom v. Hickenbottom*, 1991). Courts try to determine the extent to which the child will be harmed if the stepparent-stepchild relationship is effectively ended. In making this determination, they look at the relationship and consider information such as its length in relation to the child's age, the emotional attachment, and the amount of care provided. Some courts seem to base this analysis on the concept of the psychological parent, sometimes equating that concept to the legal doctrine of *in loco parentis* (*Carter v. Brodrick*, 1982). Courts that use this analysis occasionally will say that the stepparent who is *in loco parentis* has a right to visitation, thus changing the focus to the stepparent. However, these same courts continue to maintain that their decision about visitation is based on the child's best interest (*Spells v. Spells*, 1977).

Another factor courts consider is whether the number of persons asserting competing parental claims is too large (*Klipstein v. Zalewski*, 1988). For example, one court that denied visitation to a stepfather expressed concern that the 7-year-old child in the case had three father figures: the stepfather, the biological father, and the "present live-in boyfriend and presumably soon to be 3rd husband of the natural-mother" (*Klipstein v. Zalewski*, 1988, p. 1386). The grounds therefore were that granting visitation might result in emotional problems as well as, simply, logistical problems from trying to coordinate the child's activities with the three "fathers."

When the case involves the death of the custodial parent followed by the child's move to the house of the other biological parent, the problem of too many claimants is lessened. In some of these cases, however, the visitation is described as a way to ease the transition to the new home, implying that it would gradually decrease as the child adjusted to the change (*Collins v. Gilbreath*, 1980).

Another factor implicit in some decisions is the assumption that having at least one father is preferable to none at all (*Bryan v. Bryan*, 1982).[2] If the biological father is not part of the child's life, particularly in the case of illegitimate children, then the court may be more willing to grant visitation. For example, in the Arizona case of *Bryan v. Bryan*, the custodial mother and stepfather married in 1979 when the child was an infant. The child was apparently illegitimate, and no mention was made of the child's biological father. The stepparent "had in all respects cared for and treated the child as his own," according to the trial court. The couple divorced in 1981 and the stepparent wanted visitation. The court held that visitation rights could be granted because "the showing of an *in loco parentis* relationship between child and stepparent, together with evidence that the best interest of the child will be served by allowing a partial continuance of that relationship, may provide sufficient reason to limit the presumptive right of the natural parent to uninterrupted custody (p. 1273). Although the stepparent had been with the child since infancy, the total time spent with the child was still less than 2 years. The court's order might result in the mother being required to continue contact with the stepparent until the child reached 18. Surprisingly, the court made no mention of child support.

Financial support frequently is another factor that the courts consider when deciding stepparent visitation claims (*Klipstein v. Zalewski*, 1988). Courts may look with favor on a stepparent who supported a child during the marriage and has continued the support. Moreover, it appears likely that if a court required a stepparent to support the stepchild, the court also would grant visitation rights.

Thus, the analysis by the courts of the visitation question does not present a clear picture of the goal being sought. Some of the factors the courts consider are oriented toward the child, such as whether he or she has a close relationship with the stepparent and whether transitional visitation would be helpful for him or her. However, other factors, such as whether the stepparent is supporting the child or has a parental status, seem oriented toward stepparents' rights.

Child Support and Other Benefits

Generally, stepparents do not have a direct obligation to support their stepchildren. In those few states that do require them to provide support, the obligation usually is more limited than that imposed on biological parents. The stepparents' obligation may be secondary to that of the biological parent, or the obligation may be imposed only if the stepchild will be a public charge (Ramsey, 1986; Ramsey & Masson, 1985; Victor et al., 1991). Only one state continues a stepparent support obligation after the end of the marriage of the biological parent and stepparent. However, that obligation is imposed only if the stepparent has received the stepchild into the stepparent's family and the stepchild continues to reside there (North Dakota Century Code, 1991).

The *in loco parentis* doctrine is also a basis for a support obligation; hence, a stepparent who is *in loco parentis* can be considered responsible for the support of a stepchild. Since the *in loco parentis* relationship can be terminated at will, however, the stepparent can avoid continued financial responsibility by simply declaring that the *in loco parentis* relationship no longer exists (Buser, 1991). Therefore, the doctrine tends to be relevant only to matters related to prior support. For example, a stepparent's claim for reimbursement for expenses related to the child could be denied if the stepparent was *in loco parentis*.

Stepparents also may be required to support stepchildren if the facts of their case present a particularly compelling situation for ordering support. Thus, stepparents who promised support, treated the child as their own, and discouraged biological parent-child contact could be required to pay support based on equitable doctrines such as estoppel (Redman, 1991). However, sympathetic facts do not always result in support award (Buser, 1991).

Although the stepparent's legal obligation to support is limited, most wage-earning stepparents probably do contribute to the support of their stepchildren while they are married to the custodial parent. The financial contribution of stepparents has been recognized by both the states and the federal government for some time. Under both state Worker's Compensation acts and the federal Social Security Act, stepchildren who were dependent on a worker who was injured or killed have been ruled eligible for benefits (Chambers, 1990; Mahoney, 1987). These provisions for benefits for stepchildren have not been controversial and seem to have no negative effect on family relations. If a stepchild is dependent, then benefits are paid from the general fund.

Unfortunately, the financial contribution of stepparents also has been taken into account in a less helpful way by the federal government in cases where the children are poor. Stepparents have been expected to help support stepchildren in order to reduce government expenditures under welfare programs. For example, the amendments by the Ronald Reagan administration to the Aid to Families with Dependent Children (AFDC) program added the requirement that the states must assume that the income of stepparents who are married to the custodial parent will be available for support of the stepchild when setting AFDC benefit amounts. An AFDC grant can be reduced when a custodial parent marries, even though the new spouse has no legal obligation to support the stepchild.[3] Thus, the stepparent is indirectly responsible for support because of the reduction in family income, even when there is no direct obligation. In addition to the effect on government benefits, stepparent income also can have an effect on child support payments between parents. Stepparents can become indirectly obligated to support stepchildren if a court considers the stepparent's income to be a resource of the biological parent in deciding on a child support award. On the one hand, if the total income of the stepparent-custodial parent couple is considered, then a child support award might be less than would be the case if only the custodial parent's income were considered. On the other hand, if the income of the spouse of the noncustodial parent is taken into account, a court could order a larger support payment than one based only on the income of the noncustodial parent. However, relatively few states take the stepparent's income into account at all (Ramsey & Masson, 1985).

While it is generally assumed that stepparents support their stepchildren, for the most part child support reforms have been directed at making biological parents pay rather than at changing the stepparent's voluntary contribution to a legally enforceable one. Beginning in 1974, the federal government began forcing the states to increase the number, amount, and collection efficiency of child support awards (Krause, 1990).

The effect of this increased attention to child support on stepfamilies is not known. If parents who are forced to pay increase their contact with their children, this may be disruptive to stepfamilies who were accustomed to the noncustodial parent being absent. It also may be that the child no longer thinks of the stepparent as provider, a negative change. On the other hand, the increased income might offset any negative effects. As the research on stepfamilies increases, we should learn more about how support issues affect stepfamilies.

LAW REFORM: COMPLEX FAMILIES AND COMPETING GOALS

Why are stepparents' claims given so little recognition even though their financial contribution is generally acknowledged? Perhaps much of the rationale for the current law lies in the history of family demographics. In the past, because divorce was rare, stepfamilies were formed primarily by the death of a parent (Glick, 1988a). Consequently, the stepparent could adopt the stepchild or would be a logical person to be the child's guardian if the custodial parent died. For those stepparents who did not adopt and were not chosen as guardians, perhaps their nonstatus was an appropriate and accurate reflection of their lack of ability or interest in parenting. Now, however, most stepfamilies are not formed after the death of a parent. Instead they are formed after the biological parents divorce. Therefore, both parents have continuing rights and responsibilities related to their child. Consequently, we have a family form that was uncommon in the nineteenth century, but now is increasing common (Glick, 1989b). Yet, we have not decided how the law should respond.

Certainly, part of our difficulty in deciding what stepfamily law should be is the diversity and complexity of stepfamilies (Giles-Sims & Crosbie-Burnett, 1989b). Even if we only considered one type of stepfamily, we might still not agree on the goals and the method for achieving those goals. For example, if we are considering a stepfamily that was formed when a divorced custodial mother of a young child remarried, should we be mainly interested in the child's welfare? If so, does this mean that we should encourage multiple familial ties, or do we want to strengthen the new marriage? If strengthening the new marriage is the goal, does this mean that we should strengthen the stepparent's parental role and discourage the noncustodial parent from assuming an active coparenting arrangement, or would attaching more duties to the stepparent role actually serve to discourage remarriage?

A useful way to analyze these choices is to first list the possible goals of reforms in this area of the law. The most likely possible goals are the following:

1. Promote the child's welfare;

2. Support the custodial parent-child dyad;

3. Protect the rights and interests of the noncustodial parent;

4. Support the new marriage;

5. Reward and protect the stepparent;

6. Establish new (nonnuclear family) norms for stepfamilies;

7. Allow diversity;

8. Simplify administration (and discourage diversity); and

9. Decrease state expenditures on children.

Our present approach reflects our lack of agreement on goals. Parental rights, the child's welfare, and the state's purse seem to be the primary goals that are identified in justifying court opinions. In some areas, such as adoption, attention is given to stepparents.

This disagreement, however, may indicate that we should try to identify a solution that satisfies a number of goals rather than choosing a primary goal. I believe that the feasibility of a compromise is best assessed by considering some reform proposals. Possible approaches might be seen on a continuum in relation to stepparent claims ranging from strong support to no support at all. The strongest support of stepparents would be to facilitate adoption. This would result in the legal replacement of the parent by the stepparent. At the other end of the continuum would be a refusal to recognize any claims of the stepparents, a nonstatus for the stepparent.

What might some compromise positions be? One model worth considering is that recently adopted in England. With the passage of the Children Act 1989, England reformed its law relating to children and families. Under the new law in England, a stepparent who lives with the custodial parent can get a residence order that gives him or her almost the same authority as the parent. The rationale for this change was that it was reasonable for adults who lived with the child to have parental responsibilities. Indeed, the Children Act 1989 does not use the term *stepparent* but rather the "child of the family" concept (Masson, 1991). A person who is a party "to a marriage in relation to whom the child is a child of the family" can apply for an order (the Children Act 1989, section 10[5][a]). In addition, anyone with whom the child has lived for a period of at least 3 years also can apply (the Children Act 1989, section 10[5][b]). Hence, nonmarital partners can possibly obtain a residence order.

The granting of a residence order to a stepparent does not remove parental responsibilities from other individuals. Rather, it increases the number of persons with these responsibilities. Each person with parental responsibility may act alone, except in the few circumstances when the act requires the consent of all. Disputes between those with parental responsibilities can be brought to court and are decided based on the welfare of the child. A stepparent's rights under a residence order are not entirely coextensive with that of a parent. For example, a stepparent with parental responsibility cannot appoint a testamentary guardian, agree to the child's adoption, or consent to an order freeing the child for adoption.

Interestingly enough, this model does not represent what some English stepfamilies wanted. From 1978 to 1981 a study of English stepfamilies who had applied to adopt stepchildren was conducted by Judith Masson and her colleagues, Daphne Norbury and Sandie Chatterton, to determine the characteristics and motivations of these families (Masson, 1984; Masson, Norbury, & Chatterton, 1983). Information on the 1,733 cases in the sample came mainly from case records and reports. Masson found that usually the parents and stepparents were unsure about their legal status and the effect that adoption would have. A frequent reason for the adoption was the desire "to make the family like a proper family" (Masson, 1984,

p. 230) The families often wanted to have the same surname and the same status for both stepchildren and children born of the marriage. Other concerns were anxiety about interference from the noncustodial parent and resentment at having to explain the family composition to public institutions such as schools. As Masson pointed out, however, "for both adults and children living in a stepfamily 'a proper family' cannot be defined only in terms of a family of first marriage" (p. 231). She suggested that a solution "to the name issue may more easily be found in society's acceptance of different family patterns than new legal rules" (p. 231).

In fact, the new Children Act does not make the stepfamily a "proper family"; rather, the act expands the concept of what parent-child relations can be. Unfortunately, we do not know how typical the view of the stepfamilies in the Masson study may be of stepfamilies generally, since the individuals being studied were among the minority of stepfamilies that were applying for adoption. For that group at least the new legislation did not provide what they wanted. Indeed, under current English law, a court considering an adoption application can make a residence order instead, depending on which is better for the child (Cretney & Masson, 1990).

Several American law scholars have recommended that our laws relating to stepparents be changed. For example, Margaret Mahoney (1984) recommended that stepparents married to a custodial parent should be expected to share in the support of stepchildren, and that this obligation should continue after the end of the marriage in certain cases. She also recommended that state laws be amended so courts would have jurisdiction over stepfamily members upon the end of the marriage for the purpose of making custody and visitation decisions.

David Chambers (1990) recently recommended that the stepparent in the ongoing marriage be granted additional rights, perhaps using the British model. However, he would not require stepparents to support stepchildren upon divorce. With regard to custody and visitation after the end of the marriage, he encouraged parent figures to work cooperatively toward long-term contact. If they do not agree, he would place young children with the primary caretaker upon divorce. If the custodial parent died, he would leave the child with the stepparent, provided that the relationship between the child and stepparent was long-term and involved.

Another recent reform proposal came from the Standing Committee on Rights and Responsibilities of Stepparents of the Family Law Section of the American Bar Association (Tenenbaum, 1991). The committee's proposal would give the stepparent the right to discipline the child during the marriage. The proposal says nothing about other rights. It would require the stepparent to support the stepchild, but only if the noncustodial parent was not paying adequate support.

As can be seen from these examples, a number of variations are possible within the framework of regulating child support, custody, and visitation. An additional variation that could be allowed with any of these models would be to let the parties make private contracts that would alter the relationships imposed by law. However, traditionally courts have refused to enforce contracts governing family relations, particularly when they deal with matters related to children, such as custody and visitation. Courts and legislatures are increasingly willing to enforce prenuptial agreements and separation agreements related to financial matters.

Certainly contracts regulating family relations are problematic. One party to the contract may be especially vulnerable because the parties have an intimate relationship and may have a strong emotional investment in the outcome. There may be a substantial time gap between the time the contract was made at the beginning of the marriage, and the time of enforcement at the end of the marriage. The parties' emotional relationship may have changed from one of love and trust to one of hate and suspicion. In addition, enforcement may mean requiring a long-term interaction rather than a one-time payment of money. Perhaps most important is the concern that the courts express about the need to assess what is best for the child presently before them without regard to parental arrangements.

When a court refuses to enforce a contract, its justification is frequently a declarative statement of the court's authority rather than an analysis of the circumstances of the particular contract before it. For example, in *Klipstein v. Zalewski* (1988), the court stated:

While it is true that the mother agreed to visitation in the property settlement agreement, it is axiomatic that a mother cannot bargain away the best interests of a child. Such agreements are at best only a factor to be considered in determining the visitation rights of a stepparent. A court under its parens patriae authority always has the duty and power to disregard agreements made by parents relating to children. (p. 1389)

Which approach should we choose? Legal scholars and researchers are moving away from the first-marriage family as the only model and are encouraging more flexible and varied family structures (Bartlett, 1984; Chambers, 1990; Fine, 1989). It no longer seems appropriate to expect that a stepparent should replace the noncustodial parent. Instead, the stepparent could be viewed as an adult friend or relative rather than as a parent, or, alternatively, society could be more flexible about the number of parents a child should have. These approaches are supportive of compromise.

It may well be that neither stepfamilies nor noncustodial parents want such a compromise. Many stepfamilies may still view the nuclear family model as preferable and want to be as close to that model as possible. Perhaps, like the British stepfamilies, they want to be a "proper" family. Noncustodial parents may feel that their rights would be diminished if stepparents were given more recognition and that this would be particularly unfair if child support obligations are enforced. Certainly our consideration of stepfamily policy goals would be aided by more information about what both stepfamilies and noncustodial parents want.

Unfortunately, trying to assess the costs and benefits of these goals and the methods for achieving them is difficult at best. Assume, for example, that we choose to focus on the child and conclude that a harmonious continuing relationship with all important parental figures is beneficial and desirable. The legal system cannot deliver harmony. Instead it delivers coercive orders that require parties to do things that they do not wish to do. Although we might believe that in many cases a custodial mother should allow a stepfather to visit a stepchild after divorce, we might not feel that the child will benefit if the mother is forced to permit visitation over her strenuous objections. In other words, is the cost of conflict worth the benefit of a continuing relationship with the stepparent?

On the other hand, assume that we decide that we do want to strengthen stepfamilies. Remarriage is still a way out of poverty for many single mothers with children (Duncan, 1984). Although this fact reflects the problems of sex discrimination in our society, nonetheless it remains reality. In addition to the financial advantages of remarriage, our society generally values stable family relationships and family commitment. The first marriage, after all, is ended, and noncustodial fathers frequently do not stay in contact with the child (Furstenberg et al., 1983). If strengthening stepfamilies means following the first-marriage family model, is this an obtainable goal? The legal system has a mechanism for obtaining the legal equivalent through adoption. However, particularly for the older child, the legal rearrangement does not guarantee an emotional rearrangement.

Where does this leave us? If we take a pessimistic view, we can say we do not know what even one type of stepfamily wants or how it operates, and we cannot decide on our goals. If we decide on them, we do not know how to effectuate them. However, a more pragmatic approach suggests that some reform should be considered. As the courts hear more stepparent cases, the law is being changed anyway in a piecemeal and unpredictable fashion. Moving cautiously toward more recognition of stepparents through a compromise reform, could be a catalyst for more research and debate on these issues.

Several features of the British model would be useful in producing a compromise proposal for the legal treatment of stepparents during the marriage. Stepfamilies could choose to apply for a court order similar to the English residence order. This order would provide a means for stepparents to have their caregiving function recognized in an official way. The order would be useful in allowing them to have access to school records, consent to medical care and to do other things that are appropriately within the authority of a person who is functioning as a parent. Stepparents have complained about the inconvenience and the demeaning aspects of being denied these abilities. The issuance of an order also could be a mechanism for providing some additional rights for the child, such as a right to be treated as a child of the stepparent for purposes of inheritance if the stepparent died without a will. The order could indicate also what, if any, support obligation the stepparent would have for the stepchild.

Although this recognition of stepparents would expand the number of persons that had an official parenting role, it is less expansive than the British scheme, which includes nonmarital partners and others. Like the British scheme, the order would not directly diminish the rights of the biological parents. It would be supportive of the new family and of the stepparent. It would establish a new, nonnuclear model in law for stepfamilies. Moreover, it would provide a simple and inexpensive way for mothers of illegitimate children to have their husbands officially accept parental rights and responsibilities. The British legislative history assumes that having the child's caretaker recognized is a benefit to the child. There is no apparent reason to think otherwise, unless the noncustodial parent objects, therefore setting up a potential for family conflict.

The proper status of a stepparent after the end of a marriage is a more difficult problem because the biological parent-stepparent tie has been broken. Divorce and death need to be treated separately because of the different claimants involved.

Ideally, the divorcing parent and stepparent would voluntarily agree to continuing the relationship of the child and stepparent, if they thought that this was best for the child. If the stepparent had gotten a court order during the marriage, this order could remain in effect so the stepparent's legally recognized status would continue. The child could then continue to see the stepparent, and the stepparent would have parental responsibilities while the child was in his or her care.

A concern about this scheme would be the potential proliferation of persons with orders. For example, if the custodial mother remarried, this would mean that potentially three men would have an official parental role: the father, the first stepfather, and the second stepfather. This problem might be more theoretical than real, however, for a majority of cases. Since a majority of biological fathers seldom see their child after 2 years postdivorce (Furstenberg et al., 1983), it would seem likely that stepfathers also would fade away, and hence, would not object to termination of the court order. If a dispute did arise, the law could contain a presumption that the custodial parent's choice would control, absent extraordinary circumstances. However, if a stepparent had the role of a primary caretaker, the stepparent might be more likely to want to continue to have the child live primarily with him or at least to continue to have frequent contact. These cases might support a presumption in favor of the primary caretaker (Chambers, 1990).

If the marriage ended because of the death of the custodial parent rather than by divorce, the stepparent may be in a stronger position to establish a claim to continuing custody. Particularly when the biological parent had little contact with the child, the court might want to allow the child to continue to reside with the stepparent so the child's home, school, and friends would not be changed while the child also was dealing with the loss of a parent. Thus, continuity would prevail over biology.

The cases in which a parent had maintained contact are more difficult. My guess is that most jurisdictions would tend to favor the biological parent. Rather than leaving the courts with an indeterminate directive to decide in the child's best interests, legislation should include some guiding presumptions.

These reform proposals highlight the need for more research. We know little about what stepparents' preferences are with regard to support, visitation, custody or inheritance, and little about what tends to happen when a stepfamily experiences divorce or death. Law reform proposals now are more like trial balloons than studied responses to identified social needs. Although legislative hearings would provide an opportunity for citizen input, they should be in addition to, not instead of, well-designed research projects. We should move cautiously and with as much information as possible because of the diversity of stepfamilies, the coercive power of the law, and the indeterminacy of the best interests standard.

KEY CHAPTER POINTS

1. In most states, stepparents do not have clear rights or responsibilities in relation to their stepchildren.

2. Generally, a stepparent has no obligation to support stepchildren, either during the marriage or upon divorce from the biological parent.

3. Upon divorce, a stepparent usually is not awarded custody of a stepchild. Upon death of the custodial parent, a stepparent who lived with the child has a stronger claim than upon divorce, but courts still find blood ties compelling and tend to favor the other biological parent.

4. A stepparent who has a close relationship with the stepchild may be awarded visitation rights whether the marriage ends in divorce or death of the custodial parent. Some states have statues that specifically allow for visitation by stepparents when it is in the best interests of the child.

5. The laws relating to stepfamilies need consistent, thoughtful reform. The first step in law reform is to identify goals. Then we must develop laws that will further them.

6. Law reform that expands the number of persons who can have a recognized parental role is a good compromise between competing goals, and is recommended.

7. Additional research is needed to both refine law reform goals and decide how to achieve them.

ACKNOWLEDGEMENTS

The author is very grateful to Daan Braveman, David Chambers, Margaret Mahoney, and Judith Masson for their comments on an earlier draft of this chapter.

NOTES

1. The psychological parent is defined as "one who, on a continuing, day to day basis, through interaction, companionship, interplay, and mutuality, fulfills

the child's psychological needs for a parent, as well as the child's physical needs" (Goldstein, Freud, & Solnit, 1973, p. 98).

2. See also *Olvera v. Superior Ct.* (1991) where the discussion focuses on the lack of authority of the trial court to grant custody because the definition of parent does not include a stepparent, and custody can only be decided with regard to children of the marriage.

3. These amendments were part of the Omnibus Budget Reconciliation Act of 1981. Pub. L. No. 97-35. Tit. XXIII, 95 Stat. 357, 843-74.

Chapter 13

BUILDING BRIDGES: REFLECTIONS ON THEORY, RESEARCH, AND PRACTICE

Marilyn Ihinger-Tallman and Kay Pasley

The task we undertake in this final chapter is to synthesize the material from earlier chapters, discuss the commonalities, and assess the collective contribution to our understanding of remarriage and stepparenting. We identify the progress made toward addressing the gaps in the literature (both topical and methodological) by emphasizing the utility of the information for practice in clinical, educational, and legal settings alike. We conclude the chapter with a discussion of the issues and questions that stem from practice and need to be addressed by researchers to further inform clinical practice, educational policies and practices, and legal decisions.

CONTRIBUTIONS TO THE EXTANT LITERATURE

Several topics were identified as either adequately or under researched in Chapter 1. Profiles of the remarried population, the effects of remarriage on children, child outcomes, and the effects of remarriage on the marital dyad have been well covered. Lacunae in this body of literature include information on stepparenting, kin relations, stepfamily behaviors and activities that produce successful family functioning, and cross-national comparative studies.

All the empirical studies in this volume corrected at least one of the methodological shortcomings identified in the review chapter. Sample sizes were relatively large with over 100 respondents in each study (with two exceptions). In addition, data often were collected from more than one respondent, and in one case, documentary evidence verified respondent self-report.

Theoretical Contributions

In Chapter 2 and Chapter 3 by Fine and Kurdek and Giles-Sims, respectively, theoretical contributions were made to the literature. Both chapters offered social psychological theories with strong interactional foci. These authors sought to explain stepfamily adjustment, in one case, and marital responsibility, in the other, offering unique perspectives on what is to be explained. Both theories incorporated a temporal dimension, discussing changes over time. Both also emphasized process rather than structure.

Unique to the two chapters was the key explanatory variable. Fine and Kurdek's multidimensional, cognitive-developmental model incorporated cognitions as the explanatory variable such that cognitive consistency, similarity, and compatibility leads to better stepfamily adjustment. Giles-Sims explained how marital responsibility based on relational morality develops in families when each member is concerned with fulfilling other members' needs as well as his or her own. In this conceptualization, Giles-Sims moves beyond the self-interest focus inherent in the justice perspective to emphasize the value of care. The source of marital responsibility is cooperation and empathy, as based on attributions that affect the broader context.

Commonalities among Empirical Studies

The empirical studies in this volume focused on diverse dependent variables: marital quality and stability, role integration and marital adjustment, quality of the stepmother-stepchild relationship, relations between former spouses along with father involvement, and stepfather loyalty conflicts. However, adjustment is an underlying theme in all these studies, whether explicitly or implicitly. Adjustment is analyzed in terms of adjusting to new circumstances (e.g., studying newly remarried stepfathers at 2 months and 2.5 years following remarriage), to new people (e.g., stepchildren and stepfathers), and to former intimates in new circumstances (e.g., former spouses who have either remained unmarried or who have remarried). The ways in which remarrieds chose to bring about change in, or to adjust, their own behavior or change and adjust the behavior of other family members was studied. This idea of a thematic variable also is applicable to the practice section of the volume. Suggestions were made about how therapists, school personnel, officials deciding public policy, and workers in the legal system can change their behavior (e.g., adjust) as well as the rules of behavior in their institutional settings to better serve those who live in stepfamilies.

Consensus is a second common theme that is apparent in the research studies reported in this volume. Pasley and Sandras (Chapter 4) found that consensus on issues discriminated remarriages characterized by low quality and stability from those with high quality and stability. Bray, Berger, and Boethel (Chapter 5) found that consensus about stepparenting roles was related to marital quality early in remarriage and at 2.5 years, but not when the remarriage had lasted more than 5 years. Ganong and Coleman (Chapter 6) found that parents, stepparents, and adolescent stepchildren all preferred that the parent assume the major responsibility for limit-setting behavior. Quick, McKenry, and Newman (Chapter 7) reported that frequency of agreement between spouses regarding child rearing was the strongest and only predictor of stepmother's perception of the quality of the stepparent-stepchild relationship. Although not conceptualized as consensus, Buehler and Ryan (Chapter 8) found that cooperation between former spouses who had remarried was associated with child support compliance and more frequent and longer visitation of children by fathers.

Unique Contributions from Empirical Studies

Several unique contributions are made by the theoretical and empirical studies included in this volume. For example, Pasley and Sandras found significant differences between remarriages characterized by low marital quality and stability and those with high marital quality and stability. Their findings suggest that shared perceptions, agreement (or the lack of) on issues, and high or low salience of marriage for individual well-being may be key contributors of marital quality and stability in remarriages. These variables need further study to validate the findings reported here.

Findings from the study by Bray and his associates strengthen our confidence in findings from earlier studies showing change over time in the reported behavior and attitudes of stepparents and adolescents. In 1987 Furstenberg found that stepparents who had lived in stepfamilies for more than 7 years reported greater ease in disciplining and loving their stepchildren compared to stepparents who had lived in their stepfamily less than 3 years. Stepparents who had lived in stepfamilies of 7 years or longer duration also reported that they felt it was harder to be a stepparent than a biological parent, more so than did stepparents who had lived 3 years or less in a stepfamily. The evidence that time tempers beliefs, expectations, and experience helps family members acknowledge the fundamental differences between the position and roles of the parent and the stepparent. To the degree that this realization is patterned (e.g., a majority of stepparents who are new to the role hold the belief that stepparenting is no harder than biological parenting, while the majority of stepparents who have held the role longer voice other views), we can say stepfamily roles develop and clarify over time.

Looking at the family as a system, one sees that the developmental stages in remarriage are denoted by predictable stresses and changes. Theoretically, one developmental task that moves the family through these stresses and changes is the integration of the stepparent into a coparental role. Progress toward such integration and adjustment is denoted by stability and clarity in family role relationships.

Recall that Ganong and Coleman found that male stepchildren adjust better than female stepchildren and that females got along less well than males with both biological parents and stepparents. These findings corroborate information from several earlier studies showing a differential adjustment of boys and girls after divorce and remarriage (Clingempeel et al., 1984; Hetherington, 1987; Hetherington & Clingempeel, 1992; Santrock, Warshak, Lindberg, & Meadows, 1982). Again, the strength of the Ganong and Coleman chapter lies in its methodology. Rather than having to draw conclusions from cross-sectional data, the authors have drawn their conclusions from panel data.

The unique contribution of Quick and her associates (Chapter 6) comes from the narrowness of the study. That is, the sample was restricted to biological father-stepmother families with mid-adolescent sons and daughters who either resided in the household or visited frequently. Data were collected from two respondents, representing codependent role relationships. Findings from previous studies confirm that stepmother-stepchild relations are the most problematic ones in the stepfamily. This study reinforces the idea by showing that time may be the most important factor in developing close-knit, caring, mutually respectful step-relationships. Both patience and a strong support network are essential until sufficient time passes for collective experience to result in a shared (and, preferably positive) history.

The Buehler and Ryan study (Chapter 8) adds to the scant amount of information available on the former-spouse relationship following divorce and remarriage (see, as examples, Ahrons & Wallisch, 1987; Duran-Aydintug & Ihinger-Talllman, 1993; Masheter, 1991). Its contribution lies in the revelation of the different behaviors of fathers after their own remarriage or that of their former spouse. These data further our understanding of the effects of remarriage and stepfamily formation on adults and children. Predictably, because of this study, more questions have been raised. Do divorced fathers perceive that new stepfathers are supposed to take their place in their children's lives? What is normative in this situation? Alternatively (and/or concomitantly), when former wives remarry, do they discourage their children's biological father from maintaining a stable role in the lives of his children? Is it to a new wife's advantage for conflict to escalate between her husband and his former spouse, thus decreasing contact with his children? Future research is needed to address these questions.

The unique contribution of Clingempeel, Colyar, and Hetherington's study (Chapter 9) lies in the effort to assess the loyalty conflicts experienced by men in a stepfather position. The results of the study shed new light on stepfather loyalty conflicts and its influence on marital satisfaction and resource allocation. Here, again, time seems to be an influential factor when accounting for changes in the allocation of resources to children and stepchildren, as well as the emotional and interactional consequences of such allocation.

Contributions from the Practice Pieces

In Chapter 10, Browning provided an alternative set of guidelines for therapists so they may better serve the specific needs of stepfamilies. He emphasized the ways in which assumptions from traditional family therapy are most appropriate for use in first-marriage families. Because of the complicated and complex family system that results from remarriage, such standard interventions as inviting the entire family into therapy sessions or creating therapeutic tension may be harmful to clinical work with stepfamilies. The key contribution made by Browning is in cautioning therapists to examine carefully the assumptions underlying conventional strategies of family systems intervention; armed with a thorough understanding of the unique nature of stepfamily life, therapists must incorporate alternative strategies into the therapeutic process.

The educational institution provides fertile ground for disempowering stepfamilies due to policies and practices that are insensitive to the needs of children experiencing parental divorce and remarriage. Crosbie-Burnett (Chapter 11) recommended a series of specific changes to help those working in educational settings to gain a greater understanding of, and sensitivity to, the changing American family. Her unique contribution lies in this series of recommendations and in the belief that changes in our ideology about the family must precede any institutional change.

The uniqueness of Ramsey's discussion in Chapter 12 lies in her presentation of case law to illustrate the legal standing of parents and stepparents. This presentation helps readers who lack legal understanding to better understand how issues are interpreted and justified from a legal perspective. She advocated greater flexibility in defining parental figures and called for more consistency in the law.

In the following section, we identify the ways in which the two theoretical models and findings from empirical studies can be used to better inform practice. Practice implications are limited to three contexts: therapeutic, educational, and legal/public policy.

BUILDING A BRIDGE: FROM THEORY AND RESEARCH TO PRACTICE

The research studies presented in this volume provide fertile ground for practice implications. The theoretical model advocated by Fine and Kurdek suggests that practitioners should address ways to clarify role perceptions, set realistic expectations for stepmember behavior, develop consensus and mutual understandings about the causes of family events, and recognize the differences between first-marriage and remarriage families. Clinically, practitioners need to provide a safe environment in which different perspectives are shared and respect for such differences are modeled and encouraged until such time as the cognitions of family members become more similar. When goals differ between members of a stepfamily, such as the spouses (parent and stepparent), Browning indicated the importance of clarifying individual goals and obtaining permission from other family members to work on them. Also important is searching for a potential middle ground (Papernow, 1987) or finding an alternative solution with which all can live. When therapists are well informed about stepfamily life, they can employ another effective strategy: they can help "normalize" the experiences of clients by suggesting how their experiences are common among stepfamilies (Pasley, Dollahite, & Ihinger-Tallman, 1993). In this way, members of the stepfamily can gain a better sense of what is possible, expected, and likely to happen when people live in stepfamilies.

In educational settings, the multidimensional cognitive-developmental model of Fine and Kurdek also can be used to plan, implement, and evaluate educational interventions. For example, in anticipating the lack of role clarity for members of a stepfamily and the need for members to hold realistic and shared expectations, discussion groups can be organized to address these issues. Participants, whether adults or children, can learn the range of behaviors that stepparents are likely to enact, as well as those that characterize interactions between the stepparent and the stepchild. They can learn how these behaviors are both similar and also different from those in first-marriage families. Participants can be encouraged to explore why some expectations are more facilitative of stepfamily adjustment than others. Assuming that the groups consist of participants with varying degrees of experience in stepfamilies, ideas about what works and what does not, as well as under what conditions certain behaviors are helpful, can be offered. In other words, participants can learn from others in similar circumstances who have had more time living in a stepfamily.

Legally, policies and practices could reflect greater flexibility in the definition of a parent, as suggested by Ramsey in her discussion of the recent changes in English law in Chapter 12. Encouraging a recognition of the role of multiple adults in children's lives is warranted.

The theory of marital responsibility based on relational morality, as described by Giles-Sims in Chapter 3, suggests that care for others that is not motivated by self-interest has particular relevance for addressing issues of fairness and meeting the needs of stepfamily members. In practice, the ideas expressed in this chapter have valuable implications. Relational morality focuses on attributions, disclosure, empathy, and cooperation as factors with a positive influence on family interactions. As such, gaining skills that enhance disclosure, empathy, and cooperation is an important goal for intervention and prevention strategies. For example, disclosure is fostered by the development of effective listening skills so that when an individual paraphrases the content and affect of what is said, the sender feels heard and, in turn, is more likely to reciprocate with additional sharing (Galvin & Brommel, 1991). Similarly, empathy is demonstrated by behaviors that let the sender feel that the receiver understands the issue from the former's perspective (Galin & Brommel, 1991). Thus, training in effective communication skills will foster relational morality. Such training can occur in a variety of settings, from school environments to parent education programs and individual counseling sessions. When a member of a stepfamily is able to adopt the perspective of another member and demonstrate this understanding in a clear manner (e.g., through effective communication), then what is perceived as fair by one member is more likely to be a mutual perspective. In the long run, such positive communication may diminish the need for legal intervention

Another important point made by Giles-Sims emphasizes the role of the broader sociohistorical context and the way in which members of stepfamilies accept, reject, redefine, and respond to it. For example, gaining insight into gender differences when approaching problems may be a key to resolution. When stepfamilies encounter problems, it is common that they attributed them to stepfamily life (Pasley et al., 1993). However, in actuality, many problems result from other sources, such as gender differences or behavior that is attributable to individual developmental stages. In practice, this suggests that therapists, educators, and those in the legal profession must be mindful of the subtle, but often powerful, impact of contextual factors on stepfamily life. For example, in the case in which a stepfamily with an adolescent child comes to therapy, indicating that conflict arises from the adolescent's rejection of parental attempts to unite the family by demanding that the adolescent participate in family activities, an understanding of the context may help inform a solution. In a first-marriage family, the same adolescent behavior is accepted since this stage of individual development is characterized by the desire for increased independence and autonomy. For the stepfamily, however, a primary task is to develop some degree of cohesion or sense of "we-ness" in the family (Ihinger-Tallman & Pasley, 1987). One way to do this is to plan shared family time. In other words, the needs of the group (stepfamily) conflict with the needs of the individual (adolescent). Helping the stepfamily see the broader social context of individual and family development allows its members to redefine the problem and identify workable solutions.

In educational environments, interventions need to include information on the developmental tasks/stages of stepfamilies so that participants can learn about common stepfamily experiences. The availability of curriculum materials on step-families and of classroom activities that recognize and communicate respect for family diversity can serve as one means through which to educate children, teachers, and other school personnel to the varieties of family life.

These findings have particular relevance for clinical practice. Interventions that assist clients in gaining skills in problem solving and negotiation may be especially helpful in alleviating the stresses of adjustment that stem from stepfamily life. Programs and interventions that train individuals, couples and families to resolve problems in effective ways are likely to increase consensus and perceptions of fairness. In turn, good communication would strengthen the barriers to divorce. Some strategies could be borrowed from existing programs that have proven effective (see, as examples Buehler et al., 1992; Renick, Blumberg, & Markman, 1992).

Other skills may be helpful to members of stepfamilies. For example, Quick and her associates found that the quality of the step-relationship between adolescents and stepmothers was best explained by the use of certain coping strategies (reframing and social support) by the adolescents. Thus, these young people might benefit from clinical interventions that focus on cognitions and encourage them to consider issues in a positive light, from a different perspective, or using additional information. In addition, identifying and accessing social support (from friends, relatives, agencies, or organizations) may be another effective strategy for improving the quality of the step-relationship. Since the quality of the step-relationship has been found to be a strong predictor of overall stepfamily adjustment, clearly, strategies that enhance its quality are warranted.

In educational settings, many of the same types of interventions could be pursued. That is, school counselors could design programs that encourage students to think differently-and more positively-about stepfamily life. Negative stereotypes are still found with some regularity among teachers, college students, nurses, and counselors (Coleman & Ganong, 1987a). Such programs could also help students explore the range of possible social supports available to them within their immediate family, their extended family, and the larger community. Coaching on how to effectively access such supports also could be part of such programs.

As suggested by Crosbie-Burnett, school personnel at all levels (departments of education, school boards, teachers, etc.) can assist students if they are well-informed about stepfamily issues, the known sources of stress, and the means for alleviating it.

Pasley and her associates (1993) suggested that normative experiences of step-family members include role ambiguity, loyalty conflicts, uncertainty about adminis-tering discipline, unrealistic expectations, and stepparent-stepchild distance and/or conflict. New information resulting from the studies reported here offers additional insight into newly developing normative behavior.

Ganong and Coleman found that closeness in the stepparent-stepchild relationship decreased as the child entered adolescence. Research findings suggest that this experience is common in families with adolescents (Steinberg, 1991). They also found that conflict between parent/stepparent and child was not an overriding issue for the stepfamilies in their study. While folklore suggests that conflict permeates this stage in family development for most families, the literature again suggests that conflict is not overriding (Steinberg, 1991). Thus, it may be that stepfamilies with adolescents are more like first-marriage families with adolescents, at least where closeness and conflict are concerned. Again, normalizing the experiences for stepfamilies may be a key to helping them establish realistic expectations for family life.

The findings from Buehler and Ryan have relevance for legal decisions concerning visitation. These authors offer some basis for developing interventions aimed at divorcing spouses. Recall that in cases where neither former spouse remarried, high levels of direct competition were associated with decreased visitation. Also, recall that when the wife remarried, conflict and cooperation were associated with more frequent visitations from fathers, and the visitations were of longer duration. Of more interest to the courts is the finding that when former spouses remarried, the positive relationship between cooperation and the payment of child support was strengthened. These findings suggest that interventions that assist former spouses to resolve conflict and increase cooperation also may increase the likelihood that child support payments are made regularly. It may be that courts have it within their power to order former spouses to participate in short-term interventions that focus on teaching problem solving and negotiation skills. This recommendation is not new (see Buehler et al., 1992). If courts can order counseling, then other types of intervention (like family life education) may result in a greater commitment to financial responsibility to children in the long run.

Negotiation skills that result in "peaceful coexistence" (Nelson & Levant, 1991, p. 296) could impart knowledge to help stepfamilies set realistic goals and expectations, thus fostering the development of shared cognitions. Programs that emphasize such training have been found to increase parents' ability to reflect their children's feelings, express their own feelings, and accept their children's feelings, among other things, but it is less likely to influence undesirable behaviors, such as threatening or preaching (Nelson & Levant, 1991). Unfortunately such programs have not been shown to affect levels of family cohesion and adaptability.

Legal proceedings themselves have been noted as a reason why former spouses are identified as an obstacle to a continued relationship with children following divorce (Dudley, 1991). Decisions and events of the proceedings have been identified as problematic. For example, fathers perceived that judges disregarded their testimony. Fathers became hostile and cynical about family courts as they were perceived as biased toward mothers and insensitive to fathers needs and rights. From the fathers' perspective, the courts were insensitive to requests for the enforcement or expansion of visitation agreements. Programs that assist members of families to better understand the perspective of the legal profession concerning rights and responsibilities may decrease such frustration as solutions are worked out. In addition, programs are needed to educate members of the legal profession about the issues and concerns of family members as they make the transition from one marriage to another. In this way, the legal profession can engage clients in ways that demonstrate understanding and concern for all rather than on the basis of expediency or common practices.

BUILDING A BRIDGE IN THE OTHER DIRECTION: FROM THEORY AND PRACTICE TO RESEARCH

From the chapters that offer theoretical models and a focus on practice, a number of questions are suggested as guidepost to future research. First, from the multi-dimensional cognitive-developmental model applied to stepfamilies offered by Fine and Kurdek, the following study questions are derived:

1. How is cognitive consistency, similarity, and compatibility manifest in step-families? How can these concepts best be operationalized?

2. Is it possible to achieve such consistency, similarity, and compatibility in groups of more than two people?

3. How are members of stepfamilies socialized to have common expectations, assumptions, and standards (or norms)?

4. Is it desirable for all family members to share cognitions? If so, how does variety, diversity, and stimulus enter the family under such circumstances?

5. If conflict generates change, how can change occur when consistency and

similarity prevail?

From the chapter by Giles-Sims, which discusses the theory of marital responsibility based on relational morality, several questions were generated for future empirical study. These include:

1. How can the variables in the Justice Perspective be merged with the variables in the Care Perspective to produce a single theoretical framework with which to explain stepfamily phenomena?

2. How do stepfamilies create a climate of trust so that member needs can be met? What conditions affect the development of such a climate? How do these conditions, in turn, affect the meeting of individual and group needs?

3. How does congruency between family members regarding perceived needs affect family decisions regarding marital responsibility?

The chapter by Browning offered a critique of traditional family systems therapy for clinical work with stepfamilies. A number of questions related to the need for well-designed intervention studies emerged:

1. What is the nature of interventions that therapists use with stepfamilies when applying a systemic approach?

2. From the therapist's perspective, which interventions are most helpful? From the perspective of the various stepfamily members, which interventions are most helpful?

3. What assumptions do therapists make about stepfamily life that underlie their approach to therapy with stepfamilies?

4. Are there differences in the assumptions held, and interventions used by, therapists with greater versus lesser knowledge about stepfamily life? How do such difference influence therapeutic outcomes?

5. Under what conditions might a psycho-educational approach to work with stepfamilies be most appropriate? What outcomes will result from such an approach?

Crosbie-Burnett provided a series of recommendations regarding educational policies and practices. As in the Browning chapter, her comments resulted in the following questions for future empirical study:

1. How do negative perceptions of children from different family forms affect

the treatment they receive in classrooms? Do teachers who anticipate more behavior problems from children of divorce and remarriage also report more problem behavior? Might a trained observer who was ignorant to a child's family structure report similar behavior problems?

2. What effect does the adoption of empowerment behaviors (e.g., avoiding language that communicates that stepfamilies are deviant) on the part of educators have on children and on parent or stepparent involvement in schools?

3. Do planned interventions that focus on sensitizing educational personnel to stepfamily issues result in observable changes in classroom behavior?

4. What effect do planned interventions have on children's academic performance and attitude(s) toward the educational environment?

In Chapter 12, Ramsey examined the legal issues concerning stepfamily rights and responsibilities. Several questions to guide future research resulted from her discussion:

1. What information do legal practitioners need about stepfamily life to better inform decisions about custody, visitation, and child support following the end of the marriage?

2. What effects do legal decisions have on parents, stepparents, and children?

3. As with other professionals, what beliefs do legal practitioners hold about families and stepfamilies?

4. How do such beliefs affect the way in which legal practitioners interact with stepfamilies or the legal decisions which result?

CONCLUSIONS

We hope that the material presented in the chapters of this volume advances the understanding of the dynamics and complexity of stepfamily living. New theoretical frameworks were offered which have implications for practice and future research. The findings from methodologically sound studies were presented. Like the theoretical frameworks, these findings have particular relevance for practice and can serve as the foundation for a new generation of studies. The chapters that address issues faced by therapists, educators, and members of the legal profession are not only informative in their own right, but can also help to inform researchers about areas needing further empirical investigation. Finally, by outlining some of the linkages between theory, research, and practice in this final chapter, we have intended to strengthen the relationship between those who generate know- ledge via empirical investigation and those who apply it. We believe that this relationship, conceptualized as a bridge, goes two ways: that the findings from theoretical models and empirical research can, and do, inform practice, just as theory and practice can, and do, inform research. The connection between "real world" knowledge and "social science" knowledge is too often misperceived or ignored. This volume represents our attempt to once again focus attention on both knowledge sources, to emphasize the value derived from them, and to encourage greater dialogue between those who develop theories, those who study stepfamiles, and those work with these families.

KEY CHAPTER POINTS

1. Two common themes emerged from the theoretical models and research studies presented in the volume, including the effects of time and process on stepfamily adjustment and the role of consensus in the development and maintenance of stepfamilies.

2. Several unique contributions to understanding stepfamilies were identified, such as clarity of the stepparent role, the effects of the marital status of former spouses on the coparental relationship, and the harmfulness of clinical assumptions used in work with stepfamilies.

3. Examples are discussed that demonstrate how theory and research can be useful in practice, and questions for future research generated by theory and practice are also presented.

REFERENCES

Aguirre, B. E., & Kirwan, P. (1986). Marriage order and the quality and stability of marital relationships: A test of Lewis and Spanier's theory. *Journal of Comparative Family Studies, 27,* 247-276.

Aguirre, B. E., & Parr, W. C. (1982). Husband's marriage order and the stability of first/second marriage of white and black women. *Journal of Marriage and the Family, 44,* 605-620.

Ahrons, C. R. (1979). The binuclear family: Two households, one family. *Alternative Lifestyles, 2,* 499-515.

Ahrons, C. R. (1981). The continuing coparental relationship between divorced spouses. *American Journal of Orthopsychiatry, 5,* 415-428.

Ahrons, C. R. (1983). Predictors of paternal involvement postdivorce: Mothers' and fathers' perceptions. *Journal of Divorce, 6*(3), 55-69.

Ahrons, C. R. (1984). The binuclear family: Parenting roles and relationships. In I. Koch-Nielsen (Ed.), *Parent-child relationship, post-divorce: A seminar report* (pp. 54-79). Copenhagen, Denmark: Danish National Institute for Social Research.

Ahrons, C. R., & Rodgers, R. H. (1987). *Divorced families: A multidisciplinary developmental view.* New York: Norton.

Ahrons, C. R., & Wallisch, K. (1987). Parenting in the binuclear family: Relationships between biological and stepparents. In K. Pasley & M. Ihinger-Tallman (Eds.), *Remarriage and stepparenting: Current research and theory* (pp. 225-256). New York: Guilford Press.

Albrecht, S. (1979). Correlates of marital happiness among the remarried. *Journal of Marriage and the Family, 41,* 857-867.

Albrecht, S., Bahr, H., & Goodman, K. (1983). *Divorce and remarriage: Problems, adaptations, and adjustments.* Westport, CT: Greenwood.

Amato, P. R. (1987). Family processes in one-parent, stepparent, and intact families: The child's point of view. *Journal of Marriage and the Family, 49*, 327-337.

Amato, P. R., & Ochiltree, G. (1987). Child and adolescent competence in intact, one-parent, and step-families: An Australian study. *Journal of Divorce, 10*(3/4), 75-96.

Ambert, A. (1986). Being a stepparent: Live-in and visiting stepchildren. *Journal of Marriage and the Family, 48*, 795-804.

Ambert, A. M. (1988). Relationships with former in-laws after divorce: A research note. *Journal of Marriage and the Family, 50*, 679-686.

Anderson, J. Z., & White, G. D. (1986). An empirical investigation of interactive and relationship patterns in functional and dysfunctional nuclear families and stepfamilies. *Family Process, 25*, 407-422.

Anderson, R. F., Kinney, J., & Gerler, E. R. (1984). The effects of divorce groups on children's classroom behavior and attitudes toward divorce. *Elementary School Guidance and Counseling, 19*, 70-76.

Appel, K. W. (1985). America's changing families: A guide for educators. *Fastback 219*. Bloomington, IN: Phi Delta Kappa Educational Foundation.

Babbie, E. (1986). *The practice of social research*. Belmont, CA: Wadsworth.

Ball, D., McKenry, P. C., & Price-Bonham, S. (1983). Use of repeated-measure designs in family research. *Journal of Marriage and the Family, 45*, 885-896.

Barnes, H., & Olson, D. H. (1982). Parent-adolescent communication. In D. H. Olson & *Family Inventories*. Saint Paul, MN: Family Social Science.

Barney, J. (1990). Stepfamilies: Second chance or second rate? *Phi Delta Kappan, 72*(2), 144-147.

Bartlett, K. (1984). Rethinking parenthood as an exclusive status: The need for alternatives when the premise of the nuclear family has failed. *Virginia Law Review, 70*, 879-963.

Bartz, K. W., & Nye, F. I. (1970). Early marriage: Propositional formulation. *Journal of Marriage and the Family, 32*, 258-268.

Baucom, D. H. (1987). Attributions in distressed relations: How can we explain them? In S. Duck & D. Perlman (Eds.), *Heterosexual relations, marriage and divorce* (pp. 177-206). London: Sage.

Baucom, D. H., & Epstein, N. (1990). *Cognitive-behavioral marital therapy*. New York: Brunner/Mazel.

Baumrind, D. (1979). *Rating scales for parents of adolescent children*. Family Socialization and Developmental Competence Project. Berkeley, CA: University of California, Berkeley, Institute of Human Development.

Baydar, N. (1988). Effects of parental separation and reentry into union on the emotional well-being of children. *Journal of Marriage and the Family, 50*, 967-981.

Beck, A. T., Rush, A. J., Shaw, B. F., & Emery G. (1979). *Cognitive therapy of depression*. New York: Guilford.

Bell, J. E. (1975). *Family therapy*. New York: Jason Aronson.

Bellah, R. N., Madsen, R., Sullivan, W. M., Swidler, A., & Tipton, S. M. (1985). *Habits of the heart: Individual and commitment in American life*. Berkeley, CA: University of California Press.

Berg, B., & Kurdek, L. A. (1983). *Parent Separation Inventory*. Unpublished manuscript. Wright State University, Dayton.

Berman, W. H. (1988). The role of attachment in the post-divorce experience. *Journal of Personality and Social Psychology, 54*, 496-503.

Bernard, J. (1956). *Remarriage: A study of marriage*. New York: Russel & Russel.

Bernard, J. (1981). *The female world*. New York: Free Press.

Bertalanffy, L. von. (1968). *General systems theory: Foundation, development, applications*. New York: Brazillier.

Bitter, R. G. (1986). Late marriage and marital instability: The effects of heterogeneity an inflexibility. *Journal of Marriage and the Family, 48*, 631-640.

Blanc, A. K. (1987). The formation and dissolution of second units: Marriage and cohabitation in Sweden and Norway. *Journal of Marriage and the Family, 49*, 391-400.

Bloom, B. L., & Hodges, W. F. (1981). The predicament of the newly separated. *Community Mental Health Journal, 17*, 277-293.

Bohannon, P. (1970a). *Divorce and after*. New York: Doubleday.

Bohannon, P. (1970b). Divorce chains, households of remarriage, and multiple divorces. In P. Bohannon (Ed.), *Divorce and after* (pp. 127-139). New York: Doubleday.

Booth, A., & Edwards, J. N. (1992). Starting over: Why remarriages are more unstable. *Journal of Family Issues, 13*, 179-194.

Booth, A., Johnson, D., & Edwards, J. N. (1983). Measuring marital instability. *Journal of Marriage and the Family, 45*, 387-393.

Booth, A., Johnson, D., White, L. K., & Edwards, J. N. (1986). Divorce and marital instability over the life course. *Journal of Family Issues, 7*, 421-442.

Boss, P. (1980). Normative family stress: Family boundary changes across the life span. *Family Relations, 29*, 445-450.

Boss, P. (1987). Family stress. In M. B. Sussman & S. K. Steinmetz (Eds.), *Handbook of marriage and the family* (pp. 695-724). New York: Plenum Press.

Boss, P., & Greenberg, J. (1984). Family boundary ambiguity: A new variable in family stress. *Family Process, 23*, 535-546.

Boss, P., Pearce-McCall, D., & Greenberg, J. (1987). Normative loss in mid-life families: Rural, urban, and gender differences. *Family Relations, 36*, 437-443.

Boss, P. G., Greenberg, J., & Pearce-McCall, D. (1986). *The measurement of boundary ambiguity in families*. Unpublished manuscript, University of Minnesota, St. Paul.

Boszormenyi-Nagy, I., & Krasner, B. R. (1986). *Between give and take: A clinical guide to contextual therapy.* New York: Brunner/Mazel.

Bowen, M. A. (1960). A family concept of schizophrenia. In D. D. Jackson (Ed.), *The etiology of schizophrenia* (pp. 346-372). New York: Basic Books.

Bowen, M. A. (1972). Being and becoming a family therapist. In A. Ferber, M. Mendelson, & A. Napier (Eds.), *The book of family therapy* (pp. 134-154). New York: Science House.

Bowerman, C. E., & Irish, D. P. (1962). Some relationships of stepchildren to their parents. *Marriage and Family Living, 24,* 113-121.

Bowman, M., & Ahrons, C. R. (1985). Impact of legal custody status on fathers' parenting postdivorce. *Journal of Marriage and the Family, 47,* 481-488.

Bradbury, T. N., & Fincham, F. D. (1990). Attributions in marriage: Review and critique. *Psychological Bulletin, 107,* 3-33.

Brand, E., & Clingempeel, W. G. (1987). Interdependencies of marital and tepparent-stepchild relationships and children's psychological adjustment: Research findings and clinical implications. *Family Relations, 36,* 140-145.

Braver, S. L., Fitzpatrick, P. J., & Bay, R. C. (1991). Noncustodial parents' report f child support payment. *Family Relations, 40,* 180-185.

Bray, J. H. (1988a). Children's development in early remarriage. In E. M. Hetherington & J. Arasteh (Eds.), *The impact of divorce, single-parenting and step-parenting on children* (pp. 279-298). Hillsdale, NJ: Lawrence Earlbaum Associates.

Bray, J. H. (1988b). *Developmental issues in stepfamilies research project: Final report.* Grant Number R01 HD18025. Bethesda, MD: National Institute of Child Health and Human Development.

Bray, J. H. (1991, August). *Clinical interventions with adolescents in stepfamilies.* Paper presented at the annual convention of the American Psychological Association, San Francisco, CA.

Bray, J. H. (1992). Family relationships and children's adjustment in clinical and nonclinical stepfather families. *Journal of Family Psychology, 6,* 60-68.

Bray, J. H., & Anderson, H. (1984). Strategic interventions with single-parent families. *Psychotherapy, 21,* 101-109.

Bray, J. H., & Berger, S. H. (1990). Non-custodial father and paternal grandparent relationships in stepfamilies. *Family Relations, 39,* 414-419.

Bray, J. H., Berger, S. H., & Pollack, S. (1986, October). *Stepping forward: A developmental/intergenerational approach to working with remarried families.* Paper presented at the meeting of the American Association for Marriage and Family Therapy, Orlando, FL.

Bray, J. H., Berger, S. H., Silverblatt, A. H., & Hollier, A. (1987). Family process and organization during early remarriage: A preliminary analysis. In J. P. Vincent (Ed.), *Advances in family intervention, assessment, and theory* (pp. 253-279). Greenwich, CT: JAI Press.

Brody, G. H., Neubaum, E., & Forehand, R. (1988). Serial marriage: A heuristic analysis of an emerging family form. *Psychological Bulletin, 103,* 211-222.

Bronfenbrenner, U. (1979). *The ecology of human development.* Cambridge, MA: Harvard University Press.

Brown, A. C., Green, R. J., & Druckman, J. (1990). A comparison of stepfamilies with and without child-focused problems. *Journal of Orthopsychiatry, 60,* 556-566.

Brown, K. (1984). *Stepmothering in stepmother and combination families: The strains and satisfactions of making the role of stepmother.* Unpublished doctoral dissertation, University of Texas, Austin.

Browning, S. W. (1987). Preference prediction, empathy, and personal similarity as variables of family satisfaction in intact and stepfather families. *Dissertation Abstracts International, 47*(11), 4642B.

Bryan, S. H., Ganong, L. H., Coleman, M., & Bryan, L. R. (1985). Counselors' perceptions of stepparents and stepchildren. *Journal of Counseling Psychology, 32,* 279-282.

Bryan v. Bryan, 645 P.2d 1267 (Ariz. App. 1982).

Bryant, Z. L., Coleman, M., & Ganong, L. H. (1988). Race and family structure stereotyping: Perceptions of black and white nuclear and stepfamilies. *Journal of Black Psychology, 15,* 1-16.

Buehler, C., Betz, P., Ryan, C. M., Legg, B. H., & Trotter, B. B. (1992). Description and orientation for divorcing parents: Implications for postdivorce prevention programs. *Family Relations, 41,* 154-162.

Buehler, C., Hogan, M. J., Robinson, B., & Levy, R. J. (1986). Remarriage following divorce: Stressors and well-being of custodial and noncustodial parents. *Journal of Family Issues, 7,* 405-420.

Buehler, C., & Trotter, B. B. (1990). Nonresidential and residential parents' perception of the former spouse relationship and children's social competence following marital separation: Theory and programmed intervention. *Family Relations, 39,* 395-404.

Bulcroft, K., Bulcroft, R., Hatch, L., & Borgatta, E. F. (1989). Antecedents and consequences of remarriage in later life. *Research on Aging, 11,* 82-106.

Bumpass, L. & Call, V. (1988). *A national survey of families and households.* Madison, WI: University of Wisconsin, Center for Demography and Ecology.

Bumpass, L., Martin, T. C., & Sweet, J. A. (1991). The impact of family background and early marital factors on marital disruption. *Journal of Family Issues, 12,* 22-42.

Bumpass, L., & Sweet, J. (1989). *National estimates of cohabitation: Cohort levels and union stability.* NSFH Working Paper 2. Madison, WI: University of Wisconsin, Center for Demography and Ecology.

Bumpass, L., Sweet, J. A., & Cherlin, A. (1991). The role of cohabitation in declining rates of marriage. *Journal of Marriage and the Family, 53,* 913-927.

Bumpass, L., Sweet, J. A., & Martin, T. C. (1990). Changing patterns of remarriage. *Journal of Marriage and the Family, 52,* 747-756.

Burchinal, L. G. (1964). Characteristics of adolescents from unbroken, broken and reconstituted families. *Journal of Marriage and the Family, 24,* 44-51.

Burks, V. K., Lund, D. A., Gregg, C. H., & Bluhm, H. P. (1988). Bereavement and remarriage for older adults. *Death Studies, 12,* 51-60.

Buser, P. (1991). Introduction: The first generation of stepchildren. *Family Law Quarterly, 25,* 1-18.

Byrd, A. J., & Smith, R. M. (1988). A qualitative analysis of the decision to remarry using Gilligan's ethics of care. *Journal of Divorce, 11*(3-4), 87-102.

Camara, K. A., & Resnick, G. (1988). Interparental conflict and cooperation: Factors moderating children's post-divorce adjustment. In E. M. Hetherington & J. D. Arastah (Eds.), *Impact of divorce, single parenting, and stepparenting on children* (pp. 169-196). Hillsdale, NJ: Erlbaum.

Campbell, D. T., & Fiske, D. W. (1959). Convergent and discriminant validation by the multitrait-multimethod matrix. *Psychological Bulletin, 56,* 81-105.

Camper, P. M., Jacobson, N. S., Holtzworth-Munroe, A., & Schmaling, K. B. (1988). Causal attributions for interactional behaviors in married couples. *Cognitive Therapy and Research, 12,* 195-209.

Carter, B. (1989, October). *Clinical work with stepfamilies.* Paper presented at the 47th annual conference of the American Association for Marriage and Family Therapy, San Francisco, CA.

Carter v. Brodrick, 644 F2d 850 (Alaska, 1982).

Carter, E. A., & McGoldrick, M. (Eds.) (1980). *The family life cycle.* New York: Gardner Press.

Carter, E. A., & McGoldrick, M. (1988). *The changing family lifecycle.* New York: Gardner Press.

Cassetty, J. (1978). *Child support and public policy: Security support from absent fathers.* Lexington, MA: Heath.

Chambers, D. (1990). Stepparents, biologic parents, and the law's perception of "family" after divorce. In S. Sugarman & H. Kay (Eds.), *Divorce reform at the crossroads* (pp. 102-129). New Haven, CT: Yale University Press.

Cherlin, A. (1978). Remarriage as an incomplete institution. *American Journal of Sociology, 84,* 634-650.

Cherlin, A. (1981). *Marriage, divorce, remarriage.* Cambridge, MA: Harvard University Press.

Cherlin, A. J., & McCarthy, J. (1985). Remarried couple households: Data from the June 1980 current population survey. *Journal of Marriage and the Family, 47,* 23-30.

The Children Act 1989. (New legislation in the United Kingdom, effective October 1991).

Chilman, C. S. (1983). Remarriage and stepfamilies: Research results and implications. In E. C. Macklin, & R. H. Rubin (Eds.), *Contemporary families and alternate lifestyles: A handbook on research and theory* (pp. 147-163). Beverly Hills, CA: Sage.

Cissna, K. N., Cox, D. E., & Bochner, A. P. (1990). The dialectic of marital and parental relationships within the stepfamily. *Communication Monographs, 57*, 44-61.

Clark, H. (1988). *The law of domestic relations in the United States.* 2nd ed. Minneapolis, MN: West Publishing.

Clingempeel, W. G. (1981). Quasi-kin relationships and marital quality in stepfather families. *Journal of Personality and Social Psychology, 41*, 890-901.

Clingempeel, W. G., Brand, E., & Ievoli, R. (1984). Stepparent-stepchild relationships in stepmother and stepfather families: A multimethod study. *Family Relations, 33*, 465-473.

Clingempeel, W. G., Brand, E., & Segal, S. (1987). A multilevel-multivariate-developmental perspective for future research in stepfamilies. In K. Pasley & M. Ihinger-Tallman (Eds.), *Remarriage and stepparenting: Current research and theory* (pp. 65-93). New York: Guilford.

Clingempeel, W. G., Flesher, M., & Brand, E. (1987). Research on stepfamilies: Paradigmatic constrains and alternative proposals. In J. P. Vincent (Ed.), *Advances in family intervention: Assessment and theory*, (Vol. 4, pp. 229-251). Greenwich, CT: JAI Press.

Clingempell, W. G., Ievoli, R., & Brand, E. (1984). Structural complexity and the quality of stepfather-stepchild relationships. *Family Process, 23*, 547-560.

Clingempeel, W. G., & Reppucci, N. D. (1982). Joint custody after divorce: Major issues and goals for research. *Psychological Bulletin, 91*, 102-127.

Clingempeel, W. G., & Segal, S. (1986). Stepparent-stepchild relationships and the psychological adjustment of children in stepmother and stepfather families. *Child Development, 57*, 474-484.

Clingempeel, W. G., Segal, S., & Hetherington, E. M. (1981). *Loyalty Conflicts Assessment Questionnaire.* Unpublished questionnaire. Francis Marion University, Florence.

Coleman, M., & Ganong, L. H. (1987a). The cultural stereotyping of stepfamilies. In K. Pasley & M. Ihinger-Tallman (Eds.), *Remarriage and stepparenting: Current research and theory* (pp. 19-41). New York: Guilford Press.

Coleman, M., & Ganong, L. H. (1987b). Marital conflict in stepfamilies. *Youth and Society, 19*, 151-172.

Coleman, M., & Ganong, L. H. (1989). Financial management in stepfamilies. *Lifestyles: Family and Economic Issues, 10*, 217-232.

Coleman, M., & Ganong, L. (1990). Remarriage and stepfamily research in the 80s: New interest in an old family form. *Journal of Marriage and the Family, 52*, 925-940.

Coleman, M., & Ganong, L. H. (1992, April). *Effects of remarriage on children: Clinical implications*. Presentation at the 6th International Congress on Family Therapy, "Divorce and Remarriage Interdisciplinary Issues and Approaches," Jerusalem, Israel.

Coleman, M., Ganong, L. H., & Gingrich, R. (1985). Stepfamily strengths: A review of popular literature. *Family Relations, 34*, 583-589.

Coleman, M., Ganong, L., & Henry, J. (1984). What teachers should know about stepfamilies. *Childhood Education, 60*, 306-309.

Collins v. Gilbreath, 75 Ind. Dec. 456, 403 N.E.2d 921 (1980).

Cook, D., & Emerson, R. (1978). Power, equity and commitment in exchange networks. *American Sociological Review, 43*, 721-739.

Coombs, R. H. (1991). Marital status and personal well-being: A literature review. *Family Relations, 40*, 97-102.   •

Cooney, T. M., & Uhlenberg, P. (1989). Family building patterns of professional women: A comparison of lawyers, physicians, and postsecondary teachers. *Journal of Marriage and the Family, 51*, 749-758.

Cooper, J., & Fazio, R. H. (1984). A new look at dissonance theory. In L. Berkowitz (Ed.), *Advances in experimental social psychology*, (Vol. 17, pp. 229-266). New York: Academic Press.

Corcoran, K., & Fischer, J. (1987). *Measures for clinical practice*. New York: Free Press.

Cornell Empowerment Group (Allen, J., Barr, D., Cochran, M., Dean, C., & Greene, J.). (1989). Empowerment through family support. *Networking Bulletin, 1*(1), 2-12.

Coser, L. A. (1964). *The functions of social conflict*. Glencoe, IL: Free Press.

Coysh, W. S., Johnston, J. R., Tschann, J. M., Wallerstein, J. S., & Kline, M. (1989). Parental postdivorce adjustment in joint and sole physical custody families. *Journal of Family Issues, 10*, 52-71.

Crane, D. R., Allgood, S. M., Larson, J. H., & Griffin, W. (1990). Assessing marital quality with distressed and nondistressed couples: A comparison and equivalency table for three frequently used measures. *Journal of Marriage and the Family, 52*, 87-93.

Cretney, S. M., & Masson, J. M. (1990). *Principles of family law*. London: Sweet & Maxwell.

Cronbach, L. J., & Meehl, P. E. (1955). Construct validity in psychological tests. *Psychological Bulletin, 52*, 281-302.

Crosbie-Burnett, M. (1984). The centrality of the step relationship: A challenge to family theory and practice. *Family Relations, 33*, 459-464.

Crosbie-Burnett, M. (1987, February). *College-aged stepchildren: Understanding their unique stresses*. Paper presented at the Big 10 Counseling Center Conference, University of Wisconsin-Madison, Madison, WI.

Crosbie-Burnett, M. (1988, February). *Schools and students from non-nuclear families*. Paper presented at the Wisconsin School Counselor Internship Conference, Steven's Point, WI.

Crosbie-Burnett, M. (1989a). Application of family stress theory to remarriage: A model for assessing and helping stepfamilies. *Family Relations, 38*, 323-331.

Crosbie-Burnett, M. (1989b). Impact of custody arrangement and family structure on remarriage. *Journal of Divorce, 13*(1), 1-16.

Crosbie-Burnett, M. (1989c, November). *The Stepfamily Adjustment Scale: The development of a new instrument designed to measure the unique aspects of stepfamilies*. Paper presented at meeting of the National Council on Family Relatons, Theory Construction and Research Methodology Workshop, New Orleans, LA.

Crosbie-Burnett, M. (1992). The interface between non-traditional families and education: Empowering parents and families. *Family Science Review, 5*(1/2), 53-64.

Crosbie-Burnett, M., & Giles-Sims, J. (1991). Marital power in stepfather families: A test of normative-resource theory. *Journal of Family Psychology, 4*, 484-496.

Crosbie-Burnett, M., & Landfried, S. E. (1987). Perceptions of relations with parents and school achievement of adolescents in nuclear, single-parent, and step families. *Wisconsin Counselor, 10*(1), 16-20.

Crosbie-Burnett, M., & Lewis, E. (1993). A social cognitive behavioral model of couples and families: An integration of contributions from psychological theories. In P. Boss, W. Doherty, R. LaRossa, W. Schumm, & S. K. Steinmetz (Eds.), *Sourcebook of family theories and methods: A contextual approach* (pp. 531-558). New York: Plenum.

Crosbie-Burnett, M., & Newcomer, L. (1990). Group counseling children of divorce: The effects of a multimodal intervention. *Journal of Divorce, 13*(3), 69-78.

Crosbie-Burnett, M., & Pulvino, C. (1990). Children in nontraditional families: A classroom guidance program. *School Counselor, 37*(4), 286-292.

Crosbie-Burnett, M., & Skyles, A. (1989) Stepchild in schools and colleges: Recommendations for educational policy changes. *Family Relations, 38*, 59-64.

Crosbie-Burnett, M., Skyles, A., & Becker-Haven, J. (1988). Exploring stepfamilies from a feminist perspective. In S. Dornbusch & M. Strober (Eds.), *Feminism, children and new families* (pp. 297-326). New York: Guilford Press.

Currie, J. R. (1989). *Enriching adult-child affect in the stepfamily environment*. Ft. Lauderdale, FL: Nova University, Center for the Advancement of Education. (ERIC Document Reproduction Service No. ED 304 647).

Davis, K. (1988). Wives and work: A theory of the sex-role revolution and its consequences. In S. Dornbusch & M. Strober (Eds.), *Feminism, children and new families* (pp. 67-86). New York: Guilford Press.

Dawson, D. (1991). Family structure and children's health and well-being: Data from the 1988 National Health Interview Survey on Child Health. *Journal of Marriage and the Family, 53*, 573-584.

Deutsch, M. (1973). *The resolution of conflict.* New Haven, CT: Yale University Press.

Dix, T., Ruble, D., Grusec, J., & Nixon, S. (1986). Social cognition in parents: Inferential and affective reactions to children of three age levels. *Child Development, 57*, 879-894.

Doka, K. J., & Mertz, M. E. (1988). The meaning and significance of great-grandparenthood. *Gerontologist, 28*, 192-197.

Dornbusch, S. M., Ritter, P. L., & Fraleigh, M. J. (1987). Famly process and the schools. *Final Report to Stanford and the Schools for the Hewlett Foundation,* Stanford.

Dornbusch, S. M., Ritter, P. L., Leiderman, P. H., Roberts, D. F., & Fraleigh, M. J. (1987). The relation of parenting style to adolescent school performance. *Child Development, 58*, 1244-1257.

Duberman, L. (1973). Step-kin relationships. *Journal of Marriage and the Family, 35*, 283-292.

Duberman, L. (1975). *The reconstituted family: A study of remarried couples and their children.* Chicago: Nelson-Hall.

Dudley, J. (1991). Consequences of divorce proceedings for divorced fathers. *Journal of Divorce and Remarriage, 16*(3/4), 171-194.

Duncan, G. (1984). *Years of poverty, years of plenty.* Ann Arbor, MI: University of Michigan, Institute for Social Research.

Duran-Aydintug, C., & Ihinger-Tallman, M. (1992). Law and stepfamilies. *Marriage and Family Review.*

Eidelson, R. J., & Epstein, N. (1982). Cognitions and relationship maladjustment: Development of a measure of dysfunctional relationship beliefs. *Journal of Consulting and Clinical Psychology, 50*, 715-720.

Elkind, D. (1967). Egocentrism in adolescence. *Child Development, 38*, 1025-1034.

Emerson, R. (1976). Social exchange theory. In A. Inkeles, J. Coleman, & N. Smelser (Eds.), *Annual Review of Sociology* (pp. 335-362). Palo Alto, CA: Annual Reviews, Inc.

Emery, R. E., & Wyer, M. M. (1987). Divorce mediation. *American Psychologist, 42*, 472-480.

Epstein, N., Schlesinger, S., & Dryden, W. (1988). *Cognitive-behavioral therapy with families.* New York: Brunner/Mazel.

Erikson, E. (1968). *Identity, youth, and crisis.* New York: Norton.

Erickson, W. D., Luxenberg, M. G., Walbek, N. H., & Seely, R. K. (1987). Frequency of MMPI two-point code types among sex offenders. *Journal of Consulting and Clinical Psychology, 55*, 566-570.

Esses, L., & Campbell, R. (1984). Challenges in researching the remarried. *Family Relations, 33*, 415-424.

Farrington, K., & Foss, J. E. (1977, October). *In search of the "missing" conceptual framework in family sociology: The social conflict framework.* Paper presented at the meeting of the National Council on Family Relations, San Diego, CA.

Fast, I., & Cain, A. C. (1966). The stepparent role: Potential for disturbances in family functioning. *American Journal of Orthopsychiatry, 36*, 485-491.

Festinger, L. (1957). *A theory of cognitive dissonance.* Stanford, CA: Stanford University Press.

Fine, M. A. (1989). A social science perspective on stepfamily law: Suggestions for legal reform. *Family Relations, 38*, 53-58.

Fine, M. A., Donnelly, B., & Voydanoff, P. (1991). The relation between adolescent's perceptions of their family lives and their adjustment in stepfather families. *Journal of Adolescent Research, 6*, 423-436.

Fine, M. A., Kurdek, L. A., & Hennigen, L. (1992). Family structure, gender, perceived ambiguity of (step)parent roles, and perceived self-competence in young adolescents. *Family Perspective, 25*, 261-282.

Fisch, R. R., Weakland, J., & Segal, L. (1982). *The tactics of therapy: Doing therapy briefly.* San Francisco, CA: Jossey-Bass.

Flewelling, R., & Bauman, K. (1990). Family structure as a predictor for initial substance use and sexual intercourse in early adolescence. *Journal of Marriage and the Family, 52*, 171-181.

Flinn, M. V. (1988). Step- and genetic parent/offspring relationships in a Caribbean village. *Ethology and Sociology, 9*(6), 335-370.

Fluitt, M. S., & Paradise, L. V. (1991). The relationship of current family structures to young adults' perceptions of stepparents. *Journal of Divorce and Remarriage, 15*, 159-173.

Furstenberg, F. F., Jr. (1979). Recycling the family: Perspectives on a neglected family form. *Marriage and Family Review, 2*, 12-22.

Furstenberg, F. F., Jr. (1987). The new extended family: The experience of parents and children after remarriage. In K. Pasley & M. Ihinger-Tallman (Eds.), *Remarriage and stepparenting: Current research and theory* (pp. 42-61). New York: Guilford.

Furstenberg, F. F., Jr. (1988). Child care after divorce and remarriage. In E. M. Hetherington & J. Arasteh (Eds.), *Impact of divorce, single parenting, and stepparenting on children* (pp. 245-262). Hillsdale, NJ: Erlbaum.

Furstenberg, F. F., Jr., Morgan, S. P., & Allison, P. D. (1987). Paternal participation and children's well-being after marital disruption. *American Sociological Review, 52*, 695-701.

Furstenberg, F. F., Jr., & Nord, C. W. (1985). Parenting apart: Patterns of child rearing after marital disruption. *Journal of Marriage and the Family, 47*, 893-904.

Furstenberg, F. F., Jr., Nord, C. W., Peterson, J. L., & Zill, N. (1983). The lifecourse of children of divorce: Marital disruption and parental conflict. *American Sociological Review, 48*, 656-668.

Furstenberg, F. F., Jr., & Spanier, G. B. (1987). *Recycling the family: Remarriage after divorce.* Rev. ed. Beverly Hills, CA: Sage. (Originally published 1984)

Galligan, R. J., & Bahr, S. J. (1978). Economic well-being and marital stability: Implications for income. *Journal of Marriage and the Family, 40*, 283-290.

Galvin, K. M., & Brommel, B. J. (1991). *Family communication: Cohesion and change.* 3rd ed. New York: HarperCollins.

Ganong, L. H., & Coleman, M. (1984). The effects of remarriage on children: A review of the empirical literature. *Family Relations, 33*, 389-406.

Ganong, L., & Coleman, M. (1986a). A comparison of clinical and empirical literature on children in stepfamilies. *Journal of Marriage and the Family, 48*, 309-318.

Ganong, L., & Coleman, M. (1986b, November). *Stepchildren: Empirical examination of some clinical assumptions.* Paper presented at the annual meeting of the National Council on Family Relations, Detroit, MI.

Ganong, L. H., & Coleman, M. (1987a). Effects of parental remarriage on children: An updated comparison of theories, methods and findings from clinical and empirical research. In K. Pasley & M. Ihinger-Tallman (Eds.), *Remarriage and stepparenting: Current research and theory* (pp. 94-104). New York: Guilford.

Ganong, L., & Coleman, M. (1987b). Stepchildren's perceptions of their parents. *Journal of Genetic Psychology, 148*, 5-17.

Ganong, L. H., & Coleman, M. (1988). Do mutual children cement bonds in stepfamilies? *Journal of Marriage and the Family, 50*, 687-698.

Ganong, L. H., & Coleman, M. (1989). Preparing for remarriage: Anticipating the issue, seeking solutions. *Family Relations, 38*, 28-33.

Ganong, L. H., Coleman, M., & Jones, G. (1990). Effects of behavior and family structure on perceptions. *Journal of Educational Psychology, 82*, 820-825.

Ganong, L., Coleman, M., & Mapes, D. (1990). A meta-analytic review of family structure stereotypes. *Journal of Marriage and the Family, 52*, 287-297.

Gardner, R. A. (1984). Counseling children in stepfamilies. *Elementary School Guidance and Counseling, 19*, 40-49.

Giles-Sims, J. (1984). The stepparent role: Expectations, behavior, sanctions. *Journal of Family Issues, 5*, 116-130.

Giles-Sims, J. (1987a). Parental role sharing between remarrieds and ex-spouses. *Youth and Society, 19*, 134-150.

Giles-Sims, J. (1987b). Social exchange in remarried families. In K. Pasley & M. Ihinger-Tallman (Eds.), *Remarriage and stepparenting: Current research and theory* (pp. 141-163). New York: Guilford.

Giles-Sims, J., & Crosbie-Burnett, M. (1989a). Adolescent power in stepfather families: A test of normative resource theory. *Journal of Marriage and the Family, 54*, 1065-1078.

Giles-Sims, J., & Crosbie-Burnett, M. (1989b). Stepfamily research: Implications for policy, clinical interventions, and further research. *Family Relations, 38*, 19-23.

Gilligan, C. (1982). *In a different voice: Psychological theory and women's development*. Cambridge, MA: Harvard University Press.

Gilligan, C. (1987). Moral orientation and moral development. In E. F. Kittay & D. T. Meyers (Eds.), *Women and moral theory* (pp. 19-33). Totowa, NJ: Rowan & Littlefield.

Gilligan, C. (1988). Adolescent development reconsidered. In C. Gilligan, J. V. Ward, J. M. Taylor, & B. Bardige (Eds.), *Mapping the moral domain: A contribution of women's thinking to psychological theory and education* (pp. vii-xxxix). Cambridge, MA: Harvard University Press.

Giordano, J. A. (1988). Child abuse in stepfamilies. *Family Relations, 37*, 411-414.

Glick, P. C. (1984). Marriage, divorce, and living arrangements: Prospective changes. *Journal of Family Issues, 5*, 7-26.

Glick, P. C. (1988a). Fifty years of family demography: A record of social change. *Journal of Marriage and the Family, 50*, 861-873.

Glick, P. C. (1988b). The role of divorce in the changing family structure: Trends and variations. In S.A. Wolchik & P. Karoly (Eds.), *Children of divorce* (pp. 3-34). New York: Gardner.

Glick, P. C. (1989a). The family life cycle and social change. *Family Relations, 38*, 123-129.

Glick, P. C. (1989b). Remarried families, stepfamilies, and stepchildren: A brief demographic profile. *Family Relations, 38*, 24-27.

Glick, P. C. (1992). American families: As they are and were. In A. S. Skolnick & J. H. Skolnick (Eds.), *Family in transition* (pp. 93-105). New York: Harper Collins.

Glick, P. C., & Lin, S. L. (1987). Remarriage after divorce: Recent changes and demographic variations. *Sociological Perspectives, 30*, 162-179.

Goetting, A. (1982). The six stations of remarriage: Developmental tasks of remarriage after divorce. *Family Relations, 31*, 213-222.

Goldscheider, F. K., & Goldscheider, C. (1989). Family structure and conflict: Nest-leaving expectations of young adults and their parents. *Journal of Marriage and the Family, 51*, 87-97.

Goldstein, J., Freud, A., & Solnit, A. (1973). *Beyond the best interests of the child*. New York: Free Press.

Gollob, H. F., & Reichardt, C. C. (1987). Taking account of time lags in causal models. *Child Development, 58*, 80-92.

Gordon, M. (1989). The family environment of sexual abuse: A comparison of natal and stepfather abuse. *Child Abuse and Neglect, 13*, 121-130.

Gordon, M., & Creighton, S.J. (1988). Natal and nonnatal fathers as sexual abusers in the United Kingdom: A comparative analysis. *Journal of Marriage and the Family, 50*, 99-105.

Gottman, J. M., & Krokoff, L. J. (1989). Marital interaction and satisfaction: A longitudinal view. *Journal of Consulting and Clinical Psychology, 57*, 47-52.

Gray, B. J., & Pippin, G. D. (1984). Stepfamilies: A concern health education should address. *Journal of School Health, 54*(8), 292-294.

Green, R. G. (1983). The influence of divorce prediction variables on divorce adjustment: An expansion and test of Lewis and Spanier's theory of marital quality and marital stability. *Journal of Divorce, 7*(1), 67-81.

Guidubaldi, J., Cleminshaw, H. K., Perry, J. D., & McLoughlin, C. S. (1983). The impact of parental divorce on children: Report of the nationwide NASP study. *School Psychology Review, 12*, 300-323.

Guisinger, S., Cowan, P. A., & Schuldberg, D. (1989). Changing parent and spouse relations in the first years of remarriage of divorced fathers. *Journal of Marriage and family, 51*, 445-456.

Guttman, J. & Broudo, M. (1988-1989). The effect of children's family type on teachers' stereotypes. Special Issue: Children of divorce: Developmental and clinical issues. *Journal of Divorce, 12*(2/3), 315-328.

Haley, J. (1976). *Problem-solving therapy*. San Francisco, CA: Jossey-Bass.

Haley, J. (1981). *Reflections on therapy*. Chevey Chase, MD: Family Therapy Institute of Washington, DC.

Hareven, T. K. (1987). Historical analysis of the family. In M. B. Sussman & S. K. Steinmetz (Eds.), *Handbook of marriage and the family* (pp. 37-58). New York: Plenum Press.

Heaton, T. B. (1990). Marital stability throughout the child-rearing years. *Demography, 27*, 55-63.

Heaton, T. B., & Pratt, E. L. (1990). The effects of religious homogamy on marital satisfaction and stability. *Journal of Family Issues, 11*, 191-207.

Henry, C. S., & Ceglian, C. P. (1989). *Stepgrandmothers and grandmothers of stepfamilies: Role behaviors, role meanings, and grandmothering styles*. (ERIC Document Reproduction Service No. ED 311 383)

Herlihy, B. (1984). An Adlerian approach to helping children in transition. *Elementary School Guidance and Counseling, 19*, 62-69.

Hetherington, E. M. (1987). Family relations six years after divorce. In K. Pasley & M. Ihinger-Tallman (Eds.), *Remarriage and stepparenting today: Current research and theory* (pp. 185-205). New York: Guilford.

Hetherington, E. M. (1989). Coping with family transitions: Winners, losers, and survivors. *Child Development, 60*, 1-14.

Hetherington, E. M. (1991). The role of individual differences and family relationships in children's coping with divorce and remarriage. In P. Cowan & E.M. Hetherington (Eds.), *Family transitions* (pp. 165-194). Hillsdale, NJ: Erlbaum.

Hetherington, E. M., Arnett, J. D., & Hollier, E. A. (1988). Adjustment of parents and children to remarriage. In S. A. Wolchik & P. Karoly (Eds.), *Children of divorce* (pp. 67-107). New York: Gardner.

Hetherington, E. M., & Clingempeel, W. G. (1992). Coping with marital transitions: A family systems perspective. *Monographs of the Society for Research on Child Development, 57*(2/3, Serial no. 227)

Hetherington, E. M., Cox, M., & Cox, R. (1978). The aftermath of divorce. In J. H. Stevens & M. Mathews (Eds.), *Mother-child, father-child relations* (pp. 110-155). Washington, DC: National Association for the Education of Young Children.

Hetherington, E. M., Cox, M., & Cox, R. (1982). The effects of divorce on parents and children. In M. Lamb (Ed.), *Nontraditional families* (pp. 233-288). Hillsdale, NJ: Lawrence Earlbaum Associates.

Hetherington, E. M., Cox, M., & Cox, R. (1985). Long-term effects of divorce and remarriage on the adjustment of children. *Journal of the American Academy of Child Psychiatry, 24*, 518-530.

Hetherington, E. M., Stanley-Hagan, M., & Anderson, E. R. (1989). Marital transitions: A child's perspective. *American Psychologist, 44*, 303-312.

Hickenbottom v. Hickenbottom, 239 Neb. 579, 477 N.W. 2d 8 (1991).

Hill, R. (1949). *Families under stress*. New York: Harper & Row.

Hill, R. (1958). Generic features of families under stress. *Social Casework, 49*, 139-150.

Hobart, C. (1988). Perception of parent-child relationships in first married and remarried families. *Family Relations, 37*, 175-182.

Hobart, C. (1990). Relationships between the formerly married. *Journal of Divorce and Remarriage, 14*(2), 1-23.

Hobart, C. (1991). Conflict in remarriages. *Journal of Divorce and Remarriage, 15*(3/4), 69-86.

Hoffman, L. (1981). *Foundation of family therapy*. New York: Basic Books.

Hollingshead, A. (1957). Two-factor index of social position. Unpublished manuscript, available from August G. Hollingshead, 1965 Yale Station, New Haven, CT.

Hollingshead, A. (1975). *Four-factor index of social status*. Unpublished manuscript, Yale University, New Haven, CT.

Holman, T. B., & Woodroffe-Patrick, M. (1988). Family structure, conflict, and children self-esteem in Trinidad and Tobago. *Journal of Family Issues, 9*, 214-223.

Horowitz, I. L. (1967). Consensus, conflict, and cooperation. In N. J. Demerath & R. A. Peterson (Eds.), *Systems, change, and conflict* (pp. 265-279). New York: Free Press.

Hutchinson, R. L., Valutis, W. E., Brown, D. T., & White, J. S. (1989). The effects of family structure on institutionalized children's self-concepts. *Adolescence, 24*, 303-310.

Ihinger-Tallman, M. (1988). Research on stepfamilies. *Annual Review of Sociology, 14*, 25-48.

Ihinger-Tallman, M., & Pasley, K. (1987). *Remarriage*. Beverly Hills, CA: Sage.

Illinois Revised Statutes, 1987, ch. 40, par 601(b)(2). (This statute follows the Uniform Marriage and Divorce Act, Section 401(d)).

In re Custody of Krause, 44 N.E.2d 644 (Ill. App 1982).

In re Marriage of Carey, 188 Ill. App. 3d 1040, 544 N.E.2d 1293 (1989).

Isaacs, M. B. (1988). The visitation schedule and child adjustment: A three-year study. *Family Process, 27*, 251-256.

Jaccard, J., Turrisi, R., & Wan, C. K. (1990). *Interaction effects in multiple regression*. Beverly Hills, CA: Sage.

Jackson, D. D. (1957). The question of family homeostasis. *Psychiatric Quarter-ly Supplement, 31*, 71-90.

Jackson, D. D. (1967). The myth of normality. *Medical Opinion and Review, 3*, 28-33.

Jackson, D. D., & Weakland, J. H. (1961). Conjoint family therapy: Some considerations on theory, technique and results. *Psychiatry, 24*, 30-45.

Jacobson, D. (1978). The impact of marital separation/divorce on children: Interparent hostility and child development. *Journal of Divorce, 2*(4), 3-19.

Jacobson, D. (1979). Stepfamilies: Myths and realities. *Social Work, 24*, 202-207.

James, L. R., & Brett, J. M. (1984). Mediators, moderators, and tests for mediation. *Journal of Applied Psychology, 69*, 307-321.

James, S. D., & Johnson, D.W. (1988). Social interdependence, psychological adjustment and marital satisfaction in second marriage. *Journal of Social Psychology, 128*(3), 287-303.

Johnson, C. L. (1989). In-law relationships in the American kinship system: The impact of divorce and remarriage. *American Ethnologist, 16*(1) 87-99.

Johnston, J. R., Gonzalez, R., & Campbell, L. (1987). Ongoing post-divorce conflict and child disturbance. *Journal of Abnormal Child Psychology, 15*, 493-509.

Kaslow, F. W. (1981). Divorce and divorce therapy. In A. S. Gurman & D. P. Kniskern (Eds.), *Handbook of family therapy* (pp. 662-696). New York: Brunner/Mazel.

Kelley, E. L., & Conley, J. J. (1987). Personality and compatibility: A prospective analysis of marital stability and marital satisfaction. *Journal of Personality and Social Psychology, 52*, 27-40.

Keshet, J. K. (1980). From separation to stepfamily: A subsystem analysis. *Journal of Family Issues, 1*, 146-153.

Keshet, J. K. (1990). Cognitive remodeling of the family: How remarried people view stepfamilies. *American Journal of Orthopsychiatry, 60*, 196-203.

King, L. A., & King, D. W. (1990). Role conflict and role ambiguity: A critical assessment of construct validity. *Psychological Bulletin, 107*, 48-64.

Klipstein v. Zalewski, 230 N.J. Super. 567, 553 A.2d 1384 (1988).

Knaub, P. K., Hanna, S. L., & Stinnett, N. (1984). Strengths of remarried families. *Journal of Divorce, 7*(4), 41-55.

Koch, M. A., & Lowery, C. R. (1984). Visitation and the noncustodial father. *Journal of Divorce, 8*(2), 47-65.

Kosinski, F. A. (1983). Improving relations in stepfamilies. *Elementary School Guidance and Counseling, 17*, 200-207.

Krause, H. (1990). Child support reassessed: Limits of private and public interest. In S. Sugarman & H. Kay (Eds.), *Divorce reform at the crossroads* (pp. 166-190). New Haven, CT: Yale University Press.

Kressel, K., Jaffe, N., Tuckman, B., Watson, C., & Deutsch, M. (1980). A typology of divorcing couples: Implications for mediation and the divorce process. *Family Process, 19*, 101-116.

Kurdek, L. A. (1986). Custodial mothers' perceptions of visitation and payment of child support by noncustodial fathers in families with low and high levels of preseparation interparent conflict. *Journal of Applied Developmental Psychology, 7*, 307-323.

Kurdek, L. A. (1987). Children's adjustment to parental divorce: An ecological perspective. In J. P. Vincent (Ed.), *Advances in family intervention, assessment and theory* (Vol. 4, p. x). Greenwich, CT: JAI Press.

Kurdek, L. A. (1989a). Relationship quality for newly married husbands and wives: Martial history, stepchildren, and individual-difference predictors. *Journal of Marriage and the Family, 51*, 1047-1052.

Kurdek, L. A. (1989b). Social support and psychological distress in first-married and remarried newlywed husbands and wives. *Journal of Marriage and the Family, 51*, 1047-1052.

Kurdek, L. A. (1990). Effects of child age on the marital quality and psychological distress of newly married mothers and stepfathers. *Journal of Marriage and the Family, 52*, 81-85.

Kurdek, L. A. (1992). Assumptions versus standards: The validity of two relationship cognitions in heterosexual and homosexual couples. *Journal of Family Psychology, 6*, 164-170.

Kurdek, L. A., & Blisk, D. (1983). Dimensions and correlates of mothers' divorce experiences. *Journal of Divorce, 6*(4), 1-24.

Kurdek, L. A., & Fine, M. A. (1991). Cognitive correlates of satisfaction for mothers and stepfathers in stepfather families. *Journal of Marriage and the Family, 53*, 565-572.

Kurdek, L. A., & Sinclair, R. J. (1988). Relation of eighth graders' family structure, gender, and family environment with academic performance and school behavior. *Journal of Educational Psychology, 80*, 90-94.

Langman, L. (1987). Social stratification. In M. B. Sussman & S. K. Steinmetz (Eds.), *Handbook of marriage and the family* (pp. 211-250). New York: Plenum Press.

Larson, J. H., & Allgood, S. M. (1987). A comparison of intimacy in first-married and remarried couples. *Journal of Family Issues, 8*, 319-331.

Leigh, G. K., & Peterson, G. W. (1986). *Adolescents in families*. Cincinnati, OH: South-Western.

Leslie, L. A., & Epstein, N. (1988). Cognitive-behavioral treatment of remarried families. In N. Epstein, S. Schlesinger, & W. Dryden (Eds.), *Cognitive-behavioral therapy with families* (pp. 151-182). New York: Brunner/Mazel.

Lewis, R. A., & Spanier, G. B. (1979). Theorizing about the quality and stability of marriages. In W. R. Burr, R. Hill, F. I. Nye, & I. L. Reiss (Eds.), *Contemporary theories about the family* (Vol. 1, pp. 268-294). New York: Free Press.

Lin, S. L. (1990). Changes in the reproductive function among remarried women: The effects of spousal characteristics. *Sociological Perspectives, 33*, 501-516.

Liss, L. (1987). Families and the law. In M. B. Sussman & S. K. Steinmetz (Eds.), *Handbook of marriage and the family* (pp. 767-793). New York: Plenum.

Losh-Hesselbart, S. (1987). Development of gender roles. In M. B. Sussman & S. K. Steinmetz (Eds.), *Handbook of marriage and the family* (pp. 535-564). New York: Plenum Press.

Luepnitz, D. A. (1982). *Child custody: A study of families after divorce*. Lexington, MA: Lexington Books.

Lutz, E. P., Jacobs, E., & Masson, R. (1981). Stepfamily counseling: Issues and guidelines. *School Counselor, 28*(3), 189-194.

Lutz, E. P., Jacobs, E., & Masson, R. (1988). Stepfamily counseling: Issues and guidelines. In W. M. Walsh & N. J. Giblin (Eds.), *Family counseling in school settings* (pp. 157-165). Springfield, IL: Charles C. Thomas.

Lutz, P. (1983). The stepfamily: An adolescent perspective. *Family Relations, 32*, 367-375.

Maccoby, E. E., Depner, C. E., & Mnookin, R. H. (1990). Coparenting in the second year after divorce. *Journal of Marriage and the Family, 52*, 141-155.

Mahoney, M. (1984). Support and custody aspects of the stepparent-child relationship. *Cornell Law Review, 70*, 38-79.

Mahoney, M. (1987). Stepfamilies in the federal law. *University of Pittsburgh Law Review, 48*, 491-537.

Manning, D. T., & Wootten, M. D. (1987). What stepfamilies perceive schools should know about blended families. *Clearing-House, 60*(5), 230-235.

Marsh, H. W. (1989). *Two-parent, step-parent, and single-parent families: Changes in achievement, attitudes and behaviors during the last two years of high school*. (ERIC Document Reproduction Service No. #306 480).

Marsh, H. W. (1990). Two-parent, step-parent, and single-parent families: Changes in achievement, attitudes, and behaviors during the last two years of high school. *Journal of Educational Psychology, 82*, 327-340.

Martin, T. C., & Bumpass, L. L. (1989). Recent trends in marital disruption. *Demography, 26*, 37-51.

Masheter, C. (1991). Post-divorce relationships between ex-spouses: The roles of attachment and interpersonal conflict. *Journal of Marriage and the Family, 53*, 103-110.

Masson, J. (1984). Old families into new: Status for stepparents. In M. Freeman (Ed.), *State, law and the family: Critical perspectives* (pp. 227-243). London: Travistock Publications.

Masson, J. (1991). Stepping into the nineties: A summary of the legal implications of the Children Act 1989 for stepfamilies. In B. Dimmock (Ed.), *A step in both directions? The impact of the Children Act 1989 on stepfamilies*. London: National Stepfamily Association.

Masson, J., Norbury, D., & Chatterton, S. (1983). *Mine, yours or ours: A study of tepparent adoption*. London: Her Majesty's Stationery Office, Department of Health and Social Security.

McCubbin, H., Larsen, A., & Olson, D. H. (1981). Family crisis oriented personal evaluation scales (F-COPES). In H. McCubbin & J. Patterson (Eds.), *Systematic assessment of family stress, resources and coping* (pp. 134-140). St. Paul, MN: University of Minnesota, Family Stress Project. St. Paul, MN.

McCubbin, H., & McCubbin, M. (1987). Family stress theory and assessment: The T-Double ABCX model of family adjustment and adaptation. In H. McCubbin & A. Thompson (Eds.), *Family assessment for research and practice* (pp. -). Madison: University of Wisconsin.

McGoldrick, M., & Carter, E. A. (1980). Forming a remarried family. In E. A. Carter & M. McGoldrick (Eds.), *The family life cycle* (pp. 265-294). New York: Gardner Press.

McKenry, P. C., Price-Bonham, S., & O'Bryant, S. L. (1981). Adolescent discipline: Different family members' perception. *Journal of Youth and Adolescence, 10*, 327-337.

Medler, B. Y., Strother, J., Dameron, J. D., & DeNardo, N. B. (1987). Identification and treatment of stepfamily issues for counselors and teachers. *TACD Journal, 15*(1), 49-60.

Mensink, D. L., & Sawatzky, D. D. (1989). The impact of family form on perceptions of children's functioning. *Alberta Journal of Educational Research, 35*(3), 237-254.

Messinger, L. (1976). Remarriage between divorced people with children from previous marriages: A proposal for preparation for remarriage. *Journal of Marriage and Family Counseling, 2*, 193-200.

Messinger, L., Walker, K. N., & Freeman, S. T. (1978). Preparation for remarriage following divorce. *American Journal of Orthopsychiatry, 48*, 263-272.

Mills, D. (1984). A model for stepfamily development. *Family Relations, 33*, 365-372.

Minuchin, S. (1974). *Families and family therapy*. Cambridge, MA: Harvard University Press.

Minuchin, S., Rosman, B. L., & Baker, L. (1978). *Psychosomatic families*. Cambridge, MA: Harvard University Press.

Mitchell, B., Wister, A., & Burch, T. (1989). The family environment and leaving the parental home. *Journal of Marriage and the Family, 51*, 605-613.

Mnookin, R. (1985). *In the interest of children*. New York: W. H. Freeman & Co.

Mnookin, R., Maccoby, E., Albiston, C., & Depner, C. (1990). Private ordering revisited: What custodial arrangements are parents negotiating? In S. Sugarman & H. Kay (Eds.), *Divorce reform at the crossroads* (pp. 37-74). New Haven, CT: Yale University Press.

Montemayer, R. (1983). Parents and adolescents in conflict: All families some of the time and some families most of the time. *Journal of Early Adolescence, 9*, 83-103.

Moorman, J. E., & Hernandez, D. J. (1989). Married-couple families with step, adopted, and biological children. *Demography, 26*, 267-277.

Moos, R. H., & Moos, B. S. (1981). *Family Environment Scale manual*. Palo Alto, CA: Consulting Psychologists Press.

Morris, S. (1989). Grandparents, uncles, aunts, cousins, friends. *Family Advocate, 12*, 11-14, 42.

Nadler, J. (1976). The psychological stress of the stepmother. *Dissertation Abstracts International, 37*, 5367B.

National Conference of Commissioners on Uniform State Laws (1987). *Uniform marriage and divorce act*. St. Paul, MN: West.

Needle, R. H., Su, S. S., & Doherty, W. J. (1990). Divorce, remarriage, and adolescent substance use: A prospective longitudinal study. *Journal of Marriage and the Family, 52*, 157-169.

Nelson, W. P., & Levant, R. F. (1991). An evaluation of a skills training program for parents in stepfamilies. *Family Issues, 40*, 291-296.

Nichols, M. P. (1984). *Family therapy*. New York: Gardner Press.

Noddings, N. (1984). *Caring: A feminine approach to ethics and moral education*. Berkeley, CA: University of California Press. North Dakota Century Code § 14-09-09 (Supp. 1991).

Nunn, G. D., Parish, T. S., & Worthing, R. J. (1983). Perceptions of personal and familial adjustment by children from intact, single-parent and reconstituted families. *Psychology in the Schools, 20*, 166-174.

Nunnally, J. (1978). *Psychometric theory*. New York: McGraw-Hill.

Nye, F. (1957). Child adjustment in broken and unhappy unbroken homes. *Marriage and Family Living, 19*, 356-361.

O'Flahtery, K. M., & Odells, L. W. (1988). Courtship behavior of the remarried. *Journal of Marriage and the Family, 50*, 499-506.

Olson, M. J. (1986). An appraisal of school counseling in Wisconsin 1984-1985 by counselors and consumer groups. *Dissertation Abstracts International, 47*(4), 1194-A.

Olvera v. Superior Ct. 17 FLR 1591 (Ariz. App. 1991).

Omnibus Budget Reconciliation Act of 1981, Pub. L. No. 97-35, Tit. XXIII, 95 Stat. 357, 843-74.

Oppawsky, J. (1988/1989). Family dysfunctional patterns during divorce--from the view of the children. *Journal of Divorce, 13*(2), 271-281.

Orleans, M., Palisi, B. J., & Caddell, D. (1989). Marriage adjustment and satisfaction of stepfathers: Their feelings and perceptions of decision making and stepchildren relations. *Family Relations, 38*, 371-377.

Palisi, B. J., Orleans, M., Caddell, D., & Korn, B. (1991). Adjustment to stepfatherhood: The effects of marital history and relations with children. *Journal of Divorce and Remarriage, 14*, 89-106.

Papernow, P. (1980). A pheonomenological study of the developmental stages of becoming a stepparent: A gestalt and family systems approach. *Dissertation Abstracts International, 41*, 8B, 3192-3193.

Papernow, P. (1984). The stepfamily cycle: An experimental model of stepfamily development. *Family Relationships, 33*, 355-363.

Papernow, P. (1987). Thickening the "middle ground": Dilemmas and vulnerabilities of remarried couples. *Psychotherapy, 24*, 630-639.

Paquette v. Paquette, 499 A.2d 23 (Vt. 1985).

Parish, T. S. (1987). Children's self-concepts: Are they affected by parental divorce and remarriage? *Journal of Social Behavior and Personality, 2*, 559-562.

Parish, T. S., & Philip, M. (1982). The self-concepts of children from intact and divorced families: Can they be affected in school settings? *Education, 103*, 60-63.

Pasley, K. (1987). Family boundary ambiguity: Perceptions of adult remarried family members. In K. Pasley & M. Ihinger-Tallman (Eds.), *Remarriage and stepparenting: Current research and theory* (pp. 206-224). New York: Guilford.

Pasley, K. (1988, October). *Stepfamilies with adolescents: Managing competing needs*. Paper presented at the annual meeting of the Stepfamily Association of America, New Orleans, LA.

Pasley, K., Dollahite, D., & Ihinger-Tallman, M. (1993). Bridging the gap: Clinical applications of research findings on the spouse and stepparent roles in remarriage. *Family Relations, 42*, 315-322.

Pasley, K., & Healow, C. L . (1988). Adolescent self-esteem: A focus on children in step-families. In E.M. Hetherington & J. Arasteh (Eds.), *Impact of divorce, single parenting, and stepparenting on children* (pp. 263-278). Hillsdale, NJ: Erlbaum.

Pasley, K., & Ihinger-Tallman, M. (1982). Stress in remarried families. *Family Perspective, 16*, 181-190.

Pasley, K., & Ihinger-Tallman, M. (1986). Stepfamilies: New challenges for the schools. In T. S. Fairchild (Ed.), *Crisis intervention strategies for school-based helpers* (pp. 70-112). Springfield, IL: Charles C. Thomas.

Pasley, K., & Ihinger-Tallman, M. (1987). An evolution of a field of investigation: Issues and concerns. In K. Pasley & M. Ihinger-Tallman (Eds.), *Remarriage and stepparenting: Current research & theory* (pp. 303-313). New York: Guilford.

Pasley, K., & Ihinger-Tallman, M. (1989). Boundary ambiguity in remarriage: Does ambiguity differentiate degree of marital adjustment and integration? *Family Relations, 38*, 46-52.

Pasley, K., & Ihinger-Tallman, M. (1990). Remarriage in later adulthood: Correlates of perceptions of family adjustment. *Family Perspective, 24*, 263-274.

Pasley, K., & Ihinger-Tallman, M. (1992). Remarriage and stepparenting: What the 1980s have added to our understanding of these families. *Family Science Review, 5*, 153-174.

Pasley, K., Ihinger-Tallman, M., & Coleman, C. (1984). Consensus styles among happy and unahppy remarried couples. *Family Relations, 33*, 451-457.

Pearlin, L. I., & Schooler, C. (1978). The structure of coping. *Journal of Health and Social Behavior, 19*, 2-21.

Pearson, J., & Thoennes, N. (1988). Supporting children after divorce: The influence of custody on support levels and payments. *Family Law Quarterly, 22*, 319-339.

Pedro-Carroll, J., & Cowen, E. L. (1985). The children of divorce intervention program: An investigation of the efficacy of a school based prevention program. *Journal of Consulting and Clinical Psychology, 53*, 603-611.

Perkins, T .F., & Kahan, J. P. (1979). An empirical comparison of natural-father and stepfather family systems. *Family Process, 18*, 175-183.

Peterson, J., & Zill, N. (1986). Marital disruption, parent-child relationships, and behavior problems in children. *Journal of Marriage and the Family, 48*, 295-307.

Peterson, J. L. (1987, August). *Post-divorce, events and the provision of children support payments*. Paper presented at the annual conference of the National Child Support Enforcement Association, Washington, DC.

Pill, C. (1990). Stepfamilies: Redefining the family. *Family Relations, 39*, 186-193.

Pink, J. E., & Wampler, K. S. (1985). Problem areas in stepfamilies: Cohesion and adaptability and the stepfather-adolescent relationship. *Family Relations, 34*, 327-335.

Ponzetti, J. J., & Cate, R. M. (1986). The developmental course of conflict in the marital dissolution process. *Journal of Divorce, 10*, 1-15.

Poppen, W. A., & White, P. N. (1984). Transition to the blended family. *Elementary School Guidance and Counseling, 19*, 50-61.

Price-Bonham, S., & Balswick, J. O. (1980). The non-institutions: Divorce, desertion, and remarriage. *Journal of Marriage and the Family, 42*, 959-972.

Prince v. Massachusetts, 321 U.S. 158 (1944).

Ramsey, S., & Masson, J. (1985). Stepparent support of stepchildren: A comparative analysis of policies and problems in the American and English experience. *Syracuse Law Review, 36*, 659-714.

Ramsey, S. H. (1986). Stepparent support of stepchildren: The changing legal context and the need for empirical policy research. *Family Relations, 35*, 363-369.

Ransom, J. W., Schlesinger, S., & Derdeyn, A. P. (1979). A stepfamily information. *American Journal of Orthopsychiatry, 49*, 36-43.

Redman, M. (1991). The support of children in blended families: A call for change. *Family Law Quarterly, 25*, 83-94.

Renick, M. J., Blumberg, S. L., & Markman, H. J. (1992). The Prevention Relationship Enhancement Program (PREP): An empirically based prevention intervention program for couples. *Family Relations, 41*, 141-147.

Richards v. United States, 93 F. Supp. 208 (N.D.W.Va. 1950).

Richardson, R. A., Galambos, N. L., Schulenberg, J. E., & Peters, A. C. (1984). Young adolescents' perceptions of the family environment. *Journal of Early Adolescence, 4*, 131-153.

Risman, B. J., & Schwartz, P. (1989). *Gender in intimate relationships: A microstructural approach*. Belmont, CA: Wadsworth.

Roberts, T. W., & Price, S. J. (1987). Instant families: Divorce mothers marry never-married men. *Journal of Divorce, 11*(1), 71-92.

Roberts, T. W., & Price, S. J. (1989). Adjustment in remarriage: Communication, cohesion, marital and parental roles. *Journal of Divorce, 13*(1), 17-43.

Roehling, P. V., & Robin, A. L. (1986). Development and validation of the Family Beliefs Inventory: A measure of unrealistic beliefs among parents and adolescents. *Journal of Consulting and Clinical Psychology, 54*, 693-697.

Rosenberg, M. (1965). *Society and the adolescent self-image*. Princeton, NJ: Princeton.

Rusbult, C. E. (1983). A longitudinal test of the investment model: The development (and deterioration) of satisfaction and commitment in heterosexual involvements. *Journal of Personality and Social Psychology, 45*, 101-117.

Ryan, C. M. (1991). *The prediction of fathers' child support compliance from the quality of the former spouse relationship and psychological presence.* Unpublished doctoral dissertation, University of Tennessee, Knoxville.

Sabatelli, R. M. (1984). A marital comparison level index: A measure for assessing outcomes relative to expectations. *Journal of Marriage and the Family, 46*, 651-662.

Sager, C. J., Brown, H. S., Crohn, H., Engel, T., Rodstein, E., & Walker, E. (1983). *Treating the remarried family.* New York: Brunner/Mazel.

Sanders, G. F., & Trygstad, D. W. (1989). Stepgrandparents and grandparents: The view from young adults. *Family Relations, 38*, 71-75.

Sandler, I. N., Wolchik, S. A., & Braver, S. L. (1989). The stressors of children's post-divorce environments. In S. A. Wolchik & P. Karoly (Eds.), *Children of divorce: Empirical perspectives on adjustment* (p. x). New York: Gardner Press.

Santrock, J. W., & Sitterle, K.A. (1987). Parent-child relationships in stepmother families. In K. Pasley & M. Ihinger-Tallman (Eds.), *Remarriage and stepparenting: Current research and theory* (pp. 273-299). New York: Guilford.

Santrock, J. W., Warshak, R. A., & Elliott, G. L. (1982). Social development and parent-child interaction in father-custody and stepmother families. In M. E. Lamb (Ed.), *Nontraditional families: Parenting and child development* (pp. 289-310). Hillsdale, NJ: Lawrence Erlbaum Associates.

Santrock, J. W., Warshak, R., Lindbergh, C., & Meadows, L. (1982). Children and parents' observed social behavior in stepfather famlies. *Child Development, 53*, 472-480.

Satir, V. (1967). *Conjoint family therapy.* Palo Alto, CA: Science and Behavior Books.

Satir, V. (1972). *Peoplemaking.* Palo Alto, CA: Science and Behavior Books.

Sauer, L. E., & Fine, M. A. (1988). Parent-child relationships in stepparent families. *Journal of Family Psychology, 1*, 434-451.

Schuldberg, D., & Guisinger, S. (1991). Divorced fathers describe their former wives: Devaluation and contrast. *Journal of Divorce and Remarriage, 14* (3/4), 61-87.

Schumm, W. R., & Bugaighis, M. A. (1985). Marital quality and marital stability: Resolving a controversy. *Journal of Divorce, 9*(1), 73-77.

Schwebel, A. I., Fine, M. A., & Renner, M. A. (1991). A study of perceptions of the stepparent role. *Journal of Family Issues, 12*, 43-57.

Seltzer, J. A. (1991). Relationship between fathers and children who live apart: The father's role after separation. *Journal of Marriage and the Family, 53*, 79-101.

Seltzer, J. A., & Bianchi, S. M. (1988). Children's contact with absent parents. *Journal of Marriage and the Family, 50*, 663-677.

Seltzer, J. A., Schaeffer, N. C., & Charng, H. (1989). Family ties after divorce: The relationship between visiting and paying child support. *Journal of Marriage and the Family, 51*, 1013-1032.

Selvini Palazzoli, M. (1974). *Self starvation*. New York: Jason Aronson.

Selvini Palazzoli, M., Boscolo, L., Checcin, G., & Prata, L. (1978). *Paradox and counterparadox*. New York: Jason Aronson.

Shea, C. A. (1982). *Schools and non-nuclear families: Recasting relationships*. (Eric Document Reproduction Service No. ED 234 333 CG 016 927)

Sheppard v. Sheppard, 230 Kan. 146, 630 P.2d 1121 (1981). Cert. denied 455 U.S. 919 (1982).

Skeen, P., Robinson, B. E ., & Flake-Hobson, C. (1984, January). Blended families: Overcoming the Cinderella myth. *Young Children*, pp. 64-73.

Small, S. A. (1988). Parental self-esteem and its relationship to child rearing practices, parent-adolescent interaction, and adolescent behavior. *Journal of Marriage and the Family, 50*, 1063-1072.

Smith, K., & Sasaki, M. (1979). Decreasing multicollinearity: A method for models with multiplicative functions. *Sociological Methods and Research, 8*, 35-56.

Smith, K., Zick, C., & Duncan, G. J. (1991). Remarriage among recent widows and widowers. *Demography, 28*, 361-374.

Smith, R. M., Goslen, M. A., Byrd, A. J., & Reece, L. (1991). Self-other orientation and sex-role orientation of men and women who remarry. *Journal of Divorce and Remarriage, 14*(3/4), 3-32.

Smith, W. C. (1953). *The stepchild*. Chicago, IL: University of Chicago Press.

Spanier, G. B. (1976). Measuring dyadic adjustment: New scales for assessing the quality of marriage and similar dyads. *Journal of Marriage and the Family, 38*, 15-28.

Spanier, G. B., & Glick, P. C. (1980). Paths to remarriage. *Journal of Divorce, 3*(3), 283-298.

Spanier, G. B., & Thompson, L. (1984). *Parting: The aftermath of separation and divorce*. Beverly Hills, CA: Sage.

Speare, A., Jr., & Goldscheider, F. K. (1987). Effects of marital status change on residential mobility. *Journal of Marriage and the Family, 49*, 455-464.

Spells v. Spells, 250 Pa. Super. 168, 378 A.2d 879 (1977).

Sprey, J. (1979). Conflict theory and the study of marriage and the family. In W. R. Burr, R. H. Hill, F. I. Nye & I. L. Reiss (Eds.), *Contemporary theories about the family* (Vol. 2, pp. 130-159). New York: Free Press.

Steinberg, L. (1981). Transformations in family relations at puberty. *Developmental Psychology, 17*(6), 833-840.

Steinberg, L. (1991). *Adolescence*. 2nd ed. New York: McGraw-Hill.

Steinberg, L., & Hill, J. (1978). Patterns of family interaction as a function of age, the onset of puberty, and formal thinking. *Developmental Psychology, 14*(6), 683-684.

Steinhausen, H. C., VonAster, S., & Gobel, D. (1987). Family composition and child psychiatric disorders. *Journal of the American Academy of Child and Adolescent Psychiatry, 26*, 242-247.

Stenger, R. L. (1986). The school counselor and the law: New developments. *Journal of Law and Education, 15*, 105-116.

Stern, P. N. (1978). Stepfather families: Integration around child discipline. *Issues in Mental Health Nursing, 1*, 49-56.

Stolberg, A. J., & Garrison, K. M. (1985). Evaluating a primary prevention program for children of divorce: Divorce adjustment project. *American Journal of Community Psychology, 13*, 111-124.

Straus, M. A. (1979). Measuring intrafamily conflict and violence: The Conflict Tactics (CT) Scales. *Journal of Marriage and the Family, 41*, 75-88.

Strother, J., & Jacobs, E. (1984). Adolescent stress as it relates to stepfamily living: Implications for school counselors. *School Counselor, 32*, 97-103.

Suitor, J. J. (1991). Marital quality and satisfaction with the division of household labor across the family life cycle. *Journal of Marriage and the Family, 53*, 221-230.

Sweet, J. A. (1991, November). *The demography of one-parent and stepparent families: Changing marriage, remarriage, and reproductive patterns*. Paper presented at the Wingspread V Conference, annual meeting of the National Council on Family Relations, Denver, CO.

Sweet, J. A., & Bumpass, L. L. (1988). *American families and households*. New York: Russell Sage Foundation.

Teachman, J. D. (1990). Socioeconomic resources of parents and award of child support in the united states: Some exploratory models. *Journal of Marriage and the Family, 52*, 689-699.

Teachman, J. D. (1991). Who pays? Receipt of child support in the United States. *Journal of Marriage and the Family, 53*, 759-772.

Teachman, J. D., Polonko, K. A., & Scanzoni, J. (1987). Demography of the family. In M. B. Sussman & S. K. Steinmetz (Eds.), *Handbook of marriage and the family* (pp. 3-36). New York: Plenum Press.

Tenenbaum, J. (1991). Legislation for stepfamilies--The Family Law Section Standing Committee report. *Family Law Quarterly, 25*, 137-141.

Thompson, L. (1989, November). *Marital responsibility: Contextual and relational morality*. Paper presented at meeting of the National Council on Family Relations, Theory Construction and Research Methodology Workshop, New Orleans, LA.

Thompson, L. (1991). Family work: Women's sense of fairness. *Journal of Family Issues, 12*, 181-196.

Thompson, L., & Walker, A. J. (1989). Women and men in marriage, work, and parenthood. *Journal of Marriage and the Family, 51*, 845-872.

Thornton, A. (1991). Influence of marital history of parents on the marital and cohabitational experiences of children. *American Journal of Sociology, 94*, 868-894.

Tomm, K. (1984). On perspective on the Milan Systemic Approach: Part I, Overview of development, theory, and practice. *Journal of Marital and Family Therapy, 10*, 113-125.

Touliatos, J., & Lindholm, B. W. (1980). Teachers' perceptions of behavior problems in children from intact, single-parent, and stepparent families. *Psychology in the Schools, 17*, 264-269.

Touliatos, J., Perlmutter, B. F., & Straus, M. A. (Eds.). (1990). *Handbook of family measurement techniques*. Newbury Park, CA: Sage.

Trapp v. Trapp, 126 Misc. 2d 30, 480 N.Y.S.2d 979 (1984).

Tropf, W. (1984). An exploratory examination of the effects of remarriage on child support and personal contacts. *Journal of Divorce, 7*(3), 57-73.

Trotter, B. B. (1989). *Coparental conflict, competition, and cooperation and parents' perceptions of their children's social-emotional well-being following marital separation*. Unpublished doctoral dissertation, University of Tennessee, Knoxville.

Tschann, J. M., Johnston, J. R., Kline, M., & Wallerstein, J. S. (1989). Family process and children's functioning during divorce. *Journal of Marriage and the Family, 51*, 431-444.

Tygart, C. E. (1990). Self-reported delinquency and nature parents-stepparent youth relations. *Journal of Divorce and Remarriage, 13*, 89-99.

Tyrrell v. Tyrrell, 67 A.D.2d 247, 415 N.Y.S.2d 723 (1979).

Udry, R. J. (1983). The marital happiness/disruption relationship by level of marital alternatives. *Journal of Marriage and the Family, 45*, 221-222.

U.S. Bureau of the Census. (1990). *Child support and alimony: 1987*. Current Population Reports, Series P-23, No. 167. Washington, DC: U.S. Government Printing Office.

Vemer, E., Coleman, M., Ganong, L. H., & Cooper, H. (1989). Marital satisfaction in remarriage: A meta-analysis. *Journal of Marriage and the Family, 51*, 713-725.

Victor, R., Robbins, M., & Bassett, S. (1991). Statutory review of third-party rights regarding custody, visitation and support. *Family Law Quarterly, 25*, 19-25.

Visher, E. B., & Visher, J. S. (1979). *Stepfamilies: A guide to working with stepparents and stepchildren*. New York: Brunner/Mazel.

Visher, E. B., & Visher, J. S. (1980). *Stepfamilies: Myths and realities*. Secus, NC: Citadel Press.

Visher, E. B., & Visher, J. S. (1982a). Children in stepfamilies. *Psychiatric Annals, 12*, 832-841.

Visher, E. B., & Visher, J. S. (1982b). *How to win in a stepfamily*. New York: Dember.

Visher, E. B., & Visher, J. S. (1988a). *Old loyalties, new ties: Therapeutic strategies with stepfamilies*. Brunner/Mazel: New York.

Visher, E. B., & Visher, J. S. (1988b). Treating families and problems associated with remarriage and step relationships. In C. S. Chilman, E. W. Nunnally, & F. M. Cox (Eds.), *Variant family forms, Families in trouble series* (Vol. 5, pp. 222-244). Beverly Hills, CA: Sage.

Visher, E. B., & Visher, J. S. (1989). Parenting coalitions after remarriage: Dynamics and therapeutic guidelines. *Family Relations, 38*, 65-70.

Visher, E. B., & Visher, J. S. (1990). Dynamics of successful stepfamilies. *Journal of Divorce and Remarriage, 14*(1), 3-12.

Visher, E. B., & Visher, J. S. (1991). Therapy with stepfamily couples. *Psychiatric Annals, 21*, 462.

Vuchinich, S., Hetherington, E. M., Vuchinich, R., & Clingempeel, W. G. (1991). Parent-child interaction and gender differences in early adolescents' adaptation to stepfamilies. *Developmental Psychology, 27*, 618-626.

Wald, E. (1981). *The remarried family: Challenge and promise*. New York: Family Service Association of America.

Walker, K. N., & Messinger, L. (1979). Remarriage after divorce: Dissolution and reconstitution of family boundaries. *Family Process, 18*, 185-192.

Wallerstein, J. S., & Blakeslee, S. (1989). *Second chances: Men, women, and children a decade after divorce*. New York: Ticknor & Fields.

Wallerstein, J. S., & Bundy, M. L. (1984). Helping children of disrupted families: An interview with Judith S. Wallerstein. *Elementary School Guidance and Counseling, 19*, 19-29.

Wallerstein, J. S., & Huntington, D. S. (1983). Bread and roses: Nonfinancial issues related to fathers' economic support of their children following divorce. In J. Cassetty (Ed.), *The parental child support obligation: Research, practice, and social policy* (pp. 135-156). Lexington, MA: Heath.

Wallerstein, J. S., & Kelly, J. B. (1980). *Surviving the breakup: How children and parents cope with divorce*. New York: Basic Books.

Webber, R. P., Sharpley, C. F., & Rowley, G. L. (1988). Living in a stepfamily. *Australian Journal of Sex, Marriage and Family, 9*, 21-29.

Weiner, B. (1985). "Spontaneous" causal search. *Psychological Bulletin, 97*, 74-84.

Weiss, R. W. (1975). *Marital separation*. New York: Basic Books.

Weitzman, L. J. (1985). *The divorce revolution: The unexpected social and economic consequences for women and children in America*. New York: Free Press.

White, L. K., & Booth, A. (1985). The quality and stability of remarriages: The role of stepchildren. *American Sociological Review, 50*, 689-698.

Whiteside, M. F. (1982). Remarriage: A family developmental process. *Journal of Marital and Family Therapy, 4*, 59-68.

Wilcoxon, S. A., & Comas, R. E. (1987). Contemporary trends in family counseling: What do they mean for the school counselor? *School Counselor, 34*, 219-225.

Wilkinson, P. (1987). Ethnicity. In M. B. Sussman & S. K. Steinmetz (Eds.), *Handbook of marriage and the family* (pp. 183-210). New York: Plenum Press.

Wilson, B. F., & Clarke, S. C. (1992). Remarriages: A demographic profile. *Journal of Family Issues, 13*, 123-141.

Wineberg, H. (1990). Childbearing after remarriage. *Journal of Marriage and the Family, 52*, 31-38.

Wineberg, H. (1991). Intermarital fertility and dissolution of the second marriage. *Social Science Review, 75*, 62-65.

Wiser, A. W., & Burch, T. K. (1989). The family environment and leaving the parental home. *Journal of Marriage and the Family, 51*, 605-613.

Wright, D. W., & Price, S. J. (1986). Court-ordered child support payment: The effect of the former-spouse relationship on compliance. *Journal of Marriage and the Family, 48*, 869-874.

Yalom, I. D. (1985). *The theory and practice of group psychotherapy*. New York: Basic Books.

Zick, C. D., & Smith, K. R. (1988). Recent widowhood, remarriage, and changes in economic well-being. *Journal of Marriage and the Family, 50*, 233-244.

Zill, N. (1988). Behavior, achievement, and health problems among children in stepfamilies. In E. M. Hetherington & J. Arasteh (Eds.), *Impact of divorce, single parenting, and stepparenting on children* (pp. 325-368). Hillsdale, NJ: Erlbaum.

Zimiles, H., & Lee, V. E. (1991). Adolescent family structure and educational progress. *Developmental Psychology, 27*, 314-320.

INDEX

ABOUT THE CONTRIBUTORS

SANDRA H. BERGER is a Research Associate in the Department of Family Medicine at Baylor College of Medicine in Houston, TX. She is a co-investigator on the Developmental Issues in StepFamilies Research Project, and she has published and presented papers in the areas of divorce and remarriage.

CAROL L. BOETHEL is a Research Assistant in the Department of Family Medicine at Baylor College of Medicine in Houston, TX. She is an investigator on the Developmental Issues in StepFamilies Research Project, specializing in the training of behavioral coders and in family interviews. She has published and presented papers in the areas of divorce and remarriage.

JAMES H. BRAY is Associate Professor in the Department of Family Medicine at the Baylor College of Medicine in Houston, TX. He is the principal investigator of a federally funded longitudinal study, the Developmental Issues in StepFamilies Research Project. He has published numerous works on divorce, remarriage, custody, intergenerational family relations, and behavioral medicine. He also maintains an active clinical practice with children and families.

SCOTT BROWNING is the Coordinator of Counseling Psychology in the graduate division at Chestnut Hill College in Philadelphia, PA. His most recent work has focused on treatment issues for co-dependency and on strategic and narrative models of family therapy. His research interests include studying stepfamilies and developing innovative family therapy methods. He is a member of the Divorce and Remarriage project at the Philadelphia Child Guidance Clinic.

CHERYL BUEHLER is Associate Professor of Child and Family Studies at the University of Tennessee in Knoxville. Her major research interests include divorce, single-parenting, remarriage, and family functioning with special emphasis on child outcomes and the coparenting relationships.

W. GLENN CLINGEMPEEL is Associate Professor of Psychology at Francis Marion University and Co-Director of the Family Psychology Institute, both in Florence, SC. He is nationally noted for his research on the alterations in family dynamics associated with remarriage and the formation of stepfamilies.

MARILYN COLEMAN is Professor of Human Development and Family Studies at the University of Missouri-Columbia, and editor of the *Journal of Marriage and the Family*. Her research interests include remarriage and stepparenting, sex roles, and family stereotyping. Her ongoing collaboration with Lawrence H. Ganong began in 1977.

JOHN J. COLYAR has taught at La Salle University in Philadelphia, PA. He currently has two private practices specializing in problems of children, married couples, and families, in Philadelphia, PA, and Merchantville, NJ. His research interests focus on the influences of family processes on the psychological adjustment of children and adolescents.

MARGARET CROSBIE-BURNETT is Associate Professor of Counseling Psychology and Counselor Education at the University of Miami, Coral Gables, FL. Her research interests include stepfamily assessment, theory development regarding stepfamilies, and the relationship between nontraditional family forms and the educational environment, with a special emphasis on planned intervention.

MARK A. FINE is Associate Professor of Psychology at the University of Dayton, Dayton, OH, and editor of *Family Relations*. His research interests include factors related to adjustment in single-parent and stepparent families, social-cognitive models of family functioning, and personality disorders.

LAWRENCE H. GANONG is Professor of Nursing and Human Development and Family Studies at the University of Missouri-Columbia. His research interests include remarriage and stepparenting, sex roles, and stereotyping related to family roles and family structure. He and Marilyn Coleman have collaborated in research investigations since 1977.

JEAN GILES-SIMS is Associate Professor of Sociology at Texas Christian University in Fort Worth, TX, and is the author of numerous publications on remarriage and stepfamilies. Her research interests include stepfamily roles, adolescent and marital power in stepfamilies, social exchange theory, feminist Theory, and family violence in stepfamilies and other family types.

E. MAVIS HETHERINGTON is the James M. Page Professor of Psychology at the University of Virginia in Charlottesville, VA. She is an internationally recognized scholar and is noted for her research on family transitions (divorce and remarriage), social and personality development, and childhood psychopathology.

MARILYN IHINGER-TALLMAN is Professor and Chair of Sociology at Washington State University, Pullman, WA. Together with Kay Pasley, she has coauthored one book, coedited another volume, and published numerous articles on the subject of remarriage and stepparenting. In addition to her work in these areas, she is studying the university experience of young adults, using 5-year panel data.

LAWRENCE A. KURDEK is Professor of Psychology at Wright State University in Dayton, OH. His research interests include child/adolescent adjustment and its relation to family structure and family process, relationship satisfaction and relationship stability in homosexual and heterosexual couples, and social-cognitive development.

AMY LOFQUIST is a doctoral student at the University of North Carolina at Greensboro. Her research interests include family policy issues, especially the effects of child support on adjustment in remarriage and the factors influencing father involvement with children following divorce.

PATRICK C. McKENRY is Professor of Family Relations and Human Development and Adjunct Professor of Black Studies at the Ohio University in Columbus, OH. He has published extensively in the areas of family problems, family transitions, and adolescent stress and coping. He is the coauthor of a book on divorce and is completing a volume on contemporary families.

BARBARA M. NEWMAN is Professor of Family Relations and Human Develop-ment at the Ohio State University in Columbus, OH. She has coauthored several books on life span human development and has conducted research on adolescent development in the context of the family.

KAY PASLEY is Associate Professor of Human Development and Family Studies at the University of North Carolina at Greensboro. Much of her empirical work has focused on remarriage and stepparenting and done in collaboration with Marilyn Ihinger-Tallman. While other research interests include stress and coping in pregnant and parenting adolescents, most recently she has focused on two areas: fathering in postdivorce and remarried families and family boundary ambiguity.

DONNA S. QUICK is Associate Professor of Family Studies at the University of Kentucky in Lexington, KY. She directed a study of stepmother families titled "Divorce and the Transition to Remarriage: An Adolescent Perspective" at Ohio State University. Her research interest focus on the issues and complexity of the stepmother role.

SARAH H. RAMSEY is Professor in the College of Law at Syracuse University in Syracuse, NY, where she specializes in laws related to families and children. Her research interests include laws and legal decisions pertaining to stepfamilies and the role of the attorney in representing children in abuse and neglect cases.

CATHERINE RYAN is a Research Associate at the Survey Research Center of the University of Maryland, College Park. Her research interests include parent-child relationships in postdivorce families, homelessness, and policy issues and educational practices in early childhood education.

ERIC SANDRAS is a doctoral student at Oregon State University in Corvalis, OR. His research interests include marital quality in remarriage, factors affecting marital quality, and applications of research for improving stepfamily life.

ISBN 0-313-28502-0

9 780313 285028

HARDCOVER BAR CODE